Contents at a Glance

SAMS
Teach Yourself

More Visual Basic 6

in 21 Days

SAMS

A Division of Macmillan Computer Publishing
201 West 103rd St., Indianapolis, Indiana, 46290 USA

Sams Teach Yourself More Visual Basic® 6 in 21 Days

Copyright © 1998 by Sams

International Standard Book Number: 0-672-31307-3

Library of Congress Catalog Card Number: 98-84136

Printed in the United States of America

First Printing: September 1998

00 99 98   4   3   2   1

Trademarks

Warning and Disclaimer

EXECUTIVE EDITOR
Chris Denny

ACQUISITIONS EDITOR
Sharon Cox

DEVELOPMENT EDITOR
Tony Amico

TECHNICAL EDITOR
Rob Bernavich

MANAGING EDITOR
Jodi Jensen

PROJECT EDITOR
Maureen A. McDaniel

COPY EDITORS
San Dee Phillips
Christina L. Smith

INDEXER
Erika Millen

PRODUCTION
Marcia Deboy
Cynthia Fields
Jennifer Earhart
Susan Geiselman

Contents

Dedication

I would like to dedicate this book to my wife Barb, for allowing me to work for hours on end while writing and editing this book. Also, thanks to my children Sean and Christine, who actually left me alone more than they wanted to. And finally, to Divott, my Scottish Terrier, and to Callie, the new addition to the family, who both kept my feet warm while I worked on the computer.

About the Author

Lowell Mauer has been a programmer and instructor for 20 years. He has taught programming at Montclair State College in New Jersey, has developed and marketed a Visual Basic application for airplane pilots, and is involved in creating several corporate Web site applications. As a manager of technical support, he has attended seminars and training sessions in several countries and is an expert in more than six computer languages. He currently is a Senior Business Analyst at Cognos Corporation in New York City, N.Y., where he helps in the implementation and use of several PC-based computer products.

Tell Us What You Think!

As the reader of this book, *you* are our most important critic and commentator. We value your opinion and want to know what we're doing right, what we could do better, what areas you'd like to see us publish in, and any other words of wisdom you're willing to pass our way.

As the Executive Editor for the Visual Basic Programming team at Macmillan Computer Publishing, I welcome your comments. You can fax, e-mail, or write me directly to let me know what you did or didn't like about this book—as well as what we can do to make our books stronger.

Please note that I cannot help you with technical problems related to the topic of this book, and that due to the high volume of mail I receive, I might not be able to reply to every message.

When you write, please be sure to include this book's title and author as well as your name and phone or fax number. I will carefully review your comments and share them with the author and editors who worked on the book.

Fax: 317-817-7070

E-mail: vb@mcp.com

Mail: Executive Editor
           Visual Basic Programming
           Macmillan Computer Publishing
           201 West 103rd Street
           Indianapolis, IN 46290 USA

Introduction

Welcome to the next step in the process of learning Visual Basic. This book bridges the gap between the beginning Visual Basic programmer and the experienced one. In the process of crossing that bridge, you will learn programming design and creation concepts that you can apply to any Windows application you might create in the future. In most beginner books, you learn about the basics of the Visual Basic programming language. These books tend to teach you what the essential pieces are, but not how to put them together to make up a working application.

The promise of this book is that you will be a Visual Basic programmer capable of creating an advanced Windows program. This book starts where the original *Sams Teach Yourself Visual Basic 6 in 21 Days* ends. Now, don't think that you must read the original book before reading this one. You don't! However, it is assumed that you already have a good understanding of the basic Visual Basic concepts.

When More Really Means More

Many books promise more, but they usually fall short of that promise. With this book, you will learn all of the aspects of developing a professional Windows application. You may notice in this book that the term *application* is used instead of *program*. The reason for this is to drive home the point that a Windows application is made up of many different components—and, in some cases, several independent programs—that are combined to build the application.

What You Should Know Going In

Before using the book, you should be both familiar and comfortable with the basics of programming in Visual Basic. This book assumes you already know what properties, events, and methods are. In addition, you should know about the different types of events that are generally used in an application (such as Click, Load, etc.). Finally, you should also understand the concepts of a Visual Basic project, which include forms and modules. The remainder of this introduction mentions some of the new controls that have been added, and how this book deals with the new additions to the Visual Basic language and toolset.

Note This book is not going to take you step by step through the examples used. It is assuming that you know how to set properties and add objects to forms.

Welcome to Visual Basic 6

With the release of Visual Basic version 6, there are even more functions, features, and tools that you can use when creating an application. If you have been using VB5, then VB6 will not "look" all that different. However, Microsoft has enhanced many of the existing controls, added some new Basic language commands, and introduced several new database designers and controls to use in an application.

By far the largest changes have been made in the area of database access. There are several new data-bound controls, as well as a new ActiveX Data Control that combines the functionality of the standard Data control and the Remote Data Control. In addition, there is a Data Report Designer that allows you to design reports directly on forms. Many of these new features are discussed in this book.

With each new release of Visual Basic, I have found new and better ways of performing some basic functions, or adding new functionality to an application. Visual Basic 6 has even more neat stuff in it that makes it even easier to enhance your applications. If you are just now making the jump from Visual Basic 4, then you will notice many changes in the Visual Basic product.

One of the things in Visual Basic that has changed the most is the actual IDE. The overall look of the interface has become a single document type of display with all of the different dialog windows docked on the screen. In this author's opinion, all of these changes has made developing a Visual Basic application easier to do.

A form layout window has been added to the environment allowing you to position you application's forms by visually positioning a small representation of it in a screen display at designtime. If you are working with several different projects that will be included in a single application, such as custom controls and programs, you can now have them all included in a single project group. This allows you to work with multiple projects within a single instance of Visual Basic.

By far the most important changes in VB were made to the Code Editor. You no longer need to look up the syntax of functions such as MSGBOX. When you type in a recognized function name, the Code Editor displays the proper syntax in a ToolTip box. Also, when you are working with objects, as you type in an object and a period, a drop-down list is displayed showing all of the available properties and methods for that object. In addition, as you type in the property or method that you want, if Visual Basic can recognize it, you can hit the Tab key to complete the word.

There are many other new features that have been added to Visual Basic. Many of them are mentioned in this book. As you are introduced to them, you will see how they will make your job as a programmer easier.

Conventions Used in This Book

The following list details conventions used in the book:

- *Italic type* is used to emphasize the author's points or to introduce new terms.
- Screen messages, code listings, and command samples appear in monospace type.
- URLs, newsgroups, Internet addresses, and anything you are asked to type also appears in monospace type.

Final Words

Programming in Visual Basic has been, and continues to be, both an enjoyable and profitable experience. I hope that this book helps you along the same path that I have taken. Each chapter is meant to take one day to complete and absorb, However, there is no time clock here, so take your time and enjoy the trip.

 Note

> If you have a technical question about this book, call the technical support line at (317) 581-3833 or send e-mail to support@mcp.com.

WEEK 1

At a Glance

During Week 1, you gain the knowledge and skills to be able
to design a professional application. An application is a program or set of programs that act together to perform some
useful task or tasks. Generally, the programs that make up an
application work with the same body of data, or database. By
the end of the first week, you will understand the advanced
building blocks that you use to create Windows applications.
More importantly, you see how to use what you've previously
learned about Visual Basic. What this week does is enhance
your knowledge of Visual Basic and cover areas that are often
glossed over or ignored all together.

Day 1 – Writing Professional Visual Basic Applications

Day 1 covers the concepts of what makes a professional
application, the project life cycle, and the new controls that
have been added to Visual Basic.

Day 2 – The Windows Common Dialog in Use

Day 2 introduces you to the advanced ways of using the
Common Dialog and a method of using it without having to
include the control on a form. In addition, you see how to use
a new object to access information about the files and drives
on the computer.

1

2

3

4

5

6

7

Day 3 - Changing the Face of the Application

Day 3 covers the differences between the three types of application interface options.

Day 4 - Creating Form Templates

Day 4 introduces the concept of templates and explains how to use them. In addition, it explains how to create new templates and how to use the Template wizard to access the templates.

Day 5 - Objects, Collections, and Array Processing

Day 5 introduces the programming skills that deal with array processing, using the object collections to simplify the program code.

Day 6 - Procedures, Functions, and Logic

Day 6 explains how functions and subroutines work together in creating good applications. This chapter also takes a close look into how subroutines and functions affect the logic of a program.

Day 7 - Building Complex Forms

Day 7 introduces you to complex forms and the techniques and tips to use when creating them.

DAY 1

Writing Professional Visual Basic Applications

Today, you'll see what drives the type of application you're creating. This involves choosing an application that makes sense and creating a life cycle or project plan for the application that takes it from an idea to the final product.

Also, you'll start a new demo project in Visual Basic. Although you probably know how to do this already, it's a good idea to review it. You do this not just for the steps needed, but to discuss the options available to you with the project properties, focusing on what they can do for you during the development and testing process. Naming conventions will also be covered; however, you won't be shown lists of what they should be. Instead, you'll get an understanding of why you need them and how they should be used.

Finally, in the last section of today's lesson, some of the more advanced controls and features that are included in Visual Basic will be covered. You'll see what they are, how to use them individually and together, and—more importantly—why you should use them.

What Makes a Professional Application

If you read one or more Visual Basic books or have worked with Visual Basic for any length of time, you've probably created many small programs, trying out Visual Basic's different features. After you do this for a while, you've probably asked yourself, "What do I do now?" By using all the tools, controls, and objects that you've learned, you can really impress your friends and family with the things you can get the computer to do. To do anything useful on your computer, however, you need to create larger and more complex programs, or groups of programs called *applications*. Whether the application you're creating is a small inventory program for the house, a personal phone book, or possibly a personnel tracking system for your office, many things go into creating it. If you take a close look at most popular pieces of software on the market, such as Microsoft Money, you can see that many different related routines create the single application.

Whether you're a seasoned programmer or a newcomer to the industry, everyone dreams of creating an application they can sell. Next time you go into a computer store, look at the numerous software applications available; most of them started as one person's idea. If this is where you're heading, you need to know how to plan your application accordingly.

When developing an application, most programmers don't consider what happens when they're done creating the application. If you're working for a company, the finished application is handled differently than if you're planning to sell the application yourself. Putting everything together into one package takes patience, time, imagination, a little luck, and lots of planning. If all goes well, the finished product will look good and work well.

Application Types

You may not realize it, but you can create three distinct types of applications. If you're just starting out as a developer, this might seem a little strange. An application is an application, right? Wrong! Depending on where you work, the type of application you're creating, and the application's final audience, the package you create will be quite different.

You might create three types of applications: personal, internal, and retail:

- A personal application is one that you create for yourself and no one else. You probably won't create any help files or a manual for your own application. Also, because it's running on your own PC, you won't create any distribution disks. As you can see, a personal application is like keeping a private journal; no one else will ever know about it unless you tell them.

- When working for a company, most applications that you develop will probably be internal ones used by other employees of that company or by company clients (for example, home banking software). If the application is completely internal, you don't need to consider any issues that deal with marketing the application. However, you do need to create a help system and a manual because you aren't the only one that will be using the application. The users must have some type of documentation to refer to when using the application.

- If the application is for company clients or for retail distribution, marketing and advertising must be included in the overall process.

Picking the Right Application

Before jumping in and creating an application, you need to decide what function the application will serve. This decision isn't as easy as it might sound. For every idea that you can think up, probably 10 other people have had the same idea. Depending on whether you're creating an application to learn more about programming, something that you want to use at home, or an application to sell, you need to do some *market research* about what the application will do. If you're selling, it's very important to understand the type of person who would use it and how many you might sell. This helps you decide whether it makes any sense to go any further with the idea.

Without doing market research, you might create a great product that nobody wants, or a product with so many competitors that your product gets lost in the crowd. If you find that too many other products of the same type are already on the market, you might decide to select a different type of application or to place the finished product into the realm of shareware (discussed later in this book). For instance, you don't want to spend the time creating a word processing product with products such as Word and WordPerfect already on the market.

In short, you need to select an idea that's new—or at least different—and run with it. You also have to compare the cost of creating the product and advertising it versus your available cash and expected sales. After you decide on the application, however, jump in and start the process. You definitely want to get your product to the public as quickly as you can, with the best quality possible.

Project Life Cycle

When creating an application, you must take several steps to ensure that it's done correctly. These steps are generally grouped together and called the *project life cycle*. Although the number of steps in this cycle can change depending on the complexity of the project, every project must take several universal steps. These steps, or standard life cycle (see Figure 1.1), allow you to plan each section of work and set goals to help verify that you're ready to move on to the next step.

FIGURE 1.1.

The standard project life cycle used in the creation of most computer applications.

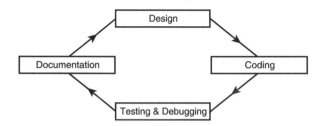

Many newer windows programmers tend to sidestep this approach and prefer to start coding their application immediately. Doing so, however, usually causes problems later on. If you don't plan or blueprint your application, you could wind up forgetting something important, thus having to redo large portions of your work just when you thought you were finished.

Design

The most difficult part of creating any application is deciding what it will do. When that's accomplished, the rest becomes relatively easy. The time you spend designing an application is the most important portion of the project. As mentioned earlier, some programmers like to jump right in and start coding. For every hour that you spend designing your application, you could wind up saving as much as a day of debugging time. If you start with a good design, you'll have considered many more of the situations that might cause problems later and resolve them before they occur.

Note   Fixing design problems on paper is always easier than after they're coded.

In reality, the design step in the life cycle is a cycle itself (see Figure 1.2). Designing an application consists of creating the application's design description, functional definitions, technical definitions, pseudocode, and finally form layouts. From all these steps your actual Visual Basic code will flow. You should expect the design phase of the life cycle to take the largest percentage of time.

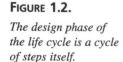

FIGURE 1.2.

The design phase of the life cycle is a cycle of steps itself.

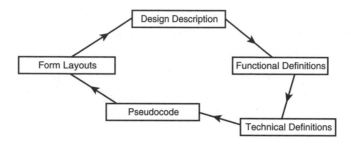

After you write down the functional definitions for your application, you would start translating them into a technical definition. As you move from one step to the next, you'll probably find things that you missed the first time; back up, rewrite that definition, and then continue forward again. In this way, when you start coding, it will be almost a line-for-line translation from your pseudocode to Visual Basic code.

If you think of designing an application the way a house is designed, you would get a good feel for the step-by-step approach you should set up before actually building the application. For example, you wouldn't put the roof of the house up before the walls are put into place, and you wouldn't put the walls up before the foundation is poured. You also wouldn't take a pile of lumber and just start nailing the wood together without a plan. If you did this, your house would not be habitable. It's the same with an application. The plan, or design, is the foundation of the application. If you start with a good foundation, your application will hold up, no matter how hard it is used.

To get a good design, you need to understand what the application will consist of. A house and an application must be built according to a carefully laid out series of steps. In a Visual Basic application, you don't want to create any code before you create the forms, or create the forms before you know what types of forms you need or their functions.

If you build the application in the wrong order or leave a part out, it will be that much harder to add the code when the rest of the application is finished. It could take longer to finish, or never work at all. To design an application correctly, you must first understand what you want it to do.

The first step in the design process is to put the overall application definition into words. This is usually done by writing a short paragraph describing exactly what the application is and what it will be able to do—for example,

> *Personal Address/Phone Book.* This application will keep track of names, addresses, and phone numbers by name. It will allow as many different addresses and phone numbers as needed. Also, it will allow the entry of some personal information (such

as birth date, spouse's name, and children's names) to be determined later. It will also provide reports in several formats and allow users to search the database for a particular person.

This example presents you with a good idea of what main functions the application will perform, giving you a final goal to aim for as you define the more detailed functions in the application. As an alternative to describing the application in a paragraph, you could list the main functions of the application in an outline format as follows:

Personal Address/Phone Book
>   Name/address/phone number entry and display
>   Personal Information entry
>   Searching for selected names, state, type, etc.
>   Reporting
>   Data backup and recovery
>   Multiple database files

This method would also give you a road map to follow when defining the functions in more technical detail. A good method for putting the functional definitions on paper is to describe each function in detail. When doing this, you should try to describe in sequence all the events, options, and results that might occur when users choose this function in the application. You might also describe how this function interacts with other functions in the application. Keeping to a conversational style when describing each function makes it easy to understand what each function will be doing. A definition of an data entry form in this type of style is as follows:

Data Entry. The data-entry form will allow entry of the following information: name, address(s), phone number(s), spouse, child names and ages, and other misc. information about the person being added.

This function must allow for as many different addresses, phone numbers, family members, and misc. information as is needed. The number can vary from entry to entry. It will also check if the input is correct (that is, validate that the phone number has the appropriate number of digits). Also, it will verify that the person being added isn't already in the database. Finally, a modification and delete function will be supported.

As you can see in this example, the main function is broken into *subfunctions,* which describe each step within the main function, such as what the application will do when the entry form's Update button is clicked.

The next step in the design process is taking these functional definitions and translating them into a technical definition or *pseudocode*. Pseudocode is a style and a technique that allows you to define a function in such great detail that you can almost write the Visual Basic code from the pseudocode. The problem with the technique is that it's not as easy as it sounds, because most of us don't think like a computer. When you force yourself to create the pseudocode, however, you'll find that many technical issues that you didn't think of are discovered and added to the design or removed from the application. The following simple function demonstrates how pseudocode would look:

```
Duplicate Name Check
Input: Name of person being added to database.
Process:
Get input name
Initialize SQL statement to query the database for the input name
Execute the SQL statement
Check the query resultset
If no records are found - return a 0 to signal that no duplicate records
were found
If a record was found - return a 1 to signal that the entry is a duplicate
Close the query
Exit function
Error Process:
If an error occurs
Display the error number and message to the user
Return the error number to indicate a problem occurred while checking the
database
```

As you can see, because this is almost Visual Basic code by itself, translating it into actual Visual Basic code will be far easier than if you didn't do this type of designing.

Finally, you need to define the forms and reports you'll need according to the functions already defined. This is more difficult to do because there's really no set way of doing this type of design. You'll find many tips, concepts, and suggestions about form design (as covered later in this book); however, it really comes down to personal choice on how the forms will look.

With all of that said, remember that the design you finally come up with isn't set in concrete. You can and should go back over the design several times, looking for possible problems before you start creating the actual application. This critical review of your plans is an important part of the design process.

Coding

Well, you've done it. You made it past the design phase of your project. Be proud that you did; more than half of all application projects never make it this far. Now you're ready to start coding, but don't bite off more than you can work on at a time. Also, you should treat the coding process like you're peeling an orange. Start by coding the main form of your application with the menu and button bar in place (see Figure 1.3). When you code your application, start with what the user will see when it's started.

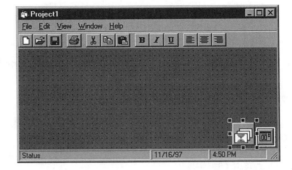

At this point, if you selected any menu or button options, nothing much would happen because you haven't written any code related to those options. Writing code for the computer isn't as simple as writing a letter. The code placed in a Visual Basic application is organized in a hierarchical fashion. An application generally consists of one or more modules, including form modules, one for each form in the application; standard modules for shared code; and possibly class modules. Determining which procedures belong in which module depends somewhat on the type of application you're creating.

There are certain ways or conventions for formatting and labeling everything in program code. Coding conventions is an attempt to standardize the structure and coding style of any application so that you and more importantly others can easily read, understand, and maintain the code. Because most applications aren't as simple as the "Hello World" example most books use to teach programming, the organization or structure of your application code becomes very important. Depending on what a section of code does and where it's used, you would place it in different areas of your application. Code is placed in three areas:

- **Event procedures** are subprograms coded to execute in response to specific events in your application.
- **Standard code modules** are subprograms not related to a specific form or control that might be used by objects in different forms.
- **Class modules** contain code and data.

By structuring your code properly and following good coding conventions, your source code would be more precise, readable, unambiguous, and as intuitive as possible.

> **Note**
>
> The object of conventions is to make the application code easy to read and understand without inhibiting your natural creativity with excessive constraints and arbitrary restrictions. For this reason, the conventions suggested here are short and entirely voluntary. This section isn't attempting to tell you how your coding should look or be done; it's only making some suggestions.

The following code listing is a *before* example of a coded function:

```
Private Sub save_but_Click()
Screen.MousePointer = 11
noupd_ent = False
If new_but.Enabled = False Then
Set logset = logdb.CreateDynaset("cdt_tbl")
logset.FindFirst "[first name] = '" & fname.Text & "' and [last name] =_
         '" & lname.Text & "'"
If Not logset.NoMatch Then
logset.Close
noupd_ent = True
Screen.MousePointer = 0
MsgBox "Duplicate Candidate Name Entered"
fname.SetFocus
Exit Sub
End If
logset.Close
End If
If data1.Recordset.EOF And data1.Recordset.BOF Then
norecs = True
Else
bk = data1.Recordset.BookMark
norecs = False
End If
If Len(lname.Text) = 0 Then
Screen.MousePointer = 0
MsgBox "You Must Enter a First and Last Name.", 32, setmsg
Exit Sub
End If
data1.Recordset.Update
loading = True
cdt_sel = data1.Recordset.Fields("cdt_id").Value
noupd_ent = False
Screen.MousePointer = 0
End Sub
```

When you enter code, the two easiest things that you can do are add comments to the code and consistently indent the code so that different logic blocks become obvious (for example, If...Then...Else...End If). Both conventions improve the overall readability of your code. To further the trend of commenting your application, you should have a brief comment box at the beginning of each procedure and function to describe what the item does (but not *how*). Any arguments passed to the procedure should be described when their usage isn't obvious or when a certain range of values is expected.

You've probably also read about the need for naming conventions. In a Visual Basic application, every object, constant, and variable needs to have a well thought-out name. Each name should include a prefix that defines the data type it's defined as. For example, strFirstname tells any programmer that the variable is defined as a string and that it's used to hold the first name for a data entry.

To show you how all this helps, the earlier sample code has been rewritten with all these conventions:

```
Private Sub cmdSaveRecord_Click()
'********
'* This routine will check to see if the person being added to
'* the database is already there. If it is not on the database then
'* it will complete the ADDNEW function by issuing an UPDATE against
'* the database.
'*
'* The variable vntBookMrk is used to pass the pointer to the current
' * record.
'* The variable intNoRecords is used to inform the calling routine if the
'*                          Record was found or not.
'*
'*********
  Screen.MousePointer = VBHourglass
'* If this is a new entry check to see if it already exists
  If cmdNewEntry.Enabled = False Then
      Set recLogRecord = dbLogBook.CreateDynaset("cdt_tbl")
      recLogRecord.FindFirst "[first name] = '" & txtFirstName & _
                          "' and [last name] = '" & txtLastName & "'"
      If Not recLogRecord.NoMatch Then
          recLogRecord.Close
          Screen.MousePointer = VBDefault
          MsgBox "Duplicate Candidate Name Entered", VBExclamation, _
          App.Title
          txtFirstName.SetFocus
          Exit Sub
      End If
      recLogRecord.Close
  End If
'* If no records were found set intNoRecords to True
  If datLogEntry.Recordset.EOF And datLogEntry.Recordset.BOF Then
      intNoRecords = True
  Else
      vntBookMrk = datLogEntry.Recordset.BookMark
      intNoRecords = False
```

```
      End If
'* If the last name was not entered then display an error message
'* to the user and exit the routine
  If Len(txtLastName) = 0 Then
      Screen.MousePointer = VBDefault
      MsgBox "You Must Enter a First and Last Name.", VBExclamation, _
      App.Title
      Exit Sub
  End If
'* if you got this far update the record.
  datLogEntry.Recordset.Update
  intEntryKey = datLogEntry.Recordset.Fields("cdt_id").Value
  Screen.MousePointer = VBDefault
End Sub
```

As you can see from this final version of the routine, the code becomes very easy to follow. Related If...End If statements are easy to spot, and the comment box explains the routine's overall purpose.

In the routine, notice that two variables are *global*—meaning that they were defined outside the routine. The *scope* of your objects, constants, and variables are important. They should always be defined with the smallest scope possible. Global variables can make the logic of an application extremely difficult to follow. They also make it much more difficult to reuse functions or subprograms in other applications. The concept of scoping is covered later in this book.

Testing and Debugging

After you start coding your application, you need to start the process of testing the code to see whether it works and to fix or debug the code that doesn't. Not everyone tests as thoroughly as they should; this is demonstrated by all the fixes and upgrades to existing software. Then again, no matter how much you test, there will always be bugs that you didn't find. In addition to bugs that you didn't find in the first place are bugs introduced into an application whenever changes or other fixes are applied to the code. To prevent much of these types of bugs, you should do what's called *regression testing*—retesting everything that has been tested before.

You'll actually be doing two levels of testing:

- **Unit testing**— testing individual routines or sections of code. An example of this would be to test just the code for the data-entry routine and nothing else.

- **Integration testing**— testing all the different units as a single system.

When testing your application, try not to use data or input that you know will work. The real art in testing is to pick test data that most likely will cause errors. You also can try the "what-if" method: Ask yourself what would happen if the user does something unexpected, such as enter letters in a phone number text box. After you begin testing your code, errors will show themselves.

The other half of this team, *debugging*, is the process of identifying the cause of an error and correcting it. (Testing, on the other hand, is the process of detecting the error when it occurs.) On some projects, debugging occupies as much as half of the total development time and, for many programmers, is the hardest part of programming.

The testing and debugging process is a long and arduous task; however, Visual Basic comes with some great tools to help you test and debug your application code. On Day 18, "Testing and Debugging the Application," you'll see how to use all these tools. One thing that you must pay close attention to is the usability of the forms that you create for your application. Making sure that the application you've created is intuitive to use is part of the total testing process.

Documentation

It doesn't matter how great your forms are; sometimes users will need help. A help system for an application should include online help and a user's manual; it may also contain other features, such as ToolTips, status bars, What's This help, and wizards.

Note

> The data processing industry is moving away from the old printed version of the user's manual and replacing it with either HTML or PDF electronic format.

Online help is important for any application—it's usually the first place users go when they're having problems or have questions. Even a simple application should provide some type of help; not providing help assumes that your users will never have any questions.

Conceptual documentation, whether printed or provided in electronic format such as a Word document, is helpful for all but the simplest applications. It can provide information that might be difficult to convey in the shorter help topics. At the very least, you should provide documentation in the form of a ReadMe text file that users can print out if desired.

Starting a Demo Project

When you learned the basics of Visual Basic, you were always starting a new project, but the concept of *managing* the project was usually never covered. A Visual Basic project by definition is a collection of files used to build an application. As you work on your application, you'll be working with many different files. Your project will include:

- A project file (.VBP)
- One or more form files (.FRM)
- Binary files related to the form files (.FRX)

In addition to these required files, your project might also contain:

- One or more standard modules (.BAS)
- One or more class modules (.CLS)
- Any ActiveX controls needed (.OCX)
- One resource file (.RES)

Finally, if you are using one of the new ActiveX Designers, your project would also contain:

- A Designer file (.DSR)

To maintain your project files, you'll use the Project Explorer window, which always displays a current list of files in the project. The Project Explorer window in Figure 1.4 shows some of the different file types that you may have included in your project.

FIGURE 1.4.

Every file in your application's project is listed in the Project Explorer window.

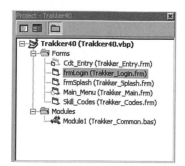

Whenever you add, remove, or modify any files in your application, you need to save your project. Each time you save the project, Visual Basic updates the project file. The project file contains the same list of files shown in the Project Explorer window, as well as references to the ActiveX controls and other objects being used in the project. Figure 1.5 shows an example of a project file's contents.

FIGURE 1.5.

A project file in Notepad showing the different information saved for the project.

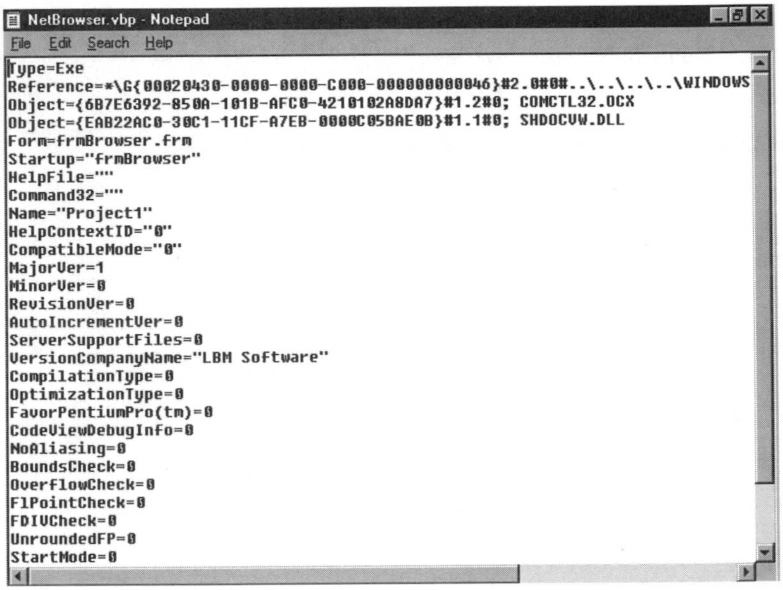

```
NetBrowser.vbp - Notepad                                              _ & X
File  Edit  Search  Help
Type=Exe
Reference=*\G{00020430-0000-0000-C000-000000000046}#2.0#0#..\..\..\..\WINDOWS
Object={6B7E6392-850A-101B-AFC0-4210102A8DA7}#1.2#0; COMCTL32.OCX
Object={EAB22AC0-30C1-11CF-A7EB-0000C05BAE0B}#1.1#0; SHDOCVW.DLL
Form=frmBrowser.frm
Startup="frmBrowser"
HelpFile=""
Command32=""
Name="Project1"
HelpContextID="0"
CompatibleMode="0"
MajorVer=1
MinorVer=0
RevisionVer=0
AutoIncrementVer=0
ServerSupportFiles=0
VersionCompanyName="LBM Software"
CompilationType=0
OptimizationType=0
FavorPentiumPro(tm)=0
CodeViewDebugInfo=0
NoAliasing=0
BoundsCheck=0
OverFlowCheck=0
FlPointCheck=0
FDIVCheck=0
UnroundedFP=0
StartMode=0
```

The Project

When you start VB6, you're presented with the New Project dialog (see Figure 1.6). This dialog allows you to choose from one of several project types, start a new project, or open an existing project on your computer. The Recent page lists the most recent projects that you've accessed. Whenever you're reopening a project, you should access this page first.

At this point, start Visual Basic 6, select a Standard EXE from the New Project dialog box and click OK. A new project starts, containing only one form. Before continuing, save the project as DEMO.VBP and the first form as FRMMAIN.FRM. This project will be used throughout the book to present features and concepts.

Note

> If you have Visual SourceSafe installed on your PC, you'll be prompted to add this project. Don't add any of the example projects in this book unless you really want to. For more information about Visual SourceSafe, see Appendix C, "Stuff Included with Visual Basic 6."

FIGURE 1.6.

The three pages of the New Project dialog box.

1

Project Properties

You can customize your application project by setting one or more properties associated with the project. To access the Project Properties dialog box, choose Project, Properties from the menu (see Figure 1.7). Any changes you make to these properties are also saved to the project file.

FIGURE 1.7.

The Project Properties dialog box allows you to customize your applications information and compile options.

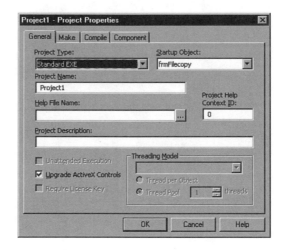

This dialog box can have three to five tabbed pages, depending on the type of application project you're creating. Each page addresses unique areas of your project's information.

The General Page

This page specifies the settings that your application needs to run properly. Figure 1.7 shows the default settings that the Demo project was created with. If your application will include an online help file, specify it in the Help File Name text box. This will set the default help file that your application will use whenever you access a help-related function or feature.

The Startup Object combo box allows you to specify the form that you want to execute first when the application is started. You also can specify a special subprogram, Main, that can execute to initialize files and setting before the first form is displayed.

The Make Page

On this page, you set the attributes for the executable file that you'll create (see Figure 1.8). This page displays the name of the current project in the title so that you can choose which project your changes will apply to. The current project is the item now selected in the Project Explorer window.

FIGURE 1.8.

The application's Make options displayed on the Make page.

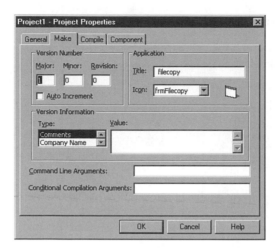

This is important if you're working with a group project that contains multiple projects. If you've ever looked at the properties of an application's executable file, you would see that the information available is directly related to this page. Figure 1.9 shows the properties dialog box for a Microsoft Word executable file (you can be view this dialog box by right-clicking a file in Windows Explorer and choosing Properties from the pop-up menu).

FIGURE 1.9.

Microsoft Word's Properties dialog box, showing current information about the executable file.

Notice the version number and a selection list at the bottom of this dialog box, which allows you to view the different information about the application.

- Application Name
- Company Name
- Description
- Copyright
- Trademark Information
- Comments

The version number of an application really consists of three separate values: a Major release number, a Minor release number, and a Revision number (if needed). The Microsoft Word version number in Figure 1.9 tells you that it's version 8 of the application, and there have been no minor releases.

The Compile Page

This page, shown in Figure 1.10, lets you set the conditions that Visual Basic uses when computing your project. The options on this page deal with the optimization or performance of your application. The differences between the settings will be discussed on Day 19, "Performance and Tuning."

FIGURE 1.10.

The Compile page allows you to control the performance of the compilation process.

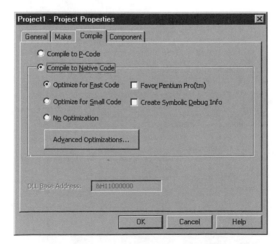

Controls Added to the Toolbox

Okay, time to take a break from all the things you should know before you start creating your application. One neat thing about installing a new version of a development tool such as Visual Basic is to see what new "stuff" has been added. Although most controls in Visual Basic have stayed pretty much the same, some additions should be mentioned before you get into the nitty-gritty of application building. All these controls are available only in the Professional and Enterprise editions of Visual Basic. In the last section of today's lesson, you'll see how to combine several of these controls with others available in Visual Basic to create more complex interactions with your application's users.

Animation

If you've been using any current version of Windows for any length of time, you're probably familiar with the animations used to inform you of some action being done, such as the delete process shown in Figure 1.11. The Animation control gives you a way to provide the same function within your application. It allows you to display silent .AVI clips, miniature movies shown sequentially to create the animation. These animations run as background tasks to allow your application to keep processing whatever is required.

FIGURE 1.11.

An animated display showing a delete process in progress.

After you add it to your toolbox, you can add the control to the form that will display the animation. Figure 1.12 shows the Animation control in the toolbox.

The Animation control is one of two controls contained in the Windows Common Controls 2 set (MSCOMCT2.OCX).

Note Starting with Visual Basic 6, the Windows Common Controls will be found in MSCOMCTL.OCX, MSCOMCT2.OCX, and MSCOMCT3.OCX. These files are replacing COMCTL32, COMCT232, and COMCT332.

The other control, UpDown, is discussed in the following section. To use the Animation control, you first need to add it to your toolbox through the Components dialog box.

FIGURE 1.12.

*The Animation control
as seen in the Visual
Basic control toolbox.*

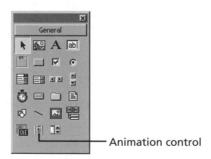

————— Animation control

Putting the Animation control on the form provides your application with a container for
the animation sequence to play in. To run the animation, however, you need to create
some code to open the .AVI file and start the playback process. The control's Open
method is used to open the file specified as the argument for the method. The .AVI files
included with VB5 are installed in the \PROGRAM FILES\MICROSOFT VISUAL
STUDIO\COMMON\GRAPHICS\VIDEOS directory. After you open the file, you need
to execute the Play method to start the animation. The following code shows how to
open and then play an animation file:

```
strAVIFile = "C:\Program Files\ MICROSOFT VISUAL
STUDIO\COMMON\GRAPHICS\\VIDEOS\Filecopy.avi"
anmAnimation1.Open strAVIFile
anmAnimation1.Play
```

When you're ready to stop the animation, you simply execute the control's Stop method:

```
anmAnimation1.Stop
```

To try out this control, add it and two command buttons to the frmMain form of your
demo project (see Figure 1.13). Next, change the names of the command buttons to
cmdStart and cmdStop, respectively. Now add the preceding code segments to the appropriate button click routines (see Figure 1.14).

FIGURE 1.13.

*Working with the
Animation control.*

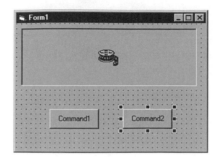

FIGURE 1.14.

Adding the code to access the Animation control.

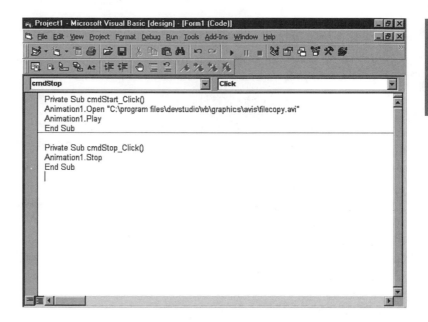

Finally, execute your application and click the Start button. You should see the file-copy animation as shown in Figure 1.15. When you're ready, click the Stop button to end the animation.

FIGURE 1.15.

Informing the user that a file-copy process is in progress.

In addition to playing the animation until your code issues the Stop method, you can set three optional parameters of the Animation control in this order:

- Repeat specifies the numbers of times the animation will be repeated.
- Start sets the frame where the animation will start.
- Stop sets the frame where the animation will end.

You can specify any or all optional parameters. If any are omitted, however, the default values are used. If you omit one of the parameters, you must use a comma as a placeholder. To modify the code in the preceding example to play the animation four times and only the first ten frames, you should change the `Play` method:

```
anmAnimation1.Open strAVIFile, 4,,10
```

Finally, it's a good practice to use the `Close` method when you're finished using an animation file. However, it's not necessary to close one file before opening another.

UpDown

The UpDown control is a new twist to an old friend. Previous releases of Visual Basic had a Spin control, which let users click an up or down arrow. What action was taken as a result was entirely up to you. If you wanted to have a number change when the Spin control was clicked (as in the number of copies in a Print dialog box), you would need the following code to perform the action:

```
Private Sub Spin1_SpinDown()
    entcopies.Text = entcopies.Text - 1
End Sub

Private Sub Spin1_SpinUp()
    entcopies.Text = entcopies.Text + 1
End Sub
```

As you can see, the code that you write controls exactly what the Spin control action will be. The UpDown control is now the control to use when this type of interaction is required. For some types of actions, such as manipulating dates, you still need to code the `UpClick` and `DownClick` routines to perform the required actions. For more basic scrolling type functionality, the UpDown control increments or decrements a value displayed in a buddy control. This control is very useful when you're asking the user to enter a number to control a certain action in the application.

To add the UpDown control to your application, make sure that the Windows Common Controls 2 file is added to your project. Then select the UpDown control from the toolbox, as shown in Figure 1.16.

FIGURE 1.16.

The UpDown control shown in Visual Basic's toolbox.

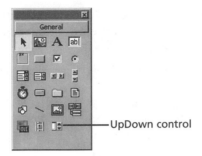

UpDown control

To see how this control works, add a Textbox control and an UpDown control to your demo form. Position these controls and label them as shown in Figure 1.17. These two controls will allow users to control a numeric value by using the built-in capabilities of the UpDown control.

FIGURE 1.17.

The demo form showing the UpDown and Textbox controls added.

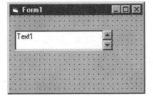

Before anything can happen when you click the UpDown buttons, you must set several properties in the control. Select the UpDown control; then right-click it and select Properties from the pop-up menu. Go to the Buddy tabbed page and set the BuddyControl property to the name of the Textbox control you added. Next, set the BuddyProperty property to Default. This will use the default property of the Textbox control, which is Text. Move to the Scrolling page to set the properties that control the behavior of the UpDown control:

- Increment, the amount that a value will change with each button click.
- Max, the maximum value that can be set.
- Min, the minimum value that can be set.
- Wrap, which tells the control to wrap from the Max value to the Min value, thus preventing invalid numbers from being selected. This property can be True or False.

Set these properties to 1, 10, and 1, respectively, and click Wrap to turn the feature on. Don't forget to set the initial value of the Textbox to a valid number in the specified Min/Max range. If you forget to do this, an error won't happen; however, the text box will contain whatever the default value was.

Run the application and click the UpDown buttons to see what happens. Don't forget that you can still use this control like the old Spin control by using the UpClick and DownClick event routines.

ImageCombo

The ImageCombo control is the newest of the list style controls and is very similar to a standard Windows ComboBox control with some interesting variations. The most visible difference is the ability to include pictures with each item in the list portion of the combo, making it easier for the user to identify and choose items from a list of possible selections. Another important difference is the way the ImageCombo manages the list portion of the control. Each item in the list is a ComboItem object, and the list itself is really a collection of ComboItem object. This makes it easy to access items individually or collectively, and assign or change the properties that determine item content and appearance.

Each item in the ImageCombo list can have three pictures associated with it, as defined by the following properties.

Note Because the items in the list are objects in a collection, several of the properties found in the standard combo box (such as List, ListIndex, and ItemData) are no longer required.

- Image—Appears in the drop-down portion of the control next to the text of the list item.
- SelImage—Specifies the picture used when an item has been selected from the list.
- OverlayImage—Provides a way to overlay an image on top of the main image, such as a check mark or an X indicating an item is unavailable.

The images themselves are defined and stored in the ImageList control and are assigned to items by using an index or key value that references a picture stored in the ImageList control. Working with the ImageCombo control is very similar to the ListView and TreeView controls. To see how to use the ImageCombo, add an ImageCombo and an ImageList control to the demo form as shown in Figure 1.18, removing any other controls and associated code.

FIGURE 1.18.

Adding the ImageCombo and ImageList controls to the demo form.

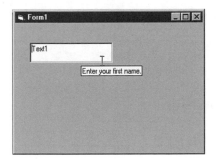

> **Note** . The ImageCombo control is included in the Windows Common Controls 6.0 (MSCOMCTL.OCX)

Before setting up the ImageCombo control, you should add the three pictures you want to the ImageList control. Once that is done, you are ready to work with the ImageCombo control. To add a new item to an ImageCombo, you would use the Add method to create a new ComboItem object in the ComboItems collection. The syntax of the Add method is as follows:

```
ImageCombo1.ComboItems(Index, Key, Text, Image, SelImage, OverlayImage, _
Indent)
```

As you can see, you can supply optional arguments to the Add method specifying many of the properties of the new item, including its Index and Key values, any pictures it will use, and the level of indentation it will have.

To see how this works, add the following code to the demo's Form_Load routine.

```
Dim objNewItem As ComboItem
Set objNewItem = ImageCombo1.ComboItems.Add(1,"Book1","Teach Yourself _
VB5",1)
Set objNewItem = ImageCombo1.ComboItems.Add(2,"Book1","Teach Yourself More _
VB5",2)
Set objNewItem = ImageCombo1.ComboItems.Add(3,"Book1","Teach Yourself _
VB6",3)
```

The preceding code will add three items to the ImageCombo control. Each of these items will appear with its own unique image next to it in the list portion of the control (see Figure 1.19). The images used were added to the Image control that was placed on the form.

FIGURE 1.19.

The ImageCombo control, showing the list portion with images, gives the user a way of visually distinguishing between list items.

Using the ImageCombo control allows you to present the user with a selection list that contains images that help to distinguish the different list items for the user.

The Two FlexGrids

Most information that's processed with computer programs is displayed in columns and rows. The most common example of such a program is Microsoft Excel, a spreadsheet application. Because the spreadsheet is one of the most successful PC programs and, with the word processor, is one of the most widely used programs in the world, it's safe to say that people have become very comfortable seeing data displayed in rows and columns. In fact, for most people, this is the preferred method of viewing any information. Figure 1.20 shows a typical view of data in a spreadsheet-type table.

Visual Basic now has several different controls for working with data in a row and column format, which include the DBGrid or DataGrid for displaying and editing the contents of a database, the MSFlexGrid for handling most other grid display needs, and the new MSHFlexGrid for displaying multiple Table queries in a hierarchical format.

Note
Both MSFlexGrid and MSHFlexGrid can be bound to a data control to display data from a database. However, the data is read-only and can't be changed as it can when using the DBGrid or Datagrid controls.

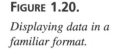

FIGURE 1.20.

Displaying data in a familiar format.

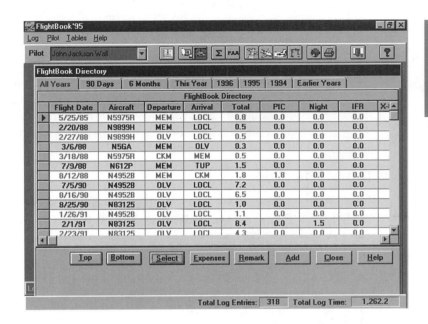

Both FlexGrid controls can display text, pictures, or both in any cells of the grid. In fact, you can give users the ability to sort information in the tables and format the information any way they require it. You can also fix the contents of rows and columns, so you can provide labels for items always displayed to users.

To use either the FlexGrid controls, you must first add them to your project's toolbox. The controls are listed in the Components dialog box as Microsoft FlexGrid Control 6.0 (MSFLXGRD.OCX) and Microsoft Hierarchical FlexGrid Control 6.0 (MSHFLXGRD.OCX). These controls will appear in the toolbox as shown in Figure 1.21.

FIGURE 1.21.

The FlexGrid controls as they appear in the Visual Basic toolbox.

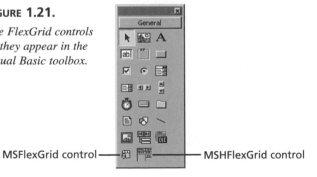

MSFlexGrid control ———   ——— MSHFlexGrid control

Because the data displayed in FlexGrid controls can't be modified directly in the grid cells, this control would require several routines to be coded for users to manipulate data. If your application requires a display-only type of format, however, you can use a FlexGrid control. The most common task you'll perform when working with a grid is setting or retrieving the value in a cell. In the FlexGrid control, the contents of all cells are treated as text strings—meaning that any data is allowed in the cell, and you must perform the appropriate edits to ensure that the correct data is being retrieved or set in the cell.

The MSFlexGrid

Three properties are available that you can use when working with cells in the FlexGrid control: Text, TextArray, and TextMatrix. You can use each property to retrieve or set the value of a single cell.

When used to retrieve a value, the Text property returns the value of the current cell. The current cell is defined by the current setting of the Row and Col properties. The following code shows how you would retrieve the value of the cell in the second row and second column of the grid:

```
MSFlexGrid1.Row = 1
MSFlexGrid1.Col = 1
txtReturn = MSFlexGrid1.Text
```

 Note   Row and column values start at zero for the FlexGrid and DBGrid controls.

The TextArray property provides a different way of accessing the value of a cell. You can use TextArray to retrieve the value of any cell, not just the current cell. This makes it easier to use than the Text property when working with multiple cells. The TextArray property uses a single index value to specify the required cell. This index is determined by multiplying the desired row number by the number of columns in the grid, and then adding the desired column number. The following code shows how to retrieve the same value as the preceding example:

```
intGetColumn = 1
```

```
intGetRow = 1
txtReturn = MSFlexGrid1.TextArray(intGetRow * MSFlexGrid1.Cols +
intGetColumn)
```

The final property is `TextMatrix`. This property requires two arguments: the index of the row and the index of the column to be retrieved. This property is probably the easiest of the three because it works the same as a standard array variable with two dimensions defined. The following code shows how `TextMatrix` would be used to retrieve the same value as the first example:

```
intGetColumn = 1
intGetRow = 1
txtReturn = MSFlexGrid1.TextMatrix(intGetRow, intGetColumn)
```

To see how this works, clear the form in your demo project and then add a FlexGrid control to the form. Set the `Row` property to 6 and the `Column` property to 4. Also, add a command button to the form and label it *Add Data*. Then in the command button's click event, add the following code:

```
Dim intC as Integer
Dim intR as Integer
For intR = 1 to 5
    For intC = 1 to 3
        MSFlexGrid1.TextMatrix(intR, intC) = intR * intC
    Next intC
Next intR
```

When you execute this code in your application, it will actually show you the order in which the cells are accessed with the `TextMatrix` property.

The MSHFlexGrid

The Microsoft Hierarchical FlexGrid control is based largely on the standard MSFlexGrid control. However, the Hierarchical FlexGrid control can present grouped and related recordsets from a Data Environment Command hierarchy. The Hierarchical FlexGrid provides you with many display options that enable you to define a custom format that best suits your application's needs.

A good example of using the Hierarchical FlexGrid is when you need to display a list of customers and all of the orders that they have in the database. The output would resemble the one shown in Figure 1.22.

The biggest difference between the two FlexGrids is the requirement to use a Data Environment object (see Figure 1.23) to define the database access and the command structure for the query. You will learn more about the Data Environment Designer in Chapter 12, "Enhancing Database Access," later in this book.

FIGURE 1.22.

Using the Hierarchical FlexGrid control to display structured information from the database.

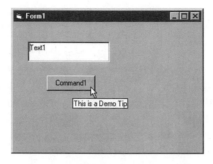

FIGURE 1.23.

The Data Environment Designer is used to define the database connection and the query specifics.

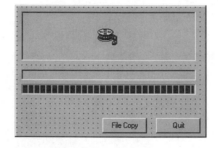

Internet Access

One of the newest things that most applications have is the ability to browse the Internet directly from the application without having to use Internet Explorer. The WebBrowser control allows you to add this capability to your application. You might think that adding the feature is very complicated and that you need to know everything involved with accessing a Web server from your computer. This isn't the case! This new control does everything for you, including interacting with whatever Internet connection you might have on your computer. The only requirement for this to work properly is that you're connected to your ISP provider when you're executing this application. The easiest way to see how to use this control is by creating a new project by using the Application Wizard on the New Project dialog box. When you select the Application Wizard, you'll be taken through several dialog boxes that ask you the type of application you want to create (see Figure 1.24).

For each different wizard dialog box, accept the default settings until you get to the Internet Connectivity dialog box. In this dialog box, select Yes to have the wizard include the Internet connect form in the application. After you click Yes, click the Finish button in the next dialog box to have the wizard complete the creation process. In Project Explorer, you should now see three forms and one module. Double-click the `frmBrowser` form to view it. As you can see in Figure 1.25, this form contains several different controls that work together to give you an Internet browser.

FIGURE 1.24.

Use the Application Wizard to create the Web browser quickly.

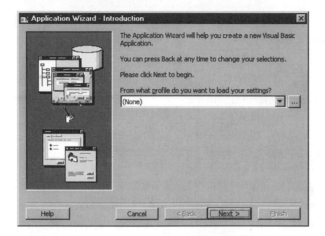

FIGURE 1.25.

The new Internet browser form created by the Application Wizard.

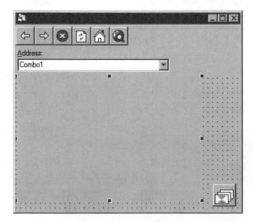

Notice that the button bar at the top of the form looks very similar to the original Internet Explorer toolbar. The WebBrowser control's `Navigate` method handles the main processing for this form. This method navigates to the resource identified by a Universal Resource Locator (URL), or to the file identified by a full path. Figure 1.26 shows what this application will look like when accessing a Web site on the Internet.

FIGURE 1.26.

Accessing Web sites on the Internet becomes a simple matter when using the WebBrowser ActiveX control.

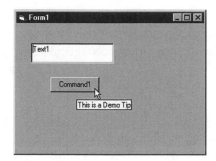

On Day 14, "Internet Programming," you get a more detailed discussion of this control and the other available Internet controls, and how to create an integrated application that can access the Internet at will.

Making Controls Come Alive

By now, you've seen other books that spend most of their time showing you controls and having you try them. At the end of the book you almost feel like saying, "Hey, its great, but what do I do with it?" Controls are used as the building blocks of all your application forms. Knowing how to use them and when to combine their functionality will help you enhance the way your application interacts with users.

ToolTips

Within the user interface are several features for providing help or tips to users. Visual Basic makes it easy to add ToolTips to your applications (see Figure 1.27). ToolTips were formerly called *Balloon Help.*

FIGURE 1.27.

ToolTips pop up whenever the mouse pointer lingers on a control that has a tip defined.

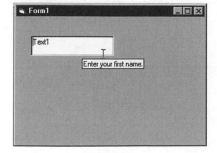

ToolTips are a terrific way to help users as they use your application. A *ToolTip* is a small label that appears when the mouse pointer is held over a control for a short period of time. It usually contains a description of the control's function. ToolTips are generally seen with the application's button bar; however, they also can work well in most any part of the form. Most Visual Basic controls now contain a single property for displaying ToolTips—ToolTipText. It can be set at designtime in the Properties window (see Figure 1.28) or during runtime by using code similar to the following code, which would implement a ToolTip for a text box named txtHomePhone:

```
txtHomePhone.ToolTipText = "Enter Home Phone Number as (222) 555-1212"
```

As with other parts of the form, make sure that the text displayed clearly conveys the correct information to users.

FIGURE 1.28.

You can set ToolTip text during design time by using the Properties window.

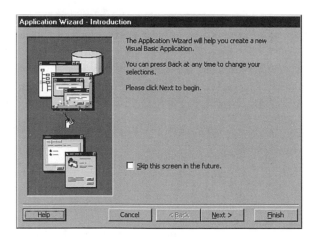

Try this just to see how easy it is to use. By using the demo project that you have open, select one of the command buttons on the form. In the Properties window for that control, find the ToolTipText property and change it to *This is a Demo Tip*. Now, run your application and move the mouse pointer over the command button you modified. After a few seconds, the ToolTip should appear (see Figure 1.29).

FIGURE 1.29.

ToolTips allow you to give users instant suggestions or help right on the forms.

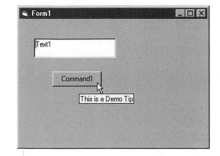

As you can see, the hardest part to this feature is making sure that the text makes some sense.

Using Controls Together

Whenever you learn about controls, the one thing left out most often is how to combine them to perform a needed function within your application. This section shows you how to create your own file-copy routine and dialog box interface that will allow users of your application to copy a file to another location and filename. At this point, however, you won't be using the CommonDialog control to allow users to select the files themselves; that's covered in Day 2's lesson, "The Windows Common Dialog in Use."

When most programmers think of copying files within a Visual Basic application, they immediately think of the FileCopy command included in the language. Although FileCopy copies the file properly, there's no way for your application to perform any other tasks while the command is executing. If you want to show your users any type of status information, it would be a before and after status only, not continuous as the command is executed. To create this type of dialog-box interface, you'll combine the following on one form:

- Animation control
- ProgressBar control
- Label control

In addition to these controls, you also have two command buttons on the form to allow users to start the process and close the form. To create this small application, start a new project and name it FILECOPY.VBP. To use the ProgressBar and Animation controls, you must add them to your project toolbox by using the Components dialog box (select the Microsoft Common Control 5.0 and Microsoft Common Control-2 5.0 components). Now, add all five controls to the form, as shown in Figure 1.30. The empty box between the Animation and ProgressBar controls is a Label control.

FIGURE 1.30.

Creating a custom File Copy dialog box function.

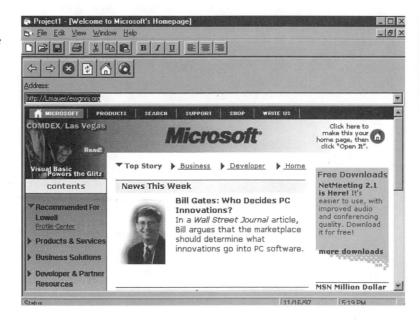

Change the properties for each control as shown in Table 1.1.

TABLE 1.1. CONTROL PROPERTIES FOR THE FILE COPY FUNCTION.

Property	Value
Form Control	
Name	frmFilecopy
BorderStyle	Fixed Dialog
ControlBox	False
MaxButton	False
MinButton	False
StartUpPosition	CenterScreen
Animation Control	
Name	anmShowAction
Center	True
Visible	False

continues

TABLE 1.1. CONTINUED

Property	*Value*Orientation Vertical or Horizontal
ProgressBar Control	
Name	prgStatus
Visible	False
Orientation	Vertical or Horizontal
Scrolling	Smooth or Standard
Label Control	
Name	lblDisplay
Caption	Leave blank
Command Button Control 1	
Name	cmdQuit
Caption	Quit
Command Button Control 2	
Name	cmdCopy
Caption	File Copy

To get the code to copy the file while your application executes other commands, use the Get and Put file statements to read data from the source file and write it to the destination file. Both files will be opened by using the Binary option of the Open file statement. Only two events need code in this application:

- For the cmdQuit_Click event, you need only the command END to finish the execution of the application.

- For the cmdCopy_Click event, add the code in Listing 1.1 to perform all the necessary tasks.

LISTING 1.1. FRMFILECOPY.TXT—THE FILE-COPY ROUTINE USED TO COPY A FILE WITHIN AN APPLICATION.

```
1: Private Sub cmdCopy_Click()
2: Dim lngFileSize As Long
3: Dim intLoopCtr As Integer
4: Dim intBufferCount As Integer
5: Dim strInByte As String * 256
6: Dim strFrom_filename As String
7: Dim strTo_filename As String
8: Dim strAvi_Filename As String
```

```
 9:
10: ' Set the file path for the animation file
11: ' Set the from and to file copy paths
12:     strAvi_Filename = "c:\program _
        files\devstudio\vb\graphics\avis\filecopy.avi"
13:     strFrom_filename = "c:\temp\Testfile.exe"
14:     strTo_filename = "d:\temp\Testfile.exe"
15:
16: ' If the destination file exists, ask the user if they
17: ' want to continue
18:     If Dir(strTo_filename) <> "" Then
19:         If MsgBox(strTo_filename & vbCrLf & _
20:             " already exists. Copy over old file?", vbOKCancel) = _
            vbCancel Then
21:             Exit Sub
22:         End If
23:     End If
24:
25: ' Get the size of the file to copy
26: ' and calculate the number of times to loop
27: ' the copy routine based on moving 256 bytes at a time
28:     lngFileSize = FileLen(strFrom_filename)
29:     intBufferCount = lngFileSize / 256
30:
31: ' Set the progressbar min and max properties
32:     prgStatus.Min = 1
33:     prgStatus.Max = i + intBufferCount
34:
35: ' Open the avi file
36:     anmShowAction.Open strAvi_Filename
37:
38: ' Open the source and destination files
39:     Open strFrom_filename For Binary As #1
40:     Open strTo_filename For Binary As #2
41:
42: ' Set the label to display the file being copied
43: ' and make all of the related controls visible
44:     lblDisplay.Caption = "Copying.. " & strFrom_filename
45:     lblDisplay.Visible = True
46:     anmShowAction.Visible = True
47:     prgStatus.Visible = True
48:
49: ' Start the animation
50:     anmShowAction.Play
51:
52: ' This routine loops until the entire file is copied
53:     For intLoopCtr = 1 To i + 1
54:         Get #1, , strInByte
55:         Put #2, , strInByte
```

continues

LISTING 1.1. continued

```
57: ' change progressbar value to indicate the status of
58: ' the copy function
59:         prgStatus.Value = intLoopCtr
60:
61: ' the DoEvents command allows Windows to update
62: ' the controls on the form
63:         DoEvents
64:     Next intLoopCtr
65:
66: ' After the copy is complete close both files
67:     Close #1    ' Close file.
68:     Close #2    ' Close file.
69:
70: ' Stop the animation and make all related controls
71: ' invisible
72:     anmShowAction.Stop
73:     anmShowAction.Visible = False
74:     prgStatus.Visible = False
75:     lblDisplay.Visible = False
76:
77: ' Inform the user that the function is complete
78:     MsgBox "Copy function complete", vbInformation
79: End Sub
```

Before executing this application, you must change the source file string to a file that exists on your computer, and change the destination file string to a valid path and file-name. Also, double-check the path of the .AVI file, in case you didn't use the default directory paths when you installed Visual Basic.

Execute the application and click the File Copy command button; what you should see should closely resemble the Windows 95 File Copy dialog box. This is only one example of what you can do when combining different controls. The only limitation you'll have is your own imagination when thinking of new combinations of controls. Of course, some combinations already exist in Visual Basic, and it's silly to reinvent the wheel. Day 2's lesson, however, will enhance this example with the Common Dialog control.

Summary

Today's lesson covered several different topics that are important to you as a Visual Basic programmer. The first is the need to properly plan out what your application will be, as well as the design of the application. This way, you can create an application that will look and perform well. It also discussed the importance of proper programming structure and conventions as you code your application. Testing and documentation was also shown to be very important to the final application. By testing the application, you'll hopefully find and fix most problems before users experience them. And if users have any questions, the documentation and online help you provide with the application should be detailed enough to answer them.

You've also reviewed the steps to take when starting a new Visual Basic project and how to manage the different components that can be included in the project. Also, the project properties that would affect your application have been discussed so that you can choose to change the ones that make sense for your application. Some of the newer controls available in Visual Basic were covered to give you a flavor for what they can do. You also saw the concept of combining controls to create a integrated, complex dialog-box function—the file-copy function example.

Q&A

Q What's the difference between a computer program and an application?

A A computer program usually   XE "programs:compared to applications" consists of one small executable file, whereas an application is made up of several programs that all contribute to an overall function. For example, Notepad is a Windows program, whereas Microsoft Word is an application with many functions.

Q Can I combine any number of controls on a form?

A Yes, you can combine as many as you might need to create a particular function on a form.

Workshop

The Workshop provides quiz questions to help solidify your understanding of the material covered, as well as exercises to provide you with experience in using what you've learned. Try to understand the quiz and exercise answers before continuing on to the next day's lesson. Answers are provided in Appendix A, "Answers to Exercises."

Quiz

1. What's an application?
2. What are the steps involved when planning a project life cycle?
3. What can the Animation control allow you to do in your application?
4. Describe the difference between testing and debugging.

Exercise

In the `FileCopy` application that you created today, change the code to move the file
rather than copy it.

DAY 2

The Windows Common Dialog in Use

Dialog boxes allow your applications to interact with users by using the same forms that Windows currently uses. Today's lesson reviews the different options available in the Common Dialog control and how to use it.

> **Note**
>
> The Common Dialog control will work in all of the latest versions of the Windows operating systems.

Now, you may be wondering why you need to review this again. If you want to create an application that closely resembles the Windows 95 standard, you want to understand and use as many of the common features available in Visual Basic as possible. In addition to the review, you'll also get an understanding of why you should use the Common Dialog control and—more importantly—when to use it.

You'll also be shown another way of accessing the Common Dialog features through the use of the Dialog Automation object available on Visual Basic's CD-ROM. You can include this object in your applications instead of the Common Dialog control.

What the Common Dialog Is All About

When the old DOS-based computers changed from black-and-white to color displays, many new commands had to be created for users to change these new properties. Then, when Windows was introduced, developers knew that users would perform many activities over and over. The outcome of this knowledge led to the creation of a "set" of Windows dialog boxes that interfaced with users. As more and more programs were written for Windows, many programmers copied the dialog boxes in this set. It was around this time that developers started calling them *common dialogs*.

When Microsoft started producing developer tools such as Visual Basic for the Windows environment, the company created a special tool—the Common Dialog control. This control, included with every version of Visual Basic, can be used by any programming language that can access an .OCX file. The Common Dialog control provides a standard set of dialog boxes for functions such as opening and saving files, setting print options, and changing colors and fonts. The control can also display help through the Windows help engine.

Why Use It?

At this point, you may be thinking that the Common Dialog control is no big deal—that if you wanted to, you could write your own interfaces for these functions. Through the years, this is exactly what many programmers did, and you could see the differences between different products. No one product looked like another, and for users this made learning how to use various products difficult. To get an idea of why this control is now used by developers, investigate what is would take to create just the open dialog. The following controls would be needed to create one version of an open dialog form:

- Two simple drop-down controls
- Toolbar with four buttons on it
- ListView control
- TextBox control
- Two Command Button controls
- Three Label controls

You also would have to access several system API functions to get some of the information you want to display.

If this all sounds difficult, it is—and you haven't even considered what the layout of the dialog box will look like yet. And remember that this is just one dialog-box interface. The Common Dialog control, on the other hand, has six different functions that you can use.

Of course, if you use the System File controls included in Visual Basic to create the Open dialog box, the process would be easier, but the resulting interface would look more like the old Windows 3.1 interface than a current Windows display (see Figure 2.1).

FIGURE 2.1.

A custom Open Dialog that uses the included System File controls in Visual Basic.

As you can see, the best way to put these functions in your application is to use the Common Dialog control. Although the simple setup is a benefit to you as a programmer, an even bigger bonus is that these dialog boxes are familiar to anyone who has used Windows 95 for more than a day, because they're the exact same dialog boxes that Windows 95 uses.

Interfacing with the Common Dialog

The actual common dialog routines are distributed in a dynamic link library file called COMDLG32.DLL. The way in which you, as the developer, interact with this library is by using the Common Dialog control. Although this control is used in almost every application that you may create, it's not one of the default controls displayed in the Visual Basic toolbox.

As a review, the Common Dialog control can access five standard Windows dialog boxes and one function:

- **Open/Save As** allows users to select files to open or choose filenames to save.
- **Font** lets users choose a base font and set any font attributes they want.
- **Color** allows users to choose from a standard color or create a custom color for

use in the program.

- **Print** lets users select a printer and set some of the printer parameters.
- **Help** accesses the Windows help engine to display the referenced help file.

To access the Common Dialog control, you have to add it to your project from the Components dialog box. You should now see the Common Dialog control in the toolbox as shown in Figure 2.2.

FIGURE 2.2.

The Common Dialog control in the toolbox.

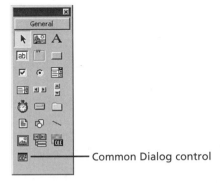

Common Dialog control

Start a new project and place the Common Dialog control on the form. To use any of the different functions, you need to set some of the control's properties by using the Properties window or the Common Dialog control's Property Pages dialog box (see Figure 2.3). The Property Pages dialog box provides you with an easy way to access the specific properties needed for each Common Dialog type. To access the Property Pages dialog box, right-click the control and select Properties from the pop-up menu. Because you need only one control to access any of the different functions available, you can set the properties for all of them at the same time.

FIGURE 2.3.

The Property Pages for the Common Dialog control allows you to change many of the control's properties.

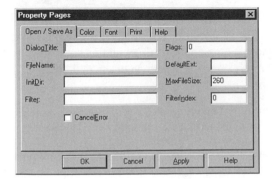

The Many Faces of the Common Dialog

One of the most commonly used functions of the Common Dialog control is the capability to select files to open or specify filenames to save. The Open and Save As dialog boxes allow users to specify a drive, directory, filename extension, and filename. If you've been using older versions of Visual Basic, you probably think that the code to display the Open dialog is the following:

```
DlgGetFile.Action =1
```

Although this code would still work, the preferred way of displaying any of the dialogs is by using one of the following methods of the control:

ShowOpen	ShowColor
ShowSave	ShowFont
ShowPrinter	ShowHelp

Using these methods makes the resulting code not only more precise, but also makes it very easy to understand.

Open/Save As

Because the Open and Save As dialog boxes perform very similar functions, this section covers them both. As mentioned earlier, the Open dialog box (see Figure 2.4) contains several different component types that work together.

FIGURE 2.4.

The Open/Save As common dialog contains several simpler controls used to interface with users.

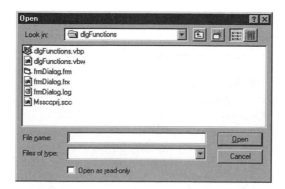

Among these components is the Toolbar control, which allows you to change the way file information is displayed, create new folders, and move up levels in the directory path. You also can use the drop-down box to select a drive or double-click a folder to move down a level in the directory path.

> **Note**
>
> Remember that the Open and Save As dialog boxes don't actually perform any function; they simply get the information from users. It's up to your application code to perform the necessary commands to complete the task.

To see how the Open and Save As dialog boxes can be used, you create a more robust version of the file copy project that you created on Day 1. This newer version will do the following:

- Allow users to pick a file
- Select whether to copy it or move it
- Specify the destination filename and path
- Check whether the file is being overwritten and warn users if it is

When you work with any of the Common Dialog control's different functions, you use several properties to set up the interface. In the case of the Open/Save As dialog boxes, these properties are as follows:

- `Filter`, which sets the file-extension filters displayed in the Type list box
- `FilterIndex`, which contains the default filter for the Open and Save As dialog boxes
- `Flags`, which sets the options for the dialog boxes
- `Filename`, which contains the path and filename of a selected file
- `DefaultExt`, which is used as the extension when a file with no extension is saved
- `InitDir`, which sets the initial file directory that's displayed
- `MaxFileSize`, which indicates the maximum string size of the data in the `Filename` property

The only two properties that require more than one or two lines to explain are `Filter` and `Flags`. The `Filter` property provides users with a list of filters to choose from. The pipe (¦) is used to separate the description and the filter values from each other. The following is an example of the syntax for setting the `Filter` property:

```
Text (*.txt)¦*.txt¦Word Documents (*.doc)¦¦*.doc¦Any Files¦*.*
```

> **Note**
>
> Don't use any spaces before or after the pipe symbol. Any spaces would be displayed with the description and filter values.

This example also allows users to display any file type by selecting the Any Files filter type.

You can change many different settings for the `Flags` property. The ones used in this example application are:

- `cdlOFNFileMustExist`. If this flag is set for the Open dialog box, users can select only files that exist.
- `cdlOFNOverwritePrompt`. This causes the Save As dialog box to confirm an over-write of an existing file.

For a complete list of these values, see the help topic for the Common Dialog control's `Flags` property.

For the enhanced version of the `FileCopy` project, you'll add a new form, as shown in Figure 2.5, as well as modify the original form and the code in the project.

FIGURE 2.5.

The new file process form interface for the FileCopy *project.*

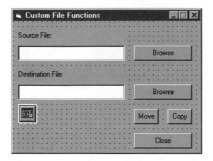

Notice that the new form has several command buttons on it as well as two text boxes and labels. Of course, it also has the Common Dialog control. In the original form, delete the command button controls from the form and reduce the size to match the form in Figure 2.6. Save this new project as `dlgFileOpenCopy`.

FIGURE 2.6.

Changing the old form to enhance the functionality of the project.

Next, rename the original form to `frmStatus` and then display its code. Rename the `FileCopy_Click` routine to `FileProcess`, and then remove all the other routines in this form. Cut the `FileProcess` routine from the `frmStatus` form and paste it into the new frmDialog form. Several changes will be made to this code for the enhanced functions. Listing 2.1 shows what the routine should look like.

 Caution

Remember that you are starting with the project that you created in Chapter 1. The FileProcess routine will reference the same controls as before.

LISTING 2.1. FILEPROCESS.BAS—THE FILE PROCESS ROUTINE FOR COPYING AND MOVING A SELECTED FILE.

```
 1: Private Sub FileProcess(FileAction As Integer)
 2:
 3: ' Set the file path for the animation file
 4: ' Set the from and to file copy paths
 5:     strAvi_Filename = "c:\program _
    files\devstudio\vb\graphics\avis\filecopy.avi"
 6:     strFrom_filename = txtSourceFile.Text
 7:     strTo_filename = txtTargetFile.Text
 8:
 9: 'add FileSystemObject code here
10:
11: ' Get the size of the file to copy
12: ' and calculate the number of times to loop
13: ' the copy routine based on moving 256 bytes at a time
14:     lngFileSize = FileLen(strFrom_filename)
15:     intBufferCount = lngFileSize / 256
16:
17: ' Set the progressbar min and max properties
18:     frmStatus.prgStatus.Min = 1
19:     frmStatus.prgStatus.Max = intBufferCount + 1
20:
21: ' Open the avi file
22:     frmStatus.anmShowAction.Open strAvi_Filename
23:
24: ' Open the source and destination files
25:     Open strFrom_filename For Binary As #1
26:     Open strTo_filename For Binary As #2
27:
28: ' Set the label to display the file being copied
29: ' and make all of the related controls visible
30:     If FileAction = ActionCopy Then
31:         frmStatus.lblDisplay.Caption = "Copying.. " & strFrom_filename
32:     Else
33:         frmStatus.lblDisplay.Caption = "Moving.. " & strFrom_filename
34:     End If
35:     frmStatus.Show
```

```
36:
37: ' Start the animation
38:     frmStatus.anmShowAction.Play
39:
40: ' This routine loops until the entire file is copied
41:     For intLoopCtr = 1 To intBufferCount + 1
42:         Get #1, , strInByte
43:         Put #2, , strInByte
44:
45: ' change progressbar value to indicate the status of
46: ' the copy function
47:         frmStatus.prgStatus.Value = intLoopCtr
48:
49: ' the DoEvents command allows Windows to update
50: ' the controls on the form
51:         DoEvents
52:     Next intLoopCtr
53:
54: ' After the copy is complete close both files
55:     Close #1     ' Close file.
56:     Close #2     ' Close file.
57:
58: 'If the function is a move, erase the source file
59:     If FileAction = ActionMove Then
60:         Kill txtSourceFile.Text
61:     End If
62:
63: ' Stop the animation and make all related controls
64: ' invisible
65:     frmStatus.anmShowAction.Stop
66:      frmStatus.Hide
67:
68: End Sub
```

The remaining code controls the action whenever any of the command buttons are clicked. When creating the frmDialog form, the names of the controls should match those in Table 2.1.

TABLE 2.1. NAME PROPERTIES FOR THE frmDialog CONTROLS.

Control	Name	Caption
Common Dialog	dlgFileSelect	
TextBox	txtSourceFile	
TextBox	txtTargetFile	
Command Button	cmdClose	Close

continues

TABLE 2.1. CONTINUED

Control	Name	Caption
Command Button	cmdMove	Move
Command Button	cmdCopy	Copy
Command Button	cmdTargetFile	Browse
Command Button	cmdSourceFile	Browse
Label	lblSourceFile	Source File:
Label	lblTargetFile	Destination File:

Listing 2.2 shows the final code. Copy it into the frmDialog form's code window; then try running the application and then copying or moving a file.

LISTING 2.2. FILEOPENCOPY.BAS—COMMAND-BUTTON PROCESSING ROUTINES.

```
 1: Private Sub cmdClose_Click()
 2:     End
 3: End Sub
 4:
 5: Private Sub cmdCopy_Click()
 6:     Call FileProcess(ActionCopy)
 7: End Sub
 8:
 9: Private Sub cmdMove_Click()
10:     Call FileProcess(ActionMove)
11: End Sub
12:
13: Private Sub cmdSourceFile_Click()
14:     dlgFileSelect.Flags = cdlOFNFileMustExist
15:     dlgFileSelect.ShowOpen
16:     txtSourceFile.Text = dlgFileSelect.filename
17:
18: End Sub
19:
20: Private Sub cmdTargetFile_Click()
21:     dlgFileSelect.Flags = cdlOFNOverwritePrompt
22:     dlgFileSelect.ShowSave
23:     txtTargetFile.Text = dlgFileSelect.filename
24: End Sub
25:
26: Private Sub Form_Load()
27:     Load frmStatus
28: End Sub
```

The definition statements are located in the General Descriptions area of the form's code. You need to add the following definitions to the form:

```
Option Explicit
Dim lngFileSize As Long
Dim intLoopCtr As Integer
Dim intBufferCount As Integer
Dim strInByte As String * 256
Dim strFrom_filename As String
Dim strTo_filename As String
Dim strAvi_Filename As String
Const ActionCopy = 1
Const ActionMove = 0
```

Notice that two constants are defined to make the code easier to understand. ActionMove and ActionCopy, instead of the sometimes cryptic 1 or 0, serve to explain what the code segments are doing.

As you can see from this example, the Open and Save As dialog boxes can perform some very needed services within your application. The trick is knowing how to use them.

Now, the application you just created enables you to copy or move any file to another location on your computer. One of the things you need to do before moving or copying a file is to check if the target drive has enough room for the file. Prior to VB6, you needed to use Windows API calls to get the available space on the drive. Included with VB6 is the File System Objects. These include objects that enable you to get information about the following:

- **Drive or Drives attached to your computer**—Enables you to get any information needed about the specified drive or drives.
- **Folder or Folders**—Enables you to create, delete, or move folders, plus access their names, paths, and so on.
- **Files**—Enables you to create, delete, or move files, plus access their names, paths, and so on.
- **FileSystemObject**—Enables you to create, delete, and get information about any of the previous objects.

To use these objects, you need to include the SCRRUN.DLL file (which can be found in the WINDOWS\SYSTEM directory) on the Project, References dialog. For the purpose of this example, use the File System Objects to get the following information:

- Available space on the target drive
- Total space on the target drive
- Total size of the file being copied

The following section of code gets the above information and then displays it to them; however, if there is not enough space for the file, the user will see an error message. You should place the following definitions at the beginning of the `FileProcess` routine that is in the application:

```
Dim Drive_TotalSpace As Long
Dim Drive_AvailableSpace As Long
Dim File_Size As Long
Dim FileInfo As Object
Dim sysInfo As New Scripting.FileSystemObject
```

The next section of code should be placed in the FileProcess routine immediately after the comment add `FileSystemObject` code here:

```
Drive_TotalSpace = SysInfo.Drives.Item(left(strTo_Filename,3)).TotalSize
Drive_AvailableSpace = _
SysInfo.Drives.Item(left(strTo_Filename,3)).AvailableSpace _
Set FileInfo = SysInfo.GetFile(strFrom_Filename)
File_Size = FileInfo.Size
If File_Size > Drive_AvailableSpace Then
    MsgBox "There is not enough space to process the
file.",vbCritical,App.Title
Else
    MsgBox "Total Drive Space: " & cstr(Drive_TotalSpace) & vbCRLF & _
"Available Drive Space: " & cstr(Drive_AvailableSpace) & vbCRLF & _
            "Source File Size is: " & Cstr(File_Size), vbInformation,
App.Title
End If
```

As you can see from this code, the File System Object makes it easy to access system information you might need for your application. Once you have added this code, try running the application to see the sizes of the drive you are using.

Colors

The Color dialog box lets you select the colors that can be used for the foreground or background colors of your forms or controls. When you use the `ShowColor` method, the Color dialog box is displayed to users (see Figure 2.7), allowing them to choose a color.

FIGURE 2.7.

The Color dialog box allows users to select a color visually, and returns a numeric value to the program.

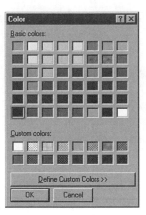

2

Setting up the Common Dialog control to work with colors requires you to set only the Flags property. The Color dialog box returns only one color at a time, requiring you to call the dialog box for every separate color that you want to be able to change. For example, add one additional command button to the existing frmDialog form, and set the Name property to cmdColor and the Caption to Change Color. Then add the following code to the form. The only flag used in this routine tells the Common Dialog control to set the initial color.

```
Private Sub cmdColor_Click()
    dlgFileSelect.Flags = cdlCCRGBInit
    dlgFileSelect.ShowColor
    frmDialog.BackColor = dlgFileSelect.Color
End Sub
```

As you can see, this code changes only the form's background color. When you run the application and change the color, you'll see that the background color of the labels don't change. That's because the code didn't assign the new color to the label's background property.

What you've just tried is the basic example of the Color dialog box that every book example uses. Now let's create a separate form that will give users a choice of objects where they can change the color. Create a new form and name it frmColor. This form will allow users to change the colors of the main form background color and the file name text box background color. To do this, use several sets of labels and command buttons, as shown in Figure 2.8.

FIGURE 2.8.

Creating a Color dialog box to interact with users.

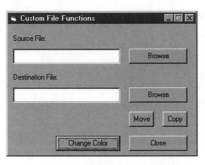

The difference with this example is that you're displaying the current color to users before it's changed and then after it changes. In the Form_Load routine, the labels used to display the current colors will be set. To see this first step in the process, add the following code to your new form:

```
lblAppBack.BackColor = frmDialog.BackColor
lblTxtBack.BackColor = frmDialog!txtSourceFile.BackColor
```

Before running the application, you must change the code in the cmdColor_Click routine to the following:

```
FrmColor.Show VBModal, Me
```

This code enables you to display the new form. It also prevents users from doing anything else until they finish with the colors. When you run the application, you'll see the default colors for these properties.

For the next step, add the following code to each of the two color labels' double-click routines, to change the label name to the respective control:

```
Private Sub lblAppBack_Click()
    dlgColor.Color = lblAppBack.BackColor
    dlgColor.ShowColor
    lblAppBack.BackColor = dlgColor.Color
End Sub

Private Sub lblTxtBack_Click()
    dlgColor.Color = lblTxtBack.BackColor
    dlgColor.ShowColor
    lblTxtBack.BackColor = dlgColor.Color
End Sub
```

This code shows the Color dialog box. When the dialog box changes, change the labels' color accordingly. Try the application again and change the colors a few times.

Up to this point, nothing is really being changed yet. You're giving users two choices when it comes to actually changing the colors:

- The Apply button changes colors without closing the Color dialog box.
- The Close button changes the colors and then closes the dialog box.

Also, a button on the form will reset the colors to the defaults for the user's computer. Using the Apply button allows users to see what the selected colors will look like before leaving the Color dialog box; if they don't like them, they can try different ones. To finish up the demo, add the following code to the frmColor code:

```
Private Sub cmdApply_Click()
    frmDialog!txtSourceFile.BackColor = lblTxtBack.BackColor
    frmDialog!txtTargetFile.BackColor = lblTxtBack.BackColor
    frmDialog.BackColor = lblAppBack.BackColor
End Sub

Private Sub cmdClose_Click()
    frmDialog!txtSourceFile.BackColor = lblTxtBack.BackColor
    frmDialog!txtTargetFile.BackColor = lblTxtBack.BackColor
    frmDialog.BackColor = lblAppBack.BackColor
    Unload Me
End Sub

Private Sub cmdReset_Click()
    lblTxtBack.BackColor = vbWindowBackground
    lblAppBack.BackColor = vbButtonFace
End Sub
```

In the cmdReset routine, constant values are used for the related Windows default colors. Try running the application one last time and see how this new form works.

 Note

When you end the application, any changes you've made to the colors, fonts, or printer options are lost. You can use several different methods to save this information. Later in this book, you'll see how to save and retrieve information related to your application properties.

Don't forget to save this project, as you'll be coming back to it later today and later in the book.

Fonts

Setting up the Common Dialog control to work with fonts is just as easy as setting it up for the Open/Save As functions. In fact, as you've seen in the preceding example, you could use the same Common Dialog control on the form for all the different functions that you might need. The first thing that you need to do with the Font dialog box is to set the Flags property. This is more important for fonts than any of the other dialog boxes. If you use the wrong settings, no fonts will be displayed to users.

Caution

If you don't set a value for the Flags property, you actually get an error message telling you that no fonts are installed on your computer.

The two most commonly used settings are:

- cdlCFBoth, which displays all available printer and screen fonts in the list box
- cdlCFEffects, which enables the strikethrough, underline, and color options on the Font dialog box

The Font dialog box is displayed by invoking the ShowFonts method (see Figure 2.9). Depending on the control you're changing the font information for, you would need to set one or more of the properties for that control.

FIGURE 2.9.

The Font dialog box allows users to modify all the different font properties available.

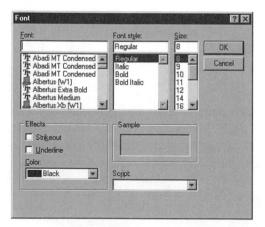

The example I'm using to show you how to use the Font dialog box makes use of a Rich TextBox control and the Open dialog box to get the text file to display. To see how to control fonts, create a new project and format the form as shown in Figure 2.10 by using the Microsoft Rich TextBox control. Then add the code in Listing 2.3 to the form.

FIGURE 2.10.

Changing fonts in the Rich TextBox control allows you to enhance text being entered.

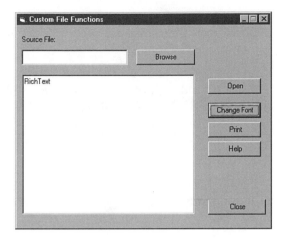

LISTING 2.3. FONTCHANGE.TXT—USING THE FONT COMMON DIALOG BOX TO CHANGE FONT PROPERTIES.

```
 1: Private Sub cmdClose_Click()
 2:     End
 3: End Sub
 4:
 5: Private Sub cmdFont_Click()
 6:     dlgFileSelect.Flags = cdlCFEffects Or cdlCFBoth
 7:     dlgFileSelect.ShowFont
 8:     rtfDisplay.SelFontName = dlgFileSelect.FontName
 9:     rtfDisplay.SelFontSize = dlgFileSelect.FontSize
10:     rtfDisplay.SelColor = dlgFileSelect.Color
11: End Sub
12:
13: Private Sub cmdOpen_Click()
14:     rtfDisplay.LoadFile txtSourceFile.Text, rtfText
15: End Sub
16:
17: Private Sub cmdSourceFile_Click()
18:     dlgFileSelect.Flags = cdlOFNFileMustExist
19:     dlgFileSelect.ShowOpen
20:     txtSourceFile.Text = dlgFileSelect.filename
21:
22: End Sub
```

By this time you should be able to set the properties for each control based on the code. The properties for the RTF control sets the font information for just the selected text. Run this application and have some fun with the fonts. You'll see the features of both the Rich TextBox control and the Font dialog box. As you've seen earlier when working with colors, you can allow users to change any of the application objects fonts by using a separate form to allow selection of each object type.

Print

The Print dialog box departs a little from the direct interaction with the visible properties that users can modify by using the Common Dialog control. This dialog box is usually displayed just before your application sends data to the printer. It allows users to choose which printer to use and also to set the options for the print process (see Figure 2.11).

FIGURE 2.11.

The Print dialog box lets users set printer options by using a consistent interface.

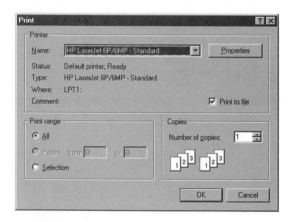

As in the other dialog boxes, the Print dialog box doesn't actually send anything to your printer; you must code the correct set of Visual Basic statements to perform that task. To the previous sample font project, add a new command button control and label it Print. Then add the following code to your form:

```
Private Sub cmdPrint_Click()
Dim FileCopies As Integer
    Dim StartPage As Integer
    Dim EndPage As Integer

    dlgFileSelect.Flags = cdlPDPrintToFile Or cdlPDCollate
    dlgFileSelect.ShowPrinter

' If this statement is true, you would need to display the Save As
' dialog box in order for the user to specify the name of the new
' saved file.
    If dlgFileSelect.Flags And cdlPDPrintToFile = cdlPDPrintToFile Then
        MsgBox "This text will be printed to a file"
    End If
```

```
' Set the nuber of copies and from/to page values before going to the
' printer.
    StartPage = dlgFileSelect.FromPage
    EndPage = dlgFileSelect.ToPage
    FileCopies = dlgFileSelect.Copies
End Sub
```

Again, you can see that the actual call to the Common Dialog control remains pretty much the same. When you need to see whether a particular value was set in the Flags property, you would use the Boolean AND function as shown in the preceding If statement code. Also, the properties for the number of copies and the pages to print are saved in variables. You would need to use them as counters in loops or pass them to the reporting tool that will actually do the printing process for you. (On Day 13, "Working with Crystal Reports," you see how to use the Printer dialog box with an advanced printing tool.) Run your application and click the Print button to see how the interaction with the Print dialog box and the related Printer Setup dialog box allows your application to have the integrated Windows 95 feel to it.

Help

You can display a help file to your user in two different ways:

- By using the help engine API functions, which requires you to define the functions and to understand how to use them
- By using the Help dialog box accessible from the Common Dialog control—a much easier method
- By using the New HTML Help pages and displaying in an HTML browser

To use this dialog box properly, you must set the help-related properties to point to a formatted Windows help file (.HLP):

- HelpFile specifies the path and filename of a Windows help file.
- HelpCommand sets the type of help display requested.

The HelpCommand settings that you'd normally use is cdlHelpContents, which tells the help engine to display the contents topic in the specified help file. To see how this works, add one last command button to the form in the open project, and then insert the following code in its Click event routine:

```
' Set the name of the help file
    dlgFileSelect.HelpFile = "c:\program files\Microsoft Visual _
    Studio\Common\Tools\Reports\crw.HLP"
    dlgFileSelect.HelpCommand = cdlHelpContents
' Display Visual Basic Help contents topic.
    dlgFileSelect.ShowHelp
```

This code displays the Contents page for the Crystal Reports help file that comes with Visual Basic. When it's displayed, users are in the standard Windows help application and can navigate to any area of the help file that they need to go.

Using the Dialog Automation Objects

Now that you've seen how to use VB's Common Dialog control, I want to show you another way of performing the set of functions *without* using this control. One tool included on Visual Basic's CD-ROM is the Microsoft Dialog Automation Objects component. This component provides the common dialog functionality without requiring that you place a control on a form.

To incorporate this object in your application, you first need to install it on your computer:

1. Copy DLGOBJS.DLL from the COMMON\TOOLS\VB\UNSUPPRT\DLGOBJ directory into your \WINDOWS\SYSTEM directory.

2. Register the design-time license for the object by merging the DLGOBJS.REG Registry file into your Registry file. (While in Explorer, right-click COMMON\TOOLS\VB\UNSUPPRT\DLGOBJ\DLGOBJS.REG and choose Merge from the menu.)

3. When the object is registered, select Microsoft Dialog Automation Objects in the Project References dialog box within the Visual Basic environment.

To access the dialog object, you need to define it in the application. Unlike the Common Dialog control, however, you need to define a different object for each function that you want to use. To use the Open and Save As dialog boxes, add the following line of code in the General area of the form:

```
Dim FileDialog as New DialogObjects.ChooseFile
```

This code will give you only the Open and Save As functionality. Open the dlgFileOpenCopy project that you modified earlier today and change the code in the cmdSourceFile_Click routine to this:

```
Private Sub cmdSourceFile_Click()
    dlgFileSelect.Flags = cdlOFNFileMustExist
    FileDialog.Save = False
    FileDialog.Center = True
    FileDialog.Directory = "c:\temp"
    FileDialog.Title = "Custom File Selection"
    FileDialog.Show
'    dlgFileSelect.ShowOpen
```

```
txtSourceFile.Text = dlgFileSelect.filename
```

End Sub

Although you have to insert several lines of code to perform the same function as the Common Dialog control, the actual execution of the object to display the dialog box is more efficient than the control. When working with this object, you can see what the different methods and properties are by using Visual Basic's Object Browser (see Figure 2.12). Also, when you're adding the code to your project, the objects references are included in the Auto List Members feature of the code editor (see Figure 2.13).

2

Note

Using the Dialog Automation Objects will also reduce the size of your final application program; in addition, you do not have to distribute the Common Dialog control with your application, reducing the number of files on the disks or CD.

FIGURE 2.12.

The Dialog Automation Objects methods and properties in the Object Browser.

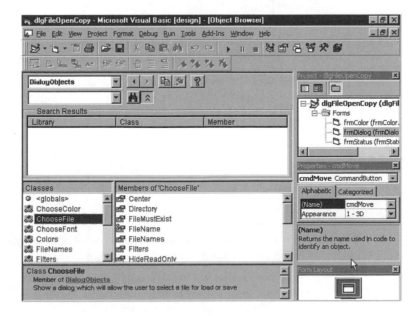

FIGURE 2.13.

The Auto List Members feature shows you what methods are available at any given moment.

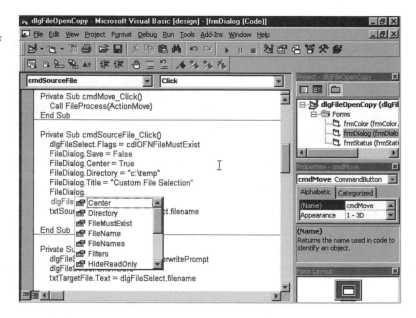

Now with this component, you have a choice in the way that you use the common dialog boxes in your application. The only down side to this component is that the help engine can't be accessed from it. If you choose not to include the Common Dialog control in your application, you need to include the help API declarations to access your application's help file.

Summary

Today you reviewed how the Common Dialog control is used; however, you've also seen how to interact with it in a real-world situation. Each different dialog box that can be used let you allow users to control the look of the application. It also gives them the control to select the printer and print options that they want when printing data from your application. The Open and Save As dialog boxes let users specify which files they want to use when working with the application. If your application allows users to have multiple files to work with, the Open and Save As dialog boxes are definitely needed. Finally, you saw another method of accessing and displaying these dialog boxes to users without adding another control to your forms.

Q&A

Q What are the five functions available from the Common Dialog control?

A The Common Dialog control lets you use the default Windows dialog boxes:

Open/Save As dialog boxes   Print dialog box

Font dialog box   Help file access

Color dialog box

Q When using the Open/Save As dialog boxes, is the file selected actually opened by the Common Dialog control?

A No, the Common Dialog control doesn't perform any actual processing.

Q How does the Dialog Automation Object vary from the Common Dialog control?

A The Dialog Automation Object performs the same functions as the Common Dialog control without you having to add a custom control to each form that needs to use these functions.

Workshop

The Workshop provides quiz questions to help solidify your understanding of the material covered, as well as exercises to provide you with experience in using what you've learned. Try to understand the quiz and exercise answers before continuing on to the next day's lesson. Answers are provided in Appendix A, "Answers to Exercises."

Quiz

1. What's the one function that the Dialog Automation Object doesn't perform?

2. What's the difference between the help function and the other Common Dialog functions that you can use?

3. When using the Common Dialog control to prompt users for a file to open, what are the properties you need to set?

Exercises

1. Use the Common Dialog control to create an application that asks users for a file to open, and then open that file in Notepad.

2. Change the preceding application to use the Dialog Automation Object.

DAY **3**

Changing the Face of the Application

When you're designing your application, remember that your user interface is probably the most important feature of the application, if not the most visible. To the users of your application, the interface *is* the application. No matter how much time and effort you put into designing, writing, and tuning your application code, the success of the application depends on the interface.

Deciding on the type of interface to use can be a little confusing. For a long time you could choose from only two types or styles: the Multiple Document Interface (MDI) and the Single Document Interface (SDI). With the release of Visual Basic 5 came a third style to choose from: the Explorer-style interface. Each style has unique features and gives users certain types of functionality. Therefore, before selecting a particular style for your application, you should be familiar with the different ways each style can be used. Today's lesson focuses on what each style lets you do within your application.

The Three Types of Applications

Before you begin the process of designing your interface, you need to think about the purpose of your application. If your application is one that will be used constantly, it should be designed differently than one that will be used only occasionally. An application that displays information has a different set of requirements for the interface than an application that gets information. Of course, the type of user that will use the application also influences what the interface will look like. An application for beginners would have a simpler interface than one designed for advanced users.

If you've been using Windows for any length of time, you probably know that not all application interfaces look or act the same. That's because some of them use the SDI interface style, whereas others use the MDI style. The SDI interface is the most straightforward of the three styles you can choose from. An SDI application contains a single data window that users work in and usually doesn't have a Window option on its menu bar (because you can't move between data windows). A good example of an SDI application is the Paint application included with Windows 95 (see Figure 3.1).

FIGURE 3.1.

A Single Document Interface application allows users to work with only a single set of data at a time.

The MDI application allows users to work with many different data sets at once. The MDI application also has a Window menu that allows users to switch between windows or documents as required. One of the best examples of an MDI application is Microsoft Word (see Figure 3.2), which allows you to have as many different documents open as you need.

FIGURE 3.2.

The MDI application allows you to work with as many documents or sets of data as you need.

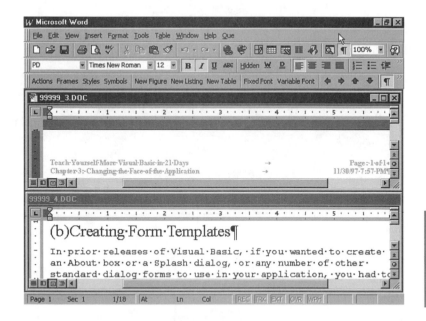

In addition to these most common interface styles, the Explorer-style interface is becoming more popular. This new interface is a single window consisting of two regions: usually a tree-style view on the left and a display or work area on the right. The simplest type of this style application is, no surprise, the Windows Explorer (see Figure 3.3), which uses a TreeView control on the left and a ListView control on the right.

FIGURE 3.3.

The Windows Explorer is the simplest of the Explorer-style applications.

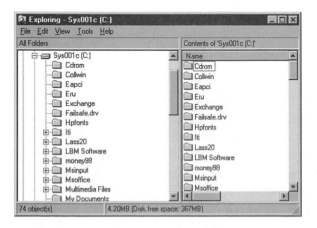

As you can see, the Explorer style is very useful to work with when the application allows users to select information from a displayed group list. This type of interface lends itself to navigating or browsing large amounts of data. Also, when users select a particular piece of information, the working interface can be displayed on the right side of the main application window. An example of this type of usage is Microsoft FrontPage 97 (see Figure 3.4), which uses the Explorer style to display information on the left of the form, and the right is used for whatever type of display or work area is needed.

FIGURE 3.4.

Microsoft FrontPage uses a more advanced Explorer-style interface.

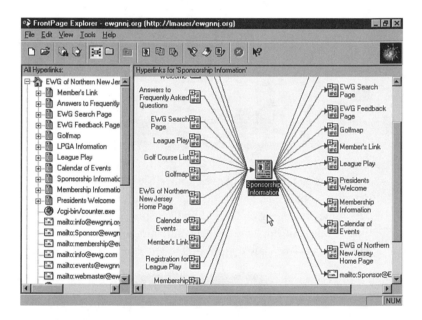

No matter which interface style you choose, be aware of several considerations and techniques:

- Creating a new MDI or SDI application is as simple as setting some of the properties for the forms that you add to your application. The Explorer-style interface, however, requires you to build a fairly complicated form with several controls on it.

- Visual Basic comes with a tool that helps you create any of the three application styles. This tool, the Application Wizard, generates a framework for the style that you select to work with. By viewing the forms and the generated code, you'll see the unique type of processing the default application styles perform.

- Finally, don't feel that if you're using the SDI interface, you can't use the Explorer style, or if you have your application start with an Explorer interface, you can't display other forms when needed. Any of the different styles can have multiple forms. The big difference with the MDI application is that it uses a controlling form (better known as a *parent form*) to hold the other forms (*child forms*) that can't appear outside the parent form's boundaries. In SDI applications, you can have as many instances of a form as you need, yet no form is a child of another.

To see how the different application styles operate, you'll build a simple Notepad-style application by using each of the three design styles.

SDI

When you use an SDI application design, what you create will contain a single form with a toolbar, menu, and other functions or features you choose to add. In fact, many of the applications that you'll create will consist of a series of independent forms. Each form is displayed separately from any other forms onscreen and is moved or resized independently. With this type of interface, there's no easy way to organize the forms into a group. Even with this limitation, it's still the interface of choice for many applications that you might use.

When using the SDI design to create a Notepad application, you'll work with only one form and add the needed controls to it. Although using the SDI design to create the actual interface is easy, SDI is the hardest type to use because the form that users interact with must be coded with great care to provide all the features users will need.

To see how an SDI application is created, start a new project and name it SDINotePad. Then, name the form frmSDINote. Now add to this form a single TextBox control named txtInput. The form in Figure 3.5 has the TextBox control on it and a simple menu defined.

FIGURE 3.5.

Creating the SDI application is as simple as one text box and a menu.

3

Besides the TextBox control, you need to add the menu as shown in Figure 3.5. To enable the initial functions, add the following code to the application:

```
Private Sub Form_Resize()
    txtinput.Height = ScaleHeight
    txtinput.Width = ScaleWidth
End Sub

Private Sub mnuFileExit_Click()
    End
End Sub

Private Sub mnuFileNew_Click()
    Dim NewNote As New frmSDINote
    NewNote.Show
End Sub
```

When you execute this application, this small amount of code will cause the text box to expand to cover the entire work area of the form, no matter what size you make the form. Although this application has only one form, you can have as many instances of it as you need (see Figure 3.6). Controlling the application's arrangement on the desktop is entirely up to users.

FIGURE 3.6.

Having multiple SDI application instances at the same time.

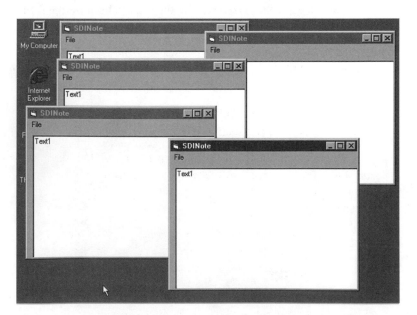

To this simple structure, you can now add any processing code that you need to perform the desired tasks. Some of the tasks you might perform in a Notepad-type application would be opening an existing or new file, saving a file, copying and pasting, and printing.

As you've just seen, the SDI design is really quite easy to put together. The next section covers how you can use the MDI interface design to create the same type of application.

MDI

Now that you've seen how to create a Notepad-type application with a Single Document Interface, see what it takes to create it with a Multiple Document Interface (MDI) design. To start, this interface allows you to create an application that contains multiple forms within a single container form, called a *parent*. When working with an MDI application, you can open multiple windows at the same time and access them from a menu; then, when you minimize the application, all the document windows are minimized with only the parent window's icon appearing in the taskbar.

Reviewing the Parent and Child Forms

The parent form is the container for all child forms in the application. This form has a number of unique characteristics that define how it behaves:

- An application can have only one MDI form.
- Only controls that support the `Align` property can be placed directly on an MDI form.
- You can't use the `Print` method or any graphics methods to display data on an MDI form.
- When you minimize the parent form, it and all its child windows are seen as a single icon on the desktop. When the parent form is restored, all the child forms are returned to their original positions and sizes.
- If the active child form has a menu, it's displayed on the MDI form's menu bar.

The child form also has certain characteristics that affect its behavior:

- Each displayed child window remains within the parent window. It also can't be moved outside the parent window's boundaries.
- When a child form is minimized, its icon is displayed within the parent window, not on the taskbar.
- A maximized child window completely fills the parent form's work area. Its title also is combined with the parent's title and displayed in the parent's title bar.
- When a child form is maximized, any other child forms are also maximized with it.

When you're designing the application, you'll work with each form, parent or child, independently of the others. To know which are child forms, standard forms, or parent forms, you just need to look at the related icon in the Project Explorer window (see Figure 3.7).

FIGURE 3.7.

Different icons identify the MDI parent and child forms as well as any standard forms included in the project.

 Note

Your MDI application can also include any number of standard forms not contained within the parent window.

Creating the MDI Notepad

After you create a new project, you next need to create the MDI parent form. To do this, choose Project, Add MDI Form, or choose MDI Form on the toolbar's Add button. When the MDI form is added to your project, it will look like the one in Figure 3.8.

FIGURE 3.8.

MDI forms have a different color background to differentiate it from any standard or child forms.

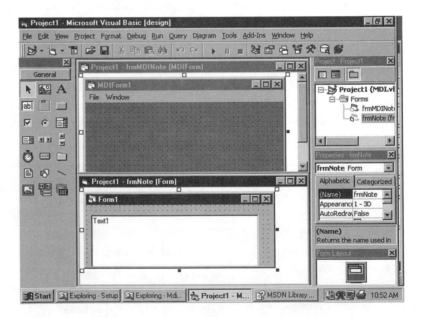

Before going any further, save the project with the name MDINOTEPAD, and name the MDI form frmMDINotepad. You also can set any of the optional properties that you might need for your application. Most of these properties are the same ones you would set to control the appearance of any form in your application.

The MDI form has two special properties that you should be aware of:

- AutoShowChildren specifies whether any child forms in the project are shown automatically as they're loaded. When this property is set, the child forms are shown as soon as they're loaded. This means that the Load statement and Show method behave the same when executed in your application.

- When ScrollBars is set to True, scrollbars appear automatically on the MDI parent form if any child form or section of a child form is moved beyond the boundary of the parent form (see Figure 3.9). If the property is set to False, scrollbars aren't displayed under any circumstances.

FIGURE 3.9.

With scrollbars, you can have the MDI form contain child forms that are larger than the parent.

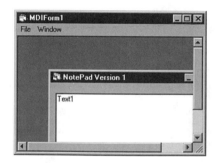

Now, add a child form to the project that contains a TextBox control. Setting up a child form is actually easier than setting up the parent form. A child form is just a standard form with its MDIChild property set to True. Thus, everything you know about working with standard forms applies to creating child forms for an MDI application.

In fact, for your application's first child form, you can use the form that's already added to your project and just change its MDIChild property to True. After you change this property, you'll see that the icon for the form changes to an MDI child icon. This is the only visible change that you see while you remain in design mode. After you have a child form, add the TextBox control to the form. Now, set the properties shown in Table 3.1 for the different objects in your project.

TABLE 3.1. MDINotepad PROJECT PROPERTIES.

Object	Property	Value
FrmMDINotepad	Caption	MDI Notepad Demo
Form1	Name	frmNote
	Caption	(blank)

continues

TABLE 3.1. CONTINUED

Object	Property	Value
TextBox1	Name	txtInput
	Left	0
	Top	0
	Text	(blank)

Then, by using the Menu Editor, add the menu options shown in Figure 3.10 to the MDI form's menu.

FIGURE 3.10.

The MDI parent menu shown in the Menu Editor.

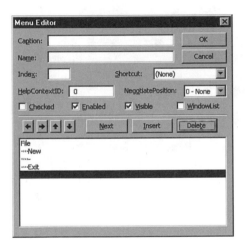

So that this application can display a child form, add the following code to the MDI parent form:

```
Dim intFormCtr As Integer

Private Sub MDIForm_Load()
intFormCtr = 1
frmNote.Caption = "NotePad Version " & intFormCtr
End Sub

Private Sub mnuFileNew_Click()
    Dim NewNote As New frmNote
    intFormCtr = intFormCtr + 1
    NewNote.Show
    NewNote.Caption = "NotePad Version " & intFormCtr
End Sub
```

This code will display a new Notepad child form every time you choose File, New from the menu. Next, add the following code to have the TextBox control cover the entire child form, no matter what size it is:

```
Private Sub Form_Resize ()
    TxtInput.Height = ScaleHeight
    TxtInput.Width = ScaleWidth
End Sub
```

Due to the way the child forms are displayed, any code that you place in the child form is shared by each instance of the form. When you have several copies of the form displayed, each unique form will recognize its own events. Because the same code is shared by each form, you might wonder how to reference the form that has actually called the code.

When you're executing the application, you can choose to have the first child form displayed automatically by setting it as the Startup form. If you want an empty MDI form shown when you start the program, you need to change the Startup setting to the MDI parent name.

Multiple Instances of the Child Form

Although the MDI form can be used to make your application more organized, this misses the real power of an MDI application. The most powerful feature of an MDI application is in its ability to create and manipulate multiple instances of the child form at the same time. In fact, many true MDI applications are made up of only two forms: the MDI parent and the template form for all the children in the application.

 Note

> Your application isn't limited to only one type of child form template. For example, the Visual Basic interface uses two basic child form types: the Form design child form and the Code child form. And as you already know, you can have as many as you need open at the same time.

After you have more than one child form created at a time, you need to use the MDI form's ActiveForm property, which returns the child form object with the focus or that's the most recently active. In the same light, when you're working with controls on the child form, you need to know exactly which control you're accessing. The ActiveControl property works the same way as the ActiveForm control by returning the control with the focus on the active child form. The following code shows an example of how to access text on the active child form:

```
frmMDINote.ActiveForm.ActiveControl.Text = "This is a Demo"
```

Note   If you don't have at least one child form loaded when you use the ActiveForm property, an error will occur.

When exiting the MDI application, you need a way to determine whether any of the data in the child form has been modified and should be saved. By using a Boolean variable, you can set its value to True in the Input control's Change event routine and reset it to False when users save the data. Then, when unloading the application, you can check this variable to see whether executing the save routine is needed.

When the MDI form is unloaded, the QueryUnload event is invoked first for the MDI form and then for every open child form. If none of the processing in this event cancels the Unload event, each child form is unloaded, and then the MDI form is finally unloaded. Because the QueryUnload event executes before the form is actually unloaded, you can give users a chance to save their data before unloading it. It's in this form that you would check to see if the Boolean variable was set to True.

Running the Application

Run the simple application to see how the child form is handled at startup time and when you choose File, New on the menu (see Figure 3.11).

FIGURE 3.11.

Creating several child forms within the MDI application.

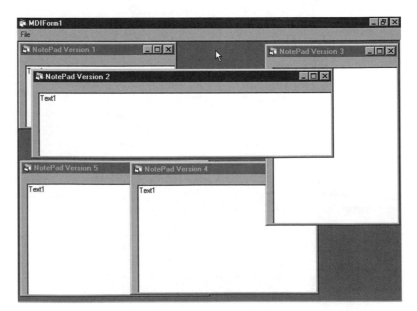

You may have noticed that each time a child form instance is created, it's placed in a different location within the parent. Actually, Windows places these forms onscreen by using a cascading windows effect, starting at the top left of the screen. To change this default placement and size, you need to place code in the load event of the child form to position and size it the way you want it.

Note

You can't change the StartUpPosition property of the child form from its default to set the initial position of the form.

One of the easier features to include in an MDI application is the ability to allow users to arrange the child forms in the parent container. The key to this feature is the MDI form's Arrange method, which organizes all the child forms in one of four very familiar patterns. Table 3.2 lists each pattern that you can use.

TABLE 3.2. USING THE Arrange METHOD SETTINGS.

Constant	Description
vbCascade	Arranges all the non-minimized forms behind one another, slightly offset to the right and down from the one behind it.
vbTileHorizontal	Each form is shown side by side, occupying the full height of the parent.
vbTileVertical	Each form is displayed on top of each other, occupying the full width of the parent.
vbArrangeIcons	This setting arranges the icons of all minimized child forms.

To add this feature to the application, add a new menu option called Window and put four suboptions in it, as shown in Figure 3.12.

FIGURE 3.12.

Adding the automatic arrangement processing to your MDI application.

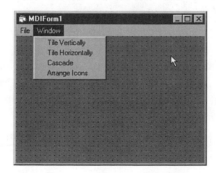

Now add the following to your MDI form code and run your application to see how this works (of course, create several child forms for the best results):

```
Private Sub mnuWindowCascade_Click()
    frmMDINote.Arrange vbCascade
End Sub

Private Sub mnuWindowHoriz_Click()
    frmMDINote.Arrange vbTileHorizontal
End Sub

Private Sub mnuWindowIcons_Click()
    frmMDINote.Arrange vbArrangeIcons
End Sub

Private Sub mnuWindowVert_Click()
    frmMDINote.Arrange vbTileVertical
End Sub
```

One of the best-kept secrets of the MDI form is its ability to keep track of all open child windows and list them in a menu option. To display a list of open child windows, simply select the WindowList check box for the Window menu item in the Menu Editor dialog box. This automatically creates a list of the child windows now in the application (see Figure 3.13).

FIGURE 3.13.

Automatically displaying all open child windows is easy when using the menu's built-in capability.

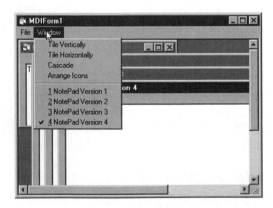

Although you've not really added any substance to this example, the main point to the section was to understand the MDI design process. Now that you've seen what it takes to create and manipulate an MDI application, move to the next section to see how to use the Explorer style for the same application design.

Note

If you're interested in seeing what a fully implemented SDI or MDI version of this Notepad example looks like, you can find the respective projects in the Samples directory that was installed with Visual Basic.

Explorer

The Explorer-style interface is the newest application style that you can use. Even though it's considered an interface, it's really a design that uses several controls on an SDI interface to give users a unique display. The controls that you'll use in creating this interface are

- TreeView
- ListView
- Image
- PictureBox
- Label

Putting these controls together to get a working Explorer interface requires some special processing to allow users to resize the tree and list areas on the form. Although you can build this interface from scratch, Microsoft did us a favor and made it a little easier to create this interface by including the Explorer interface as one of the options in the Application Wizard (see Figure 3.14).

FIGURE 3.14.

Using the Application Wizard to create an Explorer-style application.

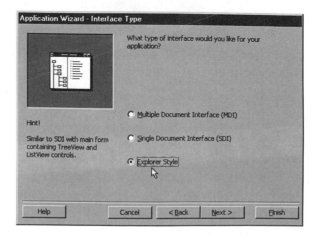

At this point, you may be wondering how this style can be used to work with document data. A good example of this usage is shown in the Visual Basic Books Online interface (see Figure 3.15).

FIGURE 3.15.

The Visual Basic Online Books interface uses the Explorer style to display the available books and topics on one side, the topic content on the other.

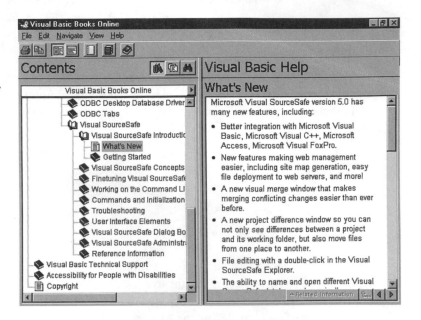

You can see that the two panes used in this application are the TreeView and an HTML-style document browser. For your example, you'll build the same type of interface by using a TextBox control and setting the ListView control's Visible property to False so that it can't be seen. The TreeView control can display a selection of documents and their related topics; when users double-click a topic, it would be displayed in the text box on the right side of the form.

To see how this interface works, start a new project, but select the Application Wizard from the New Project dialog box (see Figure 3.16).

FIGURE 3.16.

Using the Application Wizard to create the Explorer interface.

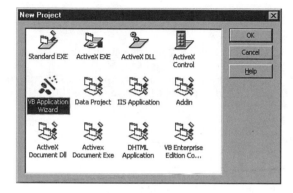

Select the Explorer style as the application type; then accept the defaults on the remaining wizard dialog boxes. This will create more the overall interface for you, including toolbars and menus. Of course, you still need to add the actual application code to this shell. Execute the application and see how the two displayed areas can be resized by simply dragging the bar between them. To add a couple of sample documents to the application, add the code in Listing 3.1 to the form and then add the following line of code to the Form_Load routine:

```
Call Add_Document
```

LISTING 3.1. ADD_DOCUMENT.TXT—ADDING NODES TO THE TREEVIEW CONTROL AND OPENING A TEXT FILE FOR DISPLAY.

```
 1: Public Sub Add_Document()
 2:     Dim MyNode As Node
 3:     'Clean out the TreeView control
 4:     tvTreeView.Nodes.Clear
 5:
 6:     'Set the Document Type
 7:     Set MyNode = tvTreeView.Nodes.Add(, , "A", "Explorer")
 8:
 9:     'Set the Documents
10:     Set MyNode = tvTreeView.Nodes.Add("A", tvwChild, "Readme", "Read Me File")
11:     Set MyNode = tvTreeView.Nodes.Add("A", tvwChild, "eula", "EULA License")
12:     MyNode.EnsureVisible
13:     tvTreeView.Style = tvwTreelinesText         ' Style 4.
14:     tvTreeView.BorderStyle = vbFixedSingle
15:
16: End Sub
17:
18: Private Sub tvTreeView_DblClick()
```

continues

LISTING 3.1. CONTINUED

```
19: Dim set_File As String
20:     set_File = "c:\temp\" & tvTreeView.SelectedItem.Key & ".txt"
21:     Open set_File For Input As #1
22:     'ToDo: add code to process the opened file
23:     lblTitle(1).Caption = "Edit Mode - " & UCase(tvTreeView.SelectedItem)
24:     txtInput.Text = Input(LOF(1), 1)
25:     Close #1
26: End Sub
```

> **Note**
>
> When inserting this code into your application, the keys in the Add state-
> ments for the TreeView control refer to two text files that reside on my
> computer. You should change these references—ReadMe and EULA—to text
> files on your computer.

This will give you the ability to select a document, double-click it to open it, and then
display the contents in the text box on the right side of the form. To get the text box to
behave properly, you must add several lines of code to the SizeControls routine.
However, it's easier to replace the entire routine with the one in Listing 3.2 than try
to tell you exactly where to add each line of code.

LISTING 3.2. SIZECONTROLS.TXT—ADDING SEVERAL LINES TO THE SizeControl ROUTINE.

```
 1: Sub SizeControls(X As Single)
 2:     On Error Resume Next
 3:
 4:     'set the width
 5:     If X < 1500 Then X = 1500
 6:     If X > (Me.Width - 1500) Then X = Me.Width - 1500
 7:     tvTreeView.Width = X
 8:     imgSplitter.Left = X
 9:     lvListView.Left = X + 40
10:     lvListView.Width = Me.Width - (tvTreeView.Width + 140)
11:     lblTitle(0).Width = tvTreeView.Width
12:     lblTitle(1).Left = lvListView.Left + 20
13:     lblTitle(1).Width = lvListView.Width - 40
14:     txtInput.Left = X + 40
15:     txtInput.Width = Me.Width - (tvTreeView.Width + 140)
16:
17:     'set the top
18:
19:     If tbToolBar.Visible Then
```

```
20:            tvTreeView.Top = tbToolBar.Height + picTitles.Height
21:        Else
22:            tvTreeView.Top = picTitles.Height
23:        End If
24:
25:    lvListView.Top = tvTreeView.Top
26:
27:      'set the height
28:      If sbStatusBar.Visible Then
29:          tvTreeView.Height = Me.ScaleHeight - (picTitles.Top + picTitles
30:          .Height + sbStatusBar.Height)
31:      Else
32:          tvTreeView.Height = Me.ScaleHeight - (picTitles.Top + picTitles
33:          .Height)
34:      End If
35:
36:      lvListView.Height = tvTreeView.Height
37:      txtInput.Top = tvTreeView.Top
38:      txtInput.Height = tvTreeView.Height
39:      imgSplitter.Top = tvTreeView.Top
40:      imgSplitter.Height = tvTreeView.Height
41: End Sub
```

3

Finally, add the TextBox control to the form and name it txtInput.

Note Don't worry about where you place the text box on the form. The SizeControls routine will resize it and place it in the correct position.

In the TreeView double-click routine, you may not recognize one line of code:

```
txtInput.Text = Input(LOF(1), 1)
```

This code line uses two built-in functions to get the total length of the file (LOF) and then input that length of data into the TextBox control (Input). If you want to allow users to open any text file on the PC, use the Common Dialog control in the application. Replace the wizard-generated mnuFileOpen_Click routine with the code in Listing 3.3 to display the File Open dialog box and then input the file into the text box.

LISTING 3.3. FILEOPEN.TXT—GIVING USERS THE ABILITY TO OPEN ANY TEXT FILE
ON THE COMPUTER.

```
 1: Private Sub mnuFileOpen_Click()
 2:     Dim sFile As String
 3:
 4:     With dlgCommonDialog
 5:         .DialogTitle = "Open"
 6:         .CancelError = False
 7:         'ToDo: set the flags and attributes of the common dialog control
 8:         .Filter = "Text Files (*.txt)¦*.txt"
 9:         .ShowOpen
10:         If Len(.filename) = 0 Then
11:             Exit Sub
12:         End If
13:         sFile = .filename
14:     End With
15:     Open sFile For Input As #1
16:     lblTitle(1).Caption = "Edit Mode - " & UCase(sFile)
17:     txtInput.Text = Input(LOF(1), 1)
18:     Close #1
19:
20: End Sub
```

Now execute the application. Double-click each of the two selections in the tree list and
see how you can work with the data in the TextBox control (see Figure 3.17). At the
same time, choose File, Open from the menu and select any other text file on your computer to see how it's displayed in the text box. Of course, you can also add code for
many menu options and buttons.

FIGURE 3.17.

The final Explorer application, showing data in the TextBox control.

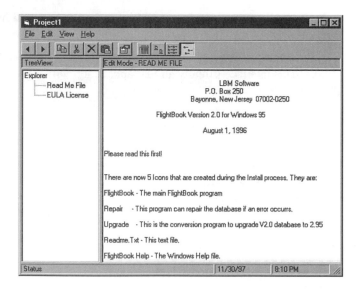

Summary

What you've seen today isn't how to design or code a particular application, but the different interface styles you can use. Deciding on the style to use depends entirely on what you want to allow users to do. Although you can use both SDI and MDI for the same type of applications, the Explorer-style interface is most useful when working with a structured application such as a phone book. You've also seen many issues that you need to deal with when using the MDI design.

Q&A

Q What makes up an SDI application?

A An SDI application usually consists of one main form where most of the application function take place.

Q How do SDI and MDI applications vary?

A An MDI application is generally written to allow users to work with multiple documents or data groups at one time, whereas an SDI application doesn't.

Q How many MDI parent forms can an application have?

A An application can have only one MDI parent form.

Q **Why is the Explorer interface different from the SDI and MDI interface styles?**

A The Explorer interface isn't actually an interface as much as it is an SDI form design. This interface is really an SDI application with a group of controls designed into a two-pane interface.

Workshop

The Workshop provides quiz questions to help solidify your understanding of the material covered, as well as exercises to provide you with experience in using what you've learned. Try to understand the quiz and exercise answers before continuing on to the next day's lesson. Answers are provided in Appendix A, "Answers to Exercises."

Quiz

1. How would you create an MDI application?
2. What controls are used when creating an Explorer interface?
3. What included Visual Basic tool helps you create any style of application interface?

Exercise

Enhance the Notepad application that you created today to use the RichTextFormat control instead of the TextBox control.

DAY 4

Creating Form Templates

Visual Basic comes with many different types of forms with some generic code already in place, for you to use as a starting point for your application forms. These forms, called *templates*, can be used independently but are also used by the Application Wizard when creating a new project.

Today's lesson focuses on several different topics related to the process of creating forms. Button bars or toolbars are essential for all new applications designed for Windows these days. Included with these controls are menus that you can add and manipulate within your application.

After you see how to use these to features to your benefit, you'll learn about the different supplied templates and see what it takes to use them. Next will be a short discussion on creating your own form templates. Finally, you'll learn about Template Manager, a tool included on Visual Basic's product CD-ROM. You'll see what it lets you do and how you can use it for applications you might create later.

Working with Toolbars

Unless you've been in a closet for the last several years, you should know that almost every Windows application available has one—if not more—toolbars to enhance the user interface. Toolbars provide users with a quick way to get at the application's commonly used functions. Depending on the application, one or more toolbars could help with specific tasks, such as the Editor Toolbar in the Visual Basic IDE. Because toolbars are so widely used, most users now expect any application they use to have them.

Adding toolbars to your application has become fairly easy with the Toolbar control supplied with Visual Basic. Creating a simple or complicated toolbar requires that you add the following controls to the form:

- The Toolbar control sets up the buttons of the actual toolbar displayed to users and handles user requests.
- The ImageList control contains the bitmaps used on the toolbar buttons.

To see how to set up a toolbar for your application, start a new project and name it TOOLBAR. To be able to add the toolbar to your forms, you need to have the controls in your Visual Basic toolbox. Because both controls are included in the Windows Common Controls 6.0 Custom controls, you simply add the one OCX file to your project.

Adding a Toolbar the Old-Fashioned Way

This section shows you how to use the Toolbar control with the ImageList control. Even though the toolbar now has a wizard associated with it to make it easy to setup the toolbar, it is a good idea to see how to set it up manually.

Note   The toolbar wizard is only displayed when you add the control to a form.

Selecting the Images for the Buttons

To create a toolbar, you first need to place an ImageList control on your form. To begin the process, add the bitmaps in the ImageList control's Property Pages dialog box (right-click the control and select Properties from the pop-up menu). The Images page is where you add the bitmaps (see Figure 4.1).

To add an image to the ImageList control, click the Insert Picture button. In the Image File Open dialog box that appears, you can choose the bitmap or icon that you want to add. After you select the image and click the Open button, it's added to the control and displayed in the images area.

FIGURE 4.1.

Adding the bitmaps to the ImageList control on the Images page of the Property Pages dialog box.

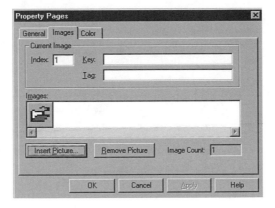

Note

Visual Basic comes with many different types of graphics files that you can use in your applications. Any of the files can be found on Visual Basic's CD-ROM in the /COMMON/GRAPHICS directory.

4

Find the New and Open bitmaps in the PROGRAM FILES/MICROSOFT VISUAL STUDIO/COMMON/GRAPHICS/BITMAPS/TLBR_W95 directory and add them to the ImageList control. When you're finished, click OK to close the Property Pages dialog box.

Now you need to add the toolbar to your project. Follow these steps:

1. Place a Toolbar control on the form. It doesn't really matter where you put it; the default Align property places it at the top of the form.

2. Right-click the control and select Properties from the pop-up menu to display the control's Property Pages dialog box (see Figure 4.2).

3. On the General page, set the ImageList property to the ImageList control that you want to use. This property identifies which ImageList control (if you have more than one on the form) the Toolbar control will use to provide the bitmaps for the buttons. (Now you can see why you had to set up the ImageList control first.)

A little later, you'll look at two other interesting properties on the General page:

- AllowCustomize specifies whether users can customize the toolbar by adding, deleting, or moving buttons.

- ShowTips determines whether ToolTips will be shown if users rest the mouse pointer on one of the buttons.

FIGURE 4.2.

Using the Toolbar con-trols Property Pages to add buttons and assign their images.

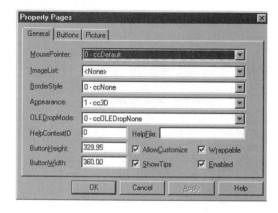

Adding the Buttons

The real action starts when you create the buttons for the toolbar. You'll actually add the buttons on the Buttons page of the Property Pages dialog box (see Figure 4.3).

FIGURE 4.3.

The Buttons page allows you to add and modify the buttons and their images that you add to the toolbar.

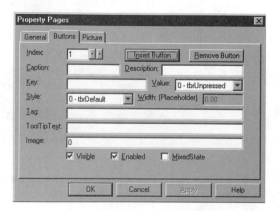

To add a button to the toolbar after the currently selected button, click the Insert button. For each button that you add, you need to specify the following properties:

- The Key property specifies a string that you can use to identify the button in your code. The value of this property must be unique for each button, and you should assign a string that's meaningful to you. This will make it easier to remember when you're writing your code.

- The Image property specifies the index of the picture you want to appear on the face of the button. The index corresponds to the index of the picture in the ImageList control. A value of zero for the Image property will give you a button lacking an image.
- The Style property determines the type of button that you're creating. The button type also determines how the button will behave in the toolbar. Table 4.1 lists the different Style property settings.

TABLE 4.1. SETTING THE BUTTON BEHAVIOR WITH THE Style PROPERTY.

Setting	Constant Name	Description
0	tbrDefault	Creates a standard push button.
1	tbrCheck	Indicates that an option is on or off.
2	tbrButtonGroup	Part of a group; only one button of the group may be selected at a time.
3	tbrSeparator	Provides a space between other buttons.
4	tbrPlaceHolder	Used to hold a space in the toolbar for other controls such as a combo box.
5	tbrDropDown	Displays a dropdown menu list when the button is clicked.

Also, you can set several optional properties for each button:

- Caption displays text beneath the picture on a button.
- Description describes the button to users when they use the Customize Toolbar dialog box.
- ToolTipText is text that appears when the mouse is placed on the button. (This text appears only if the ShowTips property of the toolbar is set to True.)
- Value sets or returns the current state of the button.
- If you set a button style property to tbrDropDown, you will then need to set the menu item for that button on the button property page as shown in Figure 4.4.

This new feature of the toolbar gives you the functionality that is included in Visual Basic (see Figure 4.5) as well as many other Microsoft products.

4

FIGURE 4.4.

Setting a menu list on the Toolbar button property page.

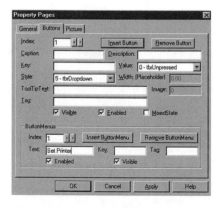

FIGURE 4.5.

Using drop-down menus from a toolbar.

After adding the buttons to your toolbar, you can click OK to close the Property Pages dialog box. You form should now look like the one in Figure 4.6.

FIGURE 4.6.

The final project form with the Toolbar and ImageList controls set.

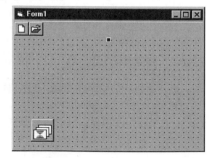

Writing the Button Code

You now have a toolbar on your form. If you execute the application, you can click the buttons and see that they respond. Until you add some code to the toolbar's events, however, the buttons won't perform any functions. The buttons of the toolbar don't have any events of their own. Instead, ButtonClick is the toolbar event in which you'll place your button code. This event passes a button object to the event procedure, which identifies the button pressed. In your code, you'll use the value of the Key property to determine which button was actually pressed. The following source code is typical for taking actions based on buttons pressed:

```
On Error Resume Next
    Select Case Button.Key
        Case "New"
            'ToDo: Add 'New' button code.
            MsgBox "Add 'New' button code."
        Case "Open"
            'ToDo: Add 'Open' button code.
            MsgBox "Add 'Open' button code."
    End Select
```

Notice that each Case statement in the Select statement will execute based on the pressed button.

Tip

> In an actual application, these Case statements should call the same code routine as the related menu options. This allows you to program the action once, and then call it from both the menu and the toolbar. Doing this makes it easier to maintain your code because any changes or corrections have to be made only once.

4

At this point, your toolbar is ready for the remaining sections of your application code to be added.

Adding a Toolbar with the Wizard

You've made it this far and have seen the hoops you have to jump through to create a toolbar. To see how the Toolbar wizard works, start a new project and place the Windows Common Controls in your toolbox. Then, place the Toolbar control on your form. When you do this, the Toolbar wizard dialog box appears (see Figure 4.7).

The Toolbar Builder dialog box displays all the bitmaps available in the /GRAPHICS/TLBR_W95 directory in the left list box. All you need to do is locate the New and Open bitmaps in the list and move them to the list box on the right. If the bitmap you want isn't shown, click the fifth button from the top as shown in Figure 4.5. This will display the Image File Open dialog box for you to select another image. After you select the two bitmaps, the Toolbar Builder should look like the one in Figure 4.8.

When you're ready, click the Finish button. The Toolbar Builder will finish the add process; you'll see that ImageList and Toolbar controls have been added to your form. If you view the code for the form, you'll also see that the Button_click routine has been added for you, saving some coding time.

FIGURE 4.7.

*Using the Toolbar
Wizard to create a
toolbar.*

Add External Image

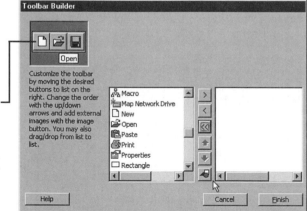

FIGURE 4.8.

*Use the Toolbar
Builder to add buttons
and images.*

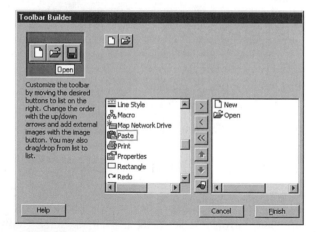

If you need to add more buttons to the toolbar, you'll need to add more images to the
ImageList control first and then add the new buttons.

 Caution

> After you connect the ImageList control to the toolbar, you can't delete any
> images from the list. If you no longer need an image, you can set the
> ImageList property of the toolbar to NONE or just leave the image in the list
> without referencing it.

Other Toolbar Features

One really great feature of any toolbar in a Windows application is your ability to customize which buttons are on the toolbar. With the Toolbar control, you can also give your

users this same ability. When the toolbar's `AllowCustomize` property is set to `True`, users can double-click anywhere on the toolbar to add, remove, or relocate buttons through the Customize Toolbar dialog box (see Figure 4.9).

FIGURE 4.9.

Customizing the toolbar is easy when using the built-in Customize Toolbar dialog box.

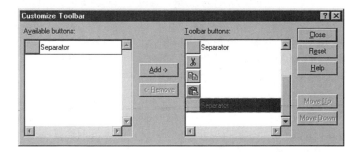

You don't need to write additional code for this capability. The only code you need is the code for each button; Visual Basic takes care of the rest.

The only thing that you must remember with the customize feature is that, unless you save the custom settings somehow, the toolbar will revert to the default view the next time the application is started. Fortunately, Visual Basic provides a way to save and retrieve these changes by using the following methods of the Toolbar control:

- At runtime, the `SaveToolbar` method saves the state of the toolbar in the Windows 95 Registry file.

- The `RestoreToolbar` method retrieves and restores the toolbar to its customized state.

Both have the same syntax, which follows (Table 4.2 explains the settings):

```
Object.<Save|Restore>Toolbar (key As String, subkey As String, value As _
String)
```

TABLE 4.2. REQUIRED `Save` AND `Restore` TOOLBAR SETTINGS.

Setting	Description
`Object`	The name of the related Toolbar control
`key`	A string that specifies the key used in the Registry when saving or retrieving toolbar information
`subkey`	A string that can be used as a secondary value under the *key* value in the Registry
`value`	A string that identifies the value under the *subkey* setting in the Registry file

Caution   When you use the RestoreToolbar method, any toolbar buttons without an
ImageList reference won't be displayed. You can make them visible again by
using the Customize Toolbar dialog box's Reset button.

If your application allows multiple users, you can use these methods to save more than
one version of the toolbar. You can change the *subkey* or *value* settings, which causes
the toolbar to keep separate settings in the Registry file.

Finally, one of the newest features to be added to Visual Basic is the ToolTip textbox feature. Almost every object and control in Visual Basic can display ToolTips. With the
toolbar, if you set the ShowTips property to True, you can then specify unique text for
each toolbar button. Text placed in the ToolTipText property for a button is displayed
during runtime when the mouse pointer remains on a button for a short period of time
(see Figure 4.10.)

FIGURE 4.10.

*Use ToolTips to inform
users what function
each button performs.*

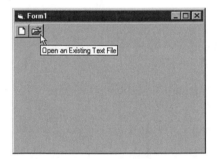

You're now halfway through the process of creating an easy-to-use form for the application. Save this project because you'll be using it to add the menu in the next section.

Using the Coolbar Control

The Coolbar control is the newest of the Visual Basic Toolbar controls that you can use
in an application. This control provides you with a toolbar that can contain multiple toolbars or bands as used in Internet Explorer (see Figure 4.11).

Actually, the Coolbar control is a container control that contains two or more bands that
can be resized and moved by the user. Each of these bands will contain a single Child
control. Depending on how you use the coolbar, the Child control can be any number of
standard controls available. However, if you want to have several different button bars
displayed on separate bands, you can use the Toolbar control to add buttons. To add

bands to the control, you would use the Bands tab on the Coolbar's property page, as shown in Figure 4.12.

FIGURE **4.11.**

Multiple toolbars contained in a coolbar for Internet Explorer.

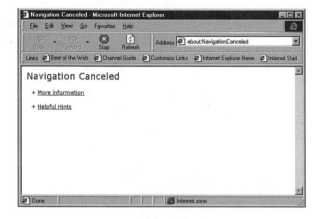

FIGURE **4.12.**

Adding bands and setting Child controls using the property page.

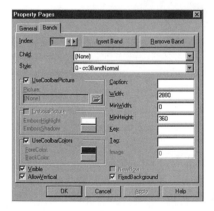

Note

In order for the Coolbar control to recognize the child controls, they must be inserted onto the coolbar itself.

To see how this works, you will create a coolbar with three bands in it. Each band will contain one toolbar. Because of the single Child control requirement, you need to add two toolbar controls to the Coolbar control. At this point, you can choose either of the following options:

- Save the current demo to use in the next section of this chapter
- Remove the toolbar from the form and add the coolbar

Note   The Coolbar control is found in the Windows Common Controls 6.0-3 (MSCOMCT3.OCX).

Start by adding the Coolbar control to the form; then draw the two toolbars onto the coolbar (see Figure 4.13). Then, set the properties of each control as shown in Table 4.3.

FIGURE 4.13.

Adding the Toolbar controls to the coolbar.

TABLE 4.3. COOLBAR PROJECT CONTROLS.

Control	Property	Value
Coolbar	Name	clbDemo
	Align	Top
Toolbar	Name	tlbBar1
	Appearance	ccFlat
Toolbar	Name	tlbBar2
	Appearance	ccFlat

Now, using the property page, assign each toolbar to a band as shown in Figure 4.14.

FIGURE 4.14.

Assigning the Child control property for each Coolbar band.

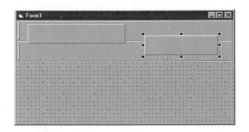

Once this is done, add a few buttons to the toolbars. Once the Toolbar controls are associated with the bands on the coolbar, you have finished the setup. Now, run the application and try opening and closing the bands as shown in Figure 4.15.

FIGURE 4.15.

Setting a menu list for the toolbar.

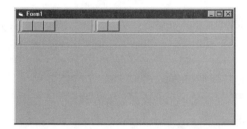

The only thing you have left to do is add the code for each of the command buttons. As you can see, this new control allows you to enhance your application so that it works very much like any other Microsoft application. This gives the user a very comfortable feeling when learning to use your application.

Adding Menus

Now that you've created a toolbar for your application, you then need to add a menu to provide a way for users to select many of the common functions easily. In most applications, you usually have file functions that let users create, edit, and save files. You also have edit functions that allow users to move data around. Then there are the functions for specific tasks in your application. For example, an application that I've written has functions for handling pilot information, aircraft data, and log entry functions. In other words, lots of things users can do.

One of the most important things in any application is allowing users to easily access all its functions. Users are accustomed to accessing most functions with a single mouse click. Also, most users want all the functions located conveniently in one place. To handle this in your application, use toolbars and menus. Visual Basic lets you quickly and easily create menus with the Menu Editor, with which you can create menu bars located at the top of a form, or pop-up menus that users typically access by right-clicking.

Creating an Application Menu

In creating any type of menu system for an application, you must first determine what functions you want or need to put on the menu and how you want to organize these functions. By looking at VB's main menu, you can see that certain functions are organized into groups of similar items (see Figure 4.16).

FIGURE 4.16.

Organizing menu items into functional groups.

Depending on the application that you're creating, you should put your similar menu items into groups. In fact, to be consistent with other Windows applications, you should use groups that your users are already familiar with. This way, they have an idea of where to find a particular menu item, even if they've never used this application before. In a Windows application, you might find the following standard menu groups:

- **File**. This menu contains any functions related to the opening and closing of files used by your application. Some of the standard items included in this menu are New, Open, Close, Save, Save As, Print, and Page Setup. The File menu is also the location of the most recently used file list that many application have. Finally, a File menu is generally where the Exit command is located.

- **Edit**. The functions on this menu are related to the editing of text and documents. Some typical Edit items are Undo, Cut, Copy, Paste, and Clear.

- **View**. This menu may be included if your program supports different views for the same document. A word processor, for example, might include a normal view for editing text and a page-layout view for positioning document elements.

- **Tools**. This menu is a catchall for any optional programs you might have available from within the application. For example, a spelling checker might be included for a word processor.

- **Window**. If your application supports working with multiple documents at the same time, you should have this menu included in your application. The Window menu is set up to let users arrange the multiple documents or switch rapidly between them.

- **Help**. The Help menu allows users to access your application's help system. It usually includes menu items for a table of contents, an index, a search feature, and an About box.

Use these six menu types as a starting point when you're creating the menu system for your application. You can include any of them as you need them, but don't feel as though you must add all six. Also, if you need other menu groups for your application, you can add whatever groups you might need.

Note

When adding other menu groups, be careful not to confuse your users. If and when possible, place as many of your menu functions in one of the standard menu groups.

Building the Menu Groups

After deciding what functions you want to include in the menu and how to group them, you can start building the menu. When creating a menu for your application, remember that every form in the application can have its own menu defined. To see how to create a menu, start with the project that you created previously for the toolbar example. (If you didn't save it, don't panic—just start a new project.) When creating a menu, you must display the form that you want to add the menu to. Only then can you start the Menu Editor by clicking the Menu Editor button on the Visual Basic toolbar (see Figure 4.17).

FIGURE 4.17.

The Menu Editor helps you create a profes-sional-looking menu system for your appli-cation.

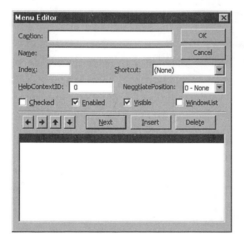

4

With the Menu Editor open, you can start adding the items that you want in the menu. For each item that you want on a menu, you must set only two properties—Caption and Name—but can accept the defaults for all other properties. The Caption property is what users see on the menu when using your application. The Name property is what you use in your application code to access the menu item.

After you enter a menu item, press Enter to accept the values for the item and placed it in the menu selection area at the bottom of the Menu Editor (see Figure 4.18). Pressing Enter also clears the input area, making it ready for the next menu item.

Note

When you work with the Menu Editor, it's very easy to enter the Caption for an item and forget to enter a Name before pressing Enter. This will generate a message that the menu control must have a name.

FIGURE 4.18.

The accepted menu items are listed in the Menu Editor.

After you finish entering the menu items for the application, click OK to close the Menu Editor. Your menu will now appear on the form exactly as you've entered it.

Adding Menu Levels

If you created a menu as shown in Figure 4.19, it will probably be very clumsy to work with. Every item that you've entered appears on the main menu bar.

FIGURE 4.19.

A menu with all the items being displayed on the main menu bar.

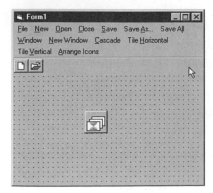

If your application has only one or two menu options, this might be acceptable to you; however, if you have many different menu items, the menu bar will run out of space. What you really need to do is set up a menu that uses multiple levels to display multiple menu items. When you click the menu item on the menu bar, the first level of the menu drops down (see Figure 4.20). This level is called a *submenu*.

FIGURE 4.20.

Multiple levels of a menu item allow for many options in a small amount of menu space.

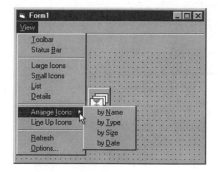

Indenting items on the menu is very easy to do. In the selection area of the Menu Editor, select the item you want to indent and then click the right arrow button directly above the selection list. This indents the item one level (see Figure 4.21) and tclls Visual Basic that the item is now part of a submenu for the main item above it. To show you that it's indented, four spaces are added to the beginning of the item's Caption.

FIGURE 4.21.

When indenting menu items, the Menu Editor visually identifies the level of the item.

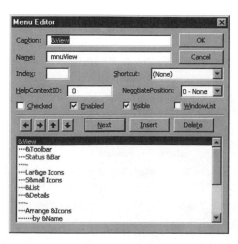

4

When you're entering new items, at a certain level each one is automatically indented to the level of the item above it in the selection list. To move a menu item up a level, click the left arrow button.

One other option available in a menu is a *separator bar*, a line that allows you to group different menu items together with a single menu item's sublevel list (see Figure 4.22). These bars break up a long list of menu items without creating submenus.

FIGURE 4.22.

Separator bars allow you to group and orga-nize menu items at the same level.

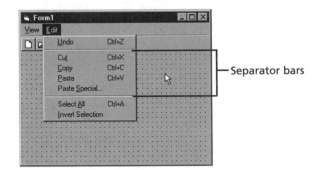

Adding a separator bar is a little tricky. You must place a hyphen (-) in the `Caption` property and enter a `Name` property for the item. I usually enter Sep*N* for the `Name` proper-ty of a separator bar, where *N* is the number of the bar I just added.

> **Note**
>
> Although separator bars a great to use, don't try to add one to the top level of the menu. You can use them only in submenus.

Enhancing the Menu

If you've been working with Windows applications for a while, you've probably noticed that you can access a menu item in several different ways. These are usually done by using a combination of keystrokes. You can include two different types of access in your menu: hotkeys and shortcuts.

Hotkeys are something you already know about and use, probably without thinking about it. A hotkey is identified by an underscore beneath the letter in the item's caption (for example, the E in Edit). To create a hotkey, place an ampersand (&) in the `Caption` prop-erty immediately before the letter you want as the hotkey. For the File menu item, the value of the `Caption` property would be &File. Hotkeys can be used for any item in your menu, including the top-level menu items.

> **Note**
>
> At any given level of a menu, only one unique value can be used as a hotkey. For example, the Visual Basic menu has File and Format at the same top-level. If you look closely at them, you'll see that the File menu item has

the F as the hotkey, but the Format menu has the o as the hotkey. If you used the F for both menu items, Windows wouldn't know which one you really wanted. The same letter can be used in items that appear in different groups, however, such as the File menu's Print option and the View menu's Page Layout option. For each group or level, you can have at most 36 hotkeys, one for each letter and one for each number.

When you've included hotkeys in your menu, you can open a top-level menu simple by holding down the Alt key and then pressing the hotkey of choice. When the menu appears, you can then press the hotkey for the menu item that you wanted to execute. For example, if you want to start a new project in Visual Basic, you could press Alt+F and then N for the File menu's New Project option.

Tip

Whenever there's no conflict with letter selection, you should use the first letter of a menu item as the hotkey. This is what users expect, and it also makes it easy to "guess" what the hotkey is for a particular function.

4

The other way to provide menu access is with shortcuts. *Shortcut keys* provide direct access to any function in a menu, no matter what level it's actually on. Shortcuts can be performed with a key combination (such as Ctrl+C for a copy function) or with a single key (such as Delete for the delete function). If you use the default shortcut keys (listed in Table 4.4), users will already know how to perform certain common tasks.

TABLE 4.4. STANDARD SHORTCUT KEYS USED BY WINDOWS APPLICATIONS.

Menu Item	Shortcut Key	Description
Edit, Cut	Ctrl+X	Removes text or a control and copies it to the Clipboard.
Edit, Copy	Ctrl+C	Copies the text or control to the Clipboard.
Edit, Paste	Ctrl+V	Pastes the contents of the Clipboard to the selected area.
Edit, Undo	Ctrl+Z	Undoes the last change.
Edit, Find	Ctrl+F	Finds a string.
File, Open	Ctrl+O	Opens a file.
File, Save	Ctrl+S	Saves the current file.
File, Print	Ctrl+P	Prints the current data.

Assigning shortcut keys is simply a process of selecting the key or keys that you want to use from the Shortcut drop-down list. Shortcut key are displayed to the right of the menu item both in the selection list (see Figure 4.23) in the Menu Editor and in the actual menu in your application.

FIGURE 4.23.

Shortcuts are displayed in the menu item selection list.

Because of the way shortcut keys work, only one shortcut key can use a given key combination. Therefore, you can have at most only 79 different shortcut keys in your application.

Just like with hotkeys, the shortcut key should correspond with the first letter of the menu item, whenever possible.

Adding the Menu Code

Adding code for the menu is the same as adding code for any other control in your application. The big difference between the menu and other controls or objects on a form is that the menu has only one event procedure—the `Click` event. This event is triggered whenever you select the menu item by clicking it, by using the hotkey, or by using the shortcut key. To display the `Click` event routine for a menu item, simply click the menu item that you want to work with; its related `Click` event will appear in the code editor window.

If you look at the code that you added to the `dlgFileOpenCopy` project in Day 1, notice that you had code in the `mnuFileOpen_Click` routine.

Optional Menu Settings

In addition to the two required properties, each menu item also has several other optional properties that you can use to control the menu item:

- Checked determines whether a check mark is displayed next to a menu item when it's selected. This is used to indicate when a particular option has been selected.
- If Enabled is False (not selected), users can see the menu item but can't access it.
- Visible allows you to hide menu items that aren't needed for a particular function or form.
- NegotiatePosition determines whether the top-level menu items are displayed while another form is active and contains its own menu.
- WindowList is available only when with MDI applications. It displays a list of the current child windows displayed.

When you want to indicate the status of a particular function, use the Checked property to show a check mark in the menu drop-down list for the item selected. Visual Basic uses this property to show which toolboxes are displayed (see Figure 4.24). This property actually toggles back and forth between True and False within the application code itself.

4

FIGURE 4.24.

Using the Checked property to display a function's status.

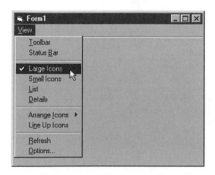

To use the Checked property, you need to add the following code to the Click event of any menu item that you want to use it with:

```
If <menu item>.Checked then
    <menu item>.Checked = True
Else
    <menu item>.Checked = False
End If
```

Note If you try to use the Checked property for a top-level menu item, you'll get an error message. You can't toggle top-level menu items on and off.

The WindowList property specifies that a list of open MDI child forms will be displayed. When this property is set to True, the menu automatically adds items as child forms are opened and removes any child forms that are closed.

Creating and Using Pop-Up Menus

Menus are generally thought of as occupying the bar at the top of an application form and usually being visible. Visual Basic allows you to create another type of menu that appears only when needed and directly next to the area you're working with. These *pop-up menus* are often used to handle functions related to a specific area of the form. For an example of this type of menu, right-click anywhere in the code editor window of Visual Basic for a code-related menu (see Figure 4.25). Pop-up menus usually appear at the mouse pointer's current location. After you select an option from the menu, it disappears from the screen.

FIGURE 4.25.

Pop-up menus give users many available options directly related to the work they're now performing.

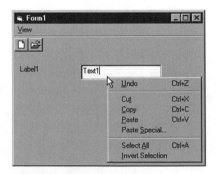

Setting Up a Pop-Up Menu

To create a pop-up menu, you use the Menu Editor in the same way you used it to create other menu and submenu items, except for one extra step: set the pop-up menu's Visible property to False (deselected). This prevents it from being displayed on the top-level menu bar.

Note If you want to have a menu item appear on the standard menu bar and use it as a pop-up menu, you wouldn't set the Visible property to False.

To see how pop-up menus work, select a menu item from the menu that you've created and set its `Visible` property to `False`. When this property is `False`, the only way you can access the `Click` routine for the menu item is by selecting the appropriate routine from the code editor's Object drop-down list.

Displaying a Pop-Up Menu

To display a pop-up menu, you need to invoke the form's `PopUpMenu` method. The syntax of this method is

```
frmForm.PopUpMenu <menu item>
```

where *menu item* is the `Name` of the top-level item that you want to display. Although you can use these pop-up menus in response to almost any action in your application, the excepted use is when the right mouse button is clicked. You can place the following code in the form's or object's `MouseDown` event:

```
Private Sub <object>_MouseDown(Button As Integer, Shift As Integer,
  X As Single, Y As Single)
If Button = vbRightButton Then
    frmMain.PopUpMenu <menu item>
End If
End Sub
```

This code will display a pop-up menu at the mouse pointer whenever users right-click. Now add this code to the form's `MouseDown` event, remembering to change the references to the form name and the menu item name. Run the application and right-click anywhere on the form; the pop-up menu should appear.

Negotiating Menus

What does negotiating menus really do for you? When you're creating an MDI application, you must take care to create your menus properly. If any of the child forms have menus of their own, you need to decide which menu bar will be displayed by your application. Whenever a child form has a menu associated with it, its menu will replace the parent form menu when the child form is displayed.

You can deal with menus in an MDI application in only two ways:

- Add all the required functions to each child form's menu. That way, whichever menu is displayed will have the correct menu items on it.

- Place all the different menu items on the main parent menu and display only the ones required at any given moment (preferred). This process is handled by using the menu item's `Visible` property to show or hide the item. When a child form is displayed, its `Form_Load` routine would set the `Visible` properties of the required menu items to `True` and the other menu items to `False`.

4

Adding Form Templates

One feature of Visual Basic taken for granted is the use of form templates in helping create an application interface. Microsoft has created many of the more standard windows forms that you can use in your application, including the following:

- **About**. This is the About dialog box displayed from the Help menu.
- **Splash**. This is the form that would appear when an application is starting up.
- **Login**. If your application requires a user ID and password, this form would provide the skeleton form and code.
- **Options**. This form provides you with the starting point of a tabbed dialog form to allow users to select from several different option sets.
- **Tip of the Day**. If you want your application to be able to display tips as Microsoft Word can do, this form will provide you with the form and starting code for the process.

You can add several other forms to your application from the template display (see Figure 4.26). These same forms are used by the Application Wizard when creating a new project.

FIGURE 4.26.

Adding a form to your application allows you to choose a blank form or one of the listed precreated forms.

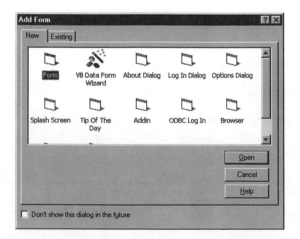

Form templates are nothing more than designed forms with or without code written for it and saved to a specified directory that Visual Basic looks in when you want to add a new form to your application. To add a new form template to this list, you simply copy the form to the FORMS directory.

Save the form you've been working with in today's lesson to this directory and then choose Project, Add Form from Visual Basic's menu. You should see your form listed in the Add Form dialog box. Of course, to use forms that you've designed previously, you don't need to add them to this directory; the Existing page in the dialog box lets you select a form from any directory on your computer.

Using the Template Manager

The Template Manager, included on Visual Basic's CD-ROM in the COMMON\TOOLS\VB\UNSUPPRT\TMPLMGR directory, is a Visual Basic add-in that lets you use three types of snippets of building blocks when creating your application. These building blocks allow you to add sections of code, menu, or controls to your application, saving you time in the process.

Installing the Template Manager

Before you can use the Template Manager, you must install it on your PC and tell Visual Basic that it exists. Follow these steps:

1. Copy the add-in file from the CD to your computer. The file can be found in COMMON\TOOLS\VB\UNSUPPRT\TMPLMGR\TEMPMGR.DLL. You can copy it anywhere, but I suggest that you copy it to your Visual Basic directory.

2. Register the add-in by using the REGSVR32.EXE program found in the \TOOLS\VB\REGUTILS directory. Copy this program to the same directory as the one you copied TEMPMGR.DLL to. Then execute the following statement from a DOS prompt:

```
regsvr32 tempmgr.dll
```

You also can drag TEMPMGR.DLL onto the REGSVR32.EXE file and drop it. Either method registers the manager on your PC.

3. Update VBADDIN.INI, a configuration file found in the Windows directory, by adding the following line to the bottom of the file:

```
TempMgr.Connect=0
```

Note

Edit this file in Notepad or Wordpad; don't edit it in any type of word processing program, as it will cause Visual Basic to operate incorrectly. This file contains many settings that Visual Basic uses to execute properly.

4. Create and copy the template directories and files. On your PC, add the following subdirectories to the TEMPLATE directory: CODE, CONTROLS, and MENUS. Then copy the contents of the corresponding directories in the COMMON\TOOLS\VB\UNSUPPRT\TMPLMGR\TEMPLATE directory on the CD-ROM.

5. Activate the add-in in Visual Basic by choosing Add-Ins, Add-In Manager from the menu, selecting VB Template Manager, and then clicking OK.

If you've completed these steps properly, you'll see three new entries on the Visual Basic Tools menu that allow you to access the Template Manager.

Working with the Template Manager

Using the Template Manager is a very simple process. To see how it works, add a new form to your open project and then select Tools, Add Menu to display the Add Menu dialog box (see Figure 4.27). The Template Manager's Add Menu dialog box displays the available choices to choose from.

FIGURE 4.27.

Choose Tools, Add Menu to open the Add Menu dialog box in the Template Manager.

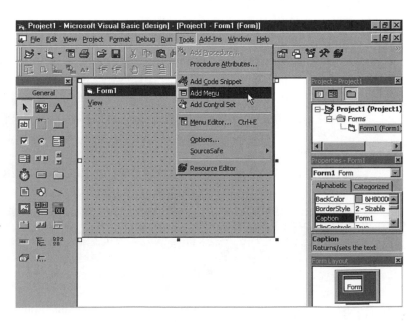

Select one of the menu items listed and click the Open button to add the menu to the current open form. The same process can be used to add controls or code sections to the form.

> **Caution**
>
> The Template Manager has a problem. If you're using the version that comes with Visual Basic and try to add control templates to your form, it won't work correctly or at all and you'll get an error message.
>
> If you choose to install the Template Manager upgrade from the Visual Basic user's Web site (http://www.microsoft.com/vstudio/owner), adding control templates will work correctly, but when you add a menu item, you'll fget only the top-level added to the form. However, all code for the It's up to you which version of the Template Manager you would prefer working with. If you want to work with menu templates more than control templates, keep the original program file. However, if you want to use control templates more, upgrade the manager to the newer version.subitems will be added.

Adding Additional Templates

To create your own templates for the Template Manager, create a form or module with just the objects that you want in the template and save it to one of the following three directories:

- \TEMPLATE\CODE
- \TEMPLATE\MENUS
- \TEMPLATE\CONTROLS

Also, the Template Manager supports wizard files (.VBZ), so you can place any wizards you want into the appropriate directory for the Template Manager to start up.

4

Summary

Today, you've seen what it takes to create toolbars and menus that you can use in your application to provide your users with a quick and easy way of accessing the application's functions and features. Also, you saw how to create pop-up menus that can be used as needed at the precise area in the application that they relate to. Finally, this lesson showed how to use templates to provide a way of reusing forms, code, controls, and menus that have been previously designed and saved. This way, you can create multiple applications with a consistent look to them.

Q&A

Q **What's the purpose of a toolbar in an application?**

A A toolbar provides users with a quick and easy way to access the most common functions of the application.

Q **What custom control file must be added to the toolbox for you to use the toolbar?**

A You must add the Windows Common Controls 6.0 - 2 (MSCOMCT2.OCX) file to the toolbox.

Q **How does a menu vary from a toolbar?**

A Because the menu has more room to work with, it can provide users with access to all functions of the application.

Q **What custom control file must be added to the toolbox for you to use the coolbar?**

A You must add the Windows Common Controls 6.0 – 3 (MSCOMCT3.OCX) file to the toolbox.

Q **How can users customize their toolbars?**

A If the toolbar's `AllowCustomize` property is set to `True`, users can double-click the toolbar to access the customize dialog box.

Q **How are form templates useful when creating an application?**

A With form templates, you can create an application where many of the forms look like standard Windows 95 dialog boxes.

Workshop

The Workshop provides quiz questions to help solidify your understanding of the material covered, as well as exercises to provide you with experience in using what you've learned. Try to understand the quiz and exercise answers before continuing on to the next day's lesson. Answers are provided in Appendix A, "Answers to Exercises."

Quiz

1. What are the two controls needed when creating a toolbar?

2. Can a toolbar display text instead of pictures in the buttons?

3. What does the Toolbar Builder do for you?

4. How many top-level menu items can you have?

5. If you use hotkeys, can you have two that start with the same letter?

6. How many shortcuts can you possibly have in your application?

Exercise

Start a new project and add the necessary controls, toolbar, and menu to allow users to select files to open and close—also when a file is selected, display the text in a control on the form. If you want, add the processing to allow users to change the font color by using a toolbar feature.

4

DAY 5

Objects, Collections, and Array Processing

You have learned a bit more about the capabilities of Visual Basic. Now, to understand the next topic you must learn some of the theory behind Visual Basic and Windows programming. Today's lesson deals with object programming using collections and arrays. You are going to see what objects really are, when to use them, and how they relate to the different controls that you use in an application. You will also see how to use collections in your application code, what makes the collection different from arrays, and how to work with both to simplify your application programming. In addition, you will learn how the different loop statements work in relation to the collections that you will be using. You will investigate how the loops differ and see when each should be used in the application process. Finally, you will create your own small object that will let you enhance an existing Visual Basic object.

What Are Objects and Collections?

Before you can understand what a collection is, you must know what an object is and what makes it a useful tool when you are developing Visual Basic applications. Objects are the central concept to Visual Basic programming. Forms, controls, and databases are considered objects. In fact, everywhere you look in Visual Basic you will see objects. When you start working directly with these objects, you need some way to keep track of them. In Visual Basic, a special object called a *collection* enables you to keep track of all the other objects that are in your application. A collection is a way to group a set of related items. In Visual Basic, collections are used to keep track of many things, such as the forms that are loaded in your program or the controls that are on a form.

Objects

Almost everything you use in Visual Basic can be considered an object. In fact, you have already worked with many objects in this book. Every control in Visual Basic is an object. When working with controls, you have seen that they all contain properties, methods, and events. Each control also contains code and data items, although you can't see the actual code that was written. In fact, each control or object, such as the TextBox control, is really a small self-contained package that is included with Visual Basic.

When you use the text box, you don't have to write any code to trigger its events or define any of its properties. The text box methods do all the work that you will need. This process is termed *encapsulation*. An object is like a space capsule; everything it needs to perform its task is included with the object. All the methods, events, and properties that an object uses are defined or coded within the object itself. All objects that share the same features (such as many text boxes on one form) are included in an object *class*. A single object is really an *instance* of its class definition. Every time you add a new control to a form, you are really creating a new instance of its class. If you go back and look at the code that you placed in the MDI project on Day 3, "Changing the Face of the Application," you will see the definition of a form object as shown in the following:

```
Dim NewNote As New frmNote
```

This code defines a new object call `NewNote` that is based on the defined form `frmNote` object. You might not realize it, but when you design a form and place controls on it, you are creating your own object. By using existing classes, you automatically inherit the properties, methods, and events from that class. To see this, you need go no further than the remaining code from the `mnuFileNew_Click` event from the MDI project as shown in the following:

```
intFormCtr = intFormCtr + 1
    NewNote.Show
    NewNote.Caption = "NotePad Version " & intFormCtr
```

Every time you execute the `NewNote.Show` method, another instance of the `frmNote` form is created. Each of these forms has associated with it all of the properties and events that you coded for the original form.

Collections

Collections are used everywhere in Visual Basic. Using the MDI project, when you have more than one `NewNote` form displayed, you can work with them from the point of view of a collection or array of forms. Unlike arrays, collections do not have to be redimensioned every time an object member is added or removed. When working in Visual Basic, you can use two collections to track the forms and controls that you use in an application. The `FORMS` collection keeps track of every loaded form in an application, whereas the `CONTROL` collection keeps track of every control that is used within an application. In addition, you can use a third built-in object to define your own collections. Using the generic `Collection` class, you can create as many different instances of the `Collection` objects as you need in your application.

The `Collection` object has three methods that you can use to add, remove, or access the objects in the collection. It also has one property that gives you the number of items in the collection. In the coming sections of this chapter, you will see how collections give you an easy way to access the objects of your application without writing large amounts of code.

Many objects in Visual Basic have default collections associated with them. One such example is the TreeView control, which has a `Nodes` collection associated with it. Each item in the `Nodes` collection has its own related properties and methods. One of the better examples of an object model is the Data Access Object (DAO) model (see Figure 5.1). The classes of the DAO are organized into a hierarchy and in turn contain collections. Each collection belongs to the class above it in the hierarchy.

FIGURE 5.1.

The classes, objects, and collections of the Data Access Object.

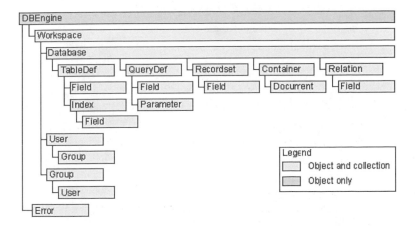

The whole concept of hierarchies simply means that objects can contain other objects, which in turn contain other objects. As you might have figured out, the terms *object* and *class* are mostly interchangeable. A class is like a data type that describes what kind of object you are referring to.

System Objects

Besides the objects that you can declare, such as forms, several other objects are included with Visual Basic to make your life as a programmer easier. These *system objects* can be used anywhere in an application. Although you can't define new instances of these objects or pass them as variables to other routines, they still are very useful. The five available system objects are listed in Table 5.1 along with some of their more important methods.

TABLE 5.1. THE AVAILABLE SYSTEM OBJECTS IN VISUAL BASIC.

Object	Description	Methods/Properties
App	The current application	EXEName returns the application's filename
		Path returns the application's path
		Title returns the startup form's title bar text
		Previnstance returns True if another instance (copy) of the application is currently running
ClipBoard	The Windows Clipboard	Clear erases the contents of the clipboard
		GetData/SetData gets or returns the graphic image stored on the clipboard
		GetText/SetText gets or returns the text on the clipboard
		GetFormat returns the format of the clipboard object
Debug	The Immediate window	Print copies information, at runtime, to the Immediate window (possible only in non-.EXE Visual Basic programs you run from Visual Basic's development environment)
		Assert suspends the execution of the application if the expression is false
Printer	The system printer	Provides printer support to the application
Screen	The user's screen	FontCount returns the number of fonts the current screen supports
		Fonts contains a list of all the screen's possible font names

Object	Description	Methods/Properties
		`Height`/`Width` returns the height or width in twips of the screen area
		`TwipsPerPixelX`/ `TwipsPerPixelY` returns the number of possible horizontal or vertical twips
		`MousePointer` sets or returns the shape of the mouse cursor

If you have worked with Visual Basic for any length of time, you might have seen some of these objects in use. For example, when using the MSGBOX statement to display a message to the user, you would want the caption to reflect the title of the application. To do this, you could enter the application title as a string every time you use a MSGBOX, or you can use the APP system object with its associated properties. The MSGBOX statement would resemble the following line of code:

```
MSGBOX "Incorrect Date entered. Try Again!", VBCritical, APP.Title
```

You can do many different things using these objects. If you want to ensure that only one instance of your application executes at a time, you could use the PrevInstance property of the APP object as follows:

```
If APP.Previnstance Then
    MSGBOX "Application is already running!", VBInformation, APP.Title
    End
End If
```

As you can see, the APP object provides runtime information about the current application. The Clipboard object gives you a way to provide users of your application with the standard Windows copy-and-paste functionality. If you decide to include the Edit, Copy and Edit, Paste menu options, then the Clipboard object would be used to provide that actual function. To see how this works, open the dlgFileOpenCopy project that you created on an earlier day. To this project, add a menu with only two main options, Copy and Paste. Then, add the following code to the form:

```
Private Sub mnuCopy_Click()
    Clipboard.Clear
    Clipboard.SetText txtSourceFile.Text
End Sub

Private Sub mnuPaste_Click()
    txtTargetFile.Text = Clipboard.GetText()
End Sub
```

When you run this application, you can copy text from the Source text box and then paste it into the Target text box. Of course, in this example, the object that is being

5

copied and pasted is hard coded into the routine. To make this a truly generic routine, you can use a property of the Form object. The ActiveControl property gives you access to whatever control is active on the form at that moment. When creating a copy-and-paste routine you must identify the type of data you are copying, because the Clipboard object handles text and graphics differently. Also, when users choose to paste the data from the clipboard, you must make sure they are pasting the data to a field that has the same data type of the data that was copied. In addition, as a rule you should empty the clipboard before copying any data into it. This entire process uses several different methods and properties of the Clipboard, Form, and Control objects. The code in Listing 5.1 shows the generic Copy/Paste routines that you can add to your application code.

LISTING 5.1. COPY_PASTE.TXT—CHECKING THE DATA TYPE BEFORE COPYING AND PASTING DATA USING THE CLIPBOARD.

```
 1: Private Sub mnuEditCopy_Click()
 2:     Clipboard.Clear
 3:     If TypeOf Form1.ActiveControl Is TextBox Then
 4:         Clipboard.SetText Form1.ActiveControl
 5:     ElseIf TypeOf Form1.ActiveControl Is PictureBox Then
 6:         Clipboard.SetData Form1.ActiveControl
 7:     End If
 8: End Sub
 9:
10: Private Sub mnuEditPaste_Click()
11:     If TypeOf Form1.ActiveControl Is TextBox Then
12:         If Clipboard.GetFormat(vbCFText) Then
13:             Form1.ActiveControl = Clipboard.GetText
14:         Else
15:             MsgBox "Invalid data in clipboard", vbInformation,
App.Title
16:         End If
17:     ElseIf TypeOf Form1.ActiveControl Is PictureBox Then
18:         If Clipboard.GetFormat(vbCFBitmap) Then
19:             Form1.ActiveControl = Clipboard.GetData
20:         Else
21:             MsgBox "Invalid data in clipboard", vbInformation,
App.Title
22:         End If
23:     End If
24: End Sub.
```

Accessing Objects

Accessing or working with Visual Basic objects is really quite simple when you use the available statements, properties, and methods. In the previous section, you saw how to create a Copy/Paste routine using several new Visual Basic statements and functions. By using the GetFormat method of the clipboard and the TypeOf-Is expression, you can test for any type of data type or control type in the application.

Finding the Object's Class

You use the TypeOf keyword to determine the type of object with which you are working. It can be used only as part of an If-Then statement and returns True or False depending on the object you are checking. In the following code, a True condition would be returned if the active control is a check box:

```
If TypeOf Form1.ActiveControl Is Checkbox Then
```

In addition to the TypeOf keyword, if you must retrieve the type of a particular object, you can use the TypeName function. The TypeName function is much more flexible than the TypeOf keyword because you can use it anywhere in your code, and because it returns the object's class name as a string. This enables you to change a section of code from the following:

```
If TypeOf Form1.ActiveControl Is Textbox Then
    MSGBOX "This control is a Textbox."
EndIf
```

to the following:

```
MSGBOX "This control is a " & TypeName(Form1.ActiveControl)
```

By simplifying your code, you are making it easier to perform maintenance or to add new features at a later time. This also lets you modify the Copy/Paste routine once again. Now the object type of the object you are copying can be compared to the object type of the object into which you are trying to paste the data, as shown in the following code:

```
If TypeName(Form1.ActiveControl) = TypeName(CopyObj) Then
```

This statement will compare the type of the active control with the type of CopyObj. CopyObj is an object variable that you define and create in the application and set in the Copy routine using the following line of code:

```
Set CopyObj = Form1.ActiveControl
```

Both the TypeOf keyword and the TypeName function are very useful when you must know the type of the object. This is because some objects might not support a particular property or method that you must reference.

Creating Objects

There are several different ways to create an object in your application. By far the easiest way is to place a control on a form. Every time you add a form or a control to the application project, you have created another object or instance of a class. Another way to create an object requires you to add some code to your application. First, you must define the object in the declarations section of the application as shown in the following:

```
Public myForm as NEW frmNote
```

This declaration does not actually create an object until you access this variable in your application code. If you look at the code for the mnuFileNew_Click routine (shown in the following code) in the MDI project you created earlier in this book, you would see that every time you selected File New from the menu, a new instance of the form object was created:

```
Private Sub mnuFileNew_Click()
    Dim NewNote As New frmNote
    intFormCtr = intFormCtr + 1
    NewNote.Show
    NewNote.Caption = "NotePad Version " & intFormCtr
End Sub
```

The third way to create an object is also done in code using the SET command along with the NEW keyword, as shown in the following:

```
Set MyObj = New frmNote
```

Again, this does not actually create a new object until you reference the MyObj variable later in the code. This would enable you to create objects without having to define unique variables for each type of object you might create. So, the mnuFileNew_Click routine could be changed to the following:

```
Private Sub mnuFileNew_Click()
    intFormCtr = intFormCtr + 1
    Set NewNoteObj = New frmNote
    NewNote.Show
    NewNote.Caption = "NotePad Version " & intFormCtr
End Sub
```

Note When you are finished working with an object, it is good programming style to set the object to nothing, as shown here, to release the memory it was using:

```
Set <object> = Nothing
```

The NewNoteObj variable is defined in the common module (.BAS) as:

```
Public NewNoteObj as Object
```

Because the object variable, NewNoteObj, is defined as an object, it can be set to whatever object you must create for the application.

Acting on Objects and Collections

As you add more controls to a form, working with these controls becomes a little cumbersome. Because the same types of objects are members of the same class (that is, every text box on a form is a member of the text box class, sharing properties), you are able to program these objects with more flexibility than you would have thought. As an example, look at a section of code that you would normally see in almost every application. This code sets several properties for a single object, a text box. In the following code, you can see that the control name is duplicated on every line:

```
txtFirstName.Text = "Demo"
txtFirstName.Font = "Ariel"
txtFirstName.BackColor = vbRed
TxtFirstName.FontBold = True
TxtFirstName.FontSize = 12
```

By using the With-End With command set you can easily set several properties for the same object. The preceding code could be rewritten as:

```
With txtFirstName
    .Text = "Demo"
    .Font = "Ariel"
    .BackColor = vbRed
    .FontBold = True
    .FontSize = 12
End With
```

Later today you will see how to use this command in conjunction with collections to reduce the amount of code in your application and increase the performance at the same time.

Most collections that you will use in your applications will be created, destroyed, and managed by Visual Basic itself. They will take one of the following forms:

- Forms
- Controls
- Grid columns and rows
- List items
- TreeView nodes
- Data recordset fields
- Others

5

Arrays

Except for a few differences, working with collections is much the same as working with arrays. An *array* is a list of variables that are accessed using the same variable name and an index value. Using arrays, you can store many occurrences of data. Each element of an array can be treated by the application code as a standard variable. The difference is the index value that specifies which element in the array to access. One of the restrictions of an array is that all of the elements must contain the data of the same data type. Another restriction is that you must define the array with an exact number of elements before you can access it. You do this using the following line of code:

```
Public Array_Demo(9) As String
```

This will define an array, `Array_Demo`, that has 10 string elements in it. However, if you do not know the maximum number of elements you might need, you could use the `ReDim` definition statement to change the number of elements in the array, as shown here:

```
ReDim Preserve Array_Demo(25)
```

You can see that you are not redefining the array itself, just the amount of memory it needs in the application. The `Preserve` keyword tells Visual Basic not to clear any existing data from the array during the process. Finally, when you define arrays, you can specify the starting value for the array. The default value in Visual Basic is zero, unless you add the `Option Base 1` statement to the definitions area of your application.

Collections

Now that you have taken a quick look at standard arrays, see how a collection works. Collections play an important role in the programming of a Visual Basic application. They are always present and are updated automatically as things change in the application. For example, if you are running an MDI-based application and start more instances of a child form, the `Forms` collection's `Count` property is updated by Visual Basic. Besides the predefined collections, you can also define your own.

The advantage of using a collection over an array is that collections will add new elements to an application without having to code anything special as with arrays. In addition, a collection can contain almost any combination of objects, although if you are using a collection it will probably be for a specific reason; thus, the objects in it will be of the same type.

When you create your own collection, you must manage it yourself. Any collection that you create will be a member of the `Collection` class as defined by Visual Basic. To define a collection, add the following code at the module level of your application:

```
Public colMyTextInput As New Collection
```

As with any other variable definition, it could be defined as Public or Private depending on your needs. A collection is like an empty file cabinet. You can add objects, remove objects, count the number of objects in it, or reference an object. The Collection class has three methods and one property that you can use:

- **Add method**—Adds items to the collection.
- **Remove method**—Deletes items from the collection using an index or key.
- **Item method**—Accesses a collection element by index or key.
- **Count property**—Returns the current number of items in the collection.

The key to adding objects to the collection is the Add method. The syntax for this method is shown here:

```
Sub Add (item as Variant [, key As Variant] [, before As Variant]
    [, after As Variant])
```

For example, to add a new name object to a collection of names using the person's social security number as the key, you would code the following:

```
ColEmployees.Add NewName, SSNum
```

This assumes that the SSNum is a string. If the value that you are using for the key is a number, you must use CStr to convert it to a string. The key value accepts only strings as input. In addition, if you are adding objects to the collection in a particular order, you can use the before and after parameters to specify the exact position to add the object.

> **Caution**
>
> Because Collection objects maintain their numeric index numbers automatically as you add and delete items, the index of a given item will change over time. Do not save an index and expect it to retrieve the same item later in your program. Use keys for this purpose.

5

Because collections can also contain objects instead of values, you can access any of the object's properties without having to first place it in an object variable. You can reference the properties directly from the collection as in the following:

```
ColTextInputLines.Item(1).ToolTipText = "Please enter your First name."
```

The reason why this works is in the way Visual Basic processes the statement. It evaluates the expression from left to right. When it comes to the Item method for the collection, it gets the reference to the indexed item and uses it to evaluate the remaining parts of the line. Although this is a faster way of writing code to access the properties of a collection object, if you're going to use more than one property or method of an object in the collection, copy the object reference to a defined object variable first. Using an object reference while it's in the collection is slower than using it after placing it in an object variable. The following is an example of this concept:

```
Dim txtInputCurrent As TextBox
    txtInputCurrent = ColTextInputLines.Item(1)
    txtInputCurrent.ToolTipText = "Please enter your First name."
    txtInputCurrent.FontBold = True
```

In many cases, if a collection object can be used, an advanced Visual Basic programmer will never use an array. Instead of using an array that must be declared to a certain size and can contain only one data type, the collection can have items added and removed from it without having to worry about the storage that it needs. If you need the user to input an unknown number of names, phone numbers, or any other type of data, you could use an array as shown here:

```
Dim Input_List() as String
Dim Current_Value as String
Dim Counter as Long
    Counter = 0
Get_Next_Number:
    Current_Value = Inputbox("Enter the Phone Number",,"NA")
    If Current_Value <> "NA" then
        Counter = Counter + 1
        ReDim Input_List(Counter)
        Input_List(Counter) = Current_Value
    End If
    If Current_Value = "END" Then Exit Sub
    Goto Get_Next_Number
```

As you can see, when using arrays you must keep track of the index value, and you must resize it every time you need to add a new element to it. With a collection, the same routine would resemble the following code:

```
Dim Input_Col as New Collection
Dim Current_Value as String
Get_Next_Number:
    Current_Value = Inputbox("Enter the Phone Number",,"NA")
    If Current_Value <> "NA" then
        Input_List.Add = Current_Value
    End If
    If Current_Value = "END" Then Exit Sub
    Goto Get_Next_Number
```

By using the collection, the process has become simpler and easier to manage.

Control Arrays

One of the things that you can do with objects is to use them as arrays. For example, you can define an array of text boxes on a form. Because of the way objects get created, you can define the array even if the objects don't yet exist. Unfortunately, all of the issues of array processing discussed earlier are still present when working with object arrays that you define.

However, Visual Basic does support one type of object array that you will find yourself using a lot, even though collections are always available. When you copy a control and paste that control back onto the form, Visual Basic displays a message box informing you that you are about to create a control array (see Figure 5.2).

FIGURE 5.2.

Pasting several of the same controls on a form will create a control array.

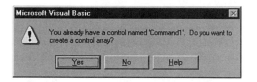

After you have a control array on the form, you can use it to manipulate all the elements. The events for a control array contain a parameter that passes the index of the current control to the event routine. Therefore, if you enter text into one of the five text boxes on a form, the `txtInput_KeyPress` routine would know which control you are typing into. As an example, if you wanted to create a keypress routine that would allow only numbers to be entered, you could code the following in the `KeyPress` event:

```
Private Sub txtInputLine_KeyPress(Index As Integer, keyascii As Integer)
    If (keyascii < 48 Or keyascii > 58) And keyascii <> 8 Then
        Beep
        keyascii = 0
    End If
End Sub
```

Of course, if this was the only thing that you needed to do in the routine, it would be better to use the Masked Edit control, which does this type of editing for you. To use this feature in a more understandable way, open the dlgFileCopyOpen project. In this application, when you allow the user to change the colors for the form and the controls, you must code each of the color statements separately for each control:

```
frmDialog!txtSourceFile.BackColor = lblTxtBack.BackColor
frmDialog!txtTargetFile.BackColor = lblTxtBack.BackColor
```

Note

Visual Basic uses the exclamation character (!) instead of the standard period (.) when referencing a form's objects from within another form or module.

Although this might be okay for a project that has only two text box controls on it, think if your application had 10 or more text box controls on a form. You can see how this would very quickly bog down your coding process, especially if you are changing several properties for the controls. By using a control array and a processing loop, you can quickly set the properties for a set of controls. The following code will set the `BackColor` property for every text box that is included in the control array:

```
Dim txtObject as Object
For each txtObject in txtInputLine
    txtObject.BackColor = lblTxtBack.BackColor
Next
```

As you can see from this simple example, this technique lets you work with the control array without having to know how many elements there are, or having to reference each one separately.

Creating Your Own Class

If you have been programming for any length of time, you know that most programmers start to collect a library of functions and routines that can be used in any application that requires them. In Visual Basic, you can define your own data types to meet certain application design requirements. You can use classes in much the same way. Although classes don't replace functions in your application code, they do provide a convenient way to organize those routines and the data they use. If you looked closely at any of the object classes that are included in Visual Basic, such as a text box, you would see that the class combines data and procedure code into one succinct unit.

Although you don't want to create a class for every routine you write, you can create a class out of it if the routine is going to be useful in many different applications. This will enable you to add the class to an application if you need it. To see how to add a class to your application, you first must create one. For the purposes of this lesson, you are going to create a small class that will calculate the age of a person based on his birthdate, and then if the age is greater than an age limit that is passed to the class, an event will be triggered to allow the application to act on that information. Although classes can become very complicated, the creation process is the same no matter what type of class procedure you create.

 Note   Don't confuse creating a class with creating a custom control. Both are classes, but a custom control can have a form interface associated with it, whereas a class module does not.

To create your class, use the Class Builder utility found in the Visual Basic Add-Ins menu. The first step is to start a Standard EXE project. Don't do anything with the form that is automatically added to the project; you will use it later. The new class, called `GetAge`, that you will build will have the properties, methods, and events listed in Table 5.2.

TABLE 5.2. NEW CLASS DEFINITIONS.

Group	Name	Data Type	Description
Property	Birthdate	String	Input date used to calculate the age of a person
	AgeLimit	Integer	Used to set the age limit for the event calculation
	Age	Integer	Read-only value containing the calculated age
Method	CalcAge		Class procedure that calculates the age
Event	Underage		This event will be triggered if the calculated age is under the AgeLimit value
	OverAge		This event will be triggered if the calculated age is over the AgeLimit value

To begin the process, start the Class Builder utility to display the Class Builder interface (see Figure 5.3).

5

FIGURE 5.3.

The Class Builder utility helps you define a new class using an Explorer-style application interface.

Add new class

Add new collection

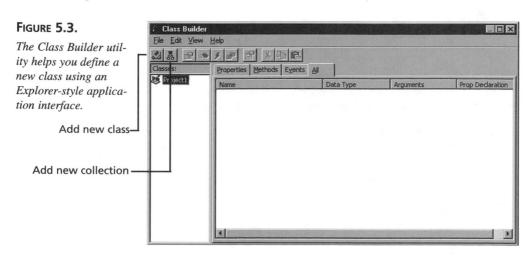

The Class Builder enables you to create a new class or a new collection. For this example, click the Add New Class button to add a new class to the project using the Class Module Builder dialog box as shown in Figure 5.4. On the Properties tab, change the class name to GetAge, then if you want, you can add a description of this class in the Description field on the Attributes tab.

FIGURE 5.4.

Creating a new class definition.

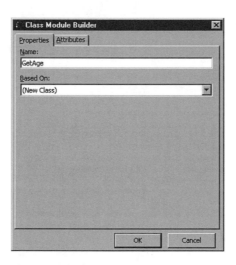

Click OK to actually add the class definition. Congratulations, you have successfully created a class!

However, this class doesn't do anything because it has no properties, methods, or events. The next step is to add the definitions for the remaining objects of the class. To add any of the objects, you can right-click the class name in the Classes list to display a drop-down menu, then select New to display the list of objects you can create (see Figure 5.5).

Select Property to display the Property Builder dialog box (see Figure 5.6), which you will use to define each of the properties required for the class.

For each property, enter the name and select the correct data type as previously listed in Table 5.2. When you have finished this task, the Class Builder dialog box should look like the one in Figure 5.7.

FIGURE 5.5.

Choosing the object to create from a drop-down submenu.

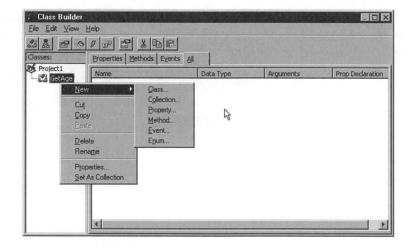

FIGURE 5.6.

The Property Builder dialog box prompts you for all the required information about the property you are creating.

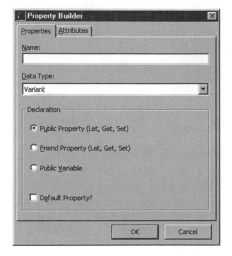

5

Now you want to add the method to the class. To add the method, right-click the class name and select New, Method from the pop-up menu to display the Method Builder dialog box shown in Figure 5.8.

FIGURE 5.7.

The new class with all of the defined properties listed.

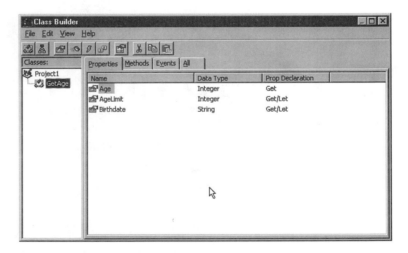

FIGURE 5.8.

You add a new method by using the Method Builder dialog box.

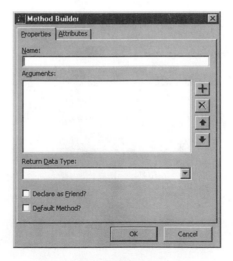

After you enter the name for the method, you must add any arguments that will be passed to the routine. No arguments are needed for this method. Click OK to add the method. The last step in this process is to add the two events to allow the calling application to take action if the age calculated is either over or under the age limit set. Again, right-click the class name and choose New, Event from the pop-up menu to display the Event Builder dialog box as shown in Figure 5.9.

As in the method, there are no arguments for this event, so enter the name and click OK to complete the task. If you click the All tab in the Class Builder dialog box, you will see all of the objects that you have added to the class (see Figure 5.10). You now are ready to add the class module to your application. Select File, Exit from the menu, and click Yes to add the class module code to your application.

FIGURE 5.9.

The Event Builder dialog box enables you to define the events that the class will use to interact with the calling application.

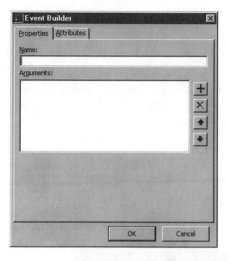

FIGURE 5.10.

The Class Builder will always list all the properties, methods, and events for a selected class.

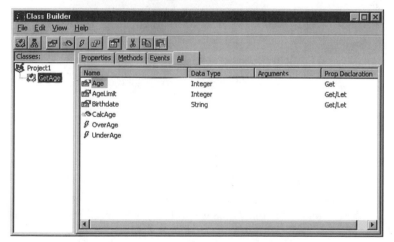

If you look in the Project window, you will now see a new folder and module added to your project. This is the new class that you just created. You still must add a few more things to the class module before you can use it. Even though you defined a method to the class, there is no code in that method's routine to perform. For this class, replace the comment Your code goes here with the following code to the CalcAge subprocedure:

```
Public Sub CalcAge()
mvarAge = DateDiff("yyyy", mvarBirthdate, Now)
    If mvarAge <= mvarAgeLimit Then
        RaiseEvent UnderAge
    Else
        RaiseEvent OverAge
```

```
    End If
End Sub
```

As you can see from this code, the age is being calculated using the built-in function DATEDIFF. Then the age is compared to the AgeLimit property value and if it is less than the age limit, the UnderAge event is triggered; otherwise, the OverAge event is triggered. You must do one last modification to the class code: Remove the Property Let routine for each property that you want to be read-only.

Now, to use the class, you will have to add a few lines of code to define the class in the application, then create a new instance of the class, and finally, you must add the code for the event routine of the class. Add a text box, Masked Edit box, two labels, and a command button to the form in the project as shown in Figure 5.11. This will allow you to enter a birth date and then call the GetAge method.

FIGURE 5.11.

Creating a form to accept a birth date to pass to the class routine.

You can see in this figure that I have also added the UpDown control to work with the age limit text box and allow the user to change the age limit value by clicking the up or down arrows. In addition, I also added some standard property settings for the form and the command button. These will center the form on the screen and set the command button to the default so the user can press Enter to calculate the age.

Now, add the code in Listing 5.2 to the form's code and run the application. This code will verify that the data entered in the text boxes has the correct data type, and if the information is okay the CalcAge method of GetAge will be invoked.

LISTING 5.2. NEWCLASS.TXT—THE APPLICATION CODE FOR THE CLASS.VBP PROJECT SHOWING HOW TO CREATE AND USE A CLASS.

```
1: Private WithEvents NewAge As GetAge
2:
3: Private Sub cmdCalcAge_Click()
4: Set NewAge = New GetAge
5:     If Not IsNumeric(txtAgeLimit.Text) Then
```

```
 6:          MsgBox "Please enter a valid age limit", vbCritical, App.Title
 7:          Exit Sub
 8:      ElseIf Not IsDate(mskDate) Then
 9:          MsgBox "An invalid date was entered.", vbCritical, App.Title
10:          Exit Sub
11:      End If
12:      NewAge.AgeLimit = CInt(txtAgeLimit.Text)
13:      NewAge.Birthdate = mskDate.Text
14:      NewAge.CalcAge
15: End Sub
16:
17: Private Sub newage_underage()
18:      MsgBox "This person is under the age limit of: " & NewAge.AgeLimit & _
19:                  " with an age of: " & NewAge.Age
20: End Sub
21:
22: Private Sub newage_overage()
23:      MsgBox "This person is over the age limit of: " & NewAge.AgeLimit & _
24:                  " with an age of: " & NewAge.Age
25: End Sub
```

Start the application, enter an age limit for the application to use, then enter a date and click the command button. If the date is less than the age limit you entered you will get the message shown in Figure 5.12.

Of course, in more sophisticated class modules, these methods and events would perform

FIGURE 5.12.

For each event of the GetAge *class, a different message box will be displayed.*

5

much more complicated processes than what is shown in this example. The neat thing about this whole topic is that after the class is created and saved, you can add it to any other application project in which you must use it.

Browsing Your Objects

When working with classes that you have created, or with any class that comes with Visual Basic, you can view all of their associated properties, methods, and events by using the Object Browser. The Object Browser tool comes with Visual Basic and gives you one single location to look for objects and object information. When you first open the Object Browser from the View, Object Browser menu option, the default browser dialog box will be displayed as shown in Figure 5.13.

The Object Browser displays information contained in type libraries. A *type library*

FIGURE 5.13.

The Object Browser displays all of your application's object information.

Navigation control buttons

Library list box

Search text list box

Classes list

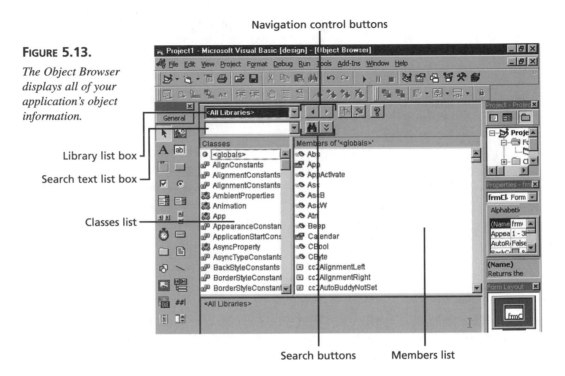

Search buttons   Members list

contains the detailed information about classes and their properties, events, methods, defined constants, and more. For every class that you create, or objects that are included in your application, or even information about other applications, such as Microsoft Excel, Visual Basic creates type library information to display. The Library list box displays each different type library that is referenced by your project (see Figure 5.14). Each of these will display the classes included in that type library.

The Object Browser will even show you the type library for your project that was created by Visual Basic. To see what is associated with the class you just created, select your project's name from the Library list box—this will display all the objects that are included in your project—and then select the new class that you have created. You will see all of the properties, methods, and events that you added to the class as shown in Figure 5.15.

This tool is very useful if you can't remember a property name; or, if you must use a Visual Basic constant, you can look it up in the Object Browser. For example, if you must know what the Select properties are, you can search for the string SELECT, and the browser will display all references that it finds as shown in Figure 5.16.

After the constants are displayed, you can select the one you want, copy it, and then paste it into the code where needed.

FIGURE 5.14.

The Object Browser will list all of the type libraries to which you have access in your application.

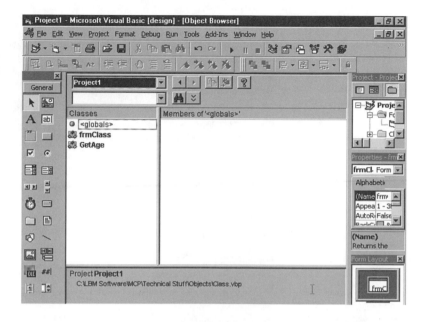

FIGURE 5.15.

Listing all the associated information for a class.

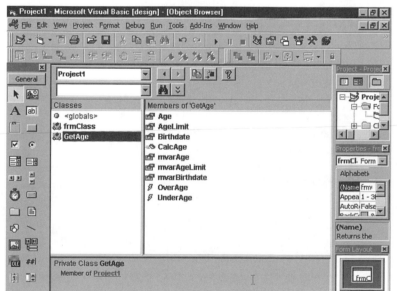

FIGURE 5.16.

*The Object Browser
will display all found
references of a search
string.*

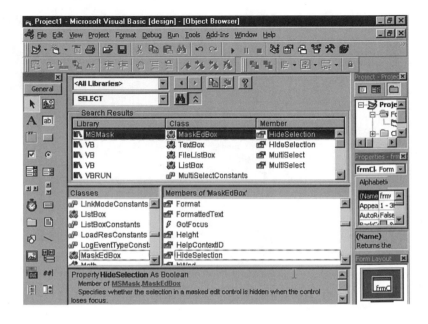

Loop Processing

One of the most useful control statements that you can use in Visual Basic is the *loop*.
Loops are used to perform most of the repetitive tasks in any application. You can use
two types of loops when creating a Visual Basic application, the counter and conditional
loops. *Conditional* loops perform a task until a specified condition occurs, and *counter*
loops will execute for a set number of times. If you search the Visual Basic Help system
for the word *loops*, several topics are listed. All of these topics fall into one of the two
mentioned loop types.

Counter Loops

In programming languages, a counter loop is usually known as a For loop or a
For...Next loop. In reference to this chapter, there is actually a third version of this
loop called a For Each...Next loop that is used specifically for collections and arrays.
Each loop is defined at the beginning with a For statement and ends with a Next statement. The syntax of a standard For...Next loop is as follows:

```
For counter = start To end [Step step]
[statements]
[Exit For]
[statements]
Next [counter]
```

In the For statement, you would specify the counter variable and the starting and ending values. At the end of the loop the Next statement instructs the computer to add 1 to the counter variable and then go back to the For statement, where the counter is compared to the ending value. If the counter is larger, the loop is ended. To see exactly what happens, a For loop can be coded without using the For...Next statements, as shown in the following code:

```
Counter = Start_Value
Top_Of_Loop:
    If Counter <=End_Value then
        [Code Statements]
        Counter = Counter + 1
        Goto Top_Of_Loop
    End If
```

As you can see, the For...Next statements do a lot of work for you. In addition, by using the Step keyword you can specify the value that is added or subtracted from the counter variable. Finally, if you must exit the loop early, you can use the Exit For statement. When the loop process is completed, program processing continues at the first line of code after the Next statement.

Tip

For debugging purposes, you should always include the counter variable name in the Next statement. This enables you to identify the For...Next relationship when several loops are nested within each other.

The other type of counter loop is the For Each...Next loop. You actually saw this loop a little earlier today, when it was used to set the BackColor properties of a text box control array. This statement enables you to use a counter loop without having to know how many elements are in the array or collection. The syntax of this statement (shown in the following code) is very similar to the first For...Next statement; however, there are a few differences:

```
For Each element In group
[statements]
[Exit For]
[statements]
Next [element]
```

In this case, you must specify a variant-defined variable as the element, and the group is either the array or the collection with which you want to work. The remaining sections of the statement are identical to the first For...Next statement.

5

Tip

> If you are going to access all of the elements in a collection, the For Each...Next statement performs better than if you use the index values with a standard For...Next loop.

This loop statement can be used in conjunction with other object-related functions mentioned earlier today to access every control on a form in order to set their properties. As an example, if you had an application in which you wanted to set the font size of all the labels, command buttons, and text boxes to a specific size, you could do it in your application code with the following routine:

```
Dim myobj As Object
    For Each myobj In Screen.ActiveForm.Controls
        If TypeOf myobj Is TextBox or _
            TypeOf myobj Is CommandButton or _
            TypeOf myobj Is Label Then
            MyObj.FontSize = 10
        End If
    Next
```

This type of programming logic enables you to create single routines that will process any object on a form.

Conditional Loops

Just like the counter loops there are several different types of conditional loops that you can use: the Do and While loops. Each of them share one key feature, which is the condition. The condition is any valid Visual Basic expression that can be evaluated to True or False. The Do statement actually has two main types that you can use, the Do While and the Do Until. The following is the syntax for both of these statements:

```
Do [{While ¦ Until} condition]
[statements]
[Exit Do]
[statements]
Loop
```

As you can see, the Do statement syntax closely resembles the For...Next syntax, and in fact, the same principles apply.

The Do While statement tells the application to process the statements in the loop while a specified condition is true. When the condition becomes false, the loop is exited. The Do Until works the same way as the Do While, except that the loop is processed until a condition becomes true. This can be seen in the following two segments of code:

```
Do While Not EOF(1)
' Process Statements
Loop

Do Until EOF(1)
' Process Statements
Loop
```

Both of these versions of the Do statement check the condition before entering the loop and then at the beginning of each iteration. As an example, in the Do Until statement, if the file was already at End of File, the code contained in the loop will not be processed. To confuse matters a little, both Do statements can be coded a different way. The syntax of this other method is as follows:

```
Do
[statements]
[Exit Do]
[statements]
Loop [{While ¦ Until} condition]
```

At first glance they might not look any different, but you should notice that the While or Until condition occurs at the bottom of the loop instead of at the top. This allows the code contained in the loop process to be executed at least once no matter what the state of the condition is.

Depending on the type of loop processing you must do, you must select the appropriate type of loop statement. For example, most file access routines that will loop reading records from the file usually use the Do Until method checking for the End of File condition to be True. Many times the type of loop you use is more for documentation purposes than for performance.

Summary

Today you learned how to work with objects and collections in your application. Accessing collections is no harder than working with arrays, although collection objects provide better performance and easier coding compared with array processing.

In addition, you learned several different ways to work with the multiple controls, with the focus on how to simplify the code you are writing. You have also seen how to create your own classes to package a process with its related data elements so that you can use them in any application. Finally, you had a short review of the different loop processing statements that you can use when working with collections and objects.

5

Q&A

Q **What is the difference between a control array and the control collection?**

A A control array is a standard array in which the elements are controls of the same type. The control collection is a system-created array that contains all of the controls on the form, no matter what type they are.

Q **What do objects of the same class share?**

A Objects of the same class share all of their properties, methods, and events.

Q **What is the benefit of creating your own collection?**

A Because a collection can contain any type of element, you can include any of the different objects that you are working with, including forms, controls, and variables.

Q **Why should I create my own class?**

A A custom class module enables you to bundle a function as a separate unit and use it as an object in any application by adding the saved class to the new project.

Workshop

The Workshop provides quiz questions to help solidify your understanding of the material covered, as well as exercises to provide you with experience in using what you've learned. Try to understand the quiz and exercise answers before continuing on to the next day's lesson. Answers are provided in Appendix A, "Answers to Exercises."

Quiz

1. Name two different ways to programmatically check an object's class.

2. Why is using the `With...End With` statements not recommended with the following code?

```
With txtInputFile
    .Text = "TextFile.TXT"
    .Maxlength = 10
End With
```

3. Name the four objects that all collections share.

4. How do you create a new instance of an object or class?

Exercise

Write an application that will put a new TextBox control on the form every time you click the command button.

DAY 6

Procedures, Functions, and Logic

Up to this point in the book, you've seen many different tools and features that you can use when creating a Visual Basic application. By following the book's examples, you have worked with built-in functions, statements, and event procedures, and have even created your own class module. What you didn't know (or like many programmers, didn't care about) was how the information was being passed to and from the different routines in the application. You've seen routines that start like this

```
Private Sub Main()
```

but didn't understand why the parentheses were needed or what `Private` really meant. The only thing that you knew was that they were needed for the application to run properly. Today's lesson looks at how variables are declared in an application and the different ways in which Visual Basic handles them. Also, you will learn the differences between subprocedures and functions and how each are used. Finally, you will review the concept of writing a logical application and see how to use some of your old programming friends in a different way.

Scoping Out the Variables

By now you probably have noticed that a Visual Basic application has different types of source files that contain the program instructions that make up your application. These files, such as forms, code, and class modules, often contain multiple procedures. A form module might have event procedures for each control on the form. In addition, the form modules might contain general routines that are used by several of the event procedures. The standard code modules can also contain multiple procedures. These procedures might be in the form of functions or subroutines.

When a module contains multiple routines, those routines often must share data between them. Creating a variable in one routine with a `Dim` statement does not automatically make that variable available to any of the other routines. To understand how to use variables properly, you must first understand how variables can be defined in your application. *Declaring* variables simply means that the application knows that the variable exists and what values or type of data is valid for that variable. Also, how a variable is defined affects how its data can be shared within the application.

Defining the Variables

If the only routines a form module contains are the event procedures, then you would not have to worry about sharing data. As you have seen in many of the sample projects you have created, all modules, including form modules, have a Declarations section that contains the definitions for many of the variables your application is using. You can view this section by selecting General from the Object drop-down list and Declarations from the Procedure drop-down list in the Code Editor (see Figure 6.1).

With only event procedures, you would have no need to declare any variables. Any variables that you declare are generally used to store data temporarily to use when performing calculations within the application. For example, you might want to calculate several values, compare them, and then perform some operations on them, depending on the result of the comparison. You must keep the values if you want to compare them, but you don't need to store them in an object property.

Besides variables, you can also declare some data for your application as *constants*. As the name implies, these values remain constant throughout the life of the application. By using constants you can make your code more readable by providing meaningful names instead of numbers or hard-coded strings. In fact, you have been using constants, even if you haven't realized it. When you code a statement like the following you are using a built-in constant:

```
frmNote.Visible = True
```

FIGURE 6.1.

Displaying the Declarations section of any module in the application in the Code Editor.

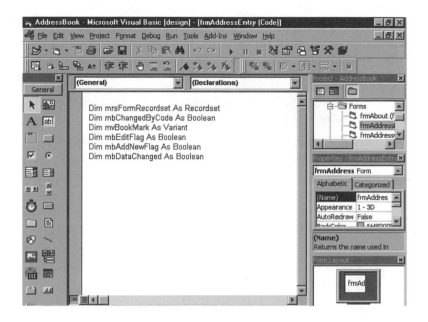

FIGURE 6.1.

Displaying the Declarations section of any module in the application in the Code Editor.

The variable name `True` is really a constant with a value of –1. You could have written this line of code as follows:

```
frmNote.Visible = -1
```

Of course, the first version of the statement is much more readable, even if you knew the –1 meant `True`.

As you begin to add code to the event procedures in your application, you might find that you want several procedures to work with data in the same variable. As an example, you could store the value of a text box in a variable when a command button is clicked. However, suppose you declared that variable inside the procedure as follows:

```
Private Sub cmdSalesComplete()
Dim Sale_Amt As Single
    Sale_Amt = Csng(txtAmt_Total.Text)
'    Any remaining code would go here
End Sub
```

Unfortunately, no other procedure would be capable of accessing this variable. `Sale_Amt` is considered local to just that procedure because you declared it inside the procedure itself. If you want other procedures to be capable of accessing the variable, you must move the declaration of it into the module's Declarations section.

As you might have discovered accidentally, there are several ways to declare variables in your application. If you just type variable names into your code as shown in the

6

following code, you don't need to declare the variable before using it unless the `Option Explicit` statement is used:

```
Private Sub cmdCalcAmt_Click()
    TempAmt = Csng(txtAmt_Total.Text)
    TempAmt = TempAmt * 1.06
    MsgBox "This is the final total: " & TempAmt
End Sub
```

However, Visual Basic will automatically create a variable that you can use, just as if you declared it yourself. Although this is convenient, it can lead to error in your code if you misspell a variable. To see how easily this could happen, try this on your computer. Start a new project and add a command button and text box to the default form. Then add the preceding code to the form. Now run the application, enter a number in the text box, and click the command button. You should see a message box with a valid number being displayed. Now, to see what would happen if you misspelled the variable somewhere in the code, change the second line to the following:

```
TempAmt = TemAmt * 1.06
```

Now, run the application again. This time, you should not see any number when the message box is displayed. Because the `TempAmt` variable was misspelled on the next-to-last line of the code, this function will always display a zero on the message box. Whenever Visual Basic encounters a new variable name, it doesn't know whether you meant to declare a new variable or you just misspelled an existing one, so it creates a new variable for you. To avoid this problem, you can tell Visual Basic to warn you whenever it encounters a name that was not explicitly declared as a variable.

When you place the `Option Explicit` statement in the `Declarations` section of any module in your application, it will prevent you from having this problem.

Tip

> You can automatically insert the `Option Explicit` statement in any new modules that you add to the application by choosing Tools, Options from the Visual Basic menu; then click the Editor tab and check the Require Variable Declaration option.

Caution

> If you already have some modules in your application, you must manually add the `Option Explicit` statement to each of them.

Where do Variables Live?

The *scope* of a variable sets which parts of your application code can access it. When you declare a variable within a procedure, only the code in that procedure can access or modify the data stored in that variable. This variable is said to have a scope that is local to that procedure. However, you might need to use a variable with a wider scope, such as one whose data is available to all the procedures within one module or to all the procedures in the entire application. Visual Basic enables you to specify the scope of any variable when you declare it. Depending on how a variable is declared, it is scoped as either a local or global variable:

- **Local (also called private)**—The variable is accessible only to the code within the procedure in which it was declared.
- **Global (also called public)**—The variable can be used by any procedure in the module in which it was declared.

As you begin to add more modules to your project, you might find that the private variables defined within the procedures are no longer enough for your applications needs. You might need to access a variable from one module in another module. To do this, you would need to declare the variable as a public variable.

> **Note**
> Public variables can be declared only in the `Declarations` section of a module. They can never be declared inside a procedure.

Besides the `Public` statement, you can also declare variables using the `Private` and `Dim` statements. The `Private` statement will declare a variable that can be accessed only in the module or procedure in which it was declared. Both the `Dim` and `Private` statements declare variables essentially the same way.

> **Tip**
> When writing code for your application, you should use the `Private` statement instead of the `Dim` statement to ensure that the scope of the variable is what you intended.

> **Note**
> Note that even the procedures with which you work have a scope. Generally, they are private to the module in which they are located, and only other procedures in that module can access each other. However, if you declare a procedure as `Public`, it will be available anywhere in the application.

6

If using public variables can cause problems in the application, why should they be used? In most cases, you should use public variables in the following situations:

- When you must access information anywhere in your application (such as custom color and font information)

- When you are creating constants to be used in your application (note that constants cannot be declared as private)

- To allow access to a database workspace without opening multiple instances of the database

- When you must access Windows API calls in the application

 Tip

If you must use any public variables, you should declare them in a standard module rather than in one of the form modules in the application. This gives you a centralized location for all of these variables. That way you would not accidentally declare another public variable with the same name.

Watching Out for Problems

The more public a variable becomes, the more cluttered your programs become and the easier it is for bugs to enter the picture. Despite the fact that public variables sound useful, you do not want to use them unless doing so is absolutely necessary. Typically, only a few procedures must share the same data values; most procedures don't need to share data at all.

One of the most common mistakes a programmer can make is to use the same variable name in multiple places for different reasons. If that variable is explicitly declared as a private variable in the different routines, then except for the issue of duplicate names from a documentation perspective, no harm is done. However, if that variable is declared as a module-level variable or as a public variable, you would wind up changing the value in the variable that might still be used in another routine in the application. This causes one of the hardest types of bugs to find and fix.

You have seen that variables can be either local (private) or global (public), and that routines often must share data among themselves. However, you now know that when you declare public variables you open yourself up to problems that could occur by reusing variable names. An overwhelming problem is that you must share data between procedures but you've been told that you shouldn't include module-level and public variables in your applications. The way around this dilemma is to pass the data that a procedure needs directly to that procedure.

```
Call Calc_Total_Sales(Units,Unit_Price)

Public Sub Calc_Total_Sales (cUnits, cUnit_Price)
```

If the parentheses are empty, nothing is being passed to the procedure. That's why many of the event routines have the parentheses in the declarations statement.

Caution   You should never pass a public variable. This would confuse Visual Basic to no end. Besides, there is no reason to pass a variable that is already accessible in the receiving routine.

Subroutines and Functions

Now that you know how to pass a variable the next step is to understand to what type of procedure you are passing the data. Since the advent of programming you could use two types of procedures: the subroutine and the function. The only difference between them is the way the data is returned to the calling routine and how the routine is accessed. You will probably code most of your application by using routines. As you design your applications you will execute many sections of code from different areas of the application (such as input edit routines). By segregating this code in routines you are making it easier to read the source code, and it will also make modifying the code easier.

Subroutines

One of the most common elements of a Visual Basic application is the *subroutine*. A subroutine is a procedure that is used to perform a certain task and return control to the routine that called it. *Calling* a subroutine refers to the transferring of execution control from the current code section to the subroutine. Suppose you have a subroutine that displays a message box saying that you got to the subroutine. Now, you want to print a text string to the form, call the subroutine, and then print another text string to the form when you click a command button. Your application would resemble the code in Listing 6.1.

LISTING 6.1. CALLSUB.TXT—CALLING A SUBROUTINE FROM THE MAIN CODE.

```
1: Private Sub cmdDemo_Click()
2:     frmDemo.Print "Starting the application"
3:     Call ShowMSGBOX
4:     frmDemo.Print "Ending the application"
5: End Sub
6:
7: Private Sub ShowMSGBOX()
8:     Msgbox "I am currently in the sub-routine"
9: End Sub
```

You should also be careful to not use the same name when you declare two separate public variables. If one variable is local in a procedure and the other is public, the lo variable will hide the scope of the public one. When the local variable is no longer accessible, the application will then use the public one. The problem here is that you probably won't realize there are two variables with the same name, and you'll use th both as if they were one variable. Of course, the results will be anything but expecte

Passing Information

Okay, now you know that working with local variables is safer than working with g or public variables. Given this fact, and that local variables can be used only by the cedure in which they were declared, what happens when you have multiple procedu that must work with the same data? Just because the procedures are separate doesn' mean they must work with separate data.

If one procedure calculates an array that is printed by another procedure later in the application but the array is local to the first routine, the second one would not be al access it. No routine can use another routine's local data until you set up some type sharing mechanism between them. When passing data between two routines, one re (the calling procedure) passes data to the second routine (the receiving procedure). receiving routine modifies or calculates a value that the calling routine needs, the r ing routine can then return that value to the calling routine.

When passing a local variable from one routine to another, you are really passing a argument from the calling routine to the receiving one. Of course, you can pass mo than one argument or variable at a time from the calling routine. The receiving rou said to *receive* a parameter or variable from the calling routine. Whether you call t passed variables arguments or parameters, the important thing is that you are sendi local variables from one routine to another.

Note   You might not realize it, but you already know how to pass arguments t routine. Every time you use the MSGBOX function you are passing data. A the information inside the parentheses are passed as arguments. The MS function will receive these values and display them.

The parentheses hold the names of the variables that you are passing or the variab are being received. To pass a local variable from one routine to another, you woul the local variable in parentheses in both the calling and receiving routines as show the following:

If you look closely at this code, you will see two separate subroutines. The first is the command button Click event routine. This routine will be executed when you click the command button. When you run this application you will see the first line being printed on the form and then a message box being displayed (see Figure 6.2). Until you click OK on the message box, the second Print statement in the main routine will not be executed.

FIGURE 6.2.

Displaying a message box in the called subroutine will halt execution until the message box is closed.

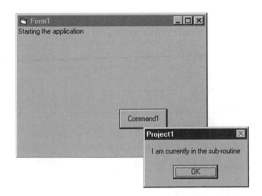

Looking at this very simple example, you could ask why not just put the line of code directly in the calling routine. In this instance, not only could you, but you should because a one-line subroutine is a very inefficient way to write code. However, if you are creating a task that requires many lines of code, using a subroutine would make your code a lot easier to understand.

When creating subroutines, you should keep the following things in mind:

- Try to group related tasks into one subroutine.
- If you have a task that is repetitive or will be called from many different places in the application, it should be created as a subroutine.

By keeping these in mind, you won't create many small subroutines that take action on the same group of information, such as a name and its related address, or retype the same section of code over and over again in different sections of the application. Another added benefit of using subroutines for complicated tasks is that if you must change the way it works, you would need to change it only in the subroutine. If you did not use a subroutine, you would need to search the entire application looking for the code to change.

Like any other procedure a subroutine starts at the top of its executable code and finishes at the bottom. If the subroutine must finish before it gets to the End Sub statement, you would add an Exit Sub statement to the code. This statement works just like the Exit

6

Do and `Exit For` statements used to end a loop early. The following code shows how the `Exit Sub` statement is used to exit a routine before reaching the end of the routine:

```
Public Sub Get_Input()
    Dim Data As Integer
    Data = InputBox("Enter a Number", App.Title)
    If Data = 0 Then
        MsgBox "Zero Entered, Process Cancelled"
        Exit Sub
    End If
    MsgBox "The number entered was: " & Data
End Sub
```

Functions

When working with subroutines, you can see that even though they can accept parameters, they return no values other than any modifications they might make to the variables that were passed. To create a subroutine that can return a value that is not a modification of a parameter that was passed, you would use a special form of the subroutine called a *function*. The only difference between a function and a subroutine is that a function can return a value to the calling routine. Both functions and subroutines can have variables passed to them, and they both accept the same types of arguments. The syntax of a function is only slightly different from a subroutine, and is shown here:

```
[Public ¦ Private ¦ Friend] [Static] Function name [(arglist)] [As type]
    [statements]
    [name = expression]
End Function
```

To return a value from a function, you only need to assign the value to the function name as in the following:

```
Public Function CalcTotal() as Single
    [Function Code]
    CalcTotal = Sale_Amount
End Function
```

This code would return the final sale amount to the calling procedure. You would call this routine as in the following line of code:

```
Invoice_Line_Amt = CalcTotal
```

If you are passing arguments to the function, the calling statement would look like this:

```
Invoice_Line_Amt = CalcTotal(Qty, Price)
```

Again, if you must exit the function before the entire routine is executed, you would use an `Exit` function.

A function's return value can be used in several different ways. It can be assigned to a variable as just shown, or the function call can be used in a statement as shown in the following:

```
If CalcTotal <= 0 Then
    Msgbox "Invalid Sale Amount Entered"
End If
```

When you create subroutines and functions, which type of routine you will create depends on whether you need a value returned. In Visual Basic, you can use several built-in functions either as a subroutine or as a function. Visual Basic figures out which way to process the routine based on its position in the code. As an example, here are two lines of code using a MsgBox. One is a subroutine and the other is a function.

```
If Msgbox("Do you want to continue?", vbQuestion + vbYesNo, App.Title)
    = vbYes Then
    Msgbox "We will continue processing the data"
End If
```

If a routine is used as a value as in the previous If statement, it is assumed to be a function. However, if no return value is expected, then it is assumed to be a subroutine. Unfortunately, you cannot create a routine that is both a subroutine and a function.

Reference or Value

You must understand only one other important issue about passing variables: how the passed data is referenced. There are two ways to reference data, by value and by reference. By default, all Visual Basic routines pass data by reference, which means that the arguments can be changed by their receiving routines. If you want to keep the data from being changed in the receiving routine, you must pass the arguments by value instead of by reference. To pass an argument by value, you would add the ByVal keyword in front of a parameter in the receiving routine's declaration statement, as shown in the following:

```
Public Sub CalcTotal (ByVal Qty, ByVal Price)
```

When you are passing a variable by reference, the subroutine is actually working with the data variable from the calling routine. In contrast, passing variables by value will pass the actual data to the receiving routine, and it will be placed into a local variable in that routine. To see the difference between these, start a new project, add two command buttons to the form, and then copy the code in Listing 6.2 to the project's code section.

6

LISTING 6.2. VALREF.TXT—PASSING VARIABLES BY REFERENCE AND BY VALUE WILL CAUSE VERY DIFFERENT RESULTS.

```
 1: Private Var1 As String
 2: Private Var2 As String
 3: Private Var3 As Integer
 4:
 5: Private Sub Command1_Click()
 6: Var1 = "This is the ByRef Demo"
 7: Var2 = "Call the demo_Reference Routine"
 8: Var3 = 10
 9: Call demo_Reference(Var1, Var2, Var3)
10: MsgBox "Var1=" & Var1 & vbCrLf & _
11:        "Var2=" & Var2 & vbCrLf & _
12:        "Var3=" & Var3
13: End Sub
14:
15: Private Sub demo_Reference(pVar1, pVar2, pVar3)
16:     pVar1 = "Var One has been changed"
17:     pVar2 = "So has Var Two"
18:     pVar3 = 33
19: End Sub
20:
21: Private Sub demo_Value(ByVal pVar1, ByVal pVar2, ByVal pVar3)
22:     pVar1 = "Var One has been changed"
23:     pVar2 = "So has Var Two"
24:     pVar3 = 33
25: End Sub
26:
27: Private Sub Command2_Click()
28: Var1 = "This is the ByVal Demo"
29: Var2 = "Call the demo_Value Routine"
30: Var3 = 10
31: Call demo_Value(Var1, Var2, Var3)
32: MsgBox "Var1=" & Var1 & vbCrLf & _
33:        "Var2=" & Var2 & vbCrLf & _
34:        "Var3=" & Var3
35: End Sub
```

Now, run the application, click the first command button, and then click the second one. As you can see, the routine passing the variables by reference is actually changing the original variable data, as shown in Figure 6.3, whereas the routine using by value does not change the original data, as shown in Figure 6.4.

FIGURE 6.3.

Passing variables by reference can cause the original data to be changed unintentionally.

FIGURE 6.4.

Unless the data must be changed in the routine, using ByVal *is the accepted method of passing arguments.*

To sum this all up, when you create routines—either subroutines or functions—you must decide how the data is going to be processed. Remember that declaring all of your variables as public will make it easier for you to write the initial code, but when you must test and fix problems, public variables will give you a very bad headache. Finally, when passing arguments, remember that if you do not explicitly set the way the arguments are passed, they will be passed by reference. If that is the case, do not modify the variables that were passed while in the routine. If you must return a new value, you should consider using a function. In addition, you can now define arguments for a Sub procedure or Function as Optional. This allows you to pass data in that parameter only when needed.

The Vulcan Way

Using functions and subroutines is but one way to affect how your application code will be processed. When designing complex database applications, many sections of code will perform the same process, just on different data. As an example, your application could accept dates as one of its inputs. Besides editing the data to see whether it is a valid date, you might have to check to see whether the date is allowed. However, you might be performing this edit check on several different data input fields at different times in the application. By calling a function, passing the date variable, and possibly the range against which to check it, would allow you to check the return value for any errors.

If the function could return more than just a True or False condition, you would need to write code that would check for each of the possible return values that might be returned. The process of checking the return value of a function or comparing any two variables or values in your application is what makes the application perform. Without the capability

6

to change the flow of execution, your application would not be very flexible and would also not work very well. The creation of your application is really the process of logically handling the data that the user will input.

Unfortunately, in programming there is no one way to do something. This still holds true even in Visual Basic. Your application will process the data that it is given by testing and comparing the data, then execute different sections of code based on the results. This process is commonly referred to as *condition execution* of the code.

Changing the Flow

To conditionally execute any code in your application, you must first be able to test it. This test is called a *condition*. If the condition is True, then the related code will be executed; if the condition is False, then the related code will be skipped. The way most programming languages, including Visual Basic, perform this testing is with one of two types of statement groups. The first and oldest of the two is the If-Then-End If statement block. The second and sexier of the two is the Select Case statement group. Both of these statement groups use the expressions that you can create using operators, variables, and functions.

If-Then, What Next?

You might think that you know the If-Then statement like the back of your hand, but you probably are not aware of a few ways to use it. In addition, several variations of the If-Then statement help when developing the application for multiple operating systems. A typical If-Then statement in an application tests a particular input data value and, if it isn't in the database, processes it accordingly. The following code uses several of the concepts that you have already seen during this first week:

```
If (keyascii < 48 Or keyascii > 58) And keyascii <> 8 Then
    Beep
    keyascii = 0
End If
```

This simple, boring way to use the If-Then statement only enables you to conditionally execute a single section of code. However, if you want to execute one section if the condition is true and another if it is false, you would use the Else clause of the If-Then statement. The code would then resemble the following:

```
If IsDate(entdate.Text) Then
      entdate.Text = DateAdd("d", 1, entdate.Text)
    Else
      Beep
End If
```

As you can see, the Else statement works as if you were talking to someone (that is, *if* the condition is true, *then* add the date, *else* if not, beep). With the Else statement you are testing for two conditions at the same time. But can you use the If-Then statement to test for multiple conditions? By using the ElseIf statement along with the rest of the If-Then-Else statements, you can test as many conditions as you need. This creates a section of code that is called a nested If statement. The following is the syntax of this extended version:

```
If condition Then
    [statements]
[ElseIf condition-n Then
    [elseifstatements] ...
[Else
    [elsestatements]]
End If
```

You might notice from the preceding code snippet that the If-Then statements to be executed are indented. The reason for this becomes very clear as you start using this extended version of the statement. If all of the code was aligned to the left of the page, finding the matching If-ElseIf-Else-End If statements would be very difficult. If you lose track of the matching statements when you are coding the application, you could wind up having some sections of code execute incorrectly. Many programmers use the If statement to test a variable that has been modified just before the If statement itself, as shown here:

```
RetCode = MsgBox("Okay to Delete Record", vbQuestion + vbOKCancel, App.Title)
If (RetCode = vbOK) Then
    'Perform delete code
End If
```

You have just seen in the previous sections in this chapter that you can use the MsgBox to return a value directly into an expression, so this code can be rewritten as

```
If (MsgBox("Okay to Delete Record", vbQuestion + vbOKCancel, App.Title) _
    = vbOK) Then
    'Perform delete code
End If
```

There is no limit to the number of nested If statements that you can string together. However, there is a mental limit. You do not want to create so complex a section of code that you cannot figure out what it does. There are other ways to create a conditional test block for many different cases.

Before leaving the If-Then statement, look at some of the other ways it can be used. You probably know that you can code an If-Then statement on one line if only one code statement must be executed. For example:

```
'If the sale was over $500 give a 10% discount
```

6

```
If Sales_Amt > 500 Then Sales_Amt = Sales_Amt * .90
```

Whenever you must execute more than one line of code, you should use the `If-Then-End If` block. Now, did you know that you can execute several lines of code on a single line? This is actually a hold-over from the old DOS Basic days. For example, the following code:

```
If (keyascii < 48 Or keyascii > 58) And keyascii <> 8 Then
    Beep
    keyascii = 0
End If
```

could have been written as follows:

```
If (keyascii < 48 Or keyascii > 58) And keyascii <> 8 Then Beep : keyascii = 0
```

By separating each statement with a colon (:), you can execute several lines of code without using the `End If` block. Most programmers have never used the `If` statement differently than the way it has been shown here. However, the statements that can be executed when a condition is true are not limited to standard lines of code. If you must test a condition and then loop through an array to process the information, you could call a subroutine that loops through the array, or you could code the following:

```
If Update_Records Then
    Do Until (EOF(1))
        'processing code
    Loop
Else
    MsgBox "No records have been updated."
End If
```

So, when needed, you can mix any type of Visual Basic statement with the `If-Then` statement block. The last version of the `If-Then` statement enables you to set sections of code to be used only when certain conditions occur. The `#If-Then-#Else` directives will instruct the Visual Basic compiler to conditionally compile different sections of code. The following code will produce different executable files depending on the operating system on which it was compiled:

```
#If Mac Then
'. Place exclusively Mac  statements here.
' Otherwise, if it is a 32-bit Windows program, do this:
#ElseIf Win32 Then
'. Place exclusively 32-bit Windows statements here.
' Otherwise, if it is neither, do this:
#Else
'. Place other platform statements here.
#End If
```

Try this code in your application. If your computer is running Windows 95 or Windows

NT, you will only have the code in the `#ElseIf` Win32 section of the statement block. This special version of the statement is typically used to compile the same application for different operating systems.

The `Select Case` Statement

The `Select Case` statement is another way to test for multiple conditions and then execute the related program code. However, it will provide a much easier section of code to maintain. The following is the syntax of the statement:

```
Select Case testexpression
[Case expressionlist-n
    [statements-n]] ...
[Case Else
    [elsestatements]]
End Select
```

If you take a moment to look at this syntax, you will probably feel like you have seen it somewhere before. In fact, if you have played with the Application Wizard and have added a toolbar to the application, the wizard uses a `Select Case` statement to test for the button that was clicked, as shown in the following:

```
Private Sub Toolbar1_ButtonClick(ByVal Button As ComctlLib.Button)
    On Error Resume Next
    Select Case Button.Key
        Case "Open"
            'ToDo: Add 'Open' button code.
            MsgBox "Add 'Open' button code."
        Case "Bold"
            'ToDo: Add 'Bold' button code.
            MsgBox "Add 'Bold' button code."
        Case "Underline"
            'ToDo: Add 'Underline' button code.
            MsgBox "Add 'Underline' button code."
    End Select
End Sub
```

Just like with the `If-Then` statement, the statements that can be executed in the `Case` block can be a mixture of any standard Visual Basic statements, including other `Select` statements. In the `Select` statement, an expression is evaluated in the opening `Select Case` statement, then the `Case` statements within the `Select-End Select` block test the resulting value against one or more values or expressions. For example, if you want to perform one section of code if an expression is zero, another if it is odd, and a third section of code if it's even, with a maximum value of 10, you could code an `If` statement with an elaborate expression to figure out whether the number is odd or even, or you could use the `Select Case` statement as shown here:

```
Select Case Input_Number
```

6

```
    Case 0
        MsgBox "The Value is Zero"
    Case 1,3,5,7,9
        MsgBox "The Value is Odd"
    Case 2,4,6,8,10
        MsgBox "The Value is Even"
    Case Else
        MsgBox "The number is invalid"
End Select
```

Again, depending on what you need for your application, the `Select Case` statement would be very useful for testing values being input into the application.

Other Functions

Finally, two other functions are worth mentioning in this section:

- `Choose`—Selects and returns a value from a list of arguments based on an index value.

- `IIf`—Returns one of two values depending on the expression.

Each of these functions provides a unique method of choosing a particular value or expression. The `Choose` function enables you to use an index value to select from a list of strings or numbers. This works particularly if the index represents the value in an option group. The following is the syntax of the `Choose` function:

```
Choose(index, choice-1[, choice-2, ... [, choice-n]])
```

This function will enable you to choose from as many different values as you need to include in the parameter list. Using the `Choose` function is quite easy. The following is an example of how to use it:

```
Shipper = Choose(index, "FedEx", "Airborne", "DHL")
```

If the index value is between 1 and 3, the appropriate string will be placed in the variable `Shipper`. If the index value is less than 1 or greater than the number of choices from which it must choose, it will return a `Null` value.

The other function, `IIf`, will return one of two expressions, depending on the value of a conditional expression. The following is the syntax of this function:

```
IIf(expr, truepart, falsepart)
```

This function is also fairly easy to use. This function represents the old two-door method of choosing. If the `expr` is true, the first value or expression is returned; if the `expr` is false, the second one is returned. This function could be used to calculate a discount based on a single condition as shown here:

```
Sales_Total = IIf( Sales_Amt>500, Sales_Amt * .90, Sales_Amt)
```

However, there is one thing to remember if you decide to use this function. The IIf function always evaluates both the true and false expressions, even though it will return only one of them. If evaluating the false expression results in an error, an error will occur even if the expr is true.

The Logical Way to Do Things

When designing your application and creating the code, you should try to keep the code's execution as logical as possible.

Summary

Today you learned what it takes to use variables properly within your application. Many things can go wrong when you are creating an application; however, if you plan and declare your variables correctly, you will have one less thing to worry about. Complex applications will usually require many types of functions and subroutines to perform specific tasks that might be repeated at different locations in the application.

You also learned the different ways to affect the application program flow. This will allow you to see how different sections of code executed depending on the current data being processed. This allows you to create a much more flexible application than if you had to anticipate everything that the user might do and code for each one separately.

Q&A

Q What two types of procedures can you use to perform tasks in Visual Basic?

A Both subroutines and functions can be used to perform tasks in an application.

Q What kind of variable has the broadest scope?

A A variable that is declared PUBLIC has the broadest scope in an application.

Q What are the different ways to change the flow of execution in the application?

A There are many different ways to change the flow of a program; however, when writing the code for an application, the best ways are by using the If-Then and Select Case statements.

Q Can a subroutine call another subroutine?

A Yes, any subroutine or function can call any other routine in the application to which it has access, according to the routine's scope.

6

Q **What is the difference between the `If-Then` and `Select Case` statements?**

A An `If-Then` statement enables you to test for different expressions on each occurrence of the `If` statement. The `Select Case` statement works with only one expression.

Workshop

The Workshop provides quiz questions to help solidify your understanding of the material covered, as well as exercises to provide you with experience in using what you've learned. Try to understand the quiz and exercise answers before continuing on to the next day's lesson. Answers are provided in Appendix A, "Answers to Exercises."

Quiz

1. How many values can a function routine return?
2. What is the difference between a subroutine and a function?
3. Why is using public variables not recommended?
4. How can you leave a subroutine before you come to the `End Sub` statement?

Exercise

Write a program that contains global variables, global constants, module-level, and procedure-level variables. Have one command button call the procedure and print all the variables in the application. Then, try having a second command button print all the variables to see what would happen.

DAY **7**

Building Complex Forms

If you are fairly new to Visual Basic programming, the forms you have created probably have a simple design. However, most applications require more than a few complex forms along with the simple ones. This chapter will discuss form design—the visual aspect of forms and also the function of each form. In addition, you will look at some built-in functions and coding techniques that can be used to enhance a form, giving the user an easier interface. Finally, you will see how to bring everything you have learned this week into well thought-out, usable forms and their related code.

Designing the Form

By now you should know that a Windows application is really a collection of related forms that enable a user to interact easily with data. As you might have seen in other Windows applications, some forms can be very useful but very boring to look at or, more importantly, to use, while others are very confusing to figure out. By using your Visual Basic knowledge and some design standards about which you'll learn, you can create an application that not only looks good, but is also easy to use. However, your application's forms will to some degree reflect your personality.

Because the form is the most important part of any application, few people will use it if the interface is not easy to follow or if it is confusing. When designing the forms, you should take into account the user's experience level. The GUI interface offers a wide variety of ways to make the user feel comfortable with the application.

The Good, the Bad, and the Ugly

Perhaps the most important concept to learn is simplicity. If the form design in your application *looks* difficult, it probably *is* difficult. Spending some time designing the forms can help you create an interface that works well and is easy to use. Also, from a visual point of view, a clean, simple design is always preferable. A common mistake that most programmers make is to design the forms after their real-world paper versions. This creates some problems for the user. The size and shape of paper forms are very different than the size and shape of a screen display; if you were to duplicate the paper form exactly, you would be limited to text boxes and check boxes. What's more, there is no added benefit to the user.

In Figure 7.1, you can see an entry form that uses several of the Visual Basic controls, which allows the form to remain on one screen.

FIGURE 7.1.

Advanced controls enable more information to be displayed on a single screen form with no scrolling required.

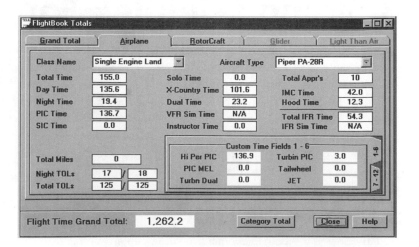

If this information were placed on the form all at the same time, not only would the user have to search for some of the fields, but he would have to scroll to see every section of the form. When designing an application that is replacing a paper-based system, you could provide the user with a version of the input form that mirrors the original paper form and could be printed. Then, this would become a reporting issue, not a form design problem.

One of the things a paper form cannot provide the user is a list of valid choices for some of the input areas. By using controls such as the list box, preloaded with choices, you can reduce the amount of typing that the user must do. In addition, you could simplify the application by moving rarely used functions to their own forms and displaying them only when needed.

With all that said, you can prevent many form problems or design issues by using the following design principles:

- Make the forms as consistent as possible within an application.
- Apply the same standards throughout the application.
- Place the command buttons on all forms in the same position and order, whenever possible.
- Use color to highlight important information.
- Don't clutter the forms with too much information.
- Group related information together on the form.
- Keep the data entry forms simple.

These design principles are not very difficult to understand when you have either seen examples of them or have used an application that doesn't conform to them.

When designing a user interface, begin by looking at some of the applications already available. You will find that they have many design concepts and objects in common. Objects such as toolbars, status bars, ToolTips, menus, and tabbed dialogs are used to enhance the interface. Therefore, it should come as no surprise that Visual Basic provides you with the capabilities to add any or all of these objects to your application.

Making Use of Space

What is space? It is not the final frontier, at least not when it comes to application design. By using space effectively in your forms, you can emphasize different controls and improve the usability of your application. This concept is generally called *whitespace*. Whitespace doesn't have to be white; it really refers to the empty areas around and between the controls on a form. If you place too many controls on a form (see Figure 7.2) the form will look cluttered, making it difficult for the user to find any single field or control. By using some of the framing type controls, such as the Tab control, you can display only sections of the form in the same space, making the display less cluttered.

7

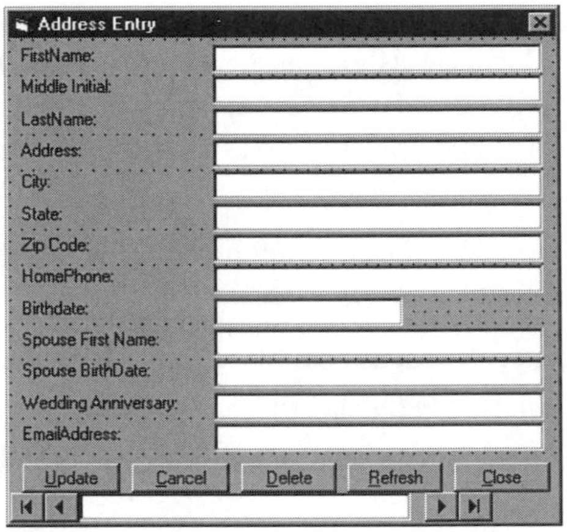

FIGURE 7.2.

Too many controls overpower the visual image of the form and make it difficult to use.

Adding Color and Pictures to Your Application

You can use color in your application to add a very appealing visual look to it. However, it is easy to go overboard with it. Color preferences are as varied as there are computers. The user's taste in color might not be the same as yours. Some colors can evoke very strong emotions, and if your application will be used overseas, some colors can have a cultural significance of which you are completely unaware. To play it safe, it's best to stay with the softer, more neutral, colors. In fact, when Windows itself was developed, color was considered very important—so much so that many different color schemes were created for the user to choose from (see Figure 7.3) in the screen settings property page.

In addition, you can change any of the individual colors in the scheme to fit your personality. Of course, the colors that you choose for your application will probably be influenced by the type of audience or the mood you are trying to convey in your application. Although using colors such as bright reds, yellows, and greens would work well for a children's application, you would not want to use them if you were creating a financial application.

Using bright colors in small doses can effectively draw the user's attention to an important area or, in the case of the form in Figure 7.4, notify the user when something requires some action to be taken.

Another feature that you can use to enhance the overall look and effectiveness of your forms is the addition of icons and pictures. As everyone knows, one picture is worth 1,000 words. Pictures can be used to convey information without the need for text. However, you must be careful about which images you choose, because images can be perceived differently by different people. Having icons in toolbar buttons to represent different functions is very useful unless the user can't identify the function represented by the icon. As you learned on Day 4, "Creating Form Templates," Visual Basic helps you in this respect by supplying the standard icons that are used in a Windows 95 application toolbar. If you decide to create your own icons or pictures, try to keep them simple. Complex, colorful images don't translate well into a 16×16-pixel icon.

FIGURE 7.3.

Windows users can choose many different color schemes for their computers.

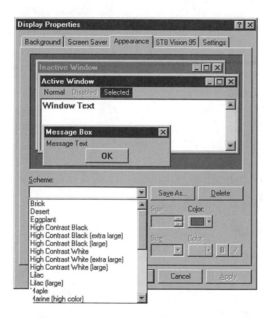

FIGURE 7.4.

Color can be used to signify exceptions in the displayed data.

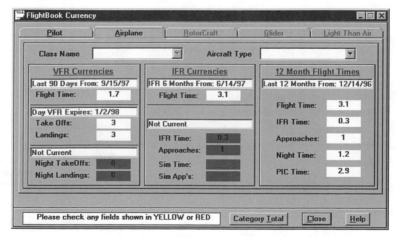

7

Consistency and Standards

Some objects in most forms that you will design will be more important than others. When actually laying out the form, you want to make sure that the more important objects are easily recognized by the user. Because of the way you learned to read (left to right and top to bottom) your eyes will be drawn to the upper-left portion of the screen first, so you should place the most important objects there. Objects such as command buttons (OK or Continue) should be placed in the lower-right portion of the screen, because users won't use those buttons until they have finished working with the form.

The way in which you group the different controls that you place on the forms is also important. Grouping the controls in a logical order according to their function or relationship with other controls on the form enables the user to work with their data in the same way. When entering name and address information, having all the fields placed in the same area of a form is far better than scattering them all over the form. In many cases, other controls such as the Frame control can be used to contain groups of controls, reinforcing the relationship of these controls. Figure 7.5 shows a form that was not designed using relationships and groupings. You can see that the input fields were placed on the form as the designer thought of them.

FIGURE 7.5.

Haphazard placement of controls on a form creates confusion for the user.

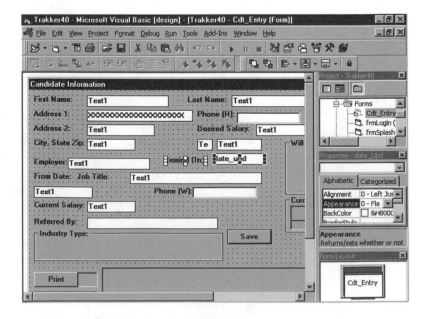

In Figure 7.6 the same form has been redesigned by placing the different input controls into logical groupings. Immediately, you can see how much easier it is to use this version of the form.

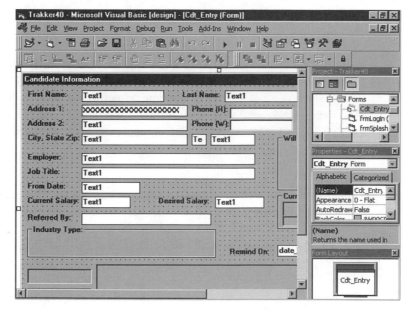

Also, because this form is used to enter date-related information, the data input field has been placed in the upper-left position of the form. If you decide on a style to use when designing your forms, stick with it. If all of your forms have a consistent look to them, the user will find them easier to use.

Consistency enables you to create harmony in your application. When the user looks at your application, everything on the forms seem to fit together. On the other hand, inconsistency can be confusing and make your application appear disorganized. The best way to provide consistency in your application is to establish a strategy and style for your forms before you begin designing them. You must consider the following elements:

- Size of the controls (command buttons, text boxes, and so on)
- Font style, size, and properties
- Types of controls to use

Because Visual Basic comes with many different controls, using all of them in an application can be very tempting for a developer. You should try to avoid this by choosing the subset of controls that best fits your application design and image that you want to present. As an example, the following controls are all used to present lists of data to the user; however, each one has specific reasons for you to select them:

- ListView
- ComboBox

7

- Grid
- TreeView

In most applications, the standard way to display a list from which to choose is by using a combo box. However, if you are displaying data from a database, the Grid control is usually the control of choice. In addition, try not to use controls for a purpose for which they were not designed. Although text box controls can be set to read-only and used to display data, a Label control is more normally used for this purpose. Not only is a label designed to display read-only information, it takes up less system resources than a TextBox control.

Unless you are planning to distribute fonts with your application, you should use only the standard Windows fonts, such as Ariel, New Times Roman, or System. If you deviate from these and the user's PC doesn't have the font that you used, it will substitute the font with the next font listed alphabetically in the font list. This can usually be fixed by installing the font, but it can be very frustrating to the user until the problem is resolved. Figure 7.7 shows how a form looks using the font Wide Latin if the font was not available on the computer. This happens because of the way Windows searched for a replacement font. The font that would be used is completely dependent on the fonts installed on the reader's computer. The next font in the list is Wing Dings, which as you can see is not exactly English.

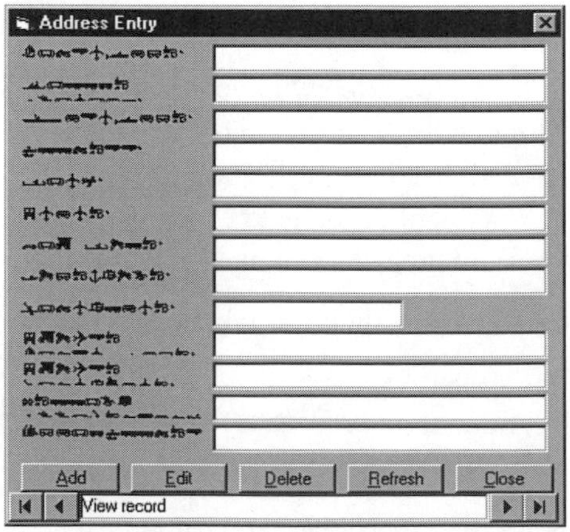

FIGURE 7.7.

Choosing standard fonts will prevent very strange substitutions by the Windows operating system.

You should keep the same style as you move from form to form. Don't change fonts, colors, or control sizes on different forms; this only annoys the user. Finally, design your forms with some thought, and then step back and look at them. If you do not think they look good, a user probably won't either.

What Size Is It?

When designing and creating forms for your application, you might want to consider what resolution users will have on their PCs. Screen resolution and color depth can be changed on every PC on which your application might run.

Even though Visual Basic handles many Windows issues for you, this is one that it doesn't handle. In Figure 7.8, you can see what happens when a form designed at 1024×768 resolution is displayed on a PC with the resolution set at 640×480.

FIGURE 7.8.

Displaying a larger form in a smaller resolution cuts off some of the form.

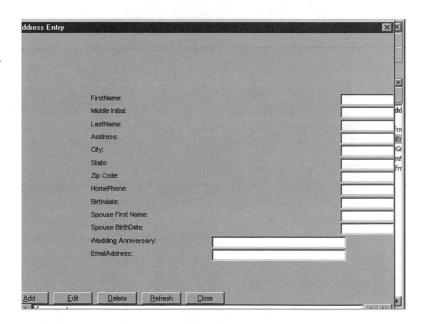

If you want to create forms and controls that have the same proportions no matter what screen resolution you use, you must either design your forms at the lowest resolution or add code to your program that changes the forms. The easiest way to prevent this type of problem is to design your forms in 640×480 resolution. However, if you prefer to work at a higher resolution, you still must be aware of how your form will look at a lower resolution.

Tip

One way to stay alert to how your form will look in a lower resolution is to create a 640×480-pixel solid color bitmap and set the form's Picture property to the bitmap. This will show you where the lower-resolution form will end. However, don't forget to remove the bitmap when you are finished designing the form.

7

There is one other way of dealing with resolution changes. That is to create different versions of each form and have the application use the correct set of forms for the resolution that is being used. If you use this method, you should realize that you will be multiplying your effort by the number of screen sizes you want to support.

Another thing that Visual Basic does for you is position your form at runtime based on its location at design time. If you are using the 1024×768 resolution at design time and you place a form in the lower-right corner of the screen, it probably will not be seen when the application is run at a lower resolution. You can avoid this by positioning your form in the Form Load event. The following code will always position the form in the top-left corner of the screen:

```
Private Sub Form_Load()
    Me.Move 0, 0
End Sub
```

The Move method has the same effect as setting both the Left and Top properties of the form to zero, but the Move method does this in one statement.

When designing your application, you must also consider the color display capabilities of the computers on which it might run. Some computers can display 256 or more colors, others are limited to 16. If you design a form that uses the 256-color palette and it is displayed on a computer that is limited to 16 colors, it will process the colors of your form by dithering the colors to simulate the ones that are not available. This will probably cause some of the controls on the form to disappear or look very strange when displayed.

To prevent this from happening, sticking with the 16 standard Windows colors is a good idea when you are creating the forms for your application. These colors are represented by the Visual Basic color constants (vbBlack, vbBlue, vbCyan, and so on). If it's necessary to use more than 16 colors in your application, you should still stick with the standard colors for text, buttons, and other interface elements.

Tip

If you must use the 256-color palette, you should use the standard colors for any text, buttons, or other important interface objects. This way the user will be guaranteed to see them no matter what colors the computer can display.

Using the Form Editor Features

When designing your forms, several features are available to you from the Visual Basic form editor. These functions are listed in the Format menu and in the Form Editor toolbar. Both of these are shown in Figure 7.9.

FIGURE 7.9.

The form editor tools are available from the toolbar and the menu.

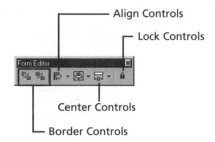

These tools enable you to simultaneously position, size, and align the controls that you place on the form. If you did not have them to use, you would have to perform these tasks manually on each control. Figure 7.10 shows a form with many text boxes that must be sized the same.

FIGURE 7.10.

Formatting the controls on the form using the editor tools.

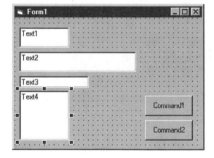

To manually size these controls, you would select each one individually and set the height and width to the required settings, or use your eyes to visually change the sizes. However, if you use the editor tools, you can select all the controls at once as shown in Figure 7.11 and then click the appropriate form editor button.

FIGURE 7.11.

Selecting all of the controls to format at once.

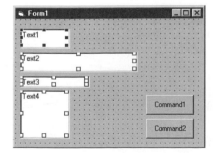

7

The only thing you must remember when using these group formatting functions is that the control selected last is the one that will be used as the template for the sizing or placement of all of the controls selected.

Tip

> The control that is used as the template can be identified by the blue sizing boxes; all the other selected controls will have white sizing boxes. This can be seen in Figure 7.11.

One other function is present on the Form Editor toolbar and the Format menu that you can use to make your design work easier. This control actually locks and unlocks controls on the form. This prevents you from accidentally moving or resizing the controls after you have positioned them all properly. Using this function will lock all the controls on the form.

Putting It All Together

Think of each form in an application as having a distinct job to do. Most applications you design will contain many types of forms. No matter which application interface style you decide to use, there will always be one main form that will act as the focal point for every function in the application. When deciding how many forms you need for your application, you should start by drawing a flowchart that lists each different form and how the user would get to it. Figure 7.12 shows a diagram for an Address Book application using the MDI style interface.

FIGURE 7.12.

When designing the form interaction, flow- charts usually help in the design process.

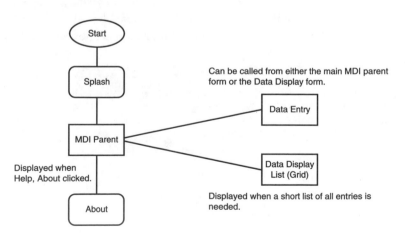

From what you've seen, designing the application form is more than just throwing controls on the form and some buttons for navigation. You want to take everything you have learned and combine it into your application. Whatever style application interface you eventually decide to use, they all have certain elements included on them.

One of the features of Visual Basic is the capability to *prototype* your application. This means to create an application structure with all of the forms and navigation in it, but none of the unique application code included. You can start this application and navigate from form to form, testing each of the command buttons or menu options without spending time on the detailed code until you are satisfied with the form's design. If you decide to use the Visual Basic Application Wizard, you can create the basic application model quickly; however, you do not really learn the different components that are used.

During this first week you have seen how to create each of the different building blocks available for your application. Now it's time to put them together and learn what happens when you do that. When you are working with only one feature during the learning process, no user issues might appear. However, when your application is finished and the user is in the middle of entering new information, for example, what happens if the user clicks the Add Entry button again? This sounds simple, but think about it. Your application is in the middle of a database add function when the user requests another add function. You have the following choices as to what the application could do:

- Cancel the previous Add, losing any data entered.
- Prompt the user to save the previous entry and then continue.
- Prevent the second add request while the entry form is in use.

Each of these choices carries with it its own set of program design issues. To see how everything comes together, you are going to build the prototype application defined in Figure 7.12. Start a new project and name it ADDRBOOK. Then add a new MDI form to the project, naming it mdiMainForm and removing the original form. Add two more forms to the project, one for the data-entry function and one for the search function. Change their properties so that they are child forms and name them frmEntry and frmSrch, respectively. The only controls that you will add to these forms will be a command-button control. Add one command button to each form that will unload that form when clicked. Don't worry about the other forms shown in the diagram, you will add them later.

Menus

You are going to add a menu to this main form, but first, you must decide which options you want to provide on the menu. An address book application usually needs the following options:

7

- Open/Save Address Book Database
- Edit Entry
- Add/Delete Entry
- Application Preferences
- Search
- Print Reports
- Help
- Back Up Database

These options would be grouped into only a few main menu options that should remain consistent with the Windows standard interface.

From this diagram, you can now add the menu to the MDI form. You must make one other design decision before actually creating the menu. That is whether to use unique names for each menu option or to create a menu collection array to work with. Each of these has good points and bad points.

Using unique names for each option will let you separate each menu option routine. This makes the maintenance of the menu code a little easier to follow because you can find a particular menu routine by clicking on the menu option directly while in design mode. It does, however, create more subroutines for the application to keep track of. On the other hand, using the collections array to handle the menu options keeps all of the menu code in one routine. This enables you to centralize the menu code; however, you must use select statements to recognize which menu option was selected. Listings 7.1 and 7.2 show you the difference between each of the coding choices.

LISTING 7.1. MENUOPTIONS.TXT—USING UNIQUE MENU OPTION NAMES REQUIRES DIFFERENT EVENT ROUTINES FOR EACH MENU OPTION.

```
 1: Private Sub mnuFileSaveAll_Click()
 2:     'ToDo: Add 'mnuFileSaveAll_Click' code.
 3:     MsgBox "Add 'mnuFileSaveAll_Click' code."
 4: End Sub
 5:
 6: Private Sub mnuFileSaveAs_Click()
 7:     'ToDo: Add 'mnuFileSaveAs_Click' code.
 8:     MsgBox "Add 'mnuFileSaveAs_Click' code."
 9: End Sub
10:
11: Private Sub mnuFileSave_Click()
12:     'ToDo: Add 'mnuFileSave_Click' code.
13:     MsgBox "Add 'mnuFileSave_Click' code."
14: End Sub
```

LISTING 7.2. MENUSELECT.TXT—BY USING THE COLLECTION ARRAY FOR THE MENU OPTIONS, ALL CODE IS KEPT WITHIN A SINGLE EVENT ROUTINE.

```
 1: Private Sub mnuArray_Click(Index As Integer)
 2:     Select Case Index
 3:         Case 1 'File, New
 4:              'ToDo: Add File New code.
 5:             MsgBox "Add File New  code."
 6:         Case 2 'File, Open
 7:              'ToDo: Add File Open code.
 8:             MsgBox "Add File Open  code."
 9:     End Select
10: End Sub.
```

Which one you choose is entirely up to you; however, this example will use the Select Case method of handling menu events. After you have designed the menu and entered it into the menu editor for the application, you should place a MSGBOX statement for each option's Click event so that when testing the prototype, you will know whether the selection process really works, as shown in the following code: .

```
MSGBOX "Place Menu Option " & <Option> & " Code Here."
```

This MSGBOX also serves as a reminder to you if you forget the code for any particular menu option as you are coding the application. After you have completed the menus, you should run the application and click each of the menu options to ensure that you did not miss one.

Besides the main form, you might want to add menu options to the child forms. However, as discussed earlier in the book, you do not really want to add menu options to the child forms if they share several of the same options as the main menu. What you should do is add the extra menu selections to the main menu and make them visible only when needed.

This brings you to the topic of which menu options are available when. If you choose the Add New Entry menu option, you can disable it so that the user cannot select it again until the entry process is completed. You do this in the menu click routine with the following code:

```
MnuFileNew.Enabled = False
```

This statement will *gray out* the menu option instead of hiding it. This is a visual cue that is used to tell the user that this option is not currently available. Then when the Entry form is unloaded, the statement setting this property to True is placed in the form's UNLOAD event. This type of process enables you to turn on and off any menu options that do not make sense to have available at a given moment.

7

However, when working with menu options that are specific for a child window, these should be hidden except when the related child window is displayed. Figure 7.13 shows the main menu with no child forms displayed, and Figure 7.14 shows the same menu with the Add child form displayed.

FIGURE 7.13.

The starting main menu with no child form menu options visible.

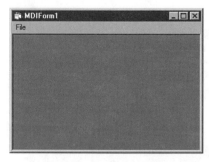

FIGURE 7.14.

When a child form is displayed, some main options will be grayed out and others will be made visible.

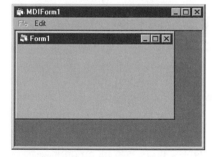

Go through the menu events and set each of them as needed, remembering to set the Add Entry event to display the Add child form and the Search event to display the Search form. In addition, in each of the child forms, add at least the Close command button to let you close the form and return to the main form. Also, add the code that will set the Enabled property for the menu option back to True. Run the application and see how the menu options work.

Toolbars

Now add the toolbar to the main menu. The first question is which options are going to be available on the toolbar. If you placed every menu option on the toolbar, it would probably take up a good percentage of the work area in the application. Therefore, most applications place only the most used options on the toolbar, enabling the users to add other menu options to the toolbar as they want. This customization is supported by the Toolbar control, so it is easy for you to give it to the user. Your only requirement is to add the initial buttons and the related code to the toolbar click event.

When you click the toolbar, only one event is triggered no matter which button you clicked. The toolbar click event uses a SELECT CASE statement to determine which button was clicked. You now have a choice to make concerning how to code the event routines for each button. This actually depends on the way you created the menu options. If you used unique names for each menu option, you can call the related menu routine from the toolbar click event routine as shown in Listing 7.3.

LISTING 7.3. TOOLOPTIONS.TXT—The toolbar routine can directly access the related unique menu option routine.

```
 1: Private Sub Toolbar1_ButtonClick(ByVal Button As ComctlLib.Button)
 2:     On Error Resume Next
 3:     Select Case Button.Key
 4:         Case "New"
 5:             Call mnuFileNew_Click
 6:         Case "Open"
 7:             Call mnuFileOpen_Click
 8:         Case "Save"
 9:             Call mnuFileSave_Click
10:     End Select
11: End Sub
```

However, if you decided to use the menu collection array for the different menu options, you would then either duplicate the menu option code in the toolbar event or call the menu click event, passing it the number that corresponds to the correct menu option. Listing 7.4 shows one way to handle the call when using collections.

LISTING 7.4. TOOLCOLLECT.TXT—Using the menu collection requires the passing of an Index value related to the menu option.

```
 1: Private Sub Toolbar1_ButtonClick(ByVal Button As ComctlLib.Button)
 2:     On Error Resume Next
 3:     Select Case Button.Key
 4:         Case "New"
 5:             Call mnuArray(1)
 6:         Case "Open"
 7:             Call mnuArray(2)
 8:         Case "Save"
 9:             Call mnuArray(3)
10:     End Select
11: End Sub
```

Your MDI parent form should now look like the one shown in Figure 7.15.

7

FIGURE 7.15.

The MDI parent form with both the menu and toolbar in place.

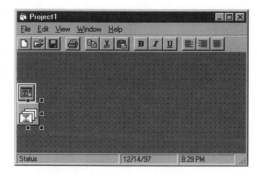

Now, if you are adding a toolbar to the child forms, you should remember that the toolbar will be shown along with the one from the MDI parent.

 Tip

It is recommended that unless you really need an extra toolbar, don't include any in the child forms.

If you decide to add a toolbar to a child form, your application could look like the one shown in Figure 7.16.

FIGURE 7.16.

Multiple toolbars do not look very good in an application.

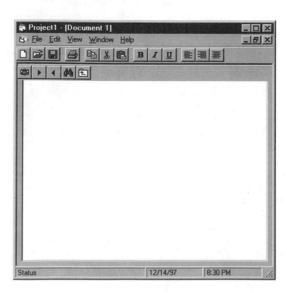

In Visual Basic 6, you can now add drop-down buttons to a toolbar that will display a menu style list to the user as shown in Figure 7.17.

FIGURE 7.17.

*Using the Toolbar to
present multiple
options.*

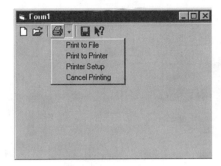

By setting the Style property of the Toolbar button to tbrButton, you can add menu items
to the button using the Toolbar button properties page (see Figure 7.18). This gives you
the ability to create toolbars that look and work exactly like the ones in Visual Basic and
other Microsoft products.

FIGURE 7.18.

*Using the Toolbar
properties page to
define a drop-down
button menu.*

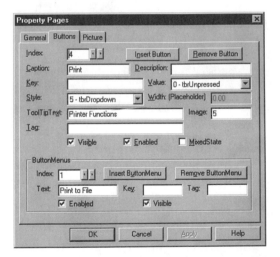

This new feature enables you to keep the toolbar small, yet still present the user with
many options to select from. In addition, you can make the buttons transparent, so that
the button will only appear when the mouse passes over it as shown in Figure 7.17.

Besides the new features of the Toolbar control, Visual Basic 6 also includes a new toolbar called the *coolbar*, which enables you to build the same type of toolbars (see Figure

7

7.19) that can be seen in newer versions of Internet Explorer or the Microsoft Office products.

FIGURE 7.19.

Using the new Coolbar control enables you to have multiple toolbars in the application.

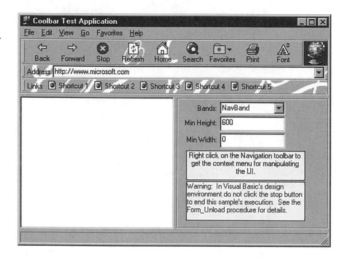

Finish adding the code you need for the toolbar `Click` event and run the application again to see how it works. You now have a good prototype for an address book application. However, a few things still must be added to the application before it is complete.

Standard Forms

Every application can have other related forms that can give the user information about the application or its status. By utilizing these form templates, you can add some flavor to your application while displaying information to the user. The splash form (see Figure 7.20) was originally created as a way to inform the user of the following while the application is starting:

- Version number
- User's name
- Serial number
- Application name
- Copyright warning

Because of its popularity, it has become a template provided with Visual Basic. To add this form to your application, choose Project, Add Form from the Visual Basic menu, and then select Splash Screen from the Add Form dialog box. This form is usually displayed while the application is performing its initialization process and is unloaded when the application is ready for use.

FIGURE 7.20.

*Using a splash form as
the main startup form
for an application tells
the user that some-
thing is happening.*

In order to use this form, you must add a code module to the project. You display a
splash form by having the SUB MAIN routine execute when the application starts. In this
routine, place the following code, which displays the splash form and then loads the
main MDI parent form:

```
Sub Main()
    frmSplash.Show
    frmSplash.Refresh
    mdiMainForm.Show
End Sub
```

Then, when the mdiMainForm has finished loading and is displayed, the splash form
will be unloaded. Depending on how long it takes for the main form to load, the splash
form might not stay on the screen for very long. To control the length of time it is visible, you could place a Timer control on the mdiMainForm and have the timer event
unload the splash form when it is triggered.

Another form template that you can add to your application is the About dialog box.
This is the same standard form that you see whenever you choose Help | About from
most Windows applications (see Figure 7.21). This dialog box is usually shown only
from the Help menu.

In addition, the About dialog box has a button on it which has code already in it that will
execute the Microsoft System Information application that displays many different types
of system-related information (see Figure 7.22).

The information displayed on both of these forms can be retrieved directly from the
application. The location of most of the information is the properties of the project.
When you create your application project, you would enter the information shown in
Figure 7.23. This information can then be accessed using the APP object properties in
your code.

7

FIGURE 7.21.

Displaying information about the application in the About help dialog box.

FIGURE 7.22.

The Microsoft System Information application displays important information about the programs that the computer is processing.

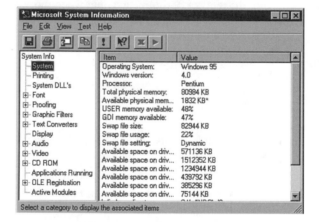

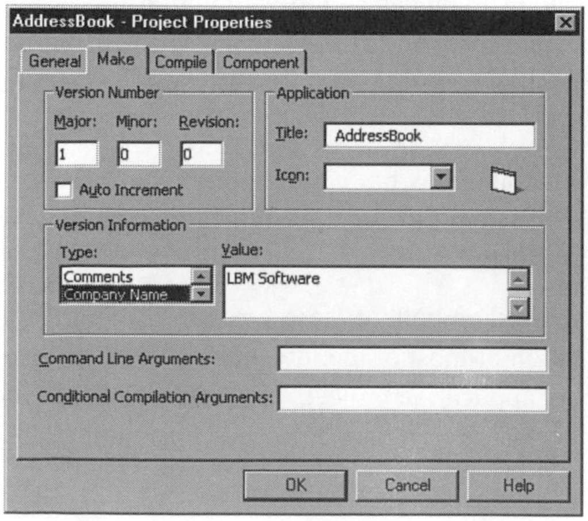

FIGURE 7.23.

The project properties to set the application information.

The following code displays the related information from the application properties in the Label controls on the splash form:

```
lblVersion.Caption = "Version " & App.Major & "." & App.Minor & "."_
    & App.Revision
lblProductName.Caption = App.Title
lblCompany.Caption = App.CompanyName
```

The APP object has several other properties that can be used for display purposes. There is one other form that you can add to your application; however, if you are like me, this form becomes annoying after it is displayed once or twice.

The *Tip of the Day* form is another template included with Visual Basic. It is different from the other two discussed in that it has some sample code in it to help you finish the coding process for it. This form (see Figure 7.24) is usually displayed after the main form is displayed but after the splash form is unloaded.

FIGURE 7.24.

The Tip of the Day form lets you give the user tips, hints, or just some comments about the application, computers, or life in general.

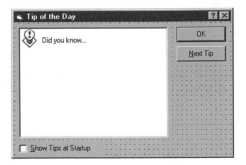

This form does require you to create a text file that contains the different tips that will be displayed. Also, a check box on the form lets the user tell the application not to display this form again. If you have been using any of the Microsoft Office tools, then you have seen this type of form and have probably turned it off. Again, using or not using these forms is your choice.

For this sample application, add both the Splash and About forms to the project. Then, add the code to the Help, About menu option to display the About form.

Tip

The About form is usually displayed as a modal form, which prevents the user from continuing until he clicks OK on the form to unload it.

7

For the Splash form, add the SUB MAIN routine as shown earlier. Also, you will need to change the Startup Object to SUB MAIN in the Project Properties dialog box. Now, run the application to see how these additions work.

Status Bars

This next feature is not a form that you can add to the application; it is a control that is included in the Windows common control that comes with Visual Basic. The status bar provides a window, usually located at the bottom of a main form, that can display various types of status information. The StatusBar control can be divided into a maximum of 16 separate Panel objects that are contained in a Panels collection. This control enables you to use one of seven values for the Style property to automatically display common data such as the system date and time or the status of the following keyboard keys:

- Scroll
- Insert
- Num Lock
- Caps Lock

The StatusBar control properties are set during design time in the control's property pages as shown in Figure 7.25.

FIGURE 7.25.

The StatusBar control's property page is used to set the initial Panel properties.

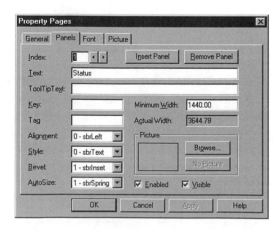

This control is used to display pertinent information about whatever form or function is being performed at the moment. Add this control to the mdiMainForm and set the Align property to the bottom. Then set three panels, one for status text, date, and time. The data and time values will be updated by the control itself when your application is executing. To use the status bar to inform the user where he is, you can simply add two lines of code for each form that is in the application. The first line of code will display text in the first panel describing what function the form performs. The following line of code should be inserted into the child form's LOAD routine:

```
StatusBar1.Panels.Item(1).Text = "Address book detail display"
```

Then in the form's UNLOAD routine, this property should be set back to blanks to remove the displayed information. At this point, your mdiMainForm should resemble the one shown in Figure 7.26.

FIGURE 7.26.

The final MDI parent form for the sample application showing the menu, toolbar, and status bar.

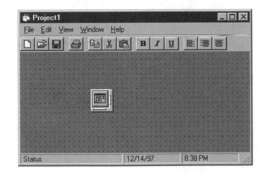

You should add only one more thing to the application prototype: the Common Dialog functions.

Common Dialog

You have already seen what you can do with the Common Dialog control. However, now you want to add these features to the application. For the File Open and Save functions, just add the code to display the common dialog form when the option is clicked. For the Color and Font functions, you really want to display a form that lists the different objects and features of these objects that can be modified using these common dialog boxes. For example, you might want to allow the user to change the background color of all the forms, or change the font style for just the command buttons, labels, or input text areas. Besides letting the user change these options, you must have a way to save the settings for the next time the application is executed. Prior to Windows 95, most applications used an initialization file or .INI to save application-related information. With the advent of Windows 95 and Visual Basic 5, programmers can also use the System Registry to save application related information instead of an .INI file. Two new functions are available to you in your application.

When you must save application-execution information in between the times you run it, you can use the SaveSetting command to save the information in the user's system

7

registry file. Conversely, you can retrieve these settings from the registry by using the
GetSetting command. The syntax is basically the same for both, as you can see here:

```
SaveSetting appname, section, key, setting
GetSetting(appname, section, key[, default])
```

The following are the parameters for each of the commands:

- appname—String containing the name of the application or project whose key
  setting is requested.
- section—String containing the section name where the key setting is found.
- key—String containing the name of the key setting to return.
- setting—Expression containing the value to which the key is being set.
- default—The value to return if no value is set in the key setting.

When the user changes any of the colors or fonts, you should save them in the registry.
When the application is started, these settings should be retrieved during the form_ini-
tialize routine to set the objects. To understand how this actually works, go back and
open the dlgFileOpenCopy project from Day 2, "The Windows Common Dialog in Use."
When you execute the application and then change the colors on the form, the changes
are not saved anywhere. So, when you close the application and restart it, the colors are
reset to the defaults. You can use the SaveSetting and GetSetting functions to save the
color change and then retrieve it when the application is started. In the cmdColor_Click
routine, place the following line of code after the call to the common dialog function:

```
SaveSetting "FileCopy", "Colors", "frmBackColor", frmDialog.BackColor
```

Then, in the form's LOAD routine, add the following line of code:

```
frmDialog.BackColor = GetSetting("FileCopy", "Colors", "frmBackColor",_
    vb3DFace)
```

This line of code will get the color value and set the application's background color
using it. Now when you run the application and change the color, it will be saved for
future use. These two lines of code must be used for every color value or font-related
value that you let the user change. In addition, you might want to set the original colors
as constants in the application. By doing this, you can enable the user to reset the colors
or fonts to the default settings.

The SSTab Control

The SSTab control allows you to add a group of tabs to a form, with each one acting as a
container for other controls. Only one tab will be active in the control at a time, displaying the controls it contains to the user while hiding the controls that are on the other tabs.

This allows you to display large numbers of controls to the user without cluttering up the form.

An SSTab control acts like the dividers in a notebook. By using the SSTab control, you can define multiple pages for the same area of a window or dialog box in your application. The properties of this control allow you to do the following:

- Set the number of tabs that are displayed
- Organize the tabs into one or more rows
- Assign the text caption for each tab
- Display a graphic on each tab
- Set the style of the tabs
- Size the tabs

When using this control, you must add it to the form before you start placing the controls you want into the tab area. Each tab can contain its own unique set of controls for the user to interact with.

Enhancing the Forms

When designing your forms, other features that you can add to them will make them even easier for the user to work with. In this section, you will see two such features that are supported either by Visual Basic or by writing program code.

Knowing what a command button does or what type of input a text box takes is very important when using the application. The `ToolTipText` property is supported by most Visual Basic controls, and by many third-party controls as well. This property contains text that is displayed whenever the user positions the mouse over the control. In addition, based on the position of the mouse, you can also display information in an area of a status bar.

Another feature that you can add to your application forms is the ability to have shortcut keys defined to input objects, such as text boxes and list boxes. You accomplish this action by using a combination of controls and program code. It lets users go directly to a particular field with which they want to work.

ToolTips

Over the years, application developers have sought a way to tell the user what function or feature a particular toolbar button or command button performs, or what type of input is required for a selected text box. There have many different solutions to this issue. One solution used for several years was to display descriptive text in a status line or bar at the

7

bottom of the main form. You can still do this by using the statusbar control and the MouseMove event of the objects on the form. However, using this method of displaying information requires you to add code to almost every object's MouseMove event. To see how this would work, start a new project and place a status bar at the bottom of the form. When you do this, you automatically get one panel set as a text panel. Now, add two command buttons to the form. This will give you enough objects to work with for this example. Now add the following code to your form:

```
Private Sub Command1_MouseMove(Button As Integer, Shift As Integer, x_
    As Single, y As Single)
      StatusBar1.Panels(1).Text = "This command button will perform task 1"
End Sub

Private Sub Command2_MouseMove(Button As Integer, Shift As Integer, X_
    As Single, Y As Single)
      StatusBar1.Panels(1).Text = "This command button will perform task 2"
End Sub

Private Sub Form_MouseMove(Button As Integer, Shift As Integer, x As_
    Single, y As Single)
      StatusBar1.Panels(1).Text = ""
End Sub

Private Sub StatusBar1_MouseMove(Button As Integer, Shift As Integer, x_
    As Single, y As Single)
      StatusBar1.Panels(1).Text = "This is the status bar used for _
      displaying text"
End Sub
```

This code will display the correct text based on the position of the mouse. However, you can see that if an object doesn't have a MouseMove event coded, the text in the status bar will not be removed or changed. This would confuse the user as to the function of that object. Another drawback to this method is that it requires the user to move his eyes and refocus on the status bar at the bottom of the form. It was this reason that prompted the development of what was termed *Balloon Help*.

Balloon Help is the little yellow box that pops up when you leave the mouse on an object for a couple of seconds. However, programming tools like Visual Basic had no way to create them. Balloon Help, or ToolTips as they are now called, have become an integral part of the Visual Basic environment. Almost every object that you can place on a form has a ToolTipText property. Setting this property is the only action you must do in order to display information to the user about the object. Visual Basic does the rest of the work. Using the open project, remove the MouseMove routines and place the following code in the Form_Load routine:

```
Command1.ToolTipText = "This command button will perform task 1"
Command2.ToolTipText = "This command button will perform task 2"
StatusBar1.Panels(1).ToolTipText = "This is the text panel"
StatusBar1.Panels(2).ToolTipText = "This is the current system date"
```

Before running the application again, add a second panel to the status bar to display the system date. Now, when you execute the application, each object on the form will display the correct information (see Figure 7.27). As you can see, this enables you to create unique messages depending on the function being performed, and additionally have tips displayed for each panel.

FIGURE 7.27.

Using ToolTip text to display related information about an object.

Object Shortcuts

Object shortcuts are a feature that you can add to your application to let the user move directly to any input field on the form. This feature is very familiar to users because it uses the same type of visual interface as the hotkeys in menus and command buttons. The difference in this method is that it uses the Ctrl key instead of the Alt key. To use this feature in your application you must associate a label control with each input control on the form. Figure 7.28 shows an example of two text boxes, a combo box, and a command button that all have a hotkey defined.

FIGURE 7.28.

Hotkeys are very useful for direct navigation within a form or to execute menu options without using the mouse.

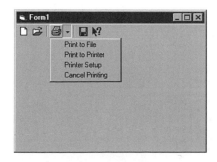

Now, by adding the following code to your application, every time the control key and the specified letter in the label are pressed, focus is set to the related input field:

```
Private Sub Form_KeyDown(KeyCode As Integer, Shift As Integer)
    If (Shift And vbCtrlMask) > 0 Then
        If KeyCode = vbKeyF Then
```

7

```
            Text1.SetFocus
        ElseIf KeyCode = vbKeyL Then
            Text2.SetFocus
        ElseIf KeyCode = vbKeyS Then
            Combo1.SetFocus
        End If
    End If
End Sub
```

Note

The KeyPreview property of the form must be set to True in order for this to work correctly.

As you can see, this feature lets you use only a certain number of letters. You can view the KeyCode constants in the Object Browser to see all of the valid keys that you can use. Run the application and try the different key combinations. You can see that if many different input fields were on the form, this navigation feature would be useful.

Summary

You have seen that designing forms takes a little more effort than just putting controls on the form. You must understand what the function of each form will be and how you want to present the information to the user. In addition, you have seen how to combine all of the different elements available in Visual Basic to create a form design that gives the user good information about the functions they are performing and a method for navigating to and from the different forms. The menus and toolbars also give users quick access to the application's functions and features without having to remember what keystroke they must make to perform the action.

Q&A

Q How can I use the Windows registry to save information from the application?

A You can access the system registry for the application by using the Visual Basic functions GetSetting and SaveSetting.

Q Are objects in Visual Basic capable of showing ToolTips?

A Most objects that have been created for Visual Basic are capable of displaying ToolTips; however, some objects do not support this feature.

Q Can an MDI parent form display a child form as Modal?

A No, child forms cannot be displayed using the Modal keyword.

Workshop

The Workshop provides quiz questions to help solidify your understanding of the material covered, as well as exercises to provide you with experience in using what you've learned. Try to understand the quiz and exercise answers before continuing on to the next day's lesson. Answers are provided in Appendix A, "Answers to Exercises."

Quiz

1. What are the six main design concepts for good forms design?
2. Can any object be placed on an MDI parent form?
3. What is the difference between an Explorer and SDI style?

Exercise

Create an application that uses MDI and contains a menu, toolbar, status bar, and one child window. Enable only the File, New menu option and the New button on the toolbar. When either of these is clicked, display another child form in the application. In addition, have the current date and time displayed on the status bar.

7

WEEK 1

In Review

What the first week has done is provide you with the knowledge and skills that you need to design a professional application. This was done by introducing you to the advanced building blocks that you can use to create a Windows application. In addition, you saw how to use what you have learned about the basic concepts of Visual Basic to enhance your applications by making both the user interface and the code easier to use and maintain.

Professional Applications and the Windows Interface

On Day 1, the concepts of deciding what type of application to create and the process you should use to design it was discussed in the idea of a project life cycle. This included design, coding, testing, debugging, and finally documentation. By following these concepts and guidelines, you can design and create a good application that will also work well. Also in Day 1 you learned about the options you can set for the entire project within Visual Basic that will help you while you are coding and testing your application. You then saw some of the newer controls that have been added to Visual Basic. Finally, you created a small application that used some of the standard programming concepts of Visual Basic and the new controls to enhance a plain file copy utility.

On Day 2, you visited with an old friend in the form of the Windows Common Dialog control. You first reviewed how this control works and then used it to enhance the file copy utility that you created in the previous chapter. Then, a new

Visual Basic object was introduced that provided you with the same functionality of the Common Dialog without having to include the control in your application. In addition, using the Dialog Automation object lets you build a more efficient application by reducing the size of the compiled executable program.

Day 3 continued by reviewing the two existing applications types, SDI and MDI, and then introduced the new Explorer-style application interface. This chapter also showed you how to use the Application wizard to build the interface with minimal effort. Finally, it went on to define and start a new address book application that you can use after you finish this book.

Chapter 5 started investigating the newer concepts of what Windows applications use to provide the user with multiple ways of accessing the application's features. The Toolbar control was covered in depth along with the new features that have been added in Visual Basic 6. One of the many new features is the ability to add buttons and drop-down menus directly onto the toolbar. In addition, the latest toolbar, or *coolbar*, was described and you saw how to use it in place of the standard toolbar to provide a Internet Explorer-style toolbar. Another important topic in this chapter was how to make use of the Menu editor to add menu functionality to your application, including the creation and use of pop-up menus within the application. The final topic in this chapter was the use and management of templates that are provided with Visual Basic. Most templates are accessible from the Visual Basic Add menu. Additionally, Visual Basic comes with an add-in that allows you to create snippets of code, menus, and controls that you can add to your application's forms without having to recreate work that you have already done. The Template Manager gives you the ability to access these templates for the application.

Using Collections and Other Visual Basic Concepts

Besides all of the Windows-oriented features of Visual Basic, there are many standard programming features that are still available to you to help create an application that performs well. Days 5 and 6 covered many topics that you may have quickly covered in previous books; however, now, you not only know *how* to use them, but *why* you should use them in certain situations. Amongst all of these features is the added ability to create your own application classes that can be used like any other object within your Visual Basic application.

Complex Forms Design

The final chapter of this week actually took a look at some topics that are usually not discussed in a "normal" Visual Basic programming book. This is what goes into designing good forms that are easy for the user to read and use. In addition, Day 7 showed you how to take all of the different features and controls that you have seen during that week and use them in a professional-style application. Finally, a couple of performance and usage tips were discussed that allow you to add easier ways for the user to access the features and data fields that appear in your application.

WEEK 2

At a Glance

During Week 2, you start by defining what databases really are, the types that are available for you to use, and how to pick the right one for your application. You also get a quick refresher on what SQL language is and how to use it. Once that is done, the actual application design process begins. You will see how to combine everything that you have learned so far into an application definition and a working prototype for that application. In addition, you see how to create ActiveX controls that can be used to enhance and simplify the application that you are building.

Next, getting the data from the database on to printed reports using Crystal Reports is discussed. In the last two days of this week, Internet access will be added to your application. You will see how to add application update capability by using the Internet file transfer features. Finally, you learn how to incorporate OLE drag and drop into your application, giving the user a quick way of performing some of the everyday tasks in the application.

Day 8 — Designing a Database Application

This chapter shows you how to design the application along with the database. This includes the application flow, the related tasks that it performs, and what forms are needed and how to create them. In addition, you see how to use some of the wizards that come with Visual Basic to simplify the tasks.

8

9

10

11

12

13

14

Day 9 — Database Processing

Day 9 reviews the concepts of database design and creation. It also gives a quick course in using the SQL to access the database. Finally, you see how to use the Visual Data Manager to create a Visual Basic Jet Database.

Day 10 — Accessing the Database

Day 10 covers the different ways to access the data from the database. You see how to use both the Data Access Objects as well as the data-bound controls. What you will also learn is how to combine both of the access methods when either one separately is not enough. In addition, the new ActiveX Data Objects and controls are introduced and compared with the standard Data Access Objects.

Day 11 — Enhancing the Application

Day 11 covers the much talked about topic of ActiveX control creation. Instead of creating a simple control that is not really useful in an actual application, this chapter shows you how to create custom controls from the data access forms you created earlier. This enables you to add these forms as another control to the Explorer interface. You also learn how to use the new ActiveX Control Test Contrainer to test your new controls.

Day 12 — Enhancing Database Access

Day 12 introduces you to several new components of Visual Basic that are used to access data in a database. You see how to use the Data Environment Designer to create database queries and then use it with the Data Reporter Designer to create reports directly on a form. In addition, you will see how to create custom control, multiple field grid displays using the Data Repeater control.

Day 13 — Working with Crystal Reports

Day 13 introduces the Crystal Reports reporting tool that is packaged with Visual Basic. Besides understanding what it does for you, you discover how to add reporting capabilities to your application using Crystal Reports.

Day 14 — Internet Programming

Day 14 discusses the latest craze in computer programming, Internet access. This chapter doesn't discuss how to create Internet applications; it does however, show you how to add Internet access to the application that you are creating—both to give users a way of browsing the Web, and to also give them a way of upgrading the application software directly from your Web site (if you have one). You will also learn how to use the new HTML Page Designer to create Web pages directly within Visual Basic. Finally, you get a brief lesson in what HTML is and how it works with a subset of Visual Basic called VBScript.

DAY 8

Designing a Database Application

In previous lessons, you've seen what makes up a good application and some of the Visual Basic tools and features that you can use to create an application. Also, some good programming concepts were reinforced. Yesterday you saw what a database is and what the issues are to build one that will allow quick access to the data. Today's lesson will bring all these building blocks together, add a few new ones, and show you the progression from the initial idea to the working prototype of an application.

You'll see that creating an application takes more effort (read: thinking) than you realize—you can't simply design and build the database, throw controls on the forms, and then expect the application to work properly. Along the way, you'll also see some of the pitfalls to watch for and some of the shortcuts that Visual Basic provides in the form of wizards.

What Is a Database?

Before you start to design a database, it's important to understand exactly what a database is and what types of databases you have to choose from. The application type will affect the database type that you choose. A database is really a system that contains many different objects used together to allow your application fast and efficient access to the data. You can use many examples of databases with your application. The most common of these are as follows:

- Microsoft Access
- Microsoft FoxPro
- Oracle Personal 7
- Sybase SQL Anywhere

All these databases can run on a standalone computer and allow you to create very complex databases for your applications. Picking the right database for your application is very important, because the wrong one will affect performance and make your job as developer that much harder.

Before starting the design process, you need to select a database. When working with Visual Basic, the databases that you can choose from fall into two distinct groups:

- *Local databases* can be accessed directly from Visual Basic through Visual Basic's database Jet engine.
- *Remote databases* can't be accessed by using Visual Basic's standard database access capabilities.

Understanding the differences will help you select the correct database for your application. However, in Visual Basic 6, there is now a way to access both local and remote databases using the same database access controls and objects known as the ActiveX Data Objects.

Understanding Universal Data Access (UDA)

As databases have grown and moved off the local computer and onto networked database servers, the methods employed to access the databases have changed. Microsoft has addressed these changes by developing a strategy to allow for any company or database to be accessed the same way. This is called Universal Data Access, or UDA. Understanding what UDA means is not as simple as understanding how to use it. The reason for this is that UDA is a set of rules and access methods that must be followed by any company that is creating a database access method to be used. This allows you, the programmer, to access any database the same way.

But, what is UDA? Universal Data Access is a platform, application, and tools concept that Microsoft has developed that defines and delivers the standards for all future application development. Using the UDA standards will provide high performance access to many types of data and information that reside on multiple platforms, and a programming interface that will work with almost any tool or language using the skills that developers already have. This is accomplished by using Microsoft's Data Access Components (MDAC), as well as an integrated set of technologies, which include ActiveX Data Objects (ADO), OLE DB, and Open Database Connectivity (ODBC). The benefits of using these standards include the following:

- **High performance access to data**—Provides the ability to scale any application or component to support concurrently connected users without losing performance.
- **Reliability**—Reduces the number of components to support on the client PC.
- **Wide industry support**—Many vendors including Microsoft have already announced support for the UDA standards.

In previous releases of Visual Basic, you needed to choose from either DAO (local) access methods to data or RDO (remote) access to data. Now, with the support of UDA, Visual Basic has a third method for data access called ADO, or ActiveX Data Objects. This allows you to combine the different ways of accessing data into one set of programming calls and objects. ADO works in conjunction with OLE DB and ODBC to provide access to any database you might be working with. Going forward, Microsoft plans to phase out ODBC in favor of OLE DB and the UDA standards. However, for the near future, both DAO and RDO, as well as ODBC, will still be supported to allow developers to slowly move up to the new standards of data access.

Local Databases

Local databases are generally much smaller than the remote type of database. The following databases fall into this category:

- Microsoft Access
- Microsoft FoxPro
- Lotus Worksheets
- Microsoft Excel Worksheets
- dBASE
- Paradox
- ASCII

As you can see, these PC-resident database types have been around for a while and are available from almost any computer software store. Accessing these databases doesn't require any other software to be installed on the PC, nor does it require special knowledge on how to work with them. However, the size of local databases is restricted. For example, Microsoft Access 97 databases can't exceed 1GB (gigabyte).

Local databases are generally used for single-user applications such as checkbooks, address books, and personal information managers. Some enterprising teenagers have created database applications that help them keep track of their baseball cards or video tapes. So in deciding what your application will address and how it will be used actually helps you in the database selection process.

Remote Databases

By definition, remote databases don't reside on the user's PC, but this isn't always true. In fact, a remote database is any type of database that requires an ODBC (Open Database Connectivity) driver for an application to access it. ODBC databases fall into two main categories: ones that run on a single PC, and the larger corporate ones that require large, very powerful computers (called *servers*) with large amounts of available disk space. Database servers are used to separate the workload between the client PC (where the application executes) and the database system (where the database queries are performed). This provides the application with fast data access without slowing down the user's PC.

Most of the large server-type databases provide versions that will run on standalone PCs. Most large corporations use one of the following database systems (though this is not to say that others aren't out there):

- Oracle
- Sybase
- Microsoft SQL Server

Using a remote database requires you to use either the remote database objects available only in the Enterprise version of Visual Basic 6 or the new ActiveX Data Objects available in all releases of Visual Basic 6. If you're designing an application that will use one of these large databases, however, the best way to create the application is to use the single-PC version during the design, development, and testing process. Then, when the application is completed, switch the ODBC connection to the larger, server-based version.

Building the Initial Design

8

Back on Day 1, "Writing Professional Visual Basic Applications," you learned that creating an application is a lot like building a house. For a well-built house, you need a blueprint to follow, but to create a good blueprint, you need to know who's going to live in the house and what their living style will be. This will help you decide the number and sizes of the rooms, what colors to use, and so on. With an application, the blueprint is the technical specs; the functional specs are what you need to know to create the technical specs. Now, many books teach the overall application design process by using very simplistic example applications. That's not what will happen here.

Let's revisit the application discussed on Day 1. The starting description of that application is as follows:

> **Personal Address/Phone Book**—This application will keep track of names, addresses, and phone numbers by name. It will allow as many different addresses and phone numbers as needed. Also, it will allow the entry of some personal information (such as birth date, spouse's name, and children's names) to be determined later. It will also provide reports in several formats and allow users to search the database for a particular person.

Although this application is fairly simple when compared with applications such as Microsoft Money or Microsoft Outlook, it still requires all the same components to perform properly. From this simple paragraph a mighty application will grow, but it takes patience and time. After you decide on the type of application you want to create, the next step is to decide the main tasks it will perform.

Choosing the Tasks

Defining the tasks for the application also defines its complexity. For example, this application is an address/phone book, if you decide to give users the ability to select a phone number and have the computer dial it for them. To add this functionality to the application, you need to know how to test for the existence of a modem, connect to that modem, and then actually dial the number. If you don't know how to add this functionality, you might consider waiting to add it after the initial version of the application is created and tested. This is what releasing new versions are all about.

Keep the initial version of this application at a simpler level. The best way to design an application is to say to yourself, "What would I want the application to do if I were the user?" Basically, you're the first and most important user of the application. This approach might not work for the larger, corporate-type application, but it does work for the smaller, more personal types.

Even before you list the different tasks that the application will perform, you need to decide what type of application interface to use for this application. For this sample application, use the Explorer-style interface. To review this style, the initial form that users see and remain in for most of the application will resemble the one shown in Figure 8.1.

FIGURE 8.1.

This interface includes many of the controls that you learned about earlier in this book, including menus, toolbars, and a status bar.

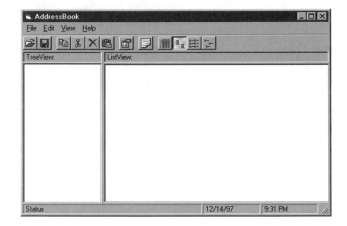

Okay, you've picked the application that you'll create—now you need to list the main functions that it will perform. Think of what the application is for and then list what you want it to do. From this reasoning, you should get the following list:

- Keep names and addresses.
- Search for a particular name.
- Print different types of reports.
- Allow for different users.
- Enable easy maintenance of the application.

Now if this list seems simplistic, it is. You would then expand each item in this list until you're satisfied with the result. Let's expand each of the preceding tasks and add a bit more detail to the definition.

Keeping Names and Addresses

What do you really mean when you say "Keep names and addresses?" It usually means that you want to keep track of the standard information found in any paper phonebook you would look at. The first step in defining all the mini-tasks required for this topic is to list the data elements you want to put in the database. Table 8.1 lists the data elements that you can use for this type of application.

TABLE 8.1. DATA ELEMENTS THAT CAN BE INCLUDED IN THE APPLICATION DATABASE.

Name	Type
First Name	String
Last Name	String
Spouse Name	String
Child Name	String
Address	String
City	String
State	String
ZIP	Integer
E-mail Address	String
Phone	Long
Birth Date	Date
Notes	String

8

This list is pretty straightforward, but look more closely at it. It has elements such as phone number and birth date. Can't a person have more than one phone number? Or, if you're allowing users to enter the names of the person's spouse and children, you could have more than one birth date to enter. When the tables for this database are created, you'll need to design the capability to handle multiple copies of these types of elements. How do you want users to see the information? This section of the application will require the following forms:

- Book Entry form
- Detailed Entry display

Although only two forms are involved with the data entry and display, each form performs quite a bit of processing. The first form gives users an easy way of entering information. Depending on how fancy you want to get, you could create a form that uses many of the more advanced Visual Basic controls. Figure 8.2 shows an example of this entry form. Notice that this form allows users to select from a list of phone number types to enter a number in. A similar approach is used for entering child and spouse information.

FIGURE 8.2.

One concept of the data-entry form, using many of the advanced Visual Basic controls.

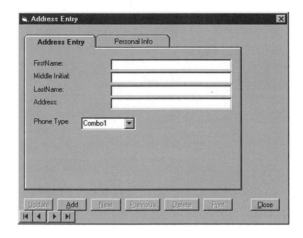

Also, you can see that the form is split in two with the TabStrip control to make unique areas for business and personal information for that entry. Now, what are the tasks that this form must perform when a new entry is added? This list is fairly standard for most database applications:

- Validate the dates entered.
- Edit the phone numbers for the correct amount of digits.
- Verify that this person isn't already in the database.
- Allow users to cancel the process, if needed.
- Provide easy ways to select static information (such as state names).
- Give positive feedback to users when the data is finally added.

Some of these tasks are code-related, whereas others are really database-related.

The second form gives users a way to display all the information in an entry without having to change sections of the display. For this to look good, you have to decide the way to display the information. Some applications use the same form as the entry form, but set it up so that the data can't be modified. Today's lesson uses the same form, with some modifications. This version of the form would have the following extra command buttons visible on the form:

- Update
- Next (entry)
- Previous (entry)
- Delete
- Print

8

Figure 8.2 shows these extra command buttons as *disabled* (grayed out), although in the actual application you would probably hide these controls unless you need them. Then again, some applications combine the Add form and the display/modify form into one single form and task by including one more command button on the form to request the add task.

 Note You should be aware that the forms, data elements, and database design in this lesson are only one way to design and create this particular application. If you choose to create this application to use, it could look vastly different from this one.

Searching for a Particular Name

The next task that this application will provide is the ability to search the database for a particular entry. Now, when you use the Explorer-style interface, it doesn't make much sense to allow users to search by a person's last name. However, you might need to find someone in the database in many other ways, including the following:

- First Name
- Zip Code
- Spouse Name
- Child Name
- City
- State

A search form is basically the same in most applications, so you can use the design concepts of any application that you use. Figure 8.3 shows the form in the sample application. Notice that a group of option buttons allows users to select the data element to search, and a text box allows users to enter the actual data to search for. This form takes the search text and then uses database functionality to perform the actual search.

FIGURE 8.3.

Search forms are very similar in design for many Windows applications.

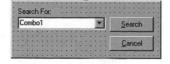

Printing Different Report Types

This task starts out simple but can quickly become the most complex task in the application. What types of reports do you want to get from this application? Is *reports* even the
correct term for this process? Reports are usually associated with bigger applications,
such as checkbooks, accounts payable, and so on.

This application will provide users with a list of the entries in the database. But what format should the list be in? Some people will want to print a list of names and numbers to
carry in their briefcase or wallet. Others will want a detailed printed copy of the entire
database information in book format. The actual creation of these lists is covered on Day
13, "Working with Crystal Reports." But you need to give users a way of selecting the
output type that they want. Different applications perform this in different ways:

- Some display a dialog box listing each available report. Users select the one they
  want and click a button to continue (see Figure 8.4).

- Other applications provide users with a way to choose from a list of options that
  would modify the application's standard reports. This way, you can design and
  create a few standard reports that users could then modify to print many different
  versions.

- Another way is to add search capability to the report selection. Each type of report
  selection ideas depend completely on the reporting tool being used to create and
  display the reports.

FIGURE 8.4.

*One method of report
selection is fairly
static, giving users a
list of available reports
but no options.*

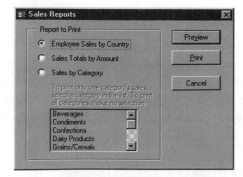

Allowing for Different Users

Many database applications can work with multiple copies of the database. This allows
more than one person in the household to use the application, yet have their own private
address/phone book database. You can go even further by requiring a password to allow
access to the database when it's first opened. This type of process is usually available
from the main application menu or toolbar, as shown in Figure 8.5.

FIGURE 8.5.

Giving users the ability to select different databases to use in the application.

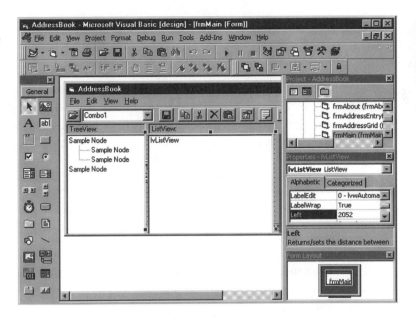

8

Of course, this capability comes with its own problems and requirements. The most important one that you need to supply with the application is an empty copy of the database that will be used to create each different working copy that users want.

Easily Maintaining the Application

What does maintenance really mean to users? The only thing they're interested in is whether the application will work every time they use it. Well, a good design and good testing should take care of this concern. But what if something goes wrong on their computer and they lose the database files, or they accidentally delete the files? Your application must allow users to create backup copies of the database files so that if the unthinkable happens, they can simply restore their data from the backup copy. Referring back to multiple databases, this backup system will have to recognize which database is being backed up.

Setting the Limits

Setting the limits of an application covers two distinct areas of the design process. When designing an application, you'll probably develop a list of functions and features that you want to see in the application but don't have the knowledge or the time to add. This type of issue really depends on whether you're planning to sell the application and when it needs to be ready for market.

One of the biggest traps developers fall into is the "one-more-feature" syndrome. Have you ever finished a project at home, sat back, and said, "That looks great, but just let me change one thing?" If you have, you already know about this deadly trap. If you keep changing "just one more thing," the application will never be completed. To prevent this from happening to you, develop the list of tasks (functions and features) for your application and stick with it. If you find something that you think would be nice to have in the application, put it on the Next Release list. This way, you don't lose the idea, yet it won't affect the initial version of the application. If you find a task that must be in the application but isn't, however, you have to add it, no matter what effect it might have on the completion date of the application.

A second limit that you need to set for the application is how much data is too much. Although you want to create a fairly flexible application, providing users with too much flexibility usually backfires in the form of errors and lost data. Imagine what would happen if you allowed users to create new phone number elements when needed. This could lead to a single entry having hundreds of phone numbers associated with it. This in turn would cause a problem with printing the entry. And how would users easily display this information?

Most times, the limits put on data in a database is a function of the database engine and how much data it can safely support. In the case of Microsoft Access 97, the database file can't exceed 1GB (gigabyte). For an application such as an address book, this is an awful lot of names.

Creating the Database

When you know what types of forms you need and how they will look, you next need to create the database that will contain the information required for this application. You've already learned that if you have information with several duplicate data elements related to it, you should create multiple tables. In this application, each entry can contain one or more of the following pieces of information:

- Addresses (Home, PO Box, Business, Shipping)
- Phone Numbers (Home, Business, Fax, Cell, Pager)
- Children's Names

The process of listing these possibilities helps in deciding how many tables you'll need in the database. In addition to these main tables in the database, you'll probably need other tables, called *reference* or *support tables*, to provide all the capabilities to users.

Building the Tables

You can build the actual tables by using the Visual Data Manager, or you can use Microsoft Access to create and define the tables. This application will need the following tables:

- Address Entry
- Phones
- Offspring
- Comments
- Reports

You also could add several optional reference tables to the application to make it easier for users to enter the information:

- A ZIP code/city cross-reference would allow users to enter a ZIP code and have the city automatically entered.
- Valid area codes would help in the validation process of phone numbers.

Of course, adding these types of reference tables requires you to type all the information or have access to a data file that contains this information for you to load into the database. For each required table, you need to define the columns that they contain. Table 8.2 lists each database table and their related columns.

TABLE 8.2. ADDING COLUMN DEFINITIONS TO THE NEW TABLES.

Column Name	Description
	Address Entry Table
	(This is the main table that will hold the basic address information)
Entry Key	Uniquely identifies each record
Date Updated	Tells you when the record was last updated
First Name	
Middle Initial	
Last Name	
Address	
City	
State	
ZIP Code	Allows for the ZIP+4 format

continues

TABLE 8.2. CONTINUED

Column Name	Description
Home Phone	Holds the area code and the phone number
Birth Date	
Spouse's First Name	
Spouse's Birth Date	
Wedding Anniversary	
E-mail Address	

Phones Table

(Each record in this table will hold one phone number that's related to a specific Address entry)

Phone Key	Uniquely identifies each record
Entry Fkey	The foreign key used to join to the Address Entry table
Phone Type	Identifies the type of phone number in the record
Phone Number	The actual phone number
Phone Ext	The extension to dial if the phone type is Business

Offspring Table

(Each record in this table will hold the information for one child who's related to a specific entry)

Offspring Key	Uniquely identifies each record
Entry Fkey	The foreign key used to join to the Address Entry table
Child First Name	
Child Birth Date	
Child Sex	Notes whether the child is a boy or a girl

Comments Table

(This table will contain any notes for the Address Entry)

Note Key	Uniquely identifies each record
Entry Fkey	The foreign key used to join to the Address Entry table
Note	Contains the actual text of the note

Reports Table

(This table maintains the list of reports available in the application. It allows future expansion of the report list)

Report Key	Uniquely identifies each record

Column Name	Description
Report Desc	Contains the description of the report
Report Filename	
Report Sort Order	Defines the sort position of the report in the display list and allows you to reorder the report list when needed

8

By looking at the information in Table 8.2, notice that only the information that can occur in multiples has been placed in their own tables. Any other information related to the address book entry is contained in the primary or master table. Also, the reports table is used only by the reporting dialog form to display the available reports to users. Finally, you should also notice that each table has two types of key fields in them: one used for system control of the records, and one used to define the relationships between tables.

Defining the Indexes

The indexes that you define for the database tables are directly related to the types of searches you'll allow users to perform in the application. If you don't define indexes, application performance slows as the database grows because, during table searches, if the field being searched isn't indexed, the database engine will have to read the entire table to find matching records. Imagine looking for a name in a phone book that isn't in alphabetical order. You would have to read every name in the book looking for the one you wanted. But with the top-of-page indexing that the phone books usually have, finding a name is easy and quick. Database indexes work the same way.

When working with indexes, don't forget that sometimes you'll need to use more than one column to create a unique index value. In this application, what happens if two people have the same last name, such as Smith? You would then need to look at the first name to see which is the one you wanted. So, for the application, you need to create at least six indexes, one for each table. For the three supporting tables, the index should be on the Entry Fkey field, which relates the record to a given address entry. Therefore, all records with the same key value should be grouped together. For the primary table, you should start by creating an index on the first and last name fields individually, and on one by using the first and last name fields together.

When combining fields into one index, it's important to remember that the order they're listed in the index affects the way the index will work.

If the index is created with the two fields in the wrong order, the returned query result will have incorrect information. For this application, add the indexes listed in Table 8.3 for much better performance when accessing the tables.

TABLE 8.3. ADDING THE NECESSARY INDEXES TO THE DATABASE.

Table Name	Index Name	Field Name
Address Entry	idxFirst	First Name
	idxLast	Last Name
	idxPrimary	Last Name; First Name
Phones	idxPhones	Entry Fkey
Offspring	idxChild	Entry Fkey
Comments	idxComment	Entry Fkey
Reports	idxReports	Report Key

If you're wondering why built-in SQL queries haven't been mentioned yet, keep in mind that these types of queries are used primarily to speed up the SQL process and to answer specific data needs in an application. Unfortunately, most query requirements aren't known until you get to that section in the application-creation process.

Note

> As you start the creation process for this application, if you decide that you want to include other data items in the address entry information, feel free to add them. Remember, however, that the forms also will have to be modified to accommodate the new fields.

Building the Application Prototype

Now that you've defined the database and have decided on each form that you need, the next step is to actually create the application prototype. At this point, you need to decide whether to use the Application Wizard to create the basic forms or create them from scratch. If you're like me, you'll use the Application Wizard. So start Visual Basic, if it's not already started, and then choose Add-Ins, Application Wizard.

Note

> If the Application Wizard on your computer looks slightly different than the figures in this lesson, don't worry. I'm using the Application Wizard installed from the Visual Basic Web site.

When the wizard starts, you'll see the Introduction dialog box. Click Next to continue. In the next dialog box, select the option to use the Explorer interface and then click Next. The next dialog lets you to select the menu options that you want in the application (see Figure 8.6). Choose the options that you know are needed in this application.

FIGURE 8.6.

Using the Application Wizard to build menu options.

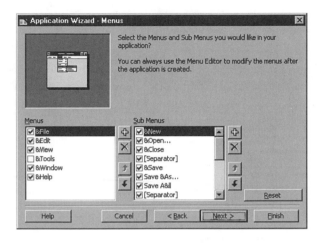

> **Note**
>
> You may notice that some menu options aren't in the order that you'd expect to see them. Selecting the Explorer-style interface changes how the menu options are displayed (each interface style has its own unique menu standards). If you want to change the order, go right ahead. If you think you'll forget an option, you can always add it later. For now, the default menu options are fine.

When you're ready, click Next to continue. The next dialog box creates the toolbar for the application (see Figure 8.7). Again, the toolbar starts with the default options for an Explorer-style interface.

FIGURE 8.7.

Adding a toolbar has become very easy when working with the Application interface.

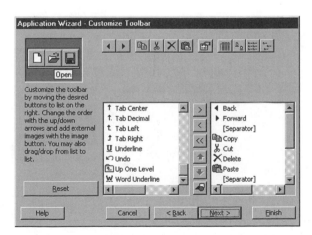

In the case of the toolbar, delete the Back and Forward arrows and put the Open and Save buttons in their place, as shown in Figure 8.7. After you finish with these changes, click Next. The next dialog box asks whether you'll use a resource file with the application. For now, the answer is no; however, resource files will be discussed on Day 19, "Performance and Tuning." After reading about resource files, you may decide to change the application. If you aren't sure, there's not harm to choose yes on this dialog box. If you do choose to use a resource file, you need to enter a path and filename. Either way, click Next to continue.

Note

> If you choose to use the resource file option, the menu captions will look a little strange at designtime. Because the actual captions are in the resource file, they're displayed only at runtime.

Now, you're asked whether you want the Internet browser included in the application. If you want to this function available for users, select Yes and click Next, keeping the default Web page as www.microsoft.com (as with anything else, you can change the reference later).

In the next dialog box, you can choose from a list of available form templates to include in the application (see Figure 8.8). For this application, choose the Splash Screen and About Dialog templates and click Next. This new dialog box allows you to add data-access forms to the application. Right now, you don't want to add any, so click Next to bypass this dialog box. (You aren't adding any data forms during this process because the next section focuses on them.)

FIGURE 8.8.

Adding any additional forms to the application from available templates.

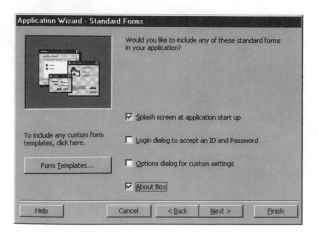

To complete the process, name the project AddressBook and click the Finish button. If you look at the Project Window, you'll see all the forms, modules, and resource files added to the project (see Figure 8.9).

FIGURE 8.9.

The Application Wizard creates all the forms and related files needed for the application prototype.

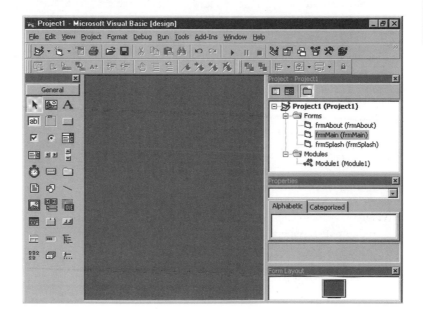

To see exactly what the Application Wizard has created for you, run your new application. Try a few of the menu options and toolbar buttons. You can see that you have a working prototype, although it's only half completed—you still need to add the search, data-entry, and report-selection forms to the application.

Using the Data Form Wizard

Adding the data-access forms to the application can be very interesting; however, just as with the application prototype, Visual Basic comes with a tool that helps you with the creation process. The Data Form Wizard takes you through several dialog boxes, in which you'll specify the database you're using and the types of forms you want to create. The final data-access forms that you'll use in the application won't resemble the forms this wizard creates. You'll use the wizard to generate the initial forms, which will have all the necessary data-access code to use as a starting point. You need to add only two forms to the application for data access: the data-entry form and a grid-style display form. Let's start with the grid-style form first.

To invoke the Data Form Wizard, choose Add-Ins, Data Form Wizard. When the introduction dialog box appears, click Next to continue. The next dialog box asks you what type of database you're using. For this application, you'll use a Visual Basic Jet database (actually, an Access database), so select Access at the top of the list and click Next. The next dialog box asks you to select the database you're using and the type of data access you want on the form (see Figure 8.10). For the grid-style form, select Data Control as the Binding Type for the new form. Click Next to continue.

FIGURE 8.10.

Entering the database filename and choosing the data binding you want to use for the new form.

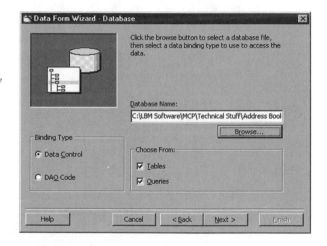

The next dialog box is pretty simple. You can create three types of form displays: a single record, a grid, or a master/detail form (such as an invoice-style display). For the grid-style form, the correct choice is pretty obvious. Then click Next.

The Record Source dialog box in Figure 8.11 lets you choose the table or query to select the columns that you want on the form. For the grid form, choose the Address Entry table, and then select the following fields to be displayed on the form. These are the main fields needed to be displayed in the grid:

- First Name
- Last Name
- Address
- City
- State
- Home Phone

FIGURE 8.11.

Selecting box the table and the columns that will be displayed from the Record Selection dialog box.

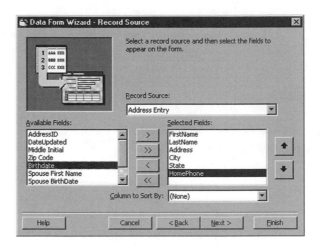

You can also choose the field to sort on. For this application, sort on the Last Name, and then click Next.

The next dialog box lets you choose the command buttons you want on the form, and whether you want the Data control to be visible. For this grid form, the only controls you want on the form are the Close command button and the Data control. Deselect the remaining buttons and click Next to finish the process. Change the form name to frmAddressGrid and click the Finish button to create the finished form. Figure 8.12 shows the resulting form.

FIGURE 8.12.

The finished data grid-display form with only the Close button and Data control displayed.

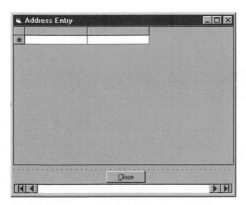

After you create this form, you need to add a menu option and a toolbar button to give users a way to display this form. Of course, in the true sense of this application interface, you'll actually incorporate the data grid display into the Explorer dialog box without using another form.

Note

On Day 11, "Enhancing the Application," you'll see how to create custom ActiveX controls. Use these data forms as a guide so that you can add these dialog boxes into the Explorer interface without it looking as though separate forms were in the application.

Next, you want to reuse the Data Form Wizard for the data-entry form; however, you want to use the DAO binding methods and a single-record display for this form (because you'll be adding more code and controls to this form later this week). By using DAO access, you get much more flexibility in design and coding. Also, you want to choose every field from the Address Entry table, except for Entry Key and the DateUpdated. These fields are used by the application, and users doesn't need to see them. You also want to sort by the Entry Key field. Finally, you want to accept the default buttons for the form. Accept the default form name and click Finish button to create the form as shown in Figure 8.13.

FIGURE 8.13.

The data-entry form has every field from the Address Entry table.

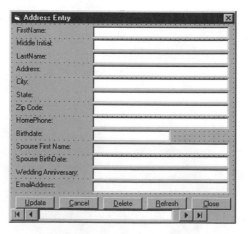

Remember to add the menu option and toolbar buttons to allow users to display the data-entry form. After you complete this step, you're almost finished. The final step is to add the unrelated forms to the application.

Adding Forms

The only forms left to add—if you haven't been keeping track—are Search and Report Selection. The Search form is pretty easy; the code behind it, however, is a bit tougher. For now, create the form as shown in Figure 8.3 earlier in this lesson. The only line of code you need to add to the form now is the code in the Close command button's click event to unload the form.

8

The Report Selection form is by far the most difficult form to create—not in what you need to place on the form, but in how you want the form to look. I'm partial to a tree-view selection list of reports (see Figure 8.14), although some developers prefer command buttons or option controls (see Figure 8.15). Either way, it's your choice. Pick one and create the form, again by adding only the code to unload it.

FIGURE 8.14.

Giving users an Explorer-style tree view to select reports from.

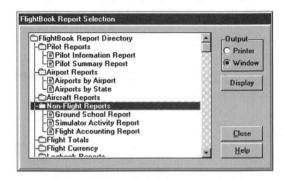

FIGURE 8.15.

With a small number of reports, option controls or command buttons work just as well.

Now that everything has been created, run the application and exercise the different options and buttons in the application to see how it all works. In the following lessons, you'll see how to add the code needed to activate the functions and features that you've created these forms for.

Summary

Today's lesson begins the process of creating a real application that you can use to keep track of phone numbers and addresses on your computer. It discusses the need to identify the different tasks that the application will do, identify the required tables and fields, and choose the indexes to create. Finally, you were shown how to create the application prototype. Every form that you need is created. Now the hard part starts—adding the code that will make this a unique, working application.

Q&A

Q **How does the Data Form Wizard help create a database application?**

A The Data Form Wizard prompts you for the necessary information and then builds a form with enough data access code already included. This gives you a head start on the modifications when customizing the form later.

Q **What are the three main form types usually included in an application?**

A An application generally has a main application interface form, such as an MDI parent or the Explorer interface form. Also, most applications have additional support forms, such as the About dialog box and splash screen. Finally, if the application uses a database, data-bound forms are also included in the application.

Workshop

The Workshop normally provides quiz questions to help solidify your understanding of the material covered, as well as exercises to provide you with experience in using what you've learned. Today's lesson is really about how to create forms based an a design that's already in place. There's nothing else I could ask you to do that you haven't already done in the lesson. For this reason, there are no quiz questions and no exercise for this lesson. However, you should take a look at the things you do at home or at work and try to envision that types of data and table structures you would create to hold this type of information.

DAY 9

Database Processing

Database processing has become an integral part of almost any type of complex application available on the market. Databases are used to store data, whether it's your address book, your checkbook, or your company's accounts payable. Even though databases can be used by any size application, the design concepts are the same, no matter what the application is that will use it.

With Visual Basic, you can create very powerful database-oriented applications with a little bit of planning and some effort. Planning a good database, however, requires that you understand exactly what a database is and what makes a good one. A poorly designed database causes even the best application to perform badly. On the other hand, a well-designed database makes the application process that much easier.

Designing a database requires you to use the same process as designing your application. The difference in designing the database and designing the application is determined by the type of application you're creating. Some applications, such as a word processor, don't use database systems at all, whereas others have a simple database and a complex user interface. Then there are those applications that make extensive use of database systems, such as an accounts payable system.

This lesson will show you how to define the data you'll need in your database, the structure of the database itself, and what it takes to actually create the working database. You'll also see how to use the Visual Data Manager included with Visual Basic. Finally, you'll get a short lesson in what SQL (Structured Query Language) is and how to use it.

Database Design

The same steps that you take to design an application can be applied to the database design as well. Before designing the first form, you must have a completed data design to work with.

> **Note**   Even though the database design is completed, changes probably will be made to it as you design the application. Don't worry about these changes; if the original design is good, the changes should be easy to apply.

When you design your application, you not only need to design your program code for performance, but you must also pay attention to the logical and physical design of the database. A good database design does the following for your application:

- Allows data to be stored efficiently so that the database doesn't get larger that absolutely necessary
- Provides for easy data updates
- Provides a flexible design to allow for the addition of new functions, tables, or data
- Allows searches to be performed quickly

All of these are provided in a relational database. Relational databases got their names because they contain tables that are *related* to one another by certain key data in the table. For example, if you kept employee records for a company, you might have two separate tables: one to keep private employee information and one to keep job-related information for each employee. The employee table would have a row for each person and columns for each unique piece of data. The job table might have multiple rows for each employee, depending on how many different jobs that person has held in the company, and of course columns to hold the specific data.

Now, if you were looking for a particular person's job description, you would go to the employee table and find the name of that person. Then by using his or her employee number, you would go to the job table, find the employee number, and look at the job description. This method of connecting data from different tables is what makes a relational database what it is.

As soon as you understand the basic idea of relational databases, you'll begin to see tables, rows, and columns everywhere. You've always seen tables; however, you probably didn't think of them as such. Everyday information that you read in the paper are actually tables of information containing rows and columns of data. Things such as the stock market report or football standings all can be placed into a database table.

Laying Out the Database Structure

You should meet several objectives when designing the tables in your database. Although it would be nice to say that you *must* meet these objectives, it's sometimes just not possible to meet all of them, as you'll see:

- Remove repetitive data
- Have the ability to find unique records quickly
- Keep the database easy to maintain
- Allow changes to the database structure easy to perform

By striving for these objectives, you'll create a database that can grow with your application. The beginning steps in designing your database actually take place in the application design itself. You must first define what tasks your application will perform. As you're defining the tasks to be performed in the functional specification, you're actually performing the first step in the database design process. These functional specifications allow you to start laying out the tables and the related data that you'll need. The remaining steps that you need to do are as follows:

1. Define the data needed for the application.
2. Organize the data into tables.
3. Set the relationships between the tables.
4. Create any table indexes that might be needed.
5. Define any data-validation requirements.
6. Define any additional queries that might be needed by the application.

After you determine the data that your application needs, you need to organize the data into groups that make it easy to retrieve the information. Within the database, the data will be stored in one or more tables.

Setting Up Tables and Columns

A *table* is really a collection of related data for a particular idea. By deciding what the main idea is for a table, you can determine whether a given piece of information belongs in that table. For example, a library wants to keep track of books and videos that it has available to loan. It might be tempted to put all the data into one table. However, when the data required for each type of record is listed, you can see that certain pieces of information aren't common for both items. In creating one table, many of the entries would be blank for the books, and there would be some blank ones for the videos as well. You also would have to add a column to distinguish between a video and a book. Creating the database this way would result in a lot of wasted space and could also result in poorer application performance. Figure 9.1 shows database table with the two types of information combined, whereas Figure 9.2 shows the same information separated into two tables.

FIGURE 9.1.

Combining information into one table can waste space.

Record Type	Name	State	Employee Number	Hours Worked
C	Barb Smith	NY		
C	Joe Minor	NJ		
E	Chris Stone	NY	012319	15
E	Mike Rogers	NY	009748	25
C	Josh Tanner	NJ		

FIGURE 9.2.

Dividing information into separate tables provides each table with only the relevant data.

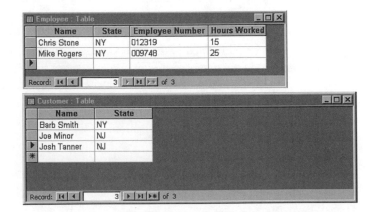

Name	State	Employee Number	Hours Worked
Chris Stone	NY	012319	15
Mike Rogers	NY	009748	25

Name	State
Barb Smith	NY
Joe Minor	NJ
Josh Tanner	NJ

As you can see, when the data is separated into two tables, the amount of wasted space is reduced to almost nothing. When deciding what data should be in which tables, the main thing to remember is that, if the information would result in wasted space for many of the rows in the table, the data doesn't belong there.

What's Normal?

Normalizing a database is the process used to reduce or eliminate any repetitive data that might be in the database. The process of normalization involves three steps. Each step reduces the amount of redundant data in the tables. Look at a table designed to keep employee information. Figure 9.3 shows the original table before the normalization process.

FIGURE 9.3.

The unnormalized Employee table.

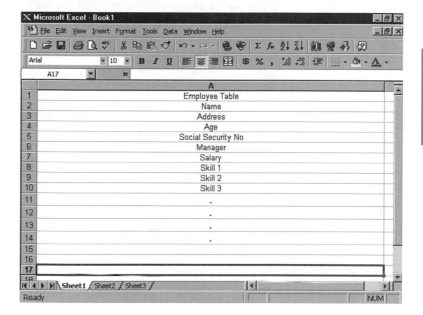

9

In this table design, what happens if the employee moves or learns a new skill? The table structure would have to be modified to allow for the new skill fields or updated for the new home address.

First Normal Form

Move the data into separate tables where the data in each table is of a similar type, and give each table a main or primary *key* (unique label or identifier). This will eliminate any repeating groups of data. After performing this process, the Employee information is now separated into two tables, as shown in Figure 9.4.

FIGURE 9.4.

*The Employee
information in
the first normal
form of design.*

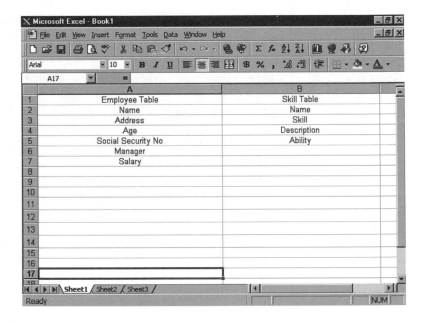

When separating the data, you can see that some information is directly related to the
employee and the other information is related to his or her skills. The Name column in
the employee table would be the key, whereas the skill table would require both the
name and the skill to define a unique row in the table. By using a name, you could get
all the skills related to that employee. If you look closely at the skills table, notice that
some information is related only to the skill, not the employee. This leads to the next
step in the process.

Second Normal Form

After you have a table with a primary key made up of more than one column, you need
to take out of that table any data that depends on only part of the key. In this example,
the skill description and the skill would be placed in a third table where the key would
be only the skill. Before this step, if only one employee knew Visual Basic and that person left the company, the employee record along with all the skills related would be
deleted from the database. When this happens, the skill and description for Visual Basic
would vanish. After applying the second normal form to the database, a skill can exist
even if no one has it. Further, your application could allow new skills to be added in
advance of anyone having them. Figure 9.5 now shows the tables in second normal form.

FIGURE 9.5.

Second normal form allows data to be kept even if it's not related to any current information.

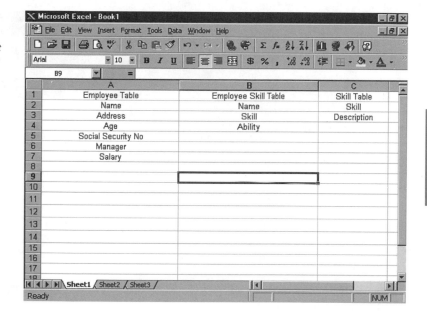

Third Normal Form

The third normal form is the final step in the process toward a well-designed database. This step gets rid of any data in the tables that doesn't solely depend on the primary key. If the employee changes jobs, you would update his or her record with the new job information. However, the job description and location isn't dependent on the employee. This is the data that would be placed into its own table. Figure 9.6 shows the final result of the normalization process.

In this form, your database can handle any changes to the information without requiring changes to the structure.

Many other tables can be added to the database. Some of these are like the skill description table in the preceding example. This type of table is called a lookup table. Lookup tables are used to store common information such as skill descriptions, or static information such as state codes and their names.

FIGURE 9.6.

Third normal form is the final step in reducing redundant data in a database.

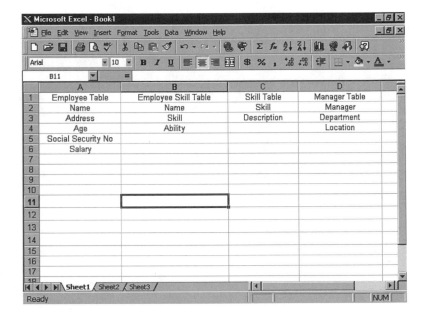

Note

Although putting your database into third normal form will completely eliminate redundant data, sometimes it's more practical to deviate from this method to improve performance. If your application tracks a salesman and you need to display a total sales amount that requires a calculation of thousands of rows of data, you might find it worthwhile to include this total column in the salesman table and update it every time a sale is made. This will affect performance a little because of the update process, but overall you'll notice better performance because the large calculations don't have to be performed. You always can make tradeoffs between application performance and database design. For every application, you must find a middle ground that you're comfortable with and that gives you the optimal performance you want.

Indexing the Information

When you put data into database tables, the individual records are usually stored in the order they were entered. This is called the *physical order* of the data. Unfortunately, you usually want to work with the data in an order different from the order in the database itself. For you to work with the data in the order you want, you need to define a *logical order* to the data. Also, you usually need to find specific records in a table quickly. Indexing the data in the tables provides you with a method of ordering the data.

An *index* is actually another database table that contains the key data for each record in the indexed table. The index itself is stored in a specific logic order maintained by the database. It also contains pointers that the database uses to find the actual record in the data table. Indexes are very similar to the index in the back of this book. To find a specific topic, you would look for it in the alphabetically listing and then, using the page number, go directly to that topic.

Because indexes are usually small tables that can be searched very quickly, they're used in all databases to provide quick access to the data and to display the data in a particular order. A table can have as many different indexes as needed; however, the more indexes a table has, the slower the database will perform when adding or deleting records from the table. This is because the database must update each index table for every change made to the actual table it references.

Another way of ordering your data is by using the ORDER BY clause of a SQL statement. This way, you can change the order of the data dynamically within your application.

Relationships

After you normalize the tables and define the required indexes, you next need to define how the tables relate to one another. This operation is usually performed on paper and added to the database diagram, as shown in Figure 9.7.

FIGURE 9.7.

Database table relationships are usually defined in the database design diagram.

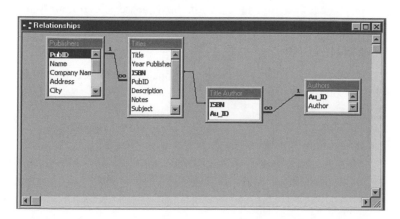

When accessing data from a database, you would have to define the relationship of the tables for every SQL statement that you would create. The relationships are actually defined in the WHERE clause of the SQL statement. The following SQL statement accesses the tables from the BIBLIO database that comes with Visual Basic:

```
SELECT Titles.ISBN, Titles.Title, Authors.[Year Born]
FROM Authors Where (Titles.ISBN = [Title Author].ISBN) and Authors.Au_ID
    = [Title Author].Au_ID;
```

As you can see, the relationship is actually defined by using the keys in the different tables that have matching information. When the database executes this SQL statement, it looks for records in the first table where the data in the key field matches the data in the second tables' key field. It returns only records where there's a match between these keys.

Queries

The problem with using databases in an application is that every time you need to access more than one table, you need to redefine the relationships and fields that you want in a SQL statement. If you're designing an application with very little database interaction, you could probably get away with doing this; a more complex application would very quickly become difficult to maintain. If you need to change what data is being retrieved, the SQL statement must be modified. Queries are a feature that you can use in most databases.

A *query* is nothing more than a SQL statement defined directly in the database. When using these defined queries, the database processes the data request faster. If you needed to access data from three tables in the BIBLIO database, you could code the following SQL statement:

```
SELECT Titles.Title, [Title Author].ISBN, Authors.Author FROM Authors
    INNER JOIN (Titles INNER JOIN [Title Author] ON Titles.ISBN
    = [Title Author].ISBN) ON Authors.Au_ID = [Title Author].Au_ID;
```

Or you could define this query in the database so that your SQL statement could be simplified:

```
Select * from ThreeTableQuery
```

Most database tools allow you to define queries in the database, allowing you to concentrate on the design of your application.

SQL: The Short Course

After you understand what goes into a database design, you need to understand the language used to access the data in the database. SQL is the language that every computer program uses to access the database. Learning to use SQL is like learning any other programming language. SQL was created and designed so that when you learn how to use it, you can access any database that supports SQL access. Just as Visual Basic conforms to standards and each command or statement has a certain syntax, so does SQL. SQL is actually divided into two types of statements:

- One used to define the database itself is called *data-definition language* (*DDL*).
- The other, used to access the database, is called *data-manipulation language* (*DML*).

This section covers a short discussion of the DML SQL language.

SQL statements allow you to perform processing in one line or a few lines of SQL code that would take you many lines of BASIC code to do. SQL statements create queries that define the fields, tables, and range of records needed in a particular process. When a query is processed, the data is usually returned in a dynaset. A *dynaset* is an updatable recordset that contains a collection of pointers to the data. SQL statements consist of the following three sections:

- **Parameter declarations** are optional parameters passed by the program code to the SQL statement.
- **Manipulative statements** tell the database engine what kind of process it will perform.
- **Options declarations** define and filter conditions, groupings, or sorts that need to be applied to the data being processed.

The syntax for a SQL statement is as follows:

```
[Parameters] Manipulative statement [Options]
```

In this section, you'll review some of the manipulative statements and a few of the options that you can use. SQL statements can perform a wide variety of tasks. These mirror the actions that users would need to perform on their data. These actions fall into one of five distinct manipulative statements:

- SELECT is used to retrieve a group of records from the database and places them into a dynaset.
- INSERT INTO adds a group of records to a table.
- UPDATE updates the values in a table.
- DELETE FROM removes the specified records from the database.
- TRANSFORM creates a new summary table by using the contents of one field as the names of the columns.

9

Although the manipulative statement tells the database engine what action to perform, the options declarations tell it what fields to process.

 Note

> You can't use SQL statements directly in a Visual Basic application. They're used with data controls or Data Access Objects.

Using the SELECT Statement

In most basic applications, the SQL statement type that you'll use most often is SELECT. The SELECT statement is used to retrieve records from the database and places them into a dynaset for access by the application code. The syntax of the SELECT statement is as follows:

```
SELECT [predicate] fieldlist FROM tablelist [table relations]
    [range options] [sort options] [group options]
```

Although you can create very complex SQL statements, as you can see from the syntax, the simplest form of the SELECT statement will retrieve all fields from a table. The following statement retrieves all fields and rows from the Contact table:

```
SELECT * FROM Contact
```

The asterisk (*) serves as a wildcard for the fieldlist section of the SELECT statement. The fieldlist defines the fields included in the output recordset. The fieldlist can include all fields in a table, only selected fields, or calculated values based on fields in the table. Also, by using the AS clause, you can rename a field to be used in the recordset.

 Caution

> Renaming fields doesn't affect the actual database field name, only the name used by the application to access that field in that particular recordset.

Because SQL allows you to retrieve data from multiple tables, you can even specify which table a field should be retrieved from. The syntax of the fieldlist section is as follows:

```
[tablename.]field1 [AS alt1][,[tablename.]field2 [AS alt2]]
```

By using this syntax, you can retrieve only the first and last name of a contact, as follows:

```
SELECT [First Name], [Last Name] from Contact
```

Note | If a field name contains blanks, you must enclose it in brackets.

Accessing Multiple Tables

Because of the normalization process, data can be placed in many different tables to reduce the amount of duplicate data. When you need to retrieve this information from the related tables, you need to create a SQL statement that will combine this information. To select data from multiple tables, you need to specify three things:

9

- The table to retrieve the field from
- The fields that need to be retrieved
- The relationship between the tables

When specifying the fields to be retrieved in the fieldlist, you need to place the table name and a period in front of the field name (for example, Contact.[First Name]). If you need to retrieve some fields from one table and all fields from another, you can still use the wildcard character (for example, Contact.[First Name], Sales.*). The next step is to specify the tables you're using in the FROM clause of the SELECT statement. Finally, the relationship between the tables is specified by using a WHERE clause of a JOIN condition. The WHERE clause is used more often than the JOIN condition when creating SQL statements. The final SQL statement would look like the following:

```
SELECT Contact.[First Name], Contact.[Last Name], Sales.* FROM Contact,
    Sales WHERE Contact.ID = Sales.ID
```

This statement retrieves the first and last name from the Contact table and all the related sales information from the Sales table.

Note | You can omit table names from the fieldlist as long as the field name is unique in the tables listed.

Creating Calculated Values

In the preceding SQL example, the sales-related information for each contact is retrieved. Suppose that you also need to work with the average sale made for that contact. You can calculate this value by dividing the two values in your program code, or you can use a calculated field in the SELECT statement. A calculated field can be the result of an arithmetic operation or the result of a string operation. In addition to the standard arithmetic and string operations, each database supports many operations and functions unique to that database. For example, Microsoft Access allows you to use the same set of functions as Visual Basic, such as MID$ or UCASE$. The following SQL statement shows how to get the average sale made for the contact as part of the query:

```
SELECT Contact.[First Name], Contact.[Last Name], Sales.*,
     Sales.[Sale Total] / Sales.[Sale Units] as [Avg Sale]
     FROM Contact, Sales WHERE Contact.ID = Sales.ID
```

Although this SQL statement will create a recordset that you can update, any calculated field in the recordset is read-only.

Changing the Tables Names

Of the names of the tables you're using, the SQL statement could get very long when supplying the table names in the fieldlist. To prevent this from happening and to simplify the SQL code, you can assign a short name to any table in the statement, much the same was that you can rename a field in the fieldlist. By using aliases in the FROM clause, you can assign a name to each table that makes sense to you. For example, the preceding SQL statement could be rewritten as follows:

```
SELECT CT.[First Name], CT.[Last Name], SA.*,
     SA.[Sale Total] / SA.[Sale Units] as [Avg Sale]
     FROM Contact as CT, Sales as SA WHERE CT.ID = SA.ID
```

As you can see, this approach makes the SQL statement a little easier to read.

Filtering the Data

One of the more powerful features of SQL is its capability to control the range of records to be processed by specifying a filter condition. You can use many types of filters, such as [Last name] = "Jones", Units > 1, or [Order Date] between #5/1/94# and #5/31/94#.

Note

> Although the SELECT statement is being reviewed, the basics of filtering can be used in other SQL statements, such as DELETE and UPDATE.

Filter conditions in a SQL command are specified in the WHERE clause. The syntax of the WHERE clause is as follows:

```
WHERE logical-expression
```

Four types of logical statements define the condition that you can use with the WHERE clause:

- A comparison is used to compare a field to another field or a given value (for example, [Sales Quantity] > 10).
- LIKE compares a field to a specified pattern (for example, SM*).
- IN is used to compare a field to a list of acceptable values (for example, State IN ("NY", "NJ", "CT")).
- BETWEEN is used to compare a field to a value range (for example, [Order Date] BETWEEN #01/01/96# and #02/28/96#).

Each predicate has many different options and wildcard values that you can use. Because some of them vary depending on the database, I suggest that you review these options for the database that you're working with.

The WHERE clause lets you specify multiple conditions to filter on more than one field at a time. Each individual condition follows the syntax discussed earlier but are combined by using the logical operators AND and OR. By using multiple-condition statements, you can find all the contacts in New York and New Jersey, or you can find anyone whose first or last name begins with Rich:

```
SELECT * FROM Contact WHERE State IN ('NY', 'NJ') or
    ([Last Name] LIKE 'RICH*' OR [First Name] = LIKE 'RICH*')
```

In addition to specifying the records to be retrieved, you can also use the SELECT statement to specify the order that you want the records to appear in the dynaset. To sort the records, you would use the ORDER BY clause of the SELECT statement. You can specify the sort order with a single field or with multiple fields. If you use multiple fields, the individual fields must be separated by commas. When specifying a sort, the default direction is ascending; to change the sort order for a given field, you use the DESC keyword after the field name. To sort contact information alphabetically by state and then by last name in a descending order, use the following SQL statement:

```
SELECT * FROM Contact WHERE State IN ('NY', 'NJ') ORDER BY State,
    [Last Name] DESC
```

Working with SQL can be very frustrating at times, but it also makes your life as a programmer easier because of the functions it performs for you. Without SQL and relational databases, every data-access function would need to be coded within your application. This review was only for the SELECT statement and a few of the many possible actions that you can perform with SQL. In the next few lessons, you'll see how to use SQL while designing the data forms and data-access processes in your application.

Creating a Database with the Visual Data Manager

After you design the database, the next step is to actually create it. When using Visual Basic, you can use two different methods to create a database: by using the Data Access Objects within a program and by using the Visual Data Manager included with Visual Basic.

You can use Visual Basic's Data Access Objects (DAO) in your application to access the data in an existing database or in a program written to create a database for use by your application. Writing programs that create databases can be an entire development effort all by itself. Unless you need to build the database when the application is executed the first time, it's usually better to create the empty database structure and include it with your application files.

 Note

> Most databases will not allow you to create new tables or columns using the Visual Basic access methods, you must use the utilities that are included with that database or you must code the SQL DDL scripts that will add the necessary objects.

The Visual Data Manager provides you with an interactive tool to create and modify databases on your computer. You can use this tool to create the database structure that you've designed for your application. However, depending on the database that you've chosen to work with, the Visual Data Manager might not be the right tool for the job.

Other databases that the Visual Data Manager can work with are as follows, although many databases come with their own tools:

- dBASE
- FoxPro
- Paradox
- Remote ODBC databases

Also, the Visual Data Manager source project is included in the Visual Basic samples directory. By examining this project, you can learn quite a bit about creating a database application.

Note

For the sake of this lesson, the database that you'll work with is the Access Jet database.

Starting the Visual Data Manager

The Visual Data Manager is automatically installed and added to Visual Basic's Add-Ins menu. The Visual Data Manager can be accessed while you're in Visual Basic, or you can run it as a standalone application. To run it without starting Visual Basic, double-click it in the /PROGRAM FILES/ directory in Windows Explorer or create a shortcut to the executable file. To see how this application works, start the Visual Data Manager. Figure 9.8 shows the initial form displayed when the application starts.

9

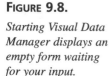

FIGURE 9.8.

Starting Visual Data Manager displays an empty form waiting for your input.

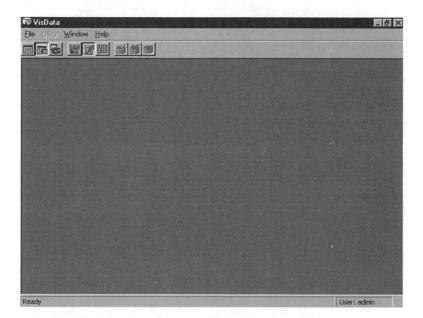

Creating the Database

When creating a new database, you first create the database file or tablespace that will contain the tables and other related information you'll add to the database. To do this with Visual Data Manager, choose File, New, Microsoft Access (see Figure 9.9). This will display another submenu that allows you to choose from the 16-bit Access 2.0 format or the newer 32-bit Access 7.0 format for the database. Because Visual Basic 5.0 is a 32-bit-only product, choose the second option to create the Access 7.0 database file.

FIGURE 9.9.

*The File, New menu
choice allow you to
choose the type of
database to create.*

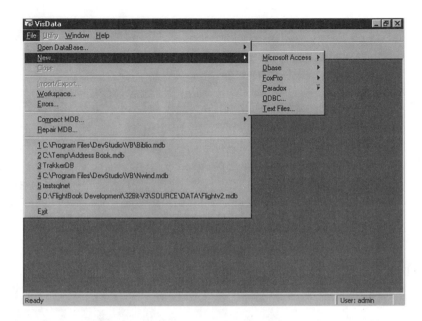

After selecting the database type, you're prompted to enter a name for the new database
file on the common dialog box displayed. After you enter a name, click the Save button
to complete the process. The Visual Data Manager displays the database information to
you in a tree view format. Initially, you can view the properties of the database file that
you just created, as shown in Figure 9.10.

FIGURE 9.10.

*Viewing the database
file properties in the
tree display.*

The Database Window will also display the tables, queries, and indexes that you'll add to the database, drilling into the views all the way to the individual fields.

Adding Tables and Columns

After you create the database file, the next step is to create the tables that you need in the database. To create a new table, right-click anywhere in the Database Window and select New Table from the pop-up menu. The Table Structure dialog box appears, showing the information about the table itself, as well as any fields and indexes already in the table (see Figure 9.11).

FIGURE 9.11.

Working with a table in the Visual Data Manager.

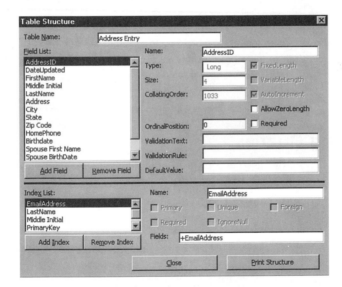

To add a field to the new table, click the Add Field button to display the Add Field dialog box (see Figure 9.12).

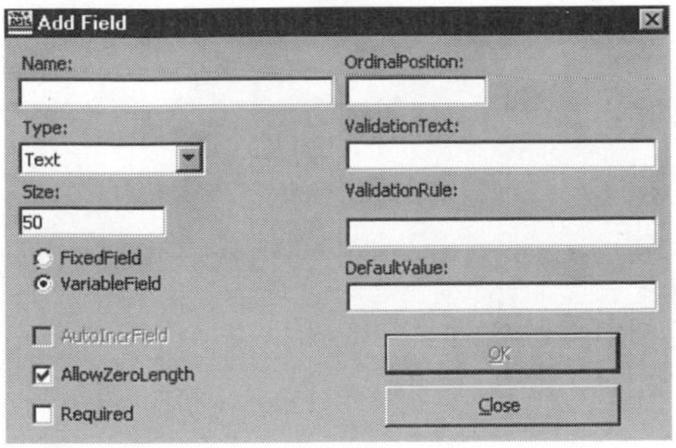

FIGURE 9.12.

Using the Add Field dialog box to add fields to the table.

In the Add Field dialog box, you need to specify the following information to actually add the field to the table:

- A name for the field
- The data type in the Type drop-down list
- The physical size of the field (if required)
- Any optional settings, such as validation rules

After you enter all the necessary information, click OK to add the field to the table. Repeat this process until you've added all the fields that you need in the table.

 Caution

Make sure that you enter the information for each field correctly. Even though you can modify some of the properties for the fields, many can't be changed. You would need to delete and re-add the field to change these settings.

Adding Queries

Another feature of the Visual Data Manager is its capability to create and store queries directly in the database. To add a query to the database, start by right-clicking in the Database Window and selecting New Query from the pop-up menu to display the Query Builder dialog box (see Figure 9.13).

FIGURE 9.13.

The Query Builder allows you to select fields from any table in the database and set the table relationships and filters.

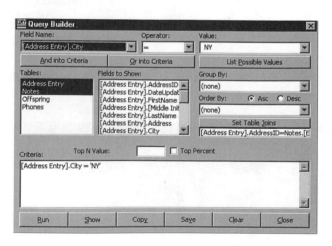

In this dialog box, you can select the required fields from each table in the database, and then define the filters needed for the query. When defining the filters for the query, you must click the And into Criteria button or the Or into Criteria button to actually add the filter to the query. Also, the Set Table Joins button displays a dialog box that allows you to define the table relationships for this query (see Figure 9.14).

FIGURE 9.14.

The Join Tables dialog box sets the table relationships for the query.

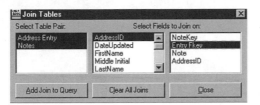

After you define the query and set the table relationships and filters, you can perform one of the following actions:

- Display the resulting query recordset (see Figure 9.15)
- Display the SQL statement generated for the query
- Copy the SQL statement to the SQL statement window
- Save the query to the database (see Figure 9.16)

FIGURE 9.15.

While designing the query, you can execute the resulting SQL to see whether the results are what you want.

Title Author.ISBN	Au_ID	Title	Year Published	Titles.ISBN
0-0038307-6-4	7576	dBASE III : A Practic	1985	0-0038307-6-4
0-0038326-7-8	7576	The dBASE Programr	1986	0-0038326-7-8
0-0038337-8-X	7661	dBASE III Plus	1987	0-0038337-8-X
0-0131985-2-1	5681	Database Manageme	1989	0-0131985-2-1
0-0131985-2-1	5684	Database Manageme	1989	0-0131985-2-1
0-0133656-1-4	1454	Wordstar 4.0-6.0 Qu	1990	0-0133656-1-4
0-0134436-3-1	128	Oracle Triggers and :	1996	0-0134436-3-1
0-0134436-3-1	132	Oracle Triggers and :	1996	0-0134436-3-1
0-0230081-2-1	203	Structured C for Eng	1995	0-0230081-2-1
0-0230081-2-1	659	Structured C for Eng	1995	0-0230081-2-1
0-0230081-2-1	1304	Structured C for Eng	1995	0-0230081-2-1
0-0230081-2-1	1306	Structured C for Eng	1995	0-0230081-2-1
0-0230362-0-6	203	An Introduction to A	1995	0-0230362-0-6
0-0230362-0-6	1273	An Introduction to A	1995	0-0230362-0-6
0-0230650-8-7	973	Applied Calculus With	1995	0-0230650-8-7

Right Click for Data Control Properties

FIGURE 9.16.

Saving the query to the database will display the query in the Database Window.

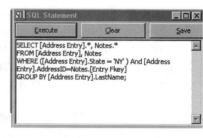

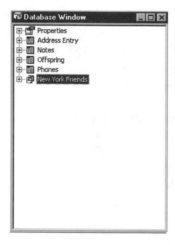

Finally, to view any of the tables or queries, all you need to do is double-click the selected item to display the data in one of three formats, as shown in Figures 9.17, 9.18, and 9.19.

FIGURE 9.17.

The default view used to display the data is a standard data grid.

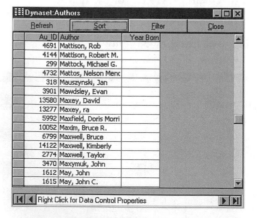

FIGURE 9.18.

By clicking the Use Data Control button on the toolbar, each record is displayed individually by using a data control.

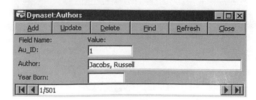

FIGURE 9.19.

You can also display the data individually by using Visual Basic's DAO features.

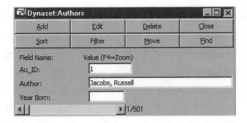

Adding an Index to a Table

The Table Structure dialog box also allows you to add, modify, or delete indexes for a table. Any indexes now in the table are displayed in the Index List at the bottom of the form (refer to Figure 9.11). To add a new index, click the Add Index button to display the Add Index dialog box (see Figure 9.20).

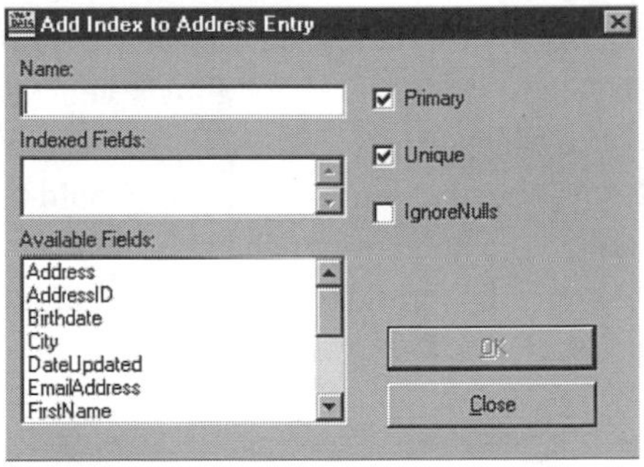

FIGURE 9.20.

The Add Index dialog box allows the creation of table indexes.

To actually add the index, you need to enter an index name, and then select the fields you want included in the index by selecting them from the Available Fields list. As you select each field, they will be added to the Indexed Fields list in the order that you selected them. After defining the fields for the index, you can specify whether you want this index to be unique or to be the primary index for the table. After you properly define the index, click OK to save it.

> **Caution**
>
> You can't edit an index after it's created. To change an index requires you to delete it and re-create it.

Using Visual Data Manager with Visual Basic

What makes the Visual Data Manager so useful is that you can access it directly from the Visual Basic development environment. While you're in the process of designing your application and coding the database access, you might have the need to test a SQL statement that you're entering or verify that the data you're testing for is actually in the database. With the Visual Data Manager, you can easily open the database you're using and execute quick SQL statements or view an entire table's worth of information. Also, if you discover that you need a new query defined in the database for you to use in the application, you can add the query without having to exit Visual Basic.

Other Database Tools

Although Visual Data Manager is a good tool to use to create and maintain databases used in your applications, you can use other available database tools. For example, when working with an Access database, everything that you've just done can also be accomplished by using Microsoft Access. In fact, Access allows you edit table, query, and field properties that the Visual Data Manager protects. Also, you can use Access to edit any indexes in the database. If you already own Access, you should use it to create the database and do any of the required maintenance or changes. When creating a new table, adding new fields is usually done in a grid-style dialog box, allowing you to position the fields as needed (see Figure 9.21).

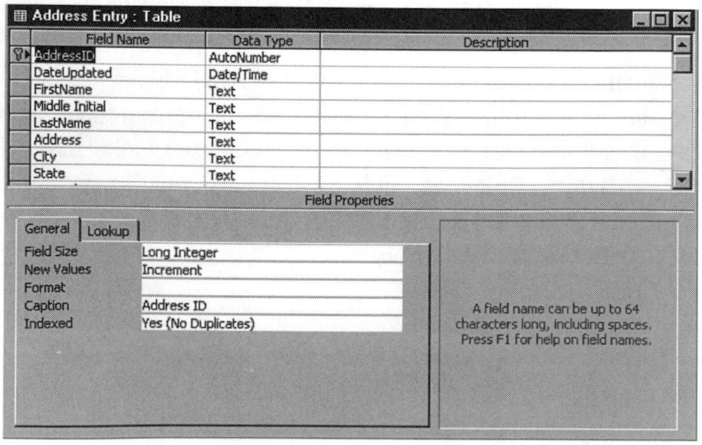

FIGURE 9.21.

Creating or modifying tables in Access is easier than using the Visual Data Manager.

But Access's power can really be seen when you add a new query to the database. Each table that you're using in the query is shown and their respective relationships are visible. You then choose the fields needed and drag them into the grid at the bottom of the form (see Figure 9.22).

FIGURE 9.22.

In Access, query creation and modification becomes a visual process.

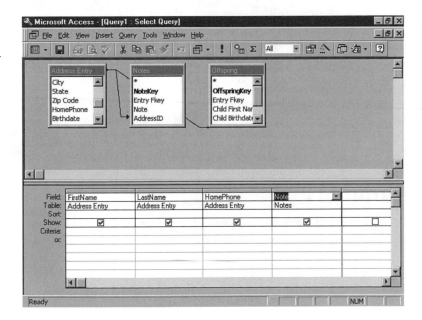

When you're working with the application project in Visual Basic, however, it's far easier to use the Visual Data Manager to test SQL and view data than it is to start Access.

Other databases also come with their own respective tools that you can use to create and modify the database tables and fields. Figure 9.23 shows the Oracle Navigator dialog box that gives access to the tables, views (queries), and other database-related information.

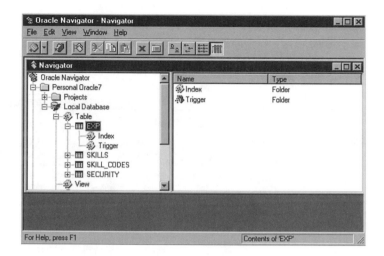

FIGURE 9.23.

Oracle provides a Windows-based tool that allows you to visually create and maintain a database.

Summary

In today's lesson, you've looked at the requirements and rules that should be followed when designing a database. The database normalization process was discussed in regards to reducing the duplicate data usually found in some databases. Also, you received a short review in what SQL is and how to code the SELECT statement. Finally, you've seen how to use the Visual Data Manager to create and maintain the database you need for your application. In the next lesson, you'll see how to design a specific database application and the database it uses.

Q&A

Q What's the difference between a local and a remote database?

A A *local database* is accessible directly from Visual Basic through the Jet database engine. A *remote database* is any other database type that uses the ODBC connections for the application to access them.

Q How many tables can there be in a database?

A Depending on the amount of storage on the computer, a database can contain as many tables as are needed for the application. For example, Access allows up to 32,768 total objects in a database.

Q What does *normalization* mean?

A Normalizing a database is the process that you use to reduce the amount of duplicate data from the tables in the database.

Q Why should indexes be used in a database?

A Indexes speed up the data-access process by creating sorted tables that the database engine uses to find the required data.

Q What is SQL?

A *SQL* stands for *Structured Query Language* and is used to access the data within a database.

Q Does Visual Basic come with a tool that can create and maintain a database?

A Visual Basic comes with the Visual Data Manager, a tool that allows you to create and maintain many different types of database.

9

Workshop

The Workshop provides quiz questions to help solidify your understanding of the material covered, as well as exercises to provide you with experience in using what you've learned. Try to understand the quiz and exercise answers before continuing on to the next day's lesson. Answers are provided in Appendix A, "Answers to Exercises."

Quiz

1. What are the four main objectives when designing a database?

2. How many different main SQL commands are there?

3. What's the difference between using the Visual Data Manager and Access to create a Jet database?

Exercise

List the tables and columns that you would want to include in a database designed for an address book application.

WEEK 2

DAY **10**

Accessing the Database

In the last few days, you've seen what a database is, how to create one, and how to use the SQL language to access the data contained in it. Also, the process of creating a database application was covered, and you used the Application Wizard to create two data forms with different access methods. Today, you'll see the different methods you can use to access the database and how you can combine them to perform complex application functions.

Visual Basic and Data Access

Visual Basic was designed to allow you to create database applications for the Windows environment quickly and easily. If you have an existing database that you want to access, Visual Basic makes it easy for you to write a complete data management application with almost no programming. You just need to drop a few controls on a form and set the properties. In fact, Visual Basic makes it so easy that it even creates the data forms for you. The components that make all these capabilities possible are the data controls to access the database and the data-bound controls to display the data. With these controls, you can create a wide variety of complex applications.

Of course, as your applications become more complex, you'll need to add code to the application. Before building complex applications, however, you should have a good understanding of the tools available for you to use.

Data Access Objects

When database access was originally added to the Visual Basic product, it came in the form of the Data Control and Access Objects. This allowed the programmer to access any type of database needed by the application. However, it worked best with Access-Jet engine databases that existed on the local PC. As the use of PCs grew in the workplace, larger, more company-wide applications were required to use databases such as Microsoft SQL Server and Oracle.

Accessing these larger, enterprisewide databases required a more robust control. Visual Basic 5 not only included the original Data Access Objects but also had a new Remote Data Control and Objects, which were specially designed to access Remote databases using an ODBC connection. However, having two separate types of access also created design issues and generated questions on which type should be used when. Once again, with the release of Visual Basic 6, Microsoft has answered this problem by adding a third data access method to the product that combines the best parts of both of its predecessors. ActiveX Data Objects and its related control provide database access to both local and remote databases without the need to choose the appropriate data access control or object. Instead of discussing the Data Access or Remote Data Controls, the remaining sections will discuss how to use the new ActiveX Data Control and ActiveX Data Objects in a Visual Basic application.

 Note   It is up to you to decide whether to use the older Data Access Control and Objects or the newer ActiveX Data Control and Objects. The size and scope of the application will usually help you to decide which to use.

The ActiveX Data Control

The Data control is the main support to a very sophisticated access method that you can easily use to access data in your application database. By setting only a few parameters of the Data control, you can attach to the database and access data from a SQL query without having to write any code at all. The ActiveX Data Control can access any database type required, either directly, for Jet supported databases', or remotely using an OLE DB supported access method. In addition to this flexibility, program code can be used to change the properties of the Data control and enhance its capabilities. In fact, set-ting up and using the Data control requires only three easy steps:

1. Place the Data control on the form.
2. Build the database connection string for the database you want to access.
3. Set the RecordSource property to the SQL query you want to access in the database.

Using the ActiveX Data Control

Because this is probably the first time you have heard about the ActiveX Data control, lets see how to use it to access the Biblio.MDB database that is included with Visual Basic. Start a new project and add the ADODC to the Toolbox using the Components dialog. Now, add the controls in Table 10.1 to the form as shown in Figure 10.1.

TABLE 10.1. ACTIVEX DATA CONTROL DEMO FORM SETUP.

Object	Property	Value
ADODC	Name	adcBooks
Textbox	Name	txtTitle
	Datasource	adcBooks
	DataField	Title
Command Button	Name	cmdQuit
	Caption	Quit
Command Button	Name	cmdNext
	Caption	Next
Command Button	Name	cmdPrev
	Caption	Previous

FIGURE 10.1.

The ActiveX Data Control Demo showing the controls to add to the Form.

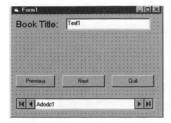

The next step in the process is to display the properties dialog (see Figure 10.2) for the ADODC by right-clicking on it and selecting properties from the displayed pop-up menu.

FIGURE 10.2.

Setting the Connection properties for the ActiveX Data Control.

For the Biblio database, you only need to specify the connection information and the RecordSource. To specify the connection, click the Build button on the General tab. This will display the connection dialogs which will help you to define the connection properly. The first dialog (see Figure 10.3) lists the available OLE DB data providers that are available on your computer.

FIGURE 10.3.

Selecting the OLE DB provider for the database used in the application.

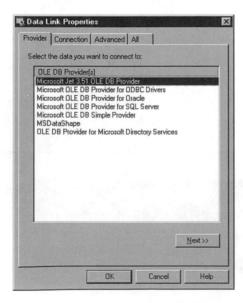

Choose the Microsoft Jet 3.51 OLE DB Provider and click Next to display the dialog to specify the database files location as shown in Figure 10.4. Enter the full path and name for Biblio.mdb.

FIGURE 10.4.

Specifying the location of the required database.

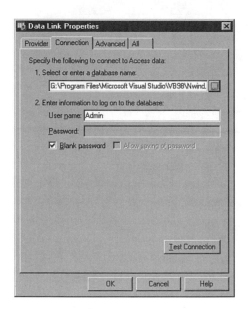

Note

There is no explorer feature for this dialog. You are required to type in the database location yourself.

Once you have entered the database name, click Next to enter a user ID and password if the database requires it. Otherwise, click Next again to continue to the last dialog (see Figure 10.5), which gives you the ability to test the connection you just created.

FIGURE 10.5.

*Finishing the
Connection definition
process by testing the
connection.*

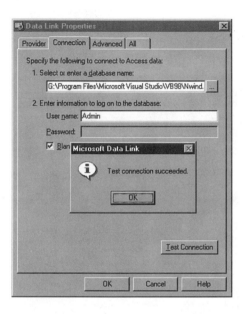

If the test passed, click Finish to return to the ADODC properties dialog. You should
now see the connection information in the dialog. The next and last step is to specify the
SQL statement that will be used by the connection as the record source. Click the
RecordSource tab, enter the SQL statement shown in Figure 10.6, and then click OK to
save the changes.

FIGURE 10.6.

*Adding the SQL query
to the ADO connection
information.*

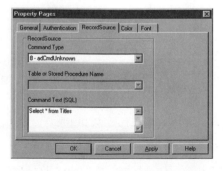

Once the connection is defined, you can set the `DataSource` and `DataField` properties
for the Textbox, as shown in Table 10.1. The last step is to add the following code to the
command buttons allowing you to navigate the SQL statement:

```
Private Sub cmdNext_Click()
adcBooks.Recordset.MoveNext
End Sub
```

```
Private Sub cmdPrev_Click()
adcBooks.Recordset.MovePrevious
End Sub

Private Sub cmdQuit_Click()
End
End Sub
```

Now, run the application and try moving around the rows. You can see that the operation of the ADODC is almost identical to the original Data control.

The ADODC also provides the record-navigation functions that users and the application need to access the data. With these buttons (refer to Figure 10.1), users can move to the first or last record in the recordset, or to the next or previous record in the recordset. The button design is similar to the buttons you would find on a VCR or CD player, making the buttons very easy to understand.

The Data control also has a `Caption` property that you can use to display any important information, such as the last name of the address record you're browsing. You can't set the `Caption` property automatically; you do it by adding the following line of code to the ADODC's `MoveComplete` routine:

```
dtaMyAddress.Caption = dtaMyAddress.Recordset.Fields("Title")
```

This is actually using the capabilities of the ActiveX Data Objects, which allow you to access the database from within your application code. As you can see, the Data control has a lot of capabilities for you to use.

 Note

> To access the ActiveX Data Objects, add the reference in the Object Browser from the Visual Basic menu.

When you invoke the Data control's `Delete` method, the current record is deleted from the database but is still held in the Data control's buffer until a `Move` method is executed. If you don't explicitly move to another record, an error will occur.

Although Data controls are covered in every book written about Visual Basic, they're always shown as a single control on a form. To make use of the capabilities to quickly add database access, many complex applications that need access to different tables and queries will use multiple Data controls on the same form. Also, in many cases, the Data control itself isn't visible on the form when the application is executing. This means that even the four functions that it supplies must be added to the form by means of additional code.

Knowing the Current Record

A recordset has a pointer that keeps track of the current record. There's only one current record for a Data control at any time. A recordset also has special positions known as beginning of file (BOF), before the first record, and end of file (EOF), after the last record. Because there's no current record when the record pointer is positioned at either of these, problems can occur.

By default, the Data control prevents these problems by setting the record pointer to the first record when the beginning of the file is reached or by setting the pointer to the last record when the end of the file is reached. This way, there's always a current record for viewing or editing. However, sometimes you need to know when you've actually reached the BOF or EOF position while using the Data control. You can control what the Data control does by setting the control's BOFAction and EOFAction properties.

The BOFAction property tells the Data control what action to take when the beginning of the file is reached. This property has two settings:

- 0 - adDoMoveFirst, the default setting, executes the MoveFirst method to set the record pointer at the first record and the BOF flag to False.
- 1 - adStayBOF sets the BOF flag to True.

The EOFAction property tells the Data control what action to take when the end of the file is reached. This property has three possible values:

- 0 - adDoMoveLast, the default setting, executes the MoveLast method to set the record pointer to the last record and the EOF flag to False.
- 1 - adStayEOF sets the EOF flag to True.
- 2 - adAddNew executes the AddNew method to prepare for the addition of a new record.

Note

The BOF and EOF actions are triggered only when users reach the beginning or end of the file by using the Data control's navigation buttons. They have no effect if you're using data-access methods (such as MoveNext) in your code.

Binding the Database

When you have the Data control on a form, you need to add one or more bound controls to connect to the Data control in order to easily access the data. Many of the controls that come with Visual Basic are set up to work with the Data control. These "bound" controls are used to create database applications. Each bound control is connected to a Data control and to a single field in the recordset specified by the Data control. The bound control automatically displays the data in the specified field for the current record. As you use the navigation buttons to move from one record to another, the data in the bound controls are updated to reflect the current record.

However, the bound controls aren't limited to displaying the data in the record—they can also be used to modify the data. This is done by editing the contents of the control; then, when the current record is changed or the form is closed, the data in the database is automatically updated to reflect the changes.

 Note   Only controls with an editable area can be used to update data.

10

Programmed Access with the Data Control

To manipulate the data accessed by a Data control, you would add code to the events for the Data control and possibly for the bound controls. Some ways that you can use code with the Data control are as follows:

- Changing the properties of the Data control or the bound controls during program execution
- Providing capabilities that the Data control doesn't have by using the recordset methods

Like any other control, you can change the properties of the Data control and bound controls at runtime. You can choose to change the Connection or RecordSource properties of the Data control to set specific conditions on the data that users want to see. This can take the form of filters or sort orders, or your application might have the filters set as part of an access control scheme.

If you need to set the properties at runtime, simply set the properties with code:

```
DtaMyDatabase.RecordSource = "Select * from Titles"
DtaMyDatabase.ReQuery
```

After setting the properties, use the Data control's Requery method to apply the changes, as shown in the last line of the code. The changes to the Data control take effect only after the Requery method is invoked.

Note When a form is loaded, any Data controls on the form will be initialized with the settings assigned at design time. To modify them before the Data control is initialized, you should place the code that modifies the control in the form's Initialize event routine.

You can also set the properties of the bound controls at runtime. The DataSource of the bound control can be changed to access a different Data control on the form. You can also change the setting of the DataField property to have the control display the contents of a different field in the recordset.

You can use several key events to manipulate the way the Data control performs:

- WillChangeRecord, WillChangeRecordset, and WillChangeFieldprocess any data before the record is updated.
- Error is triggered for any data-access error.
- MoveComplete is used to perform calculations based on data in the current record or to change the form in response to data in the current record.

Although most of the Data control's actions are handled automatically, these events can help you add enhanced capabilities to your application.

Validating the Data

When you need to add validation processing to your application, you would use the WillChangeField event, which is triggered just before a value of one or more Field objects in the Recordset is changed. However, if a method such as Update, Delete, or AddNew is executed, you would use the WillChangeRecord event to perform the validation for the entire record. This event occurs when users process a navigation button on the Data control or when the form containing the Data control is unloaded.

The WillChangeField event is triggered whenever a field in the current record is changed and an Update or Move method is executed. The parameters used by the WillChangeField event are

- cFields—Contains the number of field objects that are currently in the Fields Collection
- Fields—The collection that contains the Field objects with the pending changes
- adStatus—Contains the status of the change event

The values for the adStatus parameter let you specify whether to allow or prevent the change of the field's data. When you are using a method that affects the entire record, the

WillChangeRecord event is triggered. Besides the adStatus parameter, this event contains the parameter adReason that tells you which method invoked this event. By checking the adReason parameter, you can perform different processes depending on the type of action taken against the Data control. Table 10.2 lists the values of the adReason parameter.

TABLE 10.2. THE adReason PARAMETER VALUES FOR THE WillChangeRecord EVENT.

Constant	Value	Description
adRsnAddNew	1	AddNew
adRsnDelete	2	Delete
adRsnUpdate	3	Update
adRsnUndoUpdate	4	Undo the Update
adRsnUndoAddNew	5	Undo the AddNew
adRsnUndoDelete	6	Undo the Delete
adRsnRequery	7	Requery the database
adRsnReSync	8	Resync the query with the database
adRsnClose	9	The Close method of the Data control was used
adRsnMove	10	Move
adRsnFirstChange	11	FirstChange
adRsnMoveFirst	12	MoveFirst
adRsnMoveNext	13	MoveNext
adRsnMovePrevious	13	MovePrevious
adRsnMoveLast	15	MoveLast

The code you place in these events can be as complex as you need. An example WillChangeField routine is as follows:

```
Private Sub log_db_Validate(cFields As ??, Fields As ??, asStatus As ??,
pRecordset As ??)
    If Not IsDate(txtDate.Text) Then
            MsgBox "The Flight date you entered is Invalid" & _
                    vbCRLF & "Please Re-enter!", vbCritical, App.Title
            Action = vbDataActionCancel
            txtDate.DataChanged = False
            txtDate.Text = "??/??/??"
        End If
    End If
End Sub
```

If any of the field changes are incorrect, you would set the adStatus parameter to adStatusCancel. This would cancel the entire operation.

The Error Event

The Data control's Error event is triggered only when an error occurs during an automated process, such as the following:

- The Data control is loaded.
- A navigation button is clicked.
- The database specified in the DatabaseName property can't be found.

When the event is triggered, several parameters are returned to help you resolve the underlying cause of the problem. These parameters are

- Error Number—The native error number
- Description—Text description of the above error number
- Scode—The error code that is returned by the database server
- Source—The source of the error

If the CancelDisplay parameter is set to False, an attempt is made to continue with the next line of code. If the parameter is set to True (the default), an error message appears. When you write the code for the Error event, you can set the CancelDisplay parameter to False for those errors that can be corrected in your code, or to True for all the other errors that might occur.

The MoveComplete Event

This event is triggered after the current record pointer is moved to another record. You can use this event to control the movement of related Data controls on a form. For example, if you're creating an order-entry display and select a new customer, you might want to change the recordset of the orders Data control by changing the RecordSource property and then invoking the Requery method for the second Data control.

Data Control Methods

In addition to responding to events, the Data control also has several methods that you can use in your application code. Many of these methods are the same as the ones used with the ActiveX Data Objects, but you can use two unique ones: Requery and UpdateControls.

The Requery method tells the Data control to requery the database by using the query in the RecordSource property. You would need to use the Requery method for several reasons:

- When the Data control's RecordSource property is changed

- When the Data control is assigned to a recordset created with the ActiveX Data Objects
- To retrieve any additions, modifications, or deletions that might have been made to the data

The Update method forces the data in the bound controls to be saved to the recordset. Typically, you would have a Save or Update button on the form to execute this method, so users can save their work on the current record without having to move to another record.

The UpdateControls method redisplays the data from the current record in the bound controls. This method cancels any changes that users might have made but haven't saved yet.

ActiveX Data Objects

Now that you've seen how to access database information with Visual Basic's new ActiveX Data Control and bound controls, you can see how to use the ActiveX Data Objects to program complex database functions into your application. Visual Basic's ActiveX Data Objects (ADO) can be used to create complete database applications. ActiveX Data Objects act as an application's internal representation of the physical data stored in some type of database or data management system. The Data Objects can be thought of as special types of program variables. These "variables" represent data stored outside the application, rather than data stored in the computer's memory while the application is running.

ADO and programming code also provide the structure for many actions used by the Data control and the bound controls to access the database. To see the similarities and differences between ADO and the ADODC, you'll create the same data form as the one you created by using the Data control.

The main reason for using ActiveX Data Objects is the flexibility they give you over and above what's available with the Data control. You can perform more complex input validation than is possible with just the data engine because the commands don't directly access the database. You can also cancel changes to your edited data without using transactions. Using ADO commands also provides an efficient way to handle data input and searches that don't require user interaction. An example is looking up the price of an item in a table for the ordering process. ADO commands also allow you to do transaction processing when vneeded.

10

Opening a Database

The first step in writing most database applications is to connect or open the database you'll be working with. Opening a database is a lot like opening a file, except that you're using the ADO commands instead of the simple Basic Open statement. When you open a database, you're actually creating a Database object that will be used by the other Data Access Objects. To access the ADO command set, you must include in your project a reference for Microsoft ActiveX Data Object Library, which contains all the ADO command objects.

The database is represented in the application by the ADO Connection object. A working database session is defined by creating RecordSet objects within the Connection object. You can then open a query with the RecordSet object's Open method. To use the Open method, create a recordset object and call the method, as follows:

```
Dim cnn1 As ADODB.Connection
Dim rstEmployees As ADODB.Recordset
Dim strCnn As String
Dim varDate As Variant
' Open connection.
strCnn = "driver={SQL Server} ;server=srv;" & _
        "uid=sa;pwd=;database=pubs"
Set cnn1 = New ADODB.Connection
cnn1.Open strCnn
```

After you open the connection, only a link from your application to the database has been created. You still can't access the data in the database. To access the data, you need to create and open a Recordset object that links to the data stored in the database. When creating a Recordset object in your application, you can access an entire table, specific fields and records from a table, or a specify combination of records and fields from several tables. You can open two different types of recordsets in your application by setting the Recordsets Options parameter to one of the following values listed in Table 10.3.

TABLE 10.3. THE RECORDSET OPTIONS SETTINGS.

Option	Description
adCmdText	Indicates that a SQL statement is in the Source parameter
adCmdTable	Specifies that the ADO should create a SQL query to return the table referenced in the Source parameter

Each type has its own advantages and disadvantages when using them. Take a closer look at each to see how they work.

Using Tables

A table-type recordset is a direct link to a table in the database. Because all the data in a database is stored in tables, this recordset type is the most direct way to access the data. Because tables also are the only recordset type that supports indexes, searching a table for a specific record can be much quicker than searching a dynaset or snapshot.

When using tables, data is retrieved or modified one table at a time, one record at a time. This provides very fine control over data manipulation, but it doesn't allow you to access multiple tables at the same time. Unfortunately, you cannot set filters on a table to limit the number of records being returned.

To open a table for use, you need to define a Recordset object and then use the Open method to access the table. You also need to set the recordset type to specify that you want a table-type recordset. The adCmdTable constant in the method's parameters opens a table recordset. The following listing shows how to open a table using an already opened connection named adDbCon1.

```
Dim MyTble As Recordset
myTble.Open "Titles", adDbCon1,,,adCmdTable
```

Using SQL Queries

A *query* is a grouping of data from one or more tables in a database. This data is selected with a SQL statement that usually contains field names filters. Queries address the records present in the base tables at the time the query was created. They allow users to make changes in the data and store it back into the database. However, queries don't automatically reflect additions or deletions of records made by other code, users, or applications after the query was created.

Using queries allows you to do the following:

- Join data from multiple tables
- Limit the number of fields or records retrieved from the database
- Use filters and sort-order properties to change the data view

Queries also have a limitation that you should be aware of:

- The query won't automatically reflect any changes made to the data in the base tables. You have to "requery" it.

Opening a query is very similar to opening a table. The only real difference is the parameter that specifies the type of recordset to open. The adCmdText parameter creates a query when used in the Open method. However, the most important part of the Open method when dealing with queries is the SQL statement that defines the records to be included, the filter and sort conditions, and any join conditions to access the data from multiple tables.

The following code is the simplest form of creating a query, in which all the records and fields are selected from a table with no other condition specified. This type of query is created by a Data control as a default.

```
Dim MyDyn As Recordset
MyDynOpen "Select * from Titles", adDbCon1,,,adCmdText
```

This code gives you the same data you had when accessing the table directly by using the table-type recordset. The only difference is the type of recordset created. When you create a query, you can use any valid SQL statement that you need to select the correct data from the database.

Accessing the Data

Now that you have a understanding of what it takes to create and open recordsets, you can see how to use them in an application. As you've already seen, to display data with the Data control and bound controls, you simply draw the controls on the form and then set the appropriate data field properties for the controls. The display process itself is automatic.

With the ActiveX Data Objects, the process is only slightly more complex. You still use control objects (such as text boxes and labels) to display the data, but you assign the data to the controls manually with each record that you display. When used in this manner, the control objects are usually called *unbound controls*. One advantage of using unbound controls is that you can use any control to display data, not just the bound controls specifically meant to use with the Data control.

You can access data through a recordset's Fields collection in several ways. For example, to retrieve the contents of a field named Title in a recordset called MyDyn and place it into a text box named Text1, you could do the following:

- Use the field's ordinal position in the Fields collection as Text1.Text = MyDyn.Fields(0).
- Use the field's name to retrieve it from the Fields collection as Text1.Text = MyDyn.Fields("Title").
- Use the recordset collection's default to access the field as Text1.Text = MyDyn("Title").
- Use the recordset collection's default to access the field as Text1.Text = MyDyn!Title.

As an example, redo the demo that you created with the Data control. Start a new project and add two text boxes to the default form to hold the data from the query, as shown in Figure 10.7.

FIGURE 10.7.

Using unbound controls to display data from the Data Access Objects.

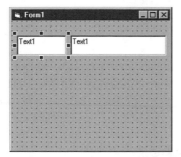

To set up the query for use, you must open a database connection and then open a recordset by using the Open method. In the General Declarations section of the form, the Dim statements that define the ActiveX Data Objects are needed by the code in the form. You then open the connection and query in the Form_Load event routine, as shown in Listing 10.1.

LISTING 10.1. ADOEX1.TXT—OPENING THE DATABASE AND RECORDSET IN THE Form_Load EVENT.

```
1: strCnn = "driver={SQL Server} ;server=srv;" & _
2:        "uid=sa;pwd=;database=pubs"
3: Set cnn1 = New ADODB.Connection
4: cnn1.Open strCnn
5: MyDyn.Open("Select * From Authors",cnn1,,,adCmdText)
6: MyDyn.MoveFirst
7: Call DisplayFields
```

Now, the query is open and you're positioned at the first record in the recordset. To display the data, assign the value of the desired data fields to the display properties of the controls containing the data. For this type of processing, it's recommended that you create a subroutine (as shown in Listing 10.2) to perform the assignment of the controls from the current record in the recordset. This same routine can be called from a number of command button events rather than repeat the code in each event. This way, the code is more efficient and easier to maintain.

10

LISTING 10.2. DAOEX2.TXT—ADDING THE DATA FIELDS TO THE DISPLAY PROPERTIES OF THE
CONTROLS.

```
1: Private Sub DisplayFields()
2: Text1(0).Text = MyDyn("AU_ID")
3: Text1(1).Text = MyDyn("Author")
4: End Sub
```

Also notice that rather than have unique names for each text box, a control array is used.
This allows you to use a loop to quickly modify some of the control's properties, if needed. When you execute the application, you would see only one record's information displayed (see Figure 10.8).

FIGURE 10.8.

*Display the informa-
tion for a single
record.*

By doing this, you can't move from one record to another in the application. You also
should have noticed in the Form_Load event that after the query was created, a
MoveFirst method was executed to ensure that the current record pointer points to the
first record. Because you're now controlling the access to the data, you must add each
navigation button that you want available to users. Generally, you would use the Move
methods to provide this functionality. To see how this is done, add four command buttons to the form, as shown in Figure 10.9.

FIGURE 10.9.

*Adding the manual
navigation buttons to
the form.*

Then add the code in Listing 10.3 to allow each button to perform the specified action.

LISTING 10.3. DAOEX3.TXT—ADDING NAVIGATION COMMAND BUTTONS TO THE FORM.

```
 1: Private Sub cmdFirst_Click()
 2:     MyDyn.MoveFirst
 3:     Call DisplayFields
 4: End Sub
 5:
 6: Private Sub cmdLast_Click()
 7:     MyDyn.MoveLast
 8:     Call DisplayFields
 9: End Sub
10:
11: Private Sub cmdNext_Click()
12:     MyDyn.MoveNext
13:     Call DisplayFields
14: End Sub
15:
16: Private Sub cmdPrevious_Click()
17:     MyDyn.MovePrevious
18:     Call DisplayFields
19: End Sub
```

Now execute the application and try using the command buttons that you just added. You should be able to move around the records in the query. You'll still have to deal with one problem, however, when you try to move past the beginning or end of the recordset. You should get an error message as shown in Figure 10.10.

FIGURE 10.10.

Trying to move past the beginning or end of a record will result in an error.

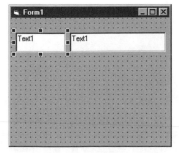

To prevent this from happening, you need to check the EOF and BOF properties of the recordset when moving forward or backward in the recordset. Listing 10.4 shows the additional code you need for this function.

LISTING 10.4. DAOEX4.TXT—CHECKING FOR THE EOF OR BOF CONDITIONS.

```
 1: Private Sub cmdNext_Click()
 2:     MyDyn.MoveNext
 3:     If MyDyn.EOF Then
 4:         MsgBox "Last record displayed", vbInformation, App.Title
 5:         MyDyn.MoveLast
 6:     End If
 7:     Call DisplayFields
 8: End Sub
 9:
10: Private Sub cmdPrevious_Click()
11:     MyDyn.MovePrevious
12:      If MyDyn.BOF Then
13:         MsgBox "First record displayed", vbInformation, App.Title
14:         MyDyn.MoveFirst
15:      End If
16:     Call DisplayFields
17: End Sub
```

Besides displaying the data on a form, you can use the ActiveX Data Objects to modify, add, or delete data in the database. The AddNew method used to add a new record to a recordset doesn't actually add the record; instead, it clears the copy buffer to allow data for the new record to be input. To add the record physically after you put data into the record's fields, you use the Update method. Listing 10.5 shows how to use the AddNew method to add a new record to the recordset.

LISTING 10.5. DAOEX5.TXT—ADDING A RECORD TO THE RECORDSET.

```
1: Private Sub cmdAdd_Click()
2:     MyDyn.AddNew
3:     Call SetFields
4:     MyDyn.Update
5: End Sub
```

Caution

> Because the new data isn't added to the database until an Update method is executed, reusing the AddNew method or moving the record pointer with any Move or Find method will clear the copy buffer, and any data that has been entered will be lost.

In the same way a routine was used to move the data from the recordset to the controls, a routine should be used to move the data from the controls to the recordset.

In order to make changes to a record, a copy of the current record is placed into the copy buffer so that data can be changed. After the user changes the data, you would need to execute the Update method. As with the AddNew method, the changes take effect only when the Update method is executed (see Listing 10.6).

LISTING 10.6. ADOEX6.TXT—ADDING THE Edit ROUTINE TO THE APPLICATION.

```
1: Private Sub cmdUpdate_Click()
2:     MyDyn!Title = "This is my Book"
3:     MyDyn.Update
4:     Call SetFields
5: End Sub
```

The Update method used with the AddNew and Edit methods writes the data from the copy buffer to the recordset. In the case of AddNew, Update also creates a blank record in the recordset to which the data is written.

Caution	When editing a record and updating it, you should never try to update the primary key fields in the data. This usually causes an error to occur.

Finally, if you need to delete a record, use the Delete method (see Listing 10.7). This method removes the record from the recordset and sets the record pointer to a null value.

LISTING 10.7. DAOEX7.TXT—ADDING THE Delete PROCESS TO THE FORM.

```
1: Private Sub cmdDelete_Click()
2:     MyDyn.Delete
3:     MsgBox "Record has been deleted", vbInformation, App.Title
4:     Call cmdNext_Click
5: End Sub
```

As you can see, after the Delete method is executed, the cmdNext click routine is called to move the current record pointer to the next valid record in the recordset. If this wasn't done, an error would occur.

To see how all this works, add three more command buttons to the form, as shown in Figure 10.11. Then, add the code for each of these actions. Now run the application again and try each action to see how it works.

10

FIGURE 10.11.

Adding the data modification processing to the example.

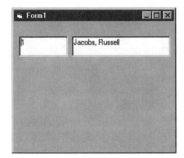

Mixing the Methods

So far, you've seen how to use the automatic data access provided by Visual Basic's Data control and bound controls, as well as how to access the data directly with more control by using the ActiveX Data Objects. However, as you might already know or have guessed, no application uses only one of these access methods. Each form or function in an application might use one method or both to provide the functionality you need.

To see this, add several routines or enhancements to the address-book application that you've been creating in this book. First, you'll see how to add information to the TreeView control, and then how to display the correct information on the ListView control. Finally, you'll make a change to the data-entry form, frmAddressEntry, to give users new ways to select information when adding or modifying a record.

Populating the TreeView Control

The TreeView control is the center of all activity in the address-book application. Initially, it will display a standard alphabetic selection list, as shown in Figure 10.12. This will allow users to go directly to a given letter in the alphabet to find a particular entry.

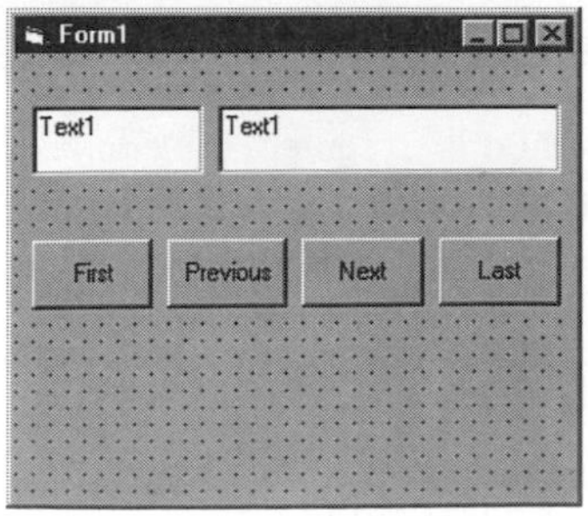

FIGURE 10.12.

The initial TreeView listing with the letters of the alphabet.

Initializing the TreeView control really has nothing to do with data access; however, it's required before adding any entry names. The code in Listing 10.8 sets the TreeView control. For each added node, the associated letter is used as the key, allowing you to access that node directly later in the process.

LISTING 10.8. ADDRDAO1.TXT—INITIALIZING THE TREEVIEW CONTROL AT THE START OF THE APPLICATION.

```
 1: Public Sub Set_NewTree()
 2: Dim Node_Letter As String * 1
 3: tvTreeView.Nodes.Clear
 4: Set MyNode = tvTreeView.Nodes.Add(, , "AB", "Address Book", 1)
 5: For I = 1 To 26
 6:     Node_Letter = Mid("ABCDEFGHIJKLMNOPQRSTUVWXYZ", I, 1)
 7:     Set MyNode = tvTreeView.Nodes.Add("AB", tvwChild, Node_Letter, _
 8:        Node_Letter, 2)
 9: Next I
10: End Sub
```

10

Note
Don't forget that the TreeView needs an Image control if you want the different nodes to have pictures associated with them.

Now that you have the TreeView control ready to accept data, you can create the code needed to perform this action. To add the entry names as shown in Figure 10.13, you need to perform the following actions:

1. Open a database connection.

2. Open a Recordset by using a SQL statement.

3. Loop through records, adding the name to the TreeView control by using the first letter of the last name as the key to the current node.

For this application, add the last name followed by the first name to the list. Also, the key to each item will be the AddressID and the last name as one string field, to provide a unique key for each node. It will also allow you to access the AddressID later in the application to display an entry.

The code in Listing 10.9 can be placed in the Form_Load routine for the application so that the TreeView control is initialized when the application is started. However, if you're allowing users to select an address book database to use, and there might be several different ones, you should place this initialization code into a separate subroutine that can be called when needed.

FIGURE 10.13.

Displaying the entry names in the TreeView.

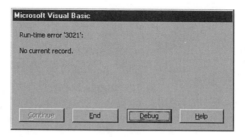

LISTING 10.9. ADDRDAO2.TXT—ADDING THE TREEVIEW CONTROL DATA INITIALIZATION CODE AS A ROUTINE CALLED FROM THE Form_Load EVENT.

```
 1: Private Sub Form_Load()
 2:     Set MyDb = OpenDatabase(App.Path & ".mdb")
 3:     Call Set_NewTree
 4:     Call Set_TreeNodes
 5: End Sub
 6:
 7: Public Sub Set_TreeNodes()
 8: Dim Node_Key As String
 9: Dim Entry_Letter As String * 1
10: Dim Node_Name As String
11:     Set MyDyn = MyDb.OpenRecordset("Select * From [Address Entry]", _
12:         dbOpenDynaset)
13:     If Not MyDyn.EOF And Not MyDyn.BOF Then
14:         MyDyn.MoveFirst
15:         Do Until MyDyn.EOF
16:             Node_Key = CStr(MyDyn.Fields(0)) & "!" & _
                MyDyn.Fields("LastName")
17:             Entry_Letter = Mid(MyDyn.Fields("LastName"), 1, 1)
18:             Node_Name = MyDyn.Fields("LastName") & ", " & _
19:               MyDyn.Fields("FirstName")
20:             Set MyNode = tvTreeView.Nodes.Add(Entry_Letter, tvwChild, _
21:                 Node_Key, Node_Name, 3)
22:             MyDyn.MoveNext
23:         Loop
24:     End If
25:     MyDyn.Close
26: End Sub
```

Tip

If you plan to use a Connection object in several different sections of the application code, open the connection once in the Form_Load routine and use the same connection object everywhere in the application.

Also, every time a new entry is added, a single new node must be added by using the same key logic (discussed in a later section). Now, add a few records to the database by using the Visual Data Manager, and then run the application to see how TreeView processing works. In the example in Figure 10.13, the TreeView control automatically provides a plus sign (+) to note which main letter nodes contain data entries.

The ListView Control

The data displayed in the ListView control will change whenever users select a different letter in the TreeView control, much the same way as Windows Explorer displays the contents of a directory that was selected. To do this, you need to know when a new letter was selected in the TreeView and then clear the ListView to reinitialize it. The first step in the process is to recognize when a node is selected; the second is to know if the selected node is a letter or a name. The NodeClick event routine is triggered whenever a node is selected in the TreeView control. The code in Listing 10.10 checks to see if the node was a letter or a name, and then calls the appropriate routines, passing the selected letter as an argument.

10

LISTING 10.10. ADDRDAO3.TXT—CHECKING FOR A LETTER NODE TO CALL THE LISTVIEW INITIALIZATION ROUTINE.

```
 1: Private Sub tvTreeView_NodeClick(ByVal Node As ComctlLib.Node)
 2: If Len(Node.Key) = 1 Then
 3:     Call Set_ListView(Node.Key)
 4: Else
 5:     If InStr(1, tvTreeView.SelectedItem.Key, "!") > 0 Then
 6:         frmAddressEntry.sqlEntry = "select * from [Address Entry] _
            Where _
 7:         [AddressID] = " & Mid(tvTreeView.SelectedItem.Key, 1, _
 8:         InStr(1, tvTreeView.SelectedItem.Key, "!") - 1)
 9:     End If
10: End If
11: End Sub
```

The ListView initialization routine takes the letter passed to it and open a dynaset by using the following SQL to retrieve the entries that start with that letter:

```
SELECT * FROM [Address Entry] WHERE [LastName] Like "M*"
```

Then, by using a loop, it adds each record to the ListView as shown in Listing 10.11.

LISTING 10.11. ADDRDAO4.TXT—INITIALIZING THE LISTVIEW CONTROL WITH DATA ACCESS OBJECTS.

```
 1: Public Sub Set_ListView(KeyCode As String)
 2: Dim listitemadd As ListItem
 3:     lvListView.ListItems.Clear
 4:     Set MyDyn = MyDb.OpenRecordset("SELECT * FROM [Address Entry] _
        WHERE _
 5:     [LastName] Like """ & KeyCode & "*""", dbOpenDynaset)
 6:     MyDyn.MoveFirst
 7:     Do Until MyDyn.EOF
 8:         Set listitemadd = lvListView.ListItems.Add(, , _
            MyDyn.Fields("LastName") _
 9:             & ", " & MyDyn.Fields("FirstName"), 1, 1)
10:         If Not IsNull(MyDyn.Fields("City")) Then
11:             listitemadd.SubItems(1) = MyDyn.Fields("City")
12:         End If
13:          If Not IsNull(MyDyn.Fields("State")) Then
14:             listitemadd.SubItems(2) = MyDyn.Fields("State")
15:         End If
16:         If Not IsNull(MyDyn.Fields("HomePhone")) Then
17:             listitemadd.SubItems(3) = MyDyn.Fields("HomePhone")
18:         End If
19:         If Not IsNull(MyDyn.Fields("EmailAddress")) Then
20:             listitemadd.SubItems(4) = MyDyn.Fields("EmailAddress")
21:         End If
22:         listitemadd.Tag = CStr(MyDyn.Fields(0)) & "!" & _
            MyDyn.Fields("LastName")
23:         MyDyn.MoveNext
24:     Loop
25:     MyDyn.Close
26: End Sub
```

For this application, the only display option that makes any sense for the ListView control is Report. It's up to you what data should be displayed for each entry. However, the minimum should be what's shown in Figure 10.14.

FIGURE 10.14.

The final ListView display showing data from the address entry table.

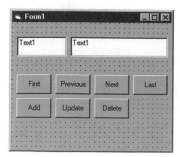

Caution If you want to restrict the ListView display option to only Report, remove any toolbar buttons or menu options that would allow users to change the display.

The other routine called from the NodeClick event displays the data-entry form for the selected name. This requires a small change to the frmAddressEntry to get the use the SQL statement that's created and display the correct record. Listing 10.12 shows this code.

LISTING 10.12. ADDRDAO5.TXT—MODIFYING THE Form_Load CODE IN THE frmAddressEntry FORM.

```
1: Private Sub Form_Load()
2:     If sqlEntry = "" Then
3:         sqlEntry = "select * from [Address Entry]"
4:     End If
5:     datPrimaryRS.RecordSource = sqlEntry
6:     datPrimaryRS.Refresh
7:      If datPrimaryRS.Recordset.RecordCount = 0 Then _
            datPrimaryRS.Recordset.AddNew
8: End Sub
```

Now, run the application again and try out the new functions you just added.

Enhancing the Entry Form

In this section, you add a combo box to allow users to select a state to add to an entry. The state abbreviations are retrieved from a reference table in the database and displayed in the drop-down list. To make the process dynamic, users also can enter state abbreviations as needed and have them added to the database. To start the process, add a data-bound combo box to the data-entry form in place of the original state text box (see Figure 10.15).

FIGURE 10.15.

Adding a combo box to the data-entry form.

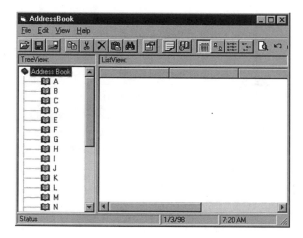

Then add another ADODC to the form and set its properties as shown in Table 10.4.

TABLE 10.4. PROPERTY SETTINGS FOR NEW DATA CONTROL.

Property	Value
Name	StateDB
RecordSource	States
Options	adCmdTable
Visible	False

The data-bound combo box (DBCombo control), similar in function to its standard counterpart, is designed to present users with a list of choices. The key difference is that a data-bound combo box control gets its list data from a recordset rather than from a series of add-item statements. The data-bound combo box is unique in that it lets you select separate fields—one to display in the list and another to add to the entry record. Table 10.5 lists the properties you would use for the data-bound combo box.

TABLE 10.5. PROPERTIES OF THE DATA-BOUND COMBO BOX.

Property	Value	Description
Name	dbCboState	The name of the control
BoundColumn	St_Abbrev	The name of the field containing the value to be copied to the other table
DataField	State	The name of the target field
DataSource	datPrimaryRS	The Data control containing the recordset that's the target of the information

Property	Value	Description
ListField	St_Desc	The field to be displayed in the list
RowSource	StatesDB	The Data control containing the data used to populate the list

For this example, set the properties of the data-bound combo box as listed in Table 10.5. Try running the application and displaying the data-entry form to see how the combo box works. Then add the code to allow users to add a new state abbreviation and its description to the reference table. After the new entry is added, the data control for the combo box is refreshed and positioned to the new entry. The code in Listing 10.13 performs these actions by using the ActiveX Data control methods and ADO commands.

LISTING 10.13. ADDRADO6.TXT—ADDING THE CODE TO ADD NEW STATES TO THE REFERENCE TABLE AS NEEDED.

10

```
 1: Private Sub dbcboState_LostFocus()
 2: Dim hold_State As String
 3:     If dbcboState.Text = " " Or IsNull(dbcboState.Text) Or _
        dbcboState.Text = "" _
 4:       Then Exit Sub
 5:     hold_State = dbcboState.BoundText
 6:     MyDyn.Open("SELECT * FROM States", MyDb,,,adCmdText
 7:     MyDyn.Find "St_Abbrev = '" & hold_State & "'", adSearchForward
 8:     If MyDyn.NoMatch Then
 9:        MyDyn.AddNew
10:        MyDyn.Fields("St_Abbrev").Value = hold_State
11:        MyDyn.Fields("St_Desc").Value = InputBox("Enter the _
           Description for: " _
12:         & hold_State, App.Title, "N/A")
13:        hold_State = MyDyn.Fields("St_Desc").Value
14:        MyDyn.Update
15:        MyDyn.Close
16:        StatesDB.Requery
17:        dbcboState.Text = hold_State
18:     End If
19: End Sub
```

In this code, you can see that although the ActiveX Data control is used to populate the combo box, ActiveX Data Objects are used to check whether the state entered by users exists and, if not, to add it to the reference table. It also prompts users for the state's full name. This whole process works because you're controlling the position of the current record pointer and the contents of the text property. Try running the application again and add a new state to an entry. You'll see it added to the drop-down list and placed in the text area so that the abbreviation is added to the address entry record.

Summary

Well, you've had a busy day. You've reviewed the two main methods of accessing data in a database from within a Visual Basic application. You've seen how to use the ActiveX Data Control and bound controls to automatically access, display, modify, and delete information. Also, you saw how to perform the same actions by using ActiveX Data Objects instead of the ActiveX Data Control.

Finally, these methods were used to add some initialization code to the address book application and to enhance the data-entry form by using a combo box and data-access commands. What all this allows you to do is create a feature-rich database application that your users can work with.

Q&A

Q Can both access methods be used in the same routine?

A Yes, you can use either or both of the access methods in the same routine. It all depends on what you need done.

Q What methods can you use to position the database to a particular record?

A You would use the `Find` and `Move` methods to position the database: `Find`, , `MoveLast`, `MoveFirst`, `MoveNext`, and `MoveLast`.

Q How do you specify a field name inside a ADO statement that includes spaces in its name?

A You must enclose the field name in square brackets (`[]`) if the field name contains blanks.

Q What do the `EOF` and `BOF` values determine?

A `EOF` determines the end of the file; `BOF` determines the beginning of the file.

Workshop

The Workshop provides quiz questions to help solidify your understanding of the material covered, as well as exercises to provide you with experience in using what you've learned. Try to understand the quiz and exercise answers before continuing on to the next day's lesson. Answers are provided in Appendix A, "Answers to Exercises."

Quiz

1. What's the difference between ActiveX Data Control access and ActiveX Data Objects?

2. What does the `MoveComplete` routine do?

3. How do you delete a record from the database?

4. What's meant by a *bound control*?

Exercise

Add a search form to the address book application that will allow users to search for a first or last name and display the results in a list box control. Then, users should be able to select a name and have it displayed in the `frmAddressEntry` form.

10

DAY **11**

Enhancing the Application

For the last few days, you've been learning about database design, data form creation, and how to access the data through code. Today, you'll switch gears a little and see what a custom control is, how to create a fairly simple one, and then—finally—how to convert an existing form into a custom control. You'll also see the reasons for converting a form into a custom control.

Custom controls are one of the most exciting features of the Visual Basic product. They allow you to combine existing controls with code and create new controls that meet your application's specific design needs. Of course, you also can create custom controls as their own application, so that other developers can use them in their applications.

You'll see how to create a custom control, but the process is by no means a simple one (even though Visual Basic provides a wizard that helps with the definition of properties, methods, and events). The best today's lesson can do is whet your appetite for more information about them.

Note

> The Standard Edition of Visual Basic can't create custom or ActiveX controls directly. However, Microsoft has a standalone Control Creation Edition that you can download from the Microsoft Web site. The steps needed to create an ActiveX control are the same across editions.
>
> If you'll be using the Control Creation Edition, you won't work directly in Visual Basic, but in the special edition of Visual Basic for the Control Creation Edition. Fortunately, the interface of both editions are identical. The Control Creation Edition isn't being used in today's lesson; however, and differences will be noted.

Using Custom Controls

Before creating a custom control, you first need to understand what they are, and the different types of custom controls you can create.

If you can create a Visual Basic form, you can create an ActiveX control. The steps and skills necessary to create controls are practically identical to those used to create a form. What's more, control creation possibilities are virtually unlimited.

Why Use Custom Controls?

Creating custom controls are like teaching an old dog a new trick. Although Visual Basic provides many different controls that you can use, and many other companies produce ActiveX controls to provide particular functionalities, at some point you'll find that you need to perform some task that the existing controls don't perform.

For example, if you want users to be able to enter a new value in a combo box, you need to have some code in the combo box's CloseUp routine. That's easy; however, if the new entry requires some additional information to actually add the new value, you need to display another form to get that information. Here's the problem: When the second form is unloaded, the new record is committed to the database with a CommitTrans command. Unfortunately, data controls all use the same workspace, so the data entry that users are working on is also committed. This causes errors when users try to finish the entry and update the database. By creating a custom control that does the initial add and update of the reference information, you aren't unloading a form and can actually code the update process differently, not to mention being able to use this control in other application.

Custom controls allow you to create any type of control that you need to solve a unique problem in your application. The only limiting factor is your own imagination.

Knowing the Models

A large part of creating a quality ActiveX control lies in the details—that is, verifying the design and runtime settings of every property, method, event, and user input. Defining these ahead of time will go a long way toward helping you succeed. Before creating the control, you should know that you can follow three different models:

- Enhancing existing controls
- Building complex controls from existing controls
- Creating user-drawn controls

Each model addresses a specific area of the design concept.

Enhancing Existing Controls

In this model, your control contains a single existing control. Most of the properties, methods, and events of the control are mapped to public properties, methods, and events of your control. Your control can add new properties or events, or otherwise modify the behavior of the standard control. For example, you could implement a text box that will convert all the text entered to uppercase characters.

The biggest advantage of enhancing an existing control is that it's extremely easy to do. The ActiveX control interface wizard can do much of the work of mapping public properties, methods, and events. Although this is the easiest method, you might want to use another approach for the following reasons:

- Each existing control defines its own behavior and drawing characteristics. There are limits to what you can do to modify the control.
- Existing controls are always in run mode when your control is active, making it impossible to set the control's design-time properties even though the new control is in design mode. For example, if you want to create an enhanced list box that supported single and multiple selection modes, you would need to place two separate list box controls into your control: one for single selection and one for multiple selection.
- As soon as you go beyond the built-in controls or redistributable controls provided by Microsoft, you run into licensing issues. For your control to work in the design environment, each existing control must be properly licensed.

Building Complex Controls from Existing Controls

This model is really a superset of the preceding model, except that rather than map your public properties and events to a single control, you map them to any or all of the existing controls in the new control. It's also possible to map the same property to more than one control.

11

Creating User-Drawn Controls

The two preceding approaches have the advantage of being incredible easy to use. User-drawn controls represent one of the most exciting approaches that you can use for control creation, although the difficulty jumps astronomically. With this type of control, you work primarily with properties and events of the UserControl object. User-drawn controls are used whenever your new control had nothing in common with any existing controls. You would actually define all the control's properties, methods, and events while drawing the control so that it looks exactly the way you want it to.

The ActiveX control that you create, with any of these three methods, will look and act like any other controls. You can insert them into the toolbox windows, double-click the control to add it to the form, and select its properties form the Properties window. Also, the control can support property pages, such as the one that appears when you click the Font property's ellipsis.

Creating a Small Custom Control

So that you can get an understanding of what it takes to create an ActiveX control, you'll create a small, fairly simple custom control with the properties, methods, events, and controls listed in Table 11.1.

TABLE 11.1. SIMPLE ACTIVEX CONTROL ELEMENTS.

Name	Description
Properties	
TableName	Contains the table name or a SQL statement
DisplayField	Contains the number of columns displayed
Methods	
Refresh	Refreshes the database control when executed
Events	
Click	Triggered when users click the control's Continue button
Controls	
Data	Accesses the table in the specified database
ComboBox	Displays the data from the specified field in the table
CommandButton	Returns control to the calling form

By combining these controls with the data-access programming you learned in yesterday's lesson, you can design a control that will solve the problem described earlier. Along the way you'll see how to use the control design and property page wizards to enhance the control you've created. In this section, you'll create the basic control interface and set the properties, methods, and events for the control. Then in the next section, you'll add code to this control to include the enhanced functionality you want.

To begin building the new control, open a new project and select ActiveX Control in the New Project dialog box. If you're using the Control Creation Edition, you can still open a new project and select the ActiveX Control icon that appears. Although Professional and Enterprise Edition programmers can access the Control Creation icon from within Visual Basic, Standard Edition programmers will have to start the separate application. The remaining steps are the same for every edition.

After you open a new ActiveX control project, you should notice some differences in the display (see Figure 11.1).

FIGURE 11.1.

The ActiveX control design window doesn't have a title bar or a border.

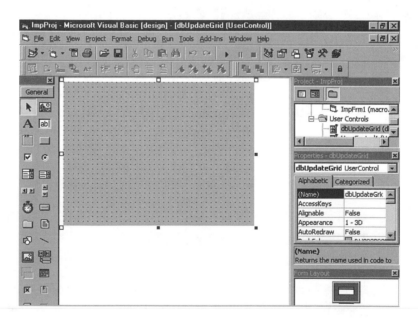

11

The biggest difference is that the displayed work area has no title bar or borders like standard form work areas. This serves as a reminder that you're not creating a form. When creating a new control, Visual Basic generates a default control class call UserControl. Visual Basic then assigns default properties, events, and methods to the control. To go beyond these defaults, you need to modify these values and routines to make the control perform the way you want it to.

Okay, now add some existing controls to the control as shown in Figure 11.2. This will give you the tools to create the unique process you need to perform.

FIGURE 11.2.

*The initial controls
added to the new
ActiveX control being
created.*

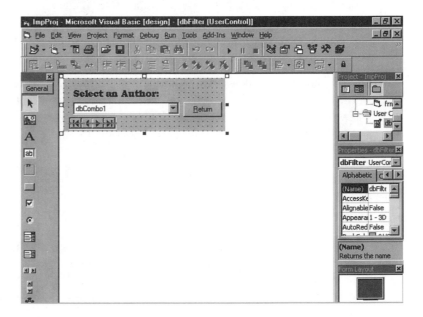

Don't forget to change the name of the project from UserControl to something a little more meaningful. For this example, name the control AdvDBAdd, referring to this control's function (Advanced Database Add). Also, you should change the control's bitmap image. This image will appear in the toolbox whenever you add the control to an application. Next, you need to activate some properties, methods, and events for the new control.

Using the ActiveX Control Interface Wizard

The ActiveX control interface wizard is a useful tool that takes some grunt work out of implementing your controls. It helps you support the standard properties, methods, and events in your control. To use the ActiveX control interface, you need to add it to the Add-Ins menu through the Add-Ins Manager, and then select it. The first dialog box that appears is the wizard's information box; you can simple click Next to continue. The wizard then displays a dialog box that lists the custom controls in the project. Select the one you just added and click Next. The next dialog box asks you which of the standard properties will be supported in your control (see Figure 11.3).

FIGURE 11.3.

Listing the standard properties available to use in your control.

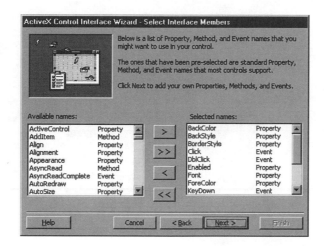

If your control is intended to be invisible at runtime, you should remove all the standard properties from the control. Otherwise, you should review the list to see which properties match the list of properties that you need in your control. The default list suggested by the wizard is a good starting point.

> **Tip**
>
> I would suggest that you add the hWnd property as well, even if you don't need it, because it will make it easier to use your control with more advanced applications that use the Win32 API calls.

> **Caution**
>
> Don't arbitrarily add every available property to the list. Some properties listed are for internal use by the control and shouldn't be exposed in the code.

Notice that many of the properties of the controls that you placed on the control are listed here. After you select the properties you want and remove the ones you don't, click Next to continue. The next dialog box prompts you for any custom properties, events, or methods that you need for the control (see Figure 11.4).

11

FIGURE 11.4.

Add your own properties, methods, and events to the new control.

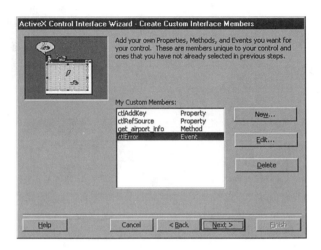

Don't worry if you forgot something; you can always add it later by modifying the control's code or by using the wizard again. Add the custom method and event for this control and click Next. The dialog box that appears (see Figure 11.5) lets you map the control's public members to those of the controls you placed on the new control or the UserControl object itself. The code produced by the wizard to map members in this manner is very educational, although it may not always match the functionality you want.

FIGURE 11.5.

Use the Procedure Attributes dialog box to verify the procedure ID for each property.

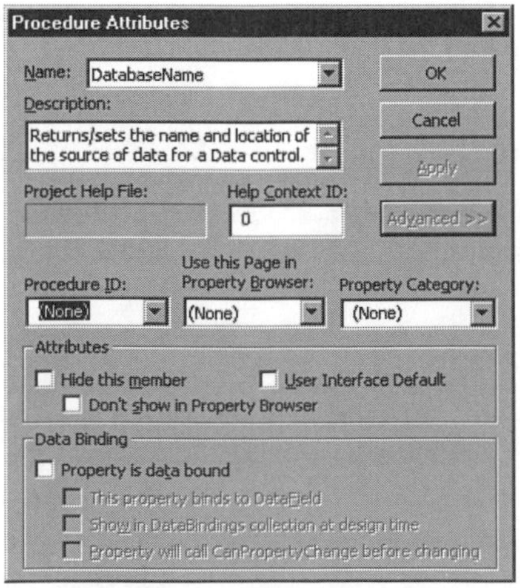

When you're satisfied with your changes, click Next to continue. The final wizard dialog box lets you specify the characteristics of unmapped members. You first should choose a property type other than the default variant type. You also can set the member description and read/write properties. You should also choose Tools, Procedures Attributes from the menu to bring up the Procedure Attributes dialog box and make sure that the procedure ID is correct for each standard property.

When you've finished, click Finish to have the wizard add the code to the new control. At this point, you should save the control project.

Well, you've created a new control, right? Wrong. All you've accomplished so far is the creation of a shell that, if executed, does very little. You still need to modify the code generated to activate this new control's features.

Changing Properties at Designtime

To make it easier to modify the properties of the new control, you can use the Properties window or create a custom Property Pages dialog box for the new ActiveX control. Property Pages offer a way to display the control's properties in a logical, easy dialog box, as shown in Figure 11.6.

FIGURE 11.6.

Using Property Pages gives you an easy way of accessing the properties of the control.

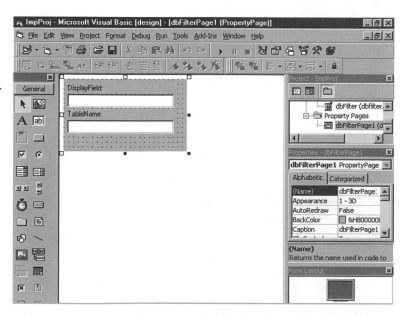

Each tab in the Property Pages dialog box represents one PropertyPage object, as shown in Figure 11.6. In the design window, the PropertyPage object doesn't display a tab or the OK, Cancel, and Apply buttons (these are provided automatically by the Property Pages dialog box and aren't part of any individual PropertyPage object). The Property Pages dialog box uses the Caption property of the PropertyPage object as the text for the tab.

Creating a Property Page is a lot like creating a form, except that a Property Page doesn't execute a Load event when it's displayed.

Your Property Pages dialog box must do only three things:

- In the SelectionChanged event, obtain the property values to be edited.
- Set the PropertyPage object's Changed property whenever users edit a property value.
- In the ApplyChanges event, copy the edited property values back to the selected control (or controls).

The SelectionChanged event occurs when the property page is displayed and when the list of currently selected controls changes.

> **Tip**
> Always treat the SelectionChanged event as though your Property Page is being loaded for the first time. As you'll see, changing the selection actually changes the state of the Property Page.

The most important thing you need to do in the SelectionChanged event is to set the values of the controls that display the property values to be edited. An example of this is as follows:

```
Private Sub PropertyPage_SelectionChanged()
    txtTableName.Text = SelectedControls(0).TableName
    txtDisplayField.Text = SelectedControls(0).DisplayField
End Sub
```

The code in the SelectionChanged event is taking the value for each property for the first control in the collection and assigning it to the appropriate control on the property page. In a single selected control, this places all the control's property values in fields where users can edit them. If a control requires a selection, you could use a combo box to display the list for users of the control to choose from. The list in the combo box would be populated in the SelectionChanged event routine.

To tell Visual Basic that one or more properties on a property page have changed, the PropertyPage object's Changed property must be set to True. Because there's really no way of knowing which property might have been changed, you would add this code for every property displayed on the page. For example, to notify the PropertyPage of changes in the ctlDatabase property, you would use the following code:

```
Private Sub ctlDatabase_Changed()
    Changed = True
End Sub
```

Note   This is exactly the same as if you coded `PropertyPage.Changed = True`.

Notifying the `PropertyPage` object that values have changed enables the Apply button on the Property Pages dialog box and causes the `ApplyChanges` event to occur when the following occurs:

- The Apply button is pressed.
- Users change pages.
- The dialog box is closed.

The last routine you need to worry about and the second most important event in a `PropertyPage` object is the `ApplyChanges` event. In this event, you copy the changed property values back to the currently selected control. The following code is an example of this routine coded for your new control:

```
Private Sub PropertyPage_ApplyChanges()
    SelectedControls(0).TableName = txtTableName.Text
    SelectedControls(0).DisplayField = txtDisplayField.Text
End Sub
```

In this example, there is little chance for an error to occur in the `ApplyChanges` event. However, if your Property Page allows users to enter values that may be rejected by the `Property Let` (or `Property Set`) procedure in the control's code, you should use error trapping in the `ApplyChanges` event. The simplest scheme is to use `On Error Resume Next` and test `Err.Number` after each property that may raise an error. When an error occurs, you should do the following:

- Stop processing the `ApplyChanges` event.
- Display an error message, so users understand what went wrong.
- Set the focus to the property that caused the error.
- Set the `Changed` property of the `PropertyPage` object to `True`.

11

Note   Setting `Changed` to `True` re-enables the Apply button and prevents the Property Pages dialog box from being closed if users click OK.

After you create the property page, you need to connect it to the control that you created
it for. To do this, you must first open the design view of the control, and then double-
click the `PropertyPages` property in the Properties window. This will display the control's Property Pages dialog box, as shown in Figure 11.7.

FIGURE 11.7.

*Connecting the new
control with its related
Property Pages that
you just created.*

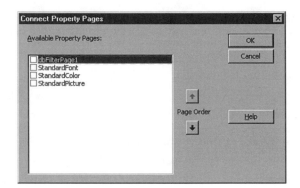

In this dialog box, check each Property Page that you want to appear when you open the
control's Property Pages dialog box. Also, you can place the pages in the order that you
want them displayed. You may have noticed in Figure 11.7 that three property pages
were listed that you didn't create. Visual Basic provides these three standard property
pages:

- `StandardFont`
- `StandardColor`
- `StandardPicture`

The Properties window automatically associates these properties with the appropriate
standard property page. They won't be automatically added to the Property Pages dialog
box, however; you must do this manually.

Using the Property Page Wizard

You haven't manually created the property page because, again, Visual Basic comes with
a wizard that does most of the work for you. Right-click the Project window, and then
choose Add, Property Page to display the Add PropertyPage dialog box (see Figure 11.8).
Select the Property Page wizard and click OK to start creating the property page.

FIGURE 11.8.

Selecting the Property Page wizard from the Add PropertyPage dialog box.

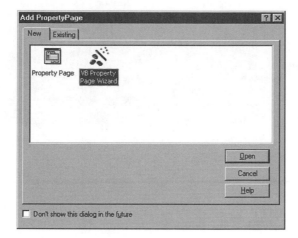

Click Next to bypass the introduction form and display the first dialog box in the wizard. This dialog box (see Figure 11.9) asks you to select a property page form the list or add a new one by clicking OK.

FIGURE 11.9.

Using the Property Page wizard to add an existing Property Page to a control, or create a new one.

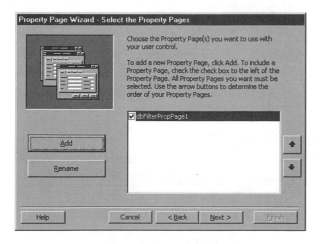

Click Add and enter myControl as the name of the new page and click OK. You'll see the new page name listed and checked in the dialog box. Click Next to continue. The Add Properties dialog box (see Figure 11.10) lists the properties of the new control you're working with.

FIGURE 11.10.

A list of the custom control's properties are displayed for selection.

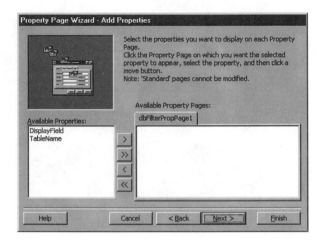

Select the properties you want on this page and add them to the list on the right side of the dialog box.

Note

Adding too many properties will clutter up the page and make it hard to use.

Now click Finish to complete the process. Congratulations! You've created an ActiveX control and added a property page to it.

Testing the Control

The way the control is defined allows you to place it on a form in a standard project, set its properties, execute its methods, and see how the default process works.

Note

You can't run an ActiveX control by choosing Debug, Run from the menu.

Depending on which version of Visual Basic you're using, you can test this new control in two ways:

- By compiling the new control, starting a new Standard EXE project (Standard Edition users will have to start Visual Basic's Standard Edition), and dropping the control into that new project

- In the Professional or Enterprise Edition of Visual Basic, by opening a second project (see Figure 11.11) and then adding the control to the default form

Either way you do this, you should wind up with a form in a standard project that looks like the one in Figure 11.12.

FIGURE 11.11.

Creating a Project group with the new custom control project and a Standard EXE project.

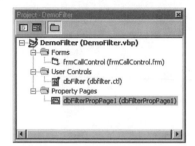

FIGURE 11.12.

Adding the custom control to a standard form.

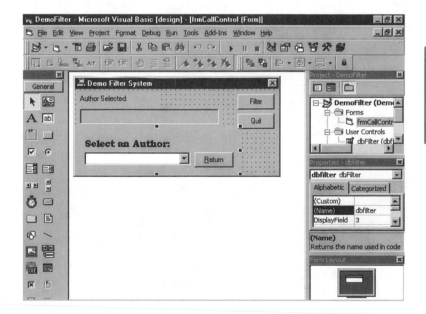

11

Note

If you compiled the control, you need to add it to the toolbox by choosing Projects, Components.

Next, open the Property Pages dialog box for the control, add the values shown in
Figure 11.13, and then click OK. Finally, run the application and test the combo box
by clicking the arrow to display the drop-down list.

FIGURE 11.13.

*Entering the properties
for the custom control
by using the new
Property Pages
dialog box.*

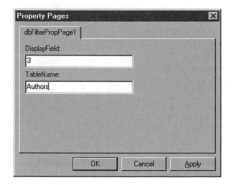

Using the ActiveX Control Test Container

Included with Visual Basic 6 is a new utility called the ActiveX Control Test Container.
This tool allows you to load an ActiveX control that you have created in order to test
each of the events that you have added to the control. This enables you to verify that the
control is setting and passing the correct information back to the application. This utility
is started from the Visual Basic Start Menu group. Once the tool is started, you can then
test any control by selecting File, New from the menu and then choosing the control to
test. The chosen control will be displayed as shown in Figure 11.14.

FIGURE 11.14.

*Using the Test
Container to ensure
that a new custom
control works properly.*

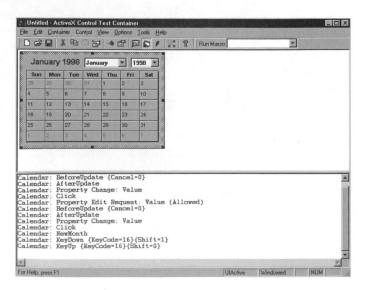

When you pass the mouse over the control or click any object on the control, the bottom work area will display the event(s) that is triggered in the appropriate order and display the data being set.

Note   In order to use this tool, you must compile the new ActiveX control into an OCX and register it.

Converting a Form to a Control

Now that you have an understanding of ActiveX control creation, look at what it takes to convert an existing form into an ActiveX control and why would you want to do it. The only time it makes sense to put the effort into converting a form is when you need to have a form's capabilities within another form's control. If you go back to the Address Book application that uses the Explorer interface, you would see that the data-entry and data-list forms need to be treated as controls in the Explorer SDI so that they can be hidden and resized as one of the panes (see Figure 11.15).

FIGURE 11.15.

Controlling the data list form as a control within the Explorer interface.

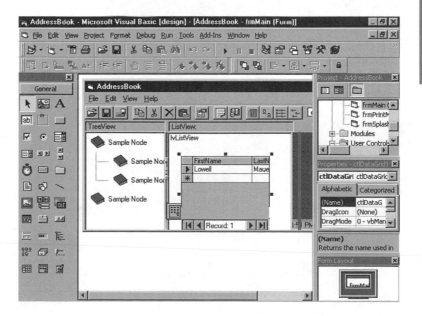

If these were treated as forms, users could keep the forms open or minimized even when they aren't needed. The other option would be to display them as modal forms. In this application design, you want them as controls. To understand the process, convert the data grid form you created in Day 9 into an ActiveX control that you'll then add to the Explorer interface. Remember, a control has no Load routine, but it has an Initialize routine. The first thing you need to do is list the routines in the form. For this example, the routines are Form_Load, datPrimaryRS_Validate, datPrimaryRS_Reposition, and datPrimaryRS_Error. Then you want to map these to their corresponding routines in the control that you'll create.

Now it's time to start a new control project while you have the Address Book project open. After you add the new project, use the ActiveX control wizard to create the members that you need to interact with the control. For this form, you'll need the sizing properties—Left, Top, Width, Height, and Visible—which are added automatically for you. You also need the Refresh method and the Click event.

The next step is to re-create the forms design on the new control. You can do this very easily by copying all the controls on the form and pasting them on the control, as shown in Figure 11.16.

FIGURE 11.16.

Using the Windows Cut and Paste functions allows you to create a control from a form fairly quickly.

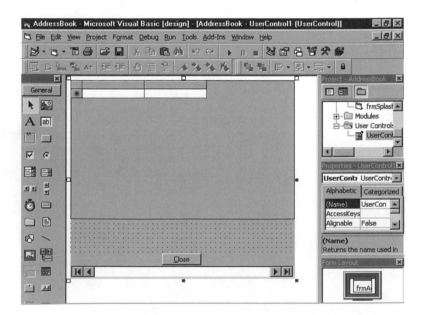

Tip

When you copy the controls, all the properties and names are copied with them.

As soon as you copy all the controls, you can start moving the code into the control. Again, you can start by copying the code from the form and modifying it. If you want, you can also create a property page for this control.

Now that you've completed the conversion process, you can add the control to the Explorer interface. The only thing left to do is add the code to the Explorer menu and toolbar to resize the control, refresh the data control it contains, and then make it visible. The code in Listing 11.1 shows you what routine this should be placed in and how to perform the resizing.

LISTING 11.1. ADDRRESIZE.TXT—ADDING THE ADDRGRID CONTROL'S PROCESSING CODE TO THE MAIN EXPLORER ROUTINES.

```
1: Case "Data Grid"
2:     ctlDataGrid1.Left = lvListView.Left
3:     ctlDataGrid1.Width = lvListView.Width
4:     ctlDataGrid1.Top = lvListView.Top
5:     ctlDataGrid1.Height = lvListView.Height
6:     ctlDataGrid1.Visible = True
```

You should add this code to the toolbar Select Case statement so that the new control will be displayed when the grid button is clicked. If you've done everything correctly, the grid should be displayed when you choose View, Book List from the menu. What you would see is shown in Figure 11.17.

11

FIGURE 11.17.

The new AddrGrid control as it's displayed in the Address Book application.

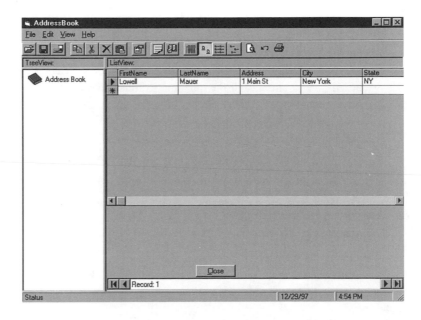

You now have a very powerful tool to use when designing and creating your own applications.

Summary

What you've seen today can be overwhelming at first, but you'll find that custom controls are just another tool now available for you to use in Visual Basic. By creating and using custom controls, you now can create a single form application that can do anything that you need done. And anytime you need a unique function for your application design, you know how to create it yourself.

Q&A

Q Why should I create my own custom controls?

A When you need a unique process for an application, you should consider creating a custom control. Also, if the process you're creating might be used in other applications, a custom control makes it easier to copy the process.

Q Are there any limitations to worry about when creating a custom control?

A You are limited only by your imagination. But before spending days or weeks creating a custom control, investigate to see if it has already been created, so you can buy it rather than waste the time and effort to create it.

Workshop

The Workshop provides quiz questions to help solidify your understanding of the material covered, as well as exercises to provide you with experience in using what you've learned. Try to understand the quiz and exercise answers before continuing on to the next day's lesson. Answers are provided in Appendix A, "Answers to Exercises."

Quiz

1. What makes up a project group?
2. What functionality does the SelectionChanged event provide in your application?
3. How do Property Pages help with a custom control?

Exercise

By using the process discussed in today's lesson, convert the address data-entry form to a custom control that can be used in the Address Book application.

DAY 12

Enhancing Database Access

When creating an application, you want to give the user as many capabilities and features as you can without making the application anymore difficult to use. In the previous chapters, you saw what it takes to design a database and access it using the new ActiveX Data Objects and Control. You also took a look at how you can enhance the application by using custom controls to add functionality to the application. In this chapter, you will take this information and combine it with the latest technologies that have been added to Visual Basic for database manipulation. Visual Basic 6 includes a new control and two new designers that will allow you to enhance data access. These new features are as follows:

- Data Environment Designer
- Data Report Designer
- Data Repeater Control

When you have completed this chapter, you will understand what these features do and how to use them effectively in an application.

Data Environment Designer

The Data Environment Designer is, in effect, a very sophisticated interface that helps you define complex database connections for use in your application. The Data Environment Designer can replace any of the three types of data access you might be using in your application. In addition, it is required if you are using the Hierarchical FlexGrid control or the Data Report Designer. This designer brings together several capabilities into one complete package. Using this designer, you can do the following:

- Define the database connection
- Create SQL commands to access the data
- Specify how separate commands are related to build complex queries
- Define aggregate functions for the query
- Specify the sort order of the data in the query

To create the connection, the Data Environment Designer displays a tabbed dialog that helps you define the connection to the database. Once the connection is defined, you can build commands by using the SQL Query Builder. Together, these give you a complete point and click method of building the SQL connections that your application needs. This section shows you how to create a Data Environment connection that will be used in the remaining sections of this chapter to demonstrate how to use the Data Report Designer and the Data Repeater control.

For the purposes of this chapter, you will build a query to access order information. This will be done by using both Parent and Child commands along with the SQL Builder. Table 12.1 lists the tables and associated columns that will be used, as well as the command they will be added to.

TABLE 12.1. NORTHWIND DATABASE INFORMATION.

Command	Query Type	Table	Column
cmdCustomers	SQL Query	Customers	CompanyName
			Address
			City
			Region
			ContactName
			Customer ID
cmdOrders	SQL Query	Orders	Customer ID
			Order ID

continues

Command	Query Type	Table	Column
			Order Date
cmdOrderDetail	Table	Order Details	<All Columns>
cmdEmployees	Table	Employees	<All Columns>

In preparation for the remaining sections of this chapter, start a new project with a single default form in it.

Defining the Connection

To define the database connection, add a Data Environment Object by right-clicking in the Project Explorer and choosing Add from the pop-up menu. Then choose More ActiveX Designers, the Data Environment as shown in Figure 12.1.

FIGURE 12.1.

Adding a Data Environment Designer to the application by using the pop-up menu in the Project Explorer.

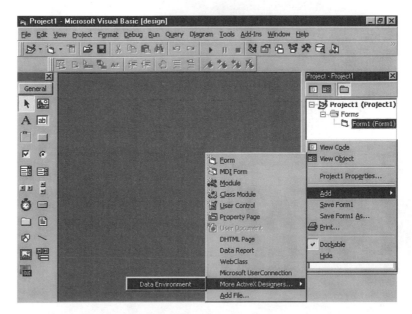

After the new Data Environment object is added to your project, right-click the Connection1 object and choose Properties to display the Connection Properties dialog. The steps defining a connection are very close to the ones used for the ActiveX Data control. When defining the connection, you can choose from either a direct connection to a Jet-supported database, a standard ODBC connection, or one of several OLE DB providers. OLE DB is the latest technique for accessing a database and provides you access to more database-supported features. On the Data Link Properties dialog (see

Figure 12.2), you first choose the database provider you will be using; and then on the Connections tab, you would specify the actual database connection.

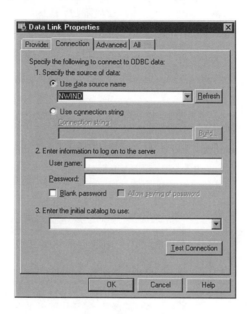

FIGURE 12.2.

Setting the Connection properties tab for the Data Environment.

The NorthWind database (NWIND.MDB) will be used in this chapter. Therefore, if you choose either the ODBC method or OLE DB method, you must define the Data Source or Data Link, respectively.

After you have defined the connection, you need to define one or more commands (SQL)

Note

I am using the OLE DB provider Data Link to allow access to the views already defined in the database.

to retrieve data from the database. To add a command, right-click the Command folder and choose Add Command (see Figure 12.3) .

FIGURE 12.3.

Adding a command to the database connection.

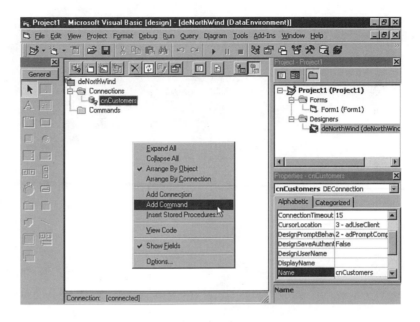

> **Note**
>
> When adding connections or commands, you must display the properties dialog—it will not be displayed automatically.

Because you can have more than one connection defined in the Data Environment, you must now select the connection that the command will use to access the database. You then have a choice between using a table, view, or stored procedure directly from the database or building your own SQL query. If you choose to use a database object, select the object type and then select the object name.

Building the SQL Command

You should use a table or predefined view from your database unless your application requires a more complex query. If you need a complex query, select SQL Statement on the General tab and hit the SQL Builder button, which will display the SQL Builder interface as shown in Figure 12.4.

12

FIGURE 12.4.

Building a SQL statement is easy using the SQL Builder interface.

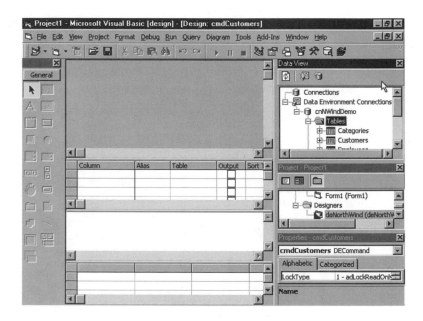

If you have ever used Microsoft Access or MSQuery, you already know how to use this SQL Builder. To add tables or views to the query, simply select the ones you want from the DataView window and drag them to the empty gray box as shown in Figure 12.5.

FIGURE 12.5.

Dragging tables into the query design area.

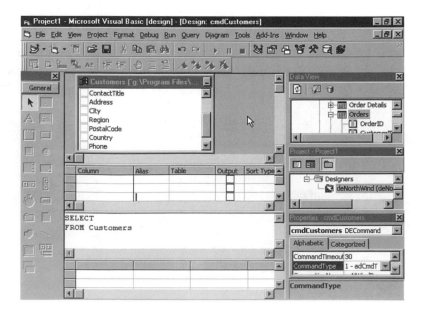

Table relationships will automatically be displayed if they already exist in the database. However, if the database you are using does not have relationship information, you need to define the relationships in the SQL Builder. As you drag tables into the work area, you should notice that a SQL statement is being built. However, there are no columns in the statement yet.

> **Note**
>
> If the database does not have relationships specified, you can add them to the query by dragging the column(s) from one table to the column(s) in the other table.

Now, to add columns, you can either click the check box for the required columns, drag each column you want to the Column area in the middle of the dialog, or use the drop-down list of all available columns, as shown in Figure 12.6.

FIGURE 12.6.

Adding columns to the query and updating the SQL statement.

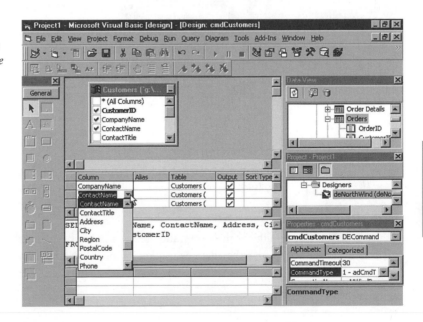

12

> **Note**
>
> Refer back to Table 12.1 for the complete list of columns to add to the primary command.

Using the SQLBuilder, you can also add any condition or sorting required for the query. After you have completed building the query, you should test it by choosing Query, Run from the Visual Basic menu. The query will be executed, with the results displayed at the bottom of the SQL Builder (see Figure 12.7).

FIGURE 12.7.

Running the completed query to test it and display the data.

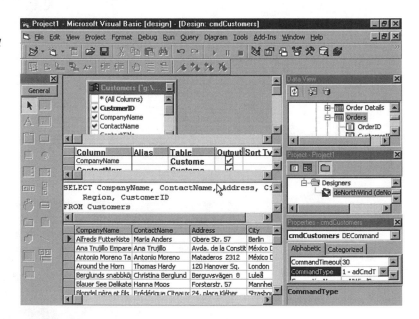

> **Note**
>
> This SQL Builder lets you design any type of SQL statement that you might need (such as Update, Insert, and Delete).

After you finish building the query and are satisfied with the results, close the builder and choose Yes to save the changes to the Command statement (see Figure 12.8).

FIGURE 12.8.

The completed SQL statement is now displayed in the Commands folder of the Data Environment.

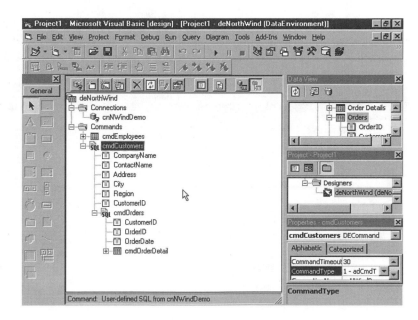

Child Commands

A Child command is nothing more than a SQL query that is dependent on a previous or Parent command to create a hierarchical query that can be used to display data in a Data Report or a Hierarchical FlexGrid control. Adding the command itself is the same as building the first query, which is as simple as right-clicking the first command and then selecting ADO Child Command from the pop-up menu. However, after the command is defined, you need to define the relationship it has with its Parent command. In the Child Command Properties dialog, go to the Relation tab. This is where you would specify the fields that relate the two commands together, creating a master/detail type relationship. Using the information in Table 12.1, define a Child command that contains the order detail for a customers order. Once you have done this, the Data Environment will show the Child command included within the Parent command as shown in Figure 12.9.

12

FIGURE 12.9.

*The Data Environment
graphically shows
which commands are
children of other com-
mands that have been
defined.*

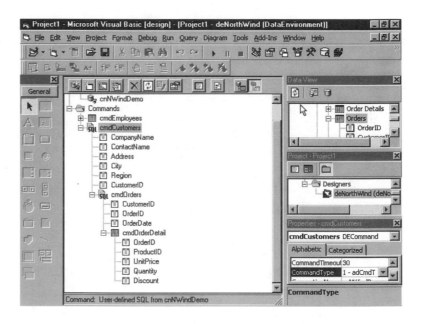

> **Caution**
>
> A Child command must contain at least one column that relates to a column in the Parent command.

To summarize the Data Environment Designer's capabilities, it provides you with database administration, enabling you to design complex queries for your application. More importantly, it provides a central repository for many commands and queries that will be used by your application. This allows you to define all the required queries in one place to simplify their maintenance.

Using the Data Environment to Access the Database

Once you add a Data Environment to your application, you can reference the connections and commands in the program code to access data in the database. At runtime, the Data Environment creates an ADO Command and Connection object for each command and connection that you defined in the Data Environment. If you mark the command object as a Recordset in the Advanced tab of the Command Properties dialog, an ADO Recordset object is also created. The ADO Command object is added as a method of the Data Environment runtime object, and the ADO Connection and Recordset objects are added as properties.

When accessing an ADO Recordset in the code, the Recordset object names are prefixed with *rs* to distinguish them from their respective Command objects. For example, a Command object named Order creates a Recordset object named rsOrder. Recordset objects are closed by default when the application is started and will be opened when the Recordset's corresponding Command method is executed. In addition, you can open a Recordset object directly by using the ADO Open method in the application code.

As a simple example of how to use the Data Environment to access data directly in your code, add a third command to the Data Environment as listed in Table 12.1. Then, add the controls listed in Table 12.2 to the default form, as shown in Figure 12.10.

TABLE 12.2. SAMPLE DATA ENVIRONMENT ACCESS FORM'S CONTROLS.

Control	Property	Value
TextBox	Name	txtEmployeeName
TextBox	Name	txtEmpId
Command	Name	cmdNext
	Caption	Next
Command	Name	cmdPrev
	Caption	Previous
Command	Name	cmdQuit
	Caption	Quit
Label	Name	lblID
	Caption	Employee ID
Label	Name	lblName
	Caption	Employee Name

FIGURE 12.10.

Creating a sample form to access the database by using the Data Environment connection.

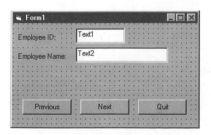

For this example, one of the textboxes will be bound to the new command, whereas the other one will be updated by using program code. In addition, the two Command buttons will allow you to move forward and backward in the query to display the data. To bind the first textbox to the customer name, the properties in Table 12.3 need to be set.

TABLE 12.3. SETTING THE PROPERTIES TO BIND A TEXTBOX TO THE DATA ENVIRONMENT.

Control	Property	Value
txtEmpID	DataSource	deNorthWind
	DataMember	cmdEmployees
	DataField	EmployeeID

The first and third properties should be familiar to you; however, the second one, DataMember, is new. When you select a Data Environment as a data source, the DataMember allows you to specify which command in the Data Environment list you want to use. Finally, add the following code to the default form:

```
Private Sub cmdNext_Click()
deNorthWind.rscmdEmployees.MoveNext
txtEmployeeName.Text = deNorthWind.rscmdEmployees.Fields!firstname & _
                " " & deNorthWind.rscmdEmployees.Fields!lastname
End Sub

Private Sub cmdPrev_Click()
deNorthWind.rscmdEmployees.MovePrevious
txtEmployeeName.Text = deNorthWind.rscmdEmployees.Fields!firstname & _
                " " & deNorthWind.rscmdEmployees.Fields!lastname
End Sub

Private Sub cmdQuit_Click()
End
End Sub

Private Sub Form_Load()
txtEmployeeName.Text = deNorthWind.rscmdEmployees.Fields!firstname & _
                " " & deNorthWind.rscmdEmployees.Fields!lastname
End Sub
```

Now run the application and try clicking the two command buttons to see how the Data Environment connection works the same as a Data control.

> **Caution**
>
> To keep this example short, you will not add any programmatic updates or EOF/BOF processing to this application. If you try to move past the End or Beginning of the query, you will receive an error message from the database.

As you can see, the Data Environment is every bit as good as the other data access methods and can be used wherever you would use a Data control or Data Access Object. Now that you have seen how you can use the Data Environment by itself in your application, continue to the next section to see how to create data reports for your application by using the Data Report Designer.

Adding Reports with the Data Report Designer

Visual Basic 6 comes with a new designer that gives you the ability to create database reports without having to use any third-party tools to design and distribute the reports with the application. The Data Report Designer gives you the ability to create a database report that can be used by your application. The Data Report Designer offers several features that give you an easy way to design the report and give the user the ability to print and/or export the report data. These features are as follows:

- Drag-and-Drop Field Placement—You can drag and drop the fields needed from the Data Environment into the Data Report Designer. Visual Basic will automatically create a text box control on the Data Report and set the DataMember and DataField properties of the field.

- Toolbox Controls—The Data Report Designer has its own set of controls that are automatically added to the toolbox on their own tab, named DataReport.

- Print Preview—The user can preview the report in its own form window before printing it.

- Print Reports—The report can be printed in code using the PrintReport method or by clicking the Print button on the toolbar when in Preview mode.

- File Export—The report can also be exported in either HTML, text, or Unicode formats using the ExportReport method.

Using the Data Report Designer requires that you define a database connection and then design the actual report. To see how to use the Data Report in your application, you will start by building a simple report and then adding more advanced features to it, such as formulas and totals. Finally, you will see how to display this report from within your application.

12

 Note If you have been using Visual Basic with Crystal Reports (see Day 13), don't panic. Crystal Reports is still included on the Visual Basic product CD-ROM. However, as the Data Report Designer is enhanced with more functionality, Crystal Reports will probably be removed altogether.

Creating the Report

The Data Report you create will use the Customers and Oruders commands that you previously defined in the Data Environment. These two commands combine to create a hierarchical query for the Data Report to use. When you have the commands defined and ready to use, you can start creating the report. Start by adding a Data Report Designer object to the project by right-clicking in the Project Explorer. Click Add and then Data Report, naming it drCustOrders. Now, set the DataSource property of the Data Report you added to deNorthWind, which is the name of the Data Environment you previously defined. Finally, set the Data Member to the Parent command, cmdCustomers.

The Data Environment Designer object must be opened to set the DataSource property to deNorthWind. In fact, it must be opened in order to use it during the Data Report design process. The best way to work with this is to tile the windows as shown in Figure 12.11.

The next step is to insert a Group section into the report. To insert the Group, right-click the Data Report Designer and click Insert Group Header/Footer (see Figure 12.11). Each Group section that you add to a report has a one-to-one relationship with a Command object in the Data Environment; in this case, the new Group will relate to the Customers command object.

FIGURE 12.11.

Inserting a Group header or footer into the Data Report.

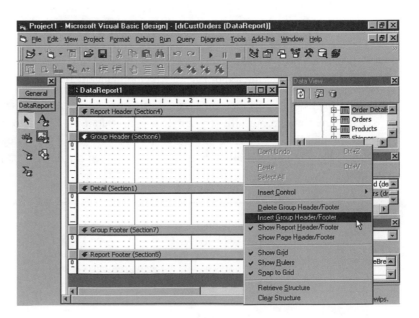

This first grouping will display the customer information, which should be displayed only once for each customer. You should also change the names of the Header and Footer sections to reflect the data that will be placed into them. To move data fields into the report, you would simply drag and drop them from the Data Environment onto the Group Header section as shown in Figure 12.12.

FIGURE 12.12.

Dragging the data columns into the report from the Data Environment.

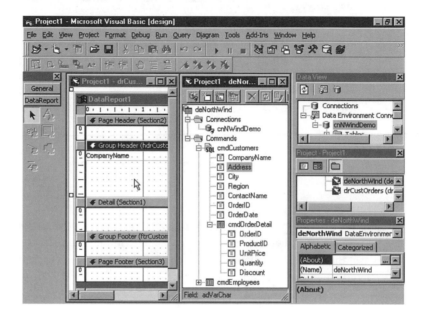

Note

The Group Header section can contain any field from the Parent command.

12

You should notice that for each field that you move into the report, a label containing the field's name is also added. For this report, you should delete the labels. Finish dragging the Customer fields into the header, as shown in Figure 12.13.

FIGURE 12.13.

The report showing the completed Header section with the customer information.

Now, you need to add the detail information to the report. The Details section represents the innermost "repeating" section of the report, and it corresponds to the lowest command object in the Data Environment parent/child hierarchy that you are using—in this case, the Orders command. When adding the detail to the report, you should resize the Details section to fit all the fields.

Note

It is important that the height of the Details section be as small as possible because the size of the section will be repeated for every unique detail row of data returned for the preceding group. Any extra space below or above the fields will result in unneeded space in the final report.

When you have added the Order ID and Date, your data report should resemble the one shown in Figure 12.14.

FIGURE 12.14.

The final data report displaying all orders for a customer.

Displaying the Form

What you have created is a fairly simple report. However, you still need to add code to the application in order to use or display it. To preview the report in your application requires that you add only a single line of code. Add a new Command button to the default form and then add the following line of code to its Click event routine:

```
drCustOrders.Show
```

When you run the application and click the Command button, the Data Report is displayed (see Figure 12.15) with the data being accessed from the database at that time.

FIGURE 12.15.

Previewing the report in the application.

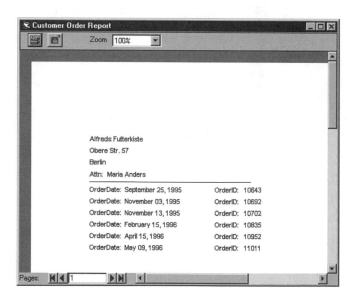

Note

If you are not using a header or footer, you can remove them from the report by simply collapsing it or reducing its height to zero.

After you have a simple data report, it is possible to extend it and make a more complex report by adding additional Child commands to the Data Environment and then inserting Group Headers and Footers for the new data as needed. Figure 12.16 shows the same report with the addition of a lower Child command to display the order detail within each order for each customer.

FIGURE 12.16.

Adding a Child command to display the order detail for each order.

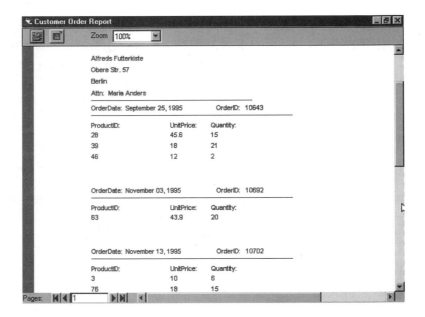

When adding another Child command, you would move the order detail to a new group header and then move the order detail to the Details section. As you can see, you can add as many Child commands and Header/Footer sections as you need to create a specific report.

Adding Functionality

The Data Report contains its own set of controls, among them is the Function control, which allows you to display data calculated at runtime by using a built-in function as the report is generated. An example is shown in Figure 12.17, where the Function control is used to display the total order value for each customer. Adding a function to a report requires you to draw a Function control in an appropriate Footer section of the Data Report. Then, you would set the `DataMember` and `DataField` properties to the field you want the function to be performed on.

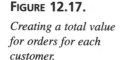

FIGURE 12.17.

Creating a total value for orders for each customer.

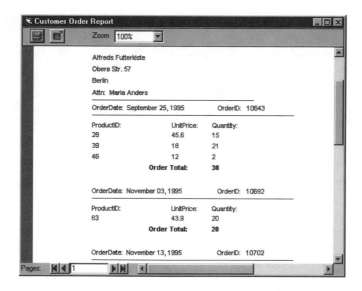

The last step is to set the FunctionType property for the function. The FunctionType property determines what operation will be performed on the data specified in the DataField. The default setting of the property is RptFuncSum, which sums the data. Other functions include Average, Minimum, and Maximum. To the Customer footer, add a function that sums the order totals, as shown in Figure 12.18, and then re-run the application to display the report with the order summary in it.

Another feature that can be used in a Data Report is the capability of creating *aggregate fields*—fields that summarize the data in a section. This may sound the same as the Function control because both are calculated as the report is generated. However, the Function control can be placed only in a Group Footer, while an Aggregate field can be placed anywhere in the Data Report. Another difference is how the two fields are created. Whereas the Function control is a feature of the Data Report itself, the Aggregate field is a feature of the Data Environment. This means that the Aggregate field can be used anywhere that the Data Environment can be used. To add an Aggregate field, you would create an Aggregate field in the Data Environment by using the Aggregate tab of the Data Environment Property dialog (see Figure 12.18).

12

FIGURE 12.18.

Adding an Aggregate field to a command in the Data Environment definition.

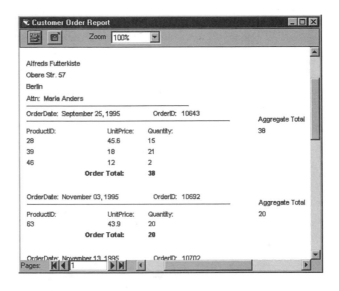

Then, you would drag the field from the Data Environment into the Data Report section in which it is needed. If your report needed a calculated field based on columns in the query, you would need to edit the SQL directly, as shown in Figure 12.19.

FIGURE 12.19.

Editing the SQL allows you to add to the query any type of calculation that is not supported directly in the Data Environment or Data Report.

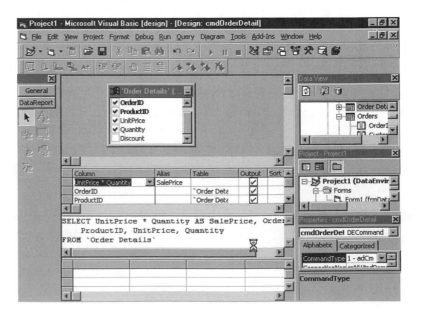

Printing and exporting the report is done by using one of two methods. The first method is done within the code and allows the user to print or export the report without previewing it—by using either the Data Reports PrintReport or ExportReport method. Using the PrintReport method is very simple; you simply add a single line of code that prints the report:

```
drCustOrders.PrintReport
```

However, the ExportReport method requires several parameters in order for it to know how to export the report and where to place it. The following is the syntax for the command:

```
object.ExportReport(index, filename, Overwrite, ShowDialog, Range,
PageFrom, PageTo)
```

Each of these parameters enables you to customize the export process. Table 12.4 lists each parameter and its description.

TABLE 12.4. THE PARAMETERS FOR THE ExportReport METHOD.

Parameter	Description
object	This references the Data Report you want to export.
index	This specifies the export format to use.
filename	This specifies the name of the file to export the report to.
overwrite	If True, the file will be overwritten.
showDialog	This specifies whether the Save As dialog should be displayed.
range	This sets an integer that determines whether all the pages in the report will be exported.
PageFrom	This is the starting page of the export.
PageTo	This is the ending page of the export.

12

An example of this command would be the following:

```
drCustOrders.ExportReport rptKeyHTML, "C:\temp\custord", True, False
```

The second way the user can print or export a report is by using the available buttons at the top of the Report Preview Form (see Figure 12.20). These provide the same functionality as the methods, only the user must first preview the report.

FIGURE **12.20.**

*Printing or exporting a
report directly from the
Report Preview Form.*

Print a Report

Export a Report

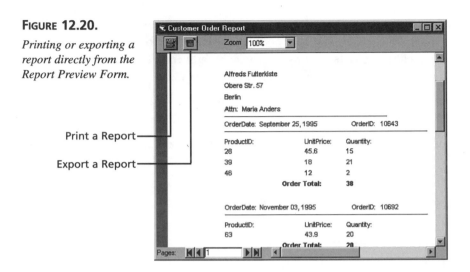

As you can see, the Data Report is a new and very powerful tool that you can add to
your application to allow the user to preview, print, and export information out of the
application.

Data Repeater

The Data Repeater functions as an advanced data-bound container control that uses a
custom data-bound control that you create. After you attach the custom control to the
Data Repeater, it will display several instances of the control, each in its own row, displaying a different record in the database, as shown in Figure 12.21.

FIGURE **12.21.**

*Displaying a formatted
data record in a grid
using the Data
Repeater control.*

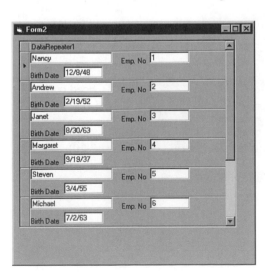

This control enables you to design complex, grid-like displays that are easier to use than a standard data grid. The reason is that when you create the custom control, you can use any available data-bound control that you need, including ComboBox, CheckBox, and OptionButton.

Building a Database OCX

Using the techniques you learned in the previous chapter, add a new ActiveX control project to the open project, naming it EmpControl. Then rename the user control ctlEmp. Now add the controls listed in Table 12.5 to the user control.

TABLE 12.5 CONTROLS FOR A DATABASE CUSTOM CONTROL.

Control	Property	Value	Mapped Value
TextBox	Name	txtEmpName	txtEmpNme
TextBox	Name	txtEmpID	txtEmpNo
TextBox	Name	txtBirthDate	txtEmpBDate
Label	Name	lblEmpNo	
	Caption	Emp. No	
Label	Name	lblBDate	
	Caption	Birth Date	

Because the custom control is going to be repeated for each record in the database, you should try to keep the height of the control as small as possible. The finished control should resemble the one shown in Figure 12.22.

Using the ActiveX Control Interface Wizard, map the Textbox and Checkbox properties to allow the application code to access them at design- and runtime, using the values in Table 12.5. Then, specify that each of the text boxes and the check box on the custom control are data-bound. To set the data-bound properties, open the Procedure Attributes dialog from the Tools menu. Then click the Advanced button at the bottom to display the full dialog form (see Figure 12.23).

12

FIGURE **12.22.**

*The new custom
control that will be
used in the Data
Repeater control.*

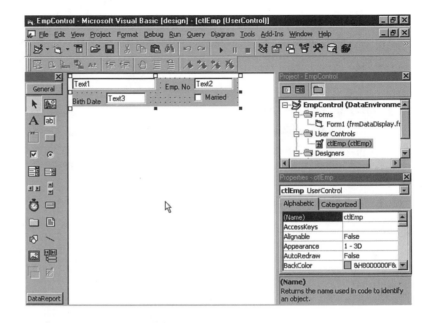

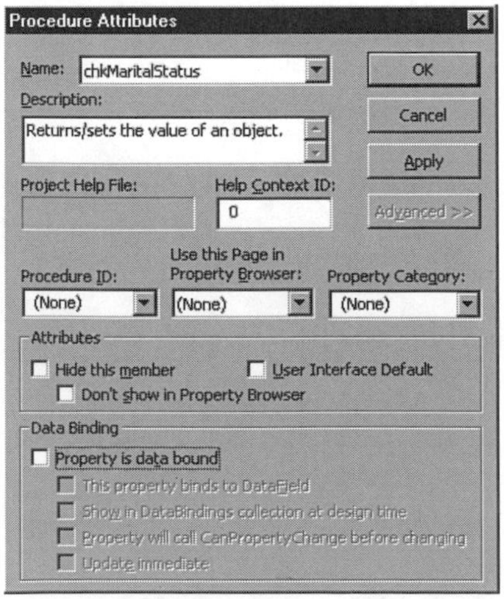

FIGURE **12.23.**

*Specifying the data-
bound properties
of the custom control.*

The Name box contains the property that you want to make data-bound and should contain txtEmpBDate as the first value. Click the Property Is Data Bound check box; then
click Show in DataBindings Collection at Design Time. These properties tell the custom
control that the property is data-bound and should be seen at designtime. Repeat these
steps for each control that is listed in the Name drop-down list. When you have finished,

click OK to close the dialog. Then, to finish the process, save the project and then compile the new control by using the File, Make EmpControl.OCX menu option. This registers the new control in Windows and makes it available to the Data Repeater control.

Repeating the OCX

After you finish building the custom control, close the project and reopen the Data Environment project from earlier in the chapter. Now, add a new form to the project, naming it `frmRepeater`. Then, add a Data Repeater control to the new form (see Figure 12.24), making it large enough to contain several rows of the control you want to repeat and naming it `drpEmployee`.

FIGURE 12.24.

Adding the Data Repeater to a form to display multiple records from a database.

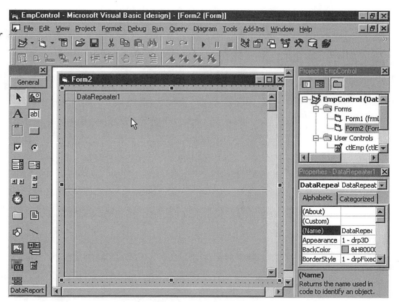

Note

Remember to add the Data Repeater control to the toolbox by using the Components dialog.

12

You could use an ADO Data Control on the form to access the database. However, for this example, you are going to use the Data Environment connection that you previously defined in this project. To connect the Data Repeater to the Data Environment, set the following properties for the Data Repeater:

| DataSource | deNorthWind |
| DataMember | cmdEmployee |

Then, click the RepeaterControlName property to display a drop-down list of all controls available on the computer. On the list, click EmpControl.ctlEmp. The selected control will be repeated in the Data Repeater control (see Figure 12.25).

FIGURE 12.25.

The Data Repeater will automatically show the custom control as many times as possible during both design- and runtime.

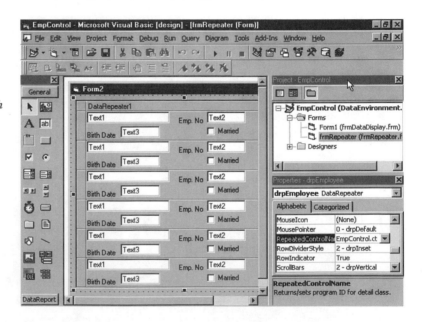

The last step in the process is to attach the custom controls properties to the record source. Open the Data Repeater Properties dialog, click the RepeaterBindings tab (see Figure 12.26) to set each of the text box and check box properties.

FIGURE 12.26.

Defining the data-bound properties of the custom repeated control.

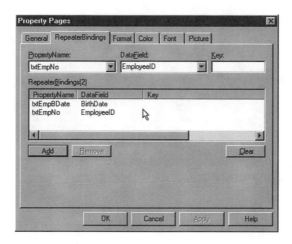

 Because the command you are using accesses a table in the database without using SQL, you can display only the FirstName or LastName field in a textbox not both as a full name. To do this, you must use a SQL query to combine the two fields together into a single field that can then be displayed in a single text box.

For each property of the custom control, add the property and data field to the RepeaterBindings collection as listed in Table 12.6. When you have finished, click OK to close the dialog. To display this form, add another Command button to the main form in the project and add a line of code to show the form frmRepeater when clicked.

TABLE 12.6. SETTING THE DATA-BINDINGS PROPERTIES FOR THE CONTROL.

PropertyName	DataField
txtEmpBDate	BirthDate
txtEmpNo	EmployeeID
txtEmpNme	FirstName

When you run the application and click the new Command button, you will see the employee data displayed in the Data Repeater control as shown in Figure 12.27.

12

FIGURE 12.27.

The final form displaying the database information repeated using the Data Repeater control.

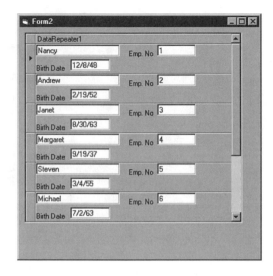

Although this example displays information from the database, you can also use the control in the Data Repeater to add or update the information displayed.

Summary

This chapter shows you some of the newest features that have been added to Visual Basic. The Data Environment Designer enables you to create a central place in the application project where you can define all the different database access commands and queries that you need for the application to perform properly. Included with this is the ability to use it in place of all the other data access methods, both the data controls and access objects. The SQL Builder that is used in the designer gives you some great tools for defining and testing the SQL queries you need.

When you have mastered the use of the Data Environment Designer, you can use it to create reports with the Data Report Designer. The Data Report Designer allows you to design reports that can be included within the application without the need of any reporting tools. Besides the standard print and preview options that all reporting tools provide, the Data Report Designer also enables the user to export the report into text or HTML formats.

Finally, using the new Data Repeater container control, you can design and create custom grid-like displays for your application that give the user a unique view of the data in the application. Together these three new features of Visual Basic give you more ways to display data to the user while providing an easier way for the user to interface with the application.

Q&A

Q **What is the difference between an ActiveX Data Control and the Data Environment Designer?**

A Although both provide the latest in database connectivity, the Data Environment Designer provides you with a tool set that helps you design and test the database commands you need for your application, whereas the ActiveX Data Control provides the database connection, with you supplying the SQL code.

Q **Can the Data Environment Designer be used in place of a data control or an access object?**

A Yes, the Data Environment Designer can be used to replace any of the three database access methods that are supported by Visual Basic.

Q **Can the Data Report be used to provide professional reports for an application?**

A The Data Report Designer is meant to supply the programmer with a way of supplying database reports from within the application.

Q **What is the difference between the Data Repeater control and a standard data-bound grid?**

A The data-bound grid displays data from the database in a single row–style layout. The Data Repeater control enables you to design a custom layout for the data to be displayed from the database.

Workshop

The Workshop provides quiz questions to help solidify your understanding of the material covered, as well as exercises to provide you with experience in using what you've learned. Try to understand the quiz and exercise answers before continuing on to the next day's lesson. Answers are provided in Appendix A, "Answers to Exercises."

12

Quiz

1. How many queries or commands can be defined and supported by the Data Environment Designer?

2. What is the benefit of using the Data Environment Designer?

3. How do you add a calculated field to a Data Environment command?

4. Can any data-bound control be used with the Data Repeater control?

5. Can the ActiveX Data Control be used with the Data Report Designer?

Exercise

Create a Data Report for the Address Book application and add the ability to run or show it to the toolbar control.

WEEK 2

DAY 13

Working with Crystal Reports

One of the most important features that you can add to an application is the capability to print the data in the application's database. In this day and age, users have come to expect professional-looking, easy-to-use reports from the applications that they use. Visual Basic 6 comes with a complete reporting tool from Seagate Software, called Crystal Reports. This product isn't a free trial or a limited feature copy; it is a full, single use copy of the Crystal Reports product. Because it comes with a runtime print engine, you can include it with any application that you develop. In the precious chapter, you learned how to create standard reports using the new Data Report Designer. However, if you need to create complex reports, you should use Crystal Reports.

Note

Crystal Reports is not included as part of the Visual Basic installation process. To install Crystal Reports, you must execute the install program CRYSTL32.EXE that can be found on the Visual Basic CD-ROM in the directory COMMON\TOOLS\VB\CRYSREPT.

In this chapter, you learn how to use Crystal Reports to design and create reports that you can add to your application. In addition, you will take a close look at how to incorporate these reports into your application by creating a report selection form. Finally, the CommonDialog Print dialog box will be added to the form, enabling the user to modify the Printer Setup options. At the end of the process the user will be able to select a report, choose some filter options, and then run the report.

What Is Crystal Reports?

Crystal Reports is a powerful program for creating custom reports, lists, and labels from the data in your application database. When Crystal Reports connects to the database, it reads in the values from the fields you selected and places them into a report, either as-is or as part of a formula that generates more complex values.

There is a wide range of built-in tools that can be used to manipulate data to fit the requirements of the report. These tools enable you to do the following:

- Create calculations
- Calculate subtotals and grand totals
- Calculate averages
- Count the total number of records in a query
- Test for the presence of specific values
- Filter database records

The data from your database can be placed and formatted exactly where you need it when designing the report. Using Crystal Reports, your reports can be as simple or as complex as your needs require. After you have designed a report for your application, you can use it within the application or as a template to create other similar reports. Although most database programs include their own report generators, they are usually too difficult for non-technical people to use, and they generally require a good understanding of how that database program works. Crystal Reports is both an end user reporting tool and a report development tool.

In keeping with the design concept of Visual Basic, Crystal Reports can connect to almost any database available. There are actually two methods of connecting to a database in Crystal Reports: the Data File and the SQL/ODBC. The first method is designed for the simpler, PC-based databases, such as dBASE and Microsoft Access. The other method is to use ODBC (Open Database Connectivity) to connect to any database that has an ODBC connection, such as Oracle, Sybase, and Microsoft SQL Server.

Note Although ODBC is generally used for more complex server databases, it can also be used to access Paradox and, if needed, Microsoft Access.

Taking a Look Around

When you start Crystal Reports, you see the plain application window shown in Figure 13.1. After you begin working with a report, Crystal Reports contains two separate tabbed windows that you will use to design and preview your reports. Both the Design and Preview windows are actually tab displays on a child window within the application. These windows have their own unique features and functions that enable you to work with your report design in slightly different ways.

FIGURE 13.1.

The Crystal Reports main form is used to access all the features when designing a report.

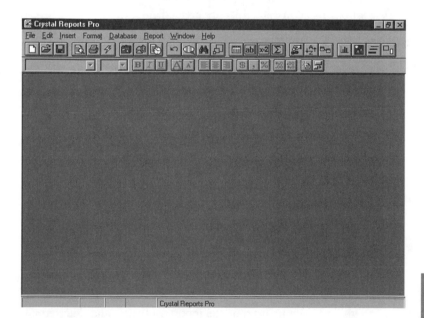

13

The Design Window

The Design window is separated into two sections that provide on-screen information that helps you design a report. The large white area of the Design window is the Edit box. This is where you design and format your report. The horizontal lines in the Edit box separate the report into several sections. As you add new data groups to your report, more sections appear in the Edit box. The gray area to the left of the Edit box displays additional information to assist you in placing the data and other objects on the report. The horizontal lines extend into the gray area, identifying which section is which.

The functions and features available in Crystal Reports are accessed via the toolbar at the top of the main window, the main menu, or by using the pop-up menus directly on the report. Crystal Reports also provides wizards to help you add the following objects to the report:

- Column Totals
- Selection Conditions
- Data Groups
- Formulas (calculated fields)
- Sort Criteria

After you select your database, the Design window is displayed to enable you to insert and format the data that you need in your report. When you start a new report, the five sections listed in Table 13.1 are created automatically in the Design window.

TABLE 13.1. DESIGN WINDOWS WORKING SECTION TYPES.

Section Name	Description
Title	Displays the report title, data, and any other information that needs to appear at the top of the report. Information displayed here is shown only once.
Page Header	Similar to the Title section; this information is displayed at the top of every page.
Details	Displays the detail information from the query.
Page Footer	Usually displays the page number and any other information that you want at the bottom of each page.
Summary	Displays information only on the last page of your report.

Reports are built by inserting data fields, formulas, and other information into one of the above sections in the Design window. You use the Insert menu to select or build the fields you want to insert on the report. Subtotals and other group values are added by selecting a field and then building the conditions to generate the new subtotal or group value (that is, change of state). These group sections are created as needed, and the values are placed in the appropriate section. If you want the value to be some other place on the report, you simply select it and drag it where you want it.

The Preview Window

You can see how your report will look when it is displayed or printed by switching to the Preview window. Whenever you select this tab, Crystal Reports retrieves the data from the database, performs any defined calculations, and then displays the report (see Figure 13.2), showing the results of all summaries, calculations, and filters. In effect, this is what the final report looks like.

FIGURE 13.2.

Using the Preview tab to see how the report will look when printed or displayed.

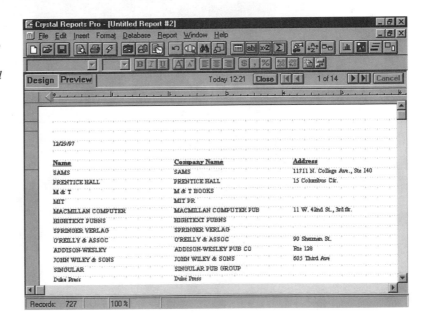

While in the Preview window, you can still modify the format of your report without having to return to the Design window. The Preview window does have a different look and feel than the Design window. Each field in the database can contain hundreds of values, depending on the number of records in the database. When you place a field in the report in the Design tab, a single field box is displayed that represents all those values. When you select this field, sizing handles appear and the border changes color as shown in Figure 13.3.

On the Preview tab, however, you are working with the actual data. Instead of a box with 9's or X's in it, the data values are displayed. When you select a field, every value from the selected field is selected. Despite the difference in look and feel, however, the process of building and modifying the report is the same in both windows.

Using the Crystal Reports Wizards

Crystal Reports contains several experts that you can use when creating reports. When you start a new report by choosing File, New, the Create New Report dialog is displayed as shown in Figure 13.4.

FIGURE 13.3.

Even though the yellow border color doesn't appear in this figure, you will see it onscreen when working with the report.

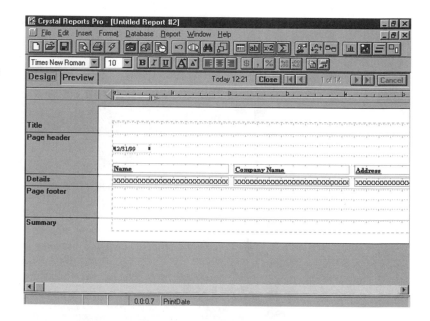

FIGURE 13.4.

The Standard Report Gallery dialog box shows each Report Expert from which you can choose.

The Report Gallery displays a series of buttons that represent the different types of report wizards that you can choose from. Each wizard takes you through the steps required to build that style report. If you want to build a new report based on an existing one, click the Another Report button. The program will make a duplicate of the original report that you can modify as needed to create the new report. If you want to build a report from scratch, click the Custom button. Several Report Type and Data Type buttons appear at the bottom of the Report Gallery as shown in Figure 13.5.

Adding Calculated Values

Crystal Reports uses formulas and functions to do the kind of number crunching and data manipulation that is needed for an advanced database report. The Edit Formula dialog box, shown in Figure 13.6, is used to create the calculated fields in the report.

FIGURE 13.5.

Custom Report buttons are displayed, enabling you to create a report from scratch.

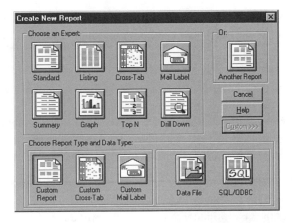

FIGURE 13.6.

Simple and complex calculations are built using the Formula Editor dialog box.

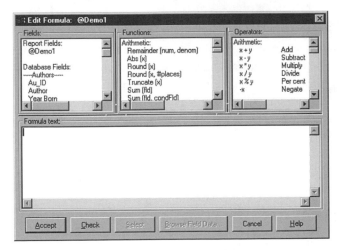

The Formula Editor enables you to work with both formulas and functions. A *formula* is a set of instructions that calculate the information you can't directly receive from the database. If a database record has two fields, Unit Price and Quantity Sold, but you need the total sales price, you would have to multiply the two fields to calculate the total sales price. This process is accomplished by using a formula that you place in the report.

This type of formula is a simple formula, because it uses the standard arithmetic operators. However, not all the calculations you need are simple formulas. There will be times when you require complex calculations or manipulations of the database fields. If you want to display the average monthly sales for the previous year, rounded to the nearest unit, you need a mathematical formula. The functions required to perform these activities involve a fair amount of data manipulation. Whereas some of this can be done using only Crystal Reports operators, many of them can't be done without the use of functions.

13

Functions are built-in procedures or subroutines that are used to evaluate, calculate, or transform data from the database. The Formula Editor is divided into four sub-windows that are used to create the calculation (see Figure 13.6). The Fields window lists all the database fields that are available to you, based on the tables you have previously selected. The Functions window lists all the functions that you can use to create a calculated field. The Operators window lists all the operators that you can use, and the largest window is the Formula Text window, where you build the actual calculation. You can choose to use the different windows to select items or if you know the correct syntax, type directly into the formula text area.

You can combine fields, functions, operators, and other calculations to create complex calculated fields. This enables you to create complex calculations in steps (small calculated fields) and then combine them together to form the finished calculation.

Filtering Your Data

When you select a field for the report, every row or query in the table will be printed. However, in many cases, you may only need specific rows of data from the database rather than including all the rows. For example, you may only a want New York customer data, or only invoices that fall within a particular range of dates. Crystal Reports includes four options, listed in Table 13.2, on the Report menu for filtering the data in your report.

TABLE 13.2. AVAILABLE OPTIONS FOR FILTERING DATA IN A REPORT.

Menu Option	Description
Select Records	Enables you to limit the number of records in your report based on a condition or conditions specified using a Selection Formula dialog box.
Edit Record Selection Formula	Uses the Formula Editor to enable you to modify the selection condition.
Select Groups	Enables you to limit your report to a specific group or groups, based on a condition or conditions specified using a Selection Formula dialog box.
Edit Group Selection Formula	Uses the Formula Editor to enable you to modify the selection condition.

Designing the Report

Of course, like anything else in the application process, designing reports requires some thought before actually creating them. For each report that you are creating, you should answer the following questions:

- What is the function of the report?
- What data will be included on the report?
- Does it need filter capabilities?
- What will be the layout of the report?

If you have the answers to these questions, your reports will perform well. Before starting Crystal Reports, you should sketch out what the report will look like and also list the fields needed for the report. The report that you design in this section will use the address book database discussed earlier in the week. An address book application usually needs several types of reports, including mailing label, phone lists, and a complete address book report.

Although you will learn enough about Crystal Reports to create most reports you need, this chapter is really meant to show you how to integrate Crystal Reports into an application while providing the user with several advanced features. The report that we will be creating is the address/phone list report, which will contain the following information:

- Name
- Address
- City
- State
- ZIP
- Home Phone
- Office Phone, if any

Although this is a fairly simple report, it will enable you to learn the necessary skills to create any type of report. After you have listed the fields, the next step is to sketch the layout of the report.

After you are satisfied with the layout, the next step is to start Crystal Reports. There are two ways to start it, either from the Visual Basic menu or the Windows 95 Start menu. If you are primarily working on reports, you might consider shutting Visual Basic until you need it, and run Crystal Reports from the Start menu. Once started, you are placed in the main window as shown earlier in Figure 13.1.

13

Creating the Report

To start the process, choose File, New from the menu to open the New Report dialog box. The standard report format is the one we will use for the example report; however, Crystal Reports can assist in creating many different styles of reports from this dialog box:

- **Standard**—Creates a standard report with rows and columns. It often has summary information at the bottom of the columns.

- **Listing**— Creates a simple row and column listing of the information in a record-set.

- **Cross-Tab**— Inverts the order of a standard columnar report. It is often used to obtain a quick summary view of a more complex set of data.

- **Mail Label**— Creates items such as mailing labels or name tags from the information in your database.

- **Summary**—Presents summary information about the data, such as total and average sales, or the number of attendees.

- **Graph**—This report shows the information in a graphical form.

- **Top N**—This report shows only a specified number of the top records in the recordset. For example, this report can be used to show the top five salespeople in the company.

- **Drill Down**—Shows the supporting information, or detail information, for each record.

After selecting the standard report option and clicking OK, the related Report Wizard is automatically started. For the style selected, there are seven steps (see Figure 13.7) involved in creating the initial report.

The logical starting point of any report is to select the database tables required for the report. The first tab will display the data access choices and any tables already included in the report. There are two choices if using the version that comes with Visual Basic, or three choices if you have purchased the professional edition of the product.

For the phone list report, select the Data File button to display the Choose Database File dialog box shown in Figure 13.8.

If you have created the Address Book database, you can select it from this dialog box, or with some minor changes to the report, you can use the Northwind database (NWIND.MDB) that is included with Visual Basic. After you have selected the database, all the tables and queries contained in the database are added to the report's table list. If you can see the wizard in the background, you should see the tables and queries listed.

Click the Done button to return to the Report Wizard. At this point, the second tab in the wizard is displayed.

FIGURE 13.7.

The Report Expert guides you through the report creation process.

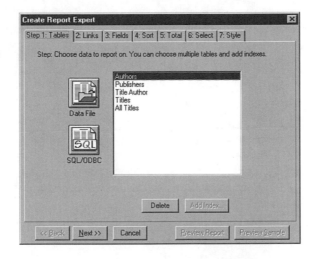

FIGURE 13.8.

Using the Choose Database File dialog box to locate and select the required database file for the report.

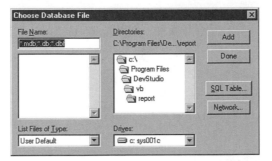

Note

If you are using an ODBC/SQL database, you will be shown a list of the tables and queries to select from. Only the tables/queries that you select will be included in the report.

13

The second tab of the Report wizard enables you to modify the join information that is already defined in the database. Because you have previously set the join information for the address book database, you will see the joins displayed as shown in Figure 13.9. When this tab is first displayed, a message is displayed, enabling you to add more tables if needed.

FIGURE 13.9.

*Defining or modifying
the join information
for a report.*

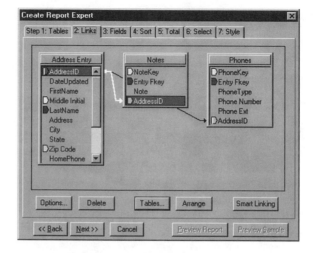

If the joins are correct, you can click the Next button to continue to the third tab. This
tab (see Figure 13.10) enables you to select the fields from each of the tables that you
need in the report.

FIGURE 13.10.

*Selecting the data
fields from the includ-
ed tables and queries.*

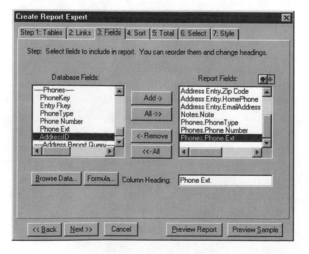

You add the fields to the report data list by double-clicking each field in the Database
Fields list or by highlighting the fields that you want and clicking the Add button. In
addition, you can set the order of the fields in the report. For each field selected, you can
also enter a custom column heading in the text box below the list. Select the fields listed
in Table 13.3 and add them to the fields list.

TABLE 13.3. REQUIRED FIELDS FOR THE ADDRESS/PHONE LIST REPORT.

Table	Field
Address Entry	First Name
	Last Name
	Address
	City
	State
	Zip
	Home Phone
	EmailAddress
Notes	Note
Phones	Phone Type
	Phone Number
	Phone Ext

You will need to set the joins for the Notes and Phones table to outer joins using the Options dialog box on the Links tab, as shown in Figure 13.11.

FIGURE 13.11.

Setting outer joins for the report query.

13

During the design of a report, you will sometimes require some manipulation of the fields that you have selected, either by performing some mathematical process or string process. Even though you will need to manipulate some of the fields, you will see how to do that a little later in this section.

After you have selected all the fields for the report, you could either preview the report or continue refining it by adding other options. By clicking the Next button, the Sort tab is displayed as shown in Figure 13.12.

FIGURE **13.12.**

Choosing the fields and sorting process using the Sort tab in the wizard.

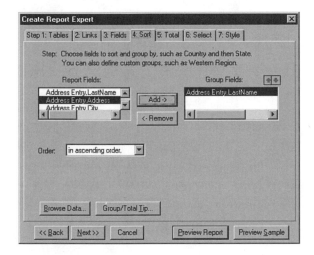

The Sort tab enables you to select the fields you want to sort, and in what order or direction to sort them. In this report, the only sort needed would be on the Last Name field. After you set the sort options, click the Next button three times to bypass the Totals and Select tabs that are not used for this example. As their names imply, the Totals tab lets you define summary fields for the report while the Select tab lets you set filter conditions for the report.

 Note   For a better learning experience, both of these options will be added to the report later.

The final tab displayed is the Style tab (see Figure 13.13), which enables you to choose from a list of default styles for your report. You can also enter a Title for your report on this tab.

Choose the Standard style and enter Personal Address Book as the title of the report. To complete the creation process, click the Finish button. You should now be in the design windows with the report layout displayed as shown in Figure 13.14.

FIGURE 13.13.

Setting the style of the report by selecting it from a list.

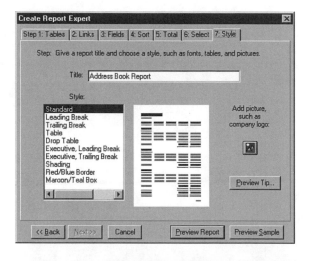

FIGURE 13.14.

The initial report shown in the Design window with the default layout.

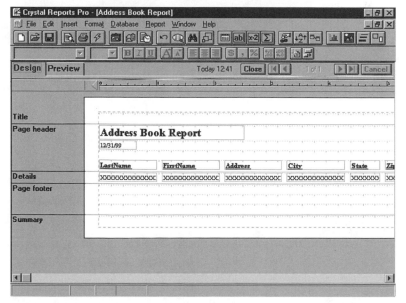

Enhancing the Output

Now that you have create the basic report, you are ready to add a few extra fields to it and enhance the format of it as well. To do this:

First, switch to the Preview tab to display the initial report, which is shown in Figure 13.15.

FIGURE 13.15.

Display the initial report layout in the Preview window with data.

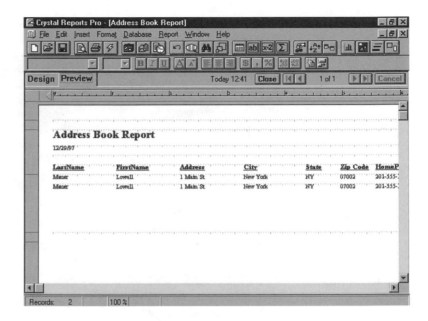

As you can see, the report still needs a little work to make it look professional. Some fields need to be formatted and the following items need to be added to the report:

- A Page Header
- A System Date
- Page numbering

These fields can be added to the report by using the Special Fields option on the Insert menu. When you select one of these fields, you then draw a box in the location that you want the field to be placed.

The most important change that we will make to the report is to create a calculated field that will take the city, state, and zip fields and put them together while removing all extra blanks. This will convert a line like:

```
New York            NY   11236
```

to a more compact, space-saving version:

```
New York, NY 11236
```

You should also notice the addition of a comma after the city name. To add a new calculated field, choose Insert, Formula from the menu or click the Insert Formula button on the toolbar. The Insert Formula dialog box will be displayed, listing any existing formulas in the report (see Figure 13.16).

Enter CityStZip as the formula name and click OK. This displays the Edit Formula dialog box, as shown in Figure 13.17, with the name of the formula in the title bar of the dialog box.

FIGURE 13.16.

Adding a new formula or choosing an existing one from the Insert Formula dialog box.

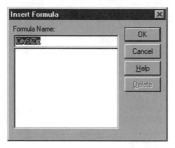

Now follow these steps create the new calculated field:

1. In the Functions list box, scroll down the list until you find the TrimRight(x) function in the Strings section and double-click it to add it to the Formula edit area.

FIGURE 13.17.

Creating a new formula with the Edit Formula dialog box.

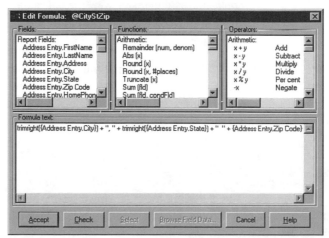

2. Find the City field in the Fields list box. In the Formula edit area, you should notice that the cursor is between the open and close parenthesis. This enables you to double-click the City field to have it placed in the function.

3. After you have added the City field, move the cursor to the end of the line and enter a plus sign (+), which can be found in the Operators list box in the Strings section, or you can just type it in. This performs a string concatenation using the trimmed City field and the next field that you will add.

13

4. At this position, you will be adding a string constant that contains a comma and a blank (,). You will need to type this in yourself. Then add another + after the string.

5. Find the State field in the Fields list box and double-click it to add it to the formula. This is assuming that the State field is two characters; if you are not sure, you should also trim the field.

6. Now, you will be adding another string constant that contains two blanks ( ), which will position the Zip field properly. You will need to type this in yourself. Remember to add a + before and after the string.

7. Finally, add the Zip field to the formula, and click the Check button to verify that there are no errors in the formula. The formula should be the same as this:

```
TrimRight ({Entry.City}) + ", "  + { Entry.State} + "  " + {
Entry.Zip}
```

If there are no errors, click the Accept button to place the new field in your report.

Note

Every formula is create the same way. The only difference is the complexity of the formula.

Depending on what type of field you are formatting, you can either right-click the field to see the pop-up menu, or if the field is a string, you need to create a calculated field that adds the required information. If the phone number fields were strings, you would need to create a formula that resembles this one:

```
"(" + {Publishers.Telephone}[1 to 3] + ") " + {Publishers.Telephone}[4 to 6]
 + "-" + {Publishers.Telephone}[7 to 10]
```

If the phone number is defined as a numeric field, you would first have to convert it to a string and then create the preceding formula. However, if you use a string, you could force the user to enter the formatted string by using the MaskedEditBox control and include the literal characters with the text.

After you have made all the changes discussed, the report should resemble the one shown in Figure 13.18.

The last thing you must do is save the report so you can access it from your Visual Basic application.

FIGURE 13.18.

The Address/Phone list report with the calculated fields added.

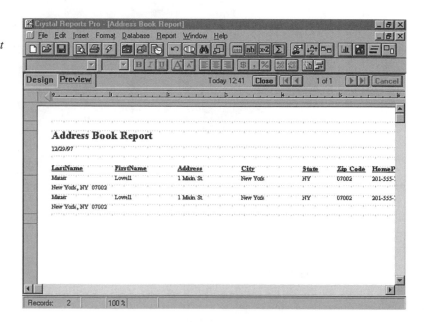

Adding the Crystal Reports Control to Your Application

Although you can run the reports you create from within Crystal Reports, you'll probably want to access them from within your Visual Basic program. Fortunately, Visual Basic and Crystal Reports has made it very easy to include the reports in a Visual Basic application. You actually have a choice of using the supplied Crystal Reports custom control, or the Crystal Reports APIs. I personally choose the custom control for its ease of use. The Crystal Reports control provides a link between the Crystal Reports engine and the reports you create with the report designer.

The first step in accessing Crystal Reports is to add the control to your project. If Visual Basic isn't started, start it and create a new project. If the Crystal Reports control (see Figure 13.19) isn't in your toolbox, add it using the Components dialog box.

13

Note

If you performed a custom setup of Visual Basic, you may have left Crystal Reports out of the initial installation. You need to rerun the Visual Basic setup program and install the Crystal Reports components.

FIGURE 13.19.

The Crystal Reports
control icon in the
Visual Basic toolbox.

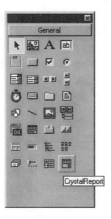

Using the Crystal Control

After the Crystal Reports control is available in your toolbox, you can use it in your program. To gain access to the control, simply select it from the toolbox and place it on the form from where you will access the reports. When that is done, you can set the control's properties to access the report you created with the report designer.

Note Because the Crystal Reports control isn't visible at runtime, it appears only as an icon on your form.

The key property that you need to specify is the ReportFileName property . This specifies the actual report that you want to run from your program. Many of the Crystal Reports properties can be modified by using the Crystal Reports Property Pages shown in Figure 13.20. From this page, you can specify the name of the report and whether the report should go to the printer, a preview window, a file, or to a message through the MAPI interface.

On the General tab of the Property Pages, either type the name of the report into the field for the ReportFileName property, or select the report from the File dialog box. Selecting the ReportFileName is the only required property that you need to specify. The other tabs on the properties dialog box, shown in the following list, enable you to customize the report to specific requirements:

Print Window	Sets the properties of the Print display window
Printer	Sets the number of copies to print

Print to File	Sets the filename and file type when printing a report to the printer
Database	Enables you to enter the UserId and connection information for a database
Selection	Enables entry of the `SelectionFormula` and `GroupSelectionFormula`
Data-Bound Report	Sets Heading for a database report

FIGURE 13.20.

Setting the report name and destination on the controls Property Pages.

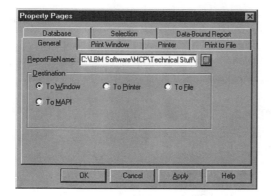

If there is nothing else you want to have the report do, you can run the report and display it by executing a single line of code in your application. Although only the `ReportFileName` is required for a report, you may want to use several optional properties with the report. The first of these properties is the `SelectionFormula` property. This property enables you to limit the number of records that will be included in the report. The `SelectionFormula` property is similar to the `Where` clause of an SQL statement, but it uses its own particular format to enter the information. To specify the `SelectionFormula`, you must enclose the name of any recordset/field combination used in the formula in curly brackets. The final result is an expression that looks like the following:

```
{AddressBook.State}="NY"
```

Of course, you can also use the `AND` or `OR` operators to create multiple expressions.

13

Caution

> If you have entered a `SelectionFormula` when designing your report, any formulas you enter in the `SelectionFormula` property of the Crystal Reports control are added as additional filters.

Another useful parameter is the `CopiesToPrinter` property. This property enables you to print multiple copies of your report easily at one time.

Modifying Report Properties

After the Crystal Reports control has been added to the form and you have set its properties, you are ready to start printing, right? Well, not quite. You still have to tell Crystal Reports when to print the report. You do this by setting the Action property of the Crystal Reports control to 1. This tells the control to execute the Crystal Reports processing engine to run the specified report.

> For easy understanding in your code, you should define a constant to use in place of the number one when requesting Crystal Reports to start.

To see how this works, add a command button to the new form and place the following line of code in its `Click` routine:

```
crReport.Action = crRunReport   'This is a constant for the value 1
```

Now execute the application and click the Command button to run the report. The report you entered in the Properties page is executed and displayed in its own window, as shown in Figure 13.21.

FIGURE 13.21.

Displaying the report on the screen from a Visual Basic application.

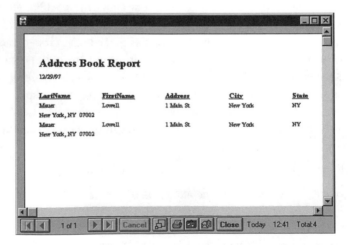

This was just a simple example of displaying a report from an application. There are many more options, properties, and methods that you can use to customize how the report looks when it is displayed, and what data will be retrieved from the database.

What you have just completed is the quickest way of executing a report from Crystal Reports. However, in most applications there is usually more than one report that the users will need to display or print, so you will need to change the Crystal Reports control's properties at runtime. Otherwise, you would need to place a separate report control for each report you supply to the user. All the major properties of the Crystal Reports control, such as ReportFileName and SelectionFormula, are available at runtime. The following example code sets up the Crystal Reports control for a new report and specifies a selection criteria based on user input:

```
crReport.ReportFileName = "AddrList.rpt"
crReport.SelectionFormula = "{EntryList.State}=" & txtStateCd
crReport.action = crRunReport  'This is a constant for the value 1
```

The other property that you may need to set at runtime is the DataFiles property. This property is not available at designtime. It specifies the name of the database file that is used by the report. Unless the user installs your application in exactly the same directory that you have on your computer, you will need to tell the Crystal Reports control the location of the database file on the users PC.

The DataFiles property is actually an array with the first element number of zero. If you're using more than one database in your report, you need to set the value of each DataFiles array element for each database. For most of your reports, however, you will be using only a single database. The following line of code shows you how to set the value of the DataFiles property for the database. This line assumes that the database file is in the same folder as your application:

```
crReport.DataFiles(0) = App.Path & "\AddressBook.mdb"
```

Creating a User Interface

In complex Visual Basic applications, you really need to give the user a good interface to select and modify the options when running reports. In an application that I developed, a Visual Basic form was used with several controls in conjunction with an input table to create the report manager shown in Figure 13.22.

This particular report manager displays report descriptions in a TreeView control with headings for each group of reports that is added to the list. It also makes use of the Common Dialog control to display the Printer dialog box. Using a TreeView control requires copious amounts of code to populate and control it. Instead you could create a simpler version of this interface, replacing the TreeView control with a ListBox control, as shown in Figure 13.23.

13

FIGURE 13.22.

*The complete report
manager from a Visual
Basic application.*

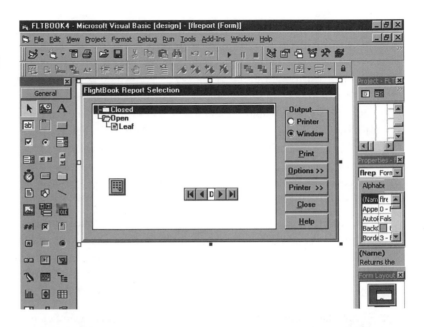

FIGURE 13.23.

*Creating another type
of report manager
using the ListBox con-
trol.*

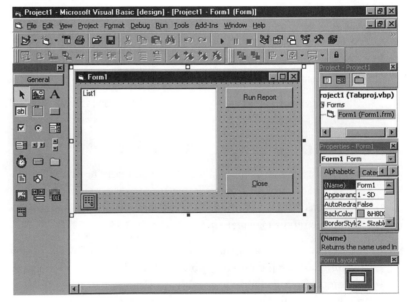

For the purposes of this chapter, you will create a report manager that will give the user
the following capabilities:

- List of reports from which to select
- Choose from display and Print
- Printer options

When you have completed this example, you will be able to include it in any application for which you need a report manager. To begin this process, start a new project and name it PRTMGR; then name the form in it frmPrintMgr. Table 13.4 lists the controls and the properties you need to set. Place them on the form as shown in Figure 13.24.

TABLE 13.4. THE REPORT MANAGER CONTROLS AND PROPERTY SETTINGS.

Control	Property	Value
ListBox	Name	lstReportName
	Multiselect	0-None
Command Button	Name	cmdCancel
	Caption	Cancel
Command Button	Name	cmdReport
	Caption	Display
Frame	Name	fraWindow
	Caption	Reports
Option Button	Name	optDisplay
	Caption	Display
	Item	0
	Value	True
Option Button	Name	optDisplay
	Caption	Print
	Item	1
	Value	False
Command Button	Name	cmdPrtSetup
	Caption	Printer
	Visible	False
Crystal Reports	Name	rptAddress
Common Dialog	Name	dlgReports

13

After you've added the controls to the form, you are ready to add the necessary code. The first section of code that should always be added is the declaration section for the variables that will be used in the code. Add the code in Listing 13.1 to the frmAddress form.

FIGURE 13.24.

*The report manager
with the controls in
design mode.*

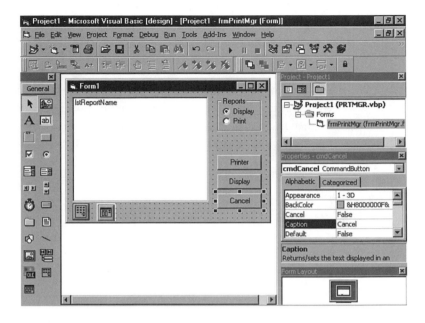

LISTING 13.1. RPTMGR01.TXT—THE DECLARATION CODE FOR THE REPORT MANAGER.

```
1: Public FilterString As String
2: Public SQLString As String
3: Public DBName As String
4: Dim I As Integer
5: Dim dbquery As Recordset
6: Dim dbTable As Database
7: Dim Total_Reports As Integer
8: Dim Report_Names() As String
```

The next section of code that has to be added is the code that initializes the form when it
is loaded. During the load routine of the report manager, you will read the report information from the database table and initialize the list box. Listing 13.2 shows the
Form_Load routine for this example.

LISTING 13.2. RPTMGR02.TXT—THE FORM_LOAD ROUTINE FROM THE REPORT MANAGER INITIALIZES
THE LIST BOX.

```
1: Private Sub Form_Load()
2: optDisplay(0).Value = True
3: cmdReport.Caption = "Display"
4: rptAddress.WindowTitle = "Demo Reporting"
5: rptAddress.WindowMinButton = False
6: cmdPrtSetup.Visible = False
```

```
 7:
 8:     Set dbTable = OpenDatabase(App.Path & "\AddressBook.mdb")
 9: 'Open table
10:     Set dbquery = dbTable.OpenRecordset("select * from reports order
by_
11: [ReportFileName]", dbOpenDynaset)
12:     dbquery.MoveLast
13:     Total_Reports = dbquery.RecordCount
14:     ReDim Report_Names(Total_Reports)
15:     dbquery.MoveFirst
16: 'Loop until there are no more reports to add
17:     For I = 1 To Total_Reports
18:         'Set the Report Names
19:         lstReportName.AddItem dbquery.Fields(1)
20:         Report_Names(lstReportName.NewIndex) = dbquery.Fields(0)
21:         dbquery.MoveNext
22:     Next I
23:     dbquery.Close
24:     dbTable.Close
25: End Sub
```

This section of code sets the report display option to Display and also sets the printer options visible property to False. When the user changes the display type by using the option buttons, the caption of the cmdReport button is changed from Display to Print. The code shown in Listing 13.3 is used to perform this action when the user clicks either of the option buttons.

LISTING 13.3. RPTMGR03.TXT—THE CLICK ROUTINE FOR THE OPTION BUTTONS ON THE FORM.

```
1: Private Sub optDisplay_Click(Index As Integer)
2:     If Index = 0 Then
3:         cmdReport.Caption = "Display"
4:         cmdPrtSetup.Visible = False
5:     Else
6:         cmdReport.Caption = "Print"
7:         cmdPrtSetup.Visible = True
8:     End If
9: End Sub
```

13

It also sets the WindowMinButton property of the Crystal Reports control to false, so that the user cannot minimize the report display. In addition, the ListItem property of the list box is used to hold the report's filename for later use. In the Load routine, you see a loop that initializes the ListBox control. The data that is placed in the list box is read from a database table that contains the following information:

Report Description	Description that the user sees in the list box.
Report File Name	If this record is for an actual report, than the filename goes here. If it isn't a report, then put spaces here.

This will help you dynamically build the list box data whenever the application is started. The next order of business is to finish the command button code. Listing 13.4 displays the code for the Close and Printer Setup buttons. The Close button is self-explanatory. However, the Printer Setup button calls the Common Dialog control to display the Printer Setup common dialog box for the user to modify. You can see from the code that the only property that can be changed is the number of copies to print. The Crystal Reports property CopiesToPrint is set to this value.

LISTING 13.4. RPTMGR04.TXT—ADDING THE CLOSE AND THE SETUP CODE FOR THE REPORT MANAGER.

```
1: Private Sub cmdPrtSetup_Click()
2:     DlgReports.ShowPrinter
3:     rptAddress.CopiesToPrinter = DlgReports.Copies
4: End Sub
5:
6: Private Sub cmdCancel_Click()
7:     Unload Me
8: End Sub
```

Of course, you can always add code to enable the user to change printers or set other options for the printing of the report.

Now, let's add the code for the Continue button next, so that you can try out the application. This routine first checks to see if a report is selected before continuing; if no report is selected, an error message is displayed to the user. If a report is selected, it checks to see if the report exists; it obtains the report name from the list box and sets the Crystal Reports properties and finally runs the report. Add the code in Listing 13.5 and try executing the application, selecting a report and displaying it.

LISTING 13.5. RPTMGR05.TXT—THE MAIN ROUTINE IN THE REPORT MANAGER THAT PRINTS THE REPORT.

```
1: Private Sub cmdReport_Click()
2:     If lstReportName.ListIndex = -1 Then
3:         MsgBox "You must first select a Report.", vbCritical, _
```

```
     App.Title
 4:          Exit Sub
 5:       End If
 6:       If Dir(App.Path & "\" & Report_Names(lstReportName.ListIndex) & ".rpt")_
 7: = "" Then
 8:          MsgBox "Report:" & Report_Names(lstReportName.ListIndex) &_
 9: "cannot be found!, vbCritical, App.Title"
10:          Exit Sub
11:       End If
12:       rptAddress.SelectionFormula = ""
13:       rptAddress.ReportFileName = App.Path & "\" &_
14: Report_Names(lstReportName.ListIndex) & ".rpt"
15:       rptAddress.WindowTitle = "Address Book Reporting"
16:       rptAddress.WindowMinButton = False
17:       If optDisplay(0).Value Then
18:          rptAddress.Destination = 0
19:       Else
20:          rptAddress.Destination = 1
21:       End If
22:       rptAddress.Action = 1
23: End Sub
```

Caution Remember to select only the report(s) that you have already created.

Now, try running the application, selecting a report, and then clicking the Display command button. You now have a working report manager to use in any application that you need to include it in.

Summary

In this chapter, you saw how to use Crystal Reports to create professional looking reports with very little effort. In addition, you added the Crystal Reports Custom Control to a Visual Basic application and used it to run, and then display, a report in a window. Finally, you saw how to build a Report manager to enable the user to select a report to run and then print or display it. What you have done in this chapter has only scratched the surface of the Crystal Reports product and how you can use it in your application. However, it has given you a solid foundation to build on when adding reporting to your application.

13

Q&A

Q What is Crystal Reports?

A Crystal Reports is a third-party application that is included with Visual Basic to enable a developer to add professional reporting directly into her applications.

Q How do I add Crystal Reports to my application?

A Crystal Reports provides a custom control that when placed on an application form, gives complete access to the properties, events, and methods of the reporting engine.

Q Can I use it in any application that I create?

A Yes, Crystal Reports can be included in any application without any problems or licensing issues.

Workshop

The Workshop provides quiz questions to help solidify your understanding of the material covered, as well as exercises to provide you with experience in using what you've learned. Try to understand the quiz and exercise answers before continuing on to the next day's lesson. Answers are provided in Appendix A, "Answers to Exercises."

Quiz

1. What databases can Crystal Reports access?
2. Do I need to know SQL to build reports using this tool?

Exercise

Take the reporting application that you created in this chapter and add it to the Address Book application and project. You will need to make some minor changes to the code when you do this.

DAY 14

Internet Programming

Internet programming has become one of the hottest skills in computer programming. With the wide acceptance of the Internet and the World Wide Web, almost every company or group and many individuals have their own Web sites. What Visual Basic enables you to do is connect to the Internet from within your application.

What's now called *Web programming* has many different aspects, and many books have been written on how to create Web-based applications or HTML pages. However, the tools included with Visual Basic 6 not only allow you to connect to the Web, they also assist you in creating Web-based applications that use a combination of Dynamic HTML and Visual Basic code that resides on the user's computer.

Today, you'll see how to use the Internet Browser control in your application and how to transfer files. You'll also get a glimpse of what HTML is all about and how to code a simple HTML page that you can view with your own application. And you'll see how to use your Visual Basic programming skills when creating Web pages by using VBScript, a subset of the full Visual Basic programming language. In addition, you will see how to use the new Dynamic HTML or DHTML to create a Web application that can dynamically interact with the user without relying on scripts or server-side processing.

Adding the Internet Controls

Among the many tools, controls, and features that Visual Basic comes with, the most intriguing are the two Internet controls: Browser and File Transfer. These controls enable you to give your application's users the ability to access the Internet from within the application.

Adding either control to your application from scratch isn't an easy proposition; however, for the Browser control, you can use the Application Wizard to include it in your application. The File Transfer control, on the other hand, requires you to understand the concepts of transferring data over the Internet and to code the process yourself.

Note

To use either control, users of your application must already have an Internet service provider (ISP). They also must have Internet Explorer 3.0, or later, installed on their PC because the controls use IE to interact with the Internet. Of course, you need to have the same tools available on your PC to develop an application that includes a Web browser or file-transfer function.

Caution

To test or use the Internet tools, you need to be either connected to the Internet or a local network with an intranet, or have Personal Web Server running on your PC while you're developing those functions.

In the following section, you'll add an Internet browser to the Address Book application that will use the Microsoft Web site as its default home page. You will also see how to let users download files from the Web. The browser itself supports file downloads specified in an HTML page, but the File Transfer control lets you code a direct download of a file without having the browser open.

Tip

The best way to develop an application that uses the Internet tools is by using the Windows 95 Personal Web Server that runs on your PC and is available as a free download from the Microsoft Products Web site (http://www.microsoft.com/products).

Internet Browser

The Internet Browser control enables you to attach to the Internet by using your PC's default Internet connection and to browse the World Wide Web. If you look at an Internet browser application such as Internet Explorer, however, you will see that it contains more than just the browser itself (see Figure 14.1).

FIGURE 14.1.

Browsing the Internet requires many more controls than the browser itself.

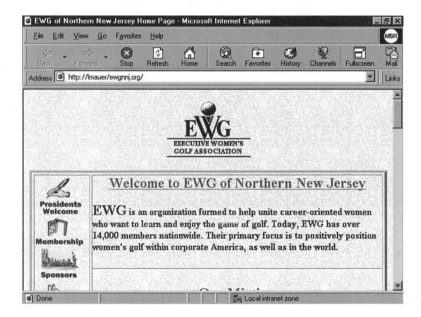

The Browser control is nothing more than a frame used to view Web pages. Although it contains the methods, properties, and events needed to perform all the required browser functions, no user interface objects are built into it. Therefore, it's up to you to design and create the necessary form for users to interact with. Because a browser can be and is an application by itself, creating a browser form for your application can be just as complicated as creating the application.

Fortunately, Visual Basic includes a form template for the browser that includes the necessary objects. You can conclude the browser in your application either by using the Application Wizard or by adding the template to your application through the Add Form dialog box. When you create an application shell with the Application Wizard, you use the Internet Connectivity dialog box (see Figure 14.2) to set up the Internet access for your application.

14

FIGURE 14.2.

Adding Web access by using the Application Wizard.

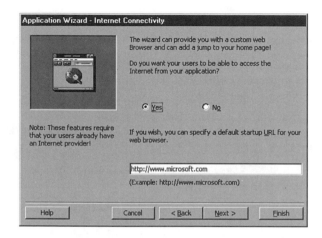

When you add Web access, the wizard actually inserts the engine for a Web browser into the new application. The browser control has several properties, methods, and events that you'll make consistent use of, as described in Table 14.1. Table 14.1 by no means lists the entire set of elements for the browser control; however, very little documentation can be found on how to use this and other included controls.

TABLE 14.1. THE INTERNET BROWSER'S MOST USED ELEMENTS.

Name	Description
Properties	
LocationURL	Contains the URL for the displayed or requested Web page
LocationName	Contains the defined name of the displayed Web page
Busy	Returns whether the browser engine is busy retrieving a Web page
Events	
DownloadComplete	Triggered whenever a Web page retrieval is completed
NavigateComplete	Triggered whenever a new URL is entered
Methods	
Navigate	Informs the browser to go to the specified URL
Stop	Stops the current browser action
GoBack	Navigates to the previously displayed Web page
GoForward	Navigates to the next Web page that was already displayed
GoHome	Navigates to the defined home page
GoSearch	Uses the Microsoft search engine to initiate an Internet search
Refresh	Refreshes the Web page now displayed

An *URL* (*Uniform Resource Locator*) is an Internet Web site address. Every Web site, if registered properly, has a unique URL assigned to it. If you add the Internet-access capability to your application, you can supply a default URL Web page for the application's browser. When users starts the browser in the application, the browser connects to the URL specified in the StartingAddress variable.

Note

Of course, the default URL assigned in the template is for Microsoft's own home page, so you need to change this if you want users to see something other than www.microsoft.com, such as your Internet home page.

Tip

Although every URL should begin with http://, many Internet browsers no longer require you to add this text; the browser will insert it for you. In fact, the browser that you create will also work without you having to include http:// at the beginning of the URL. However, it won't add the characters to the displayed URL unless you add the code to do that.

Adding the Browser

Now that you've seen some of what the browser requires to operate, you need to add the browser template to the Address Book application. Start by opening the AddressBook project. Then right-click the Project Explorer window and choose Add, Form from the pop-up menu to display the Add Form dialog box (see Figure 14.3). Select the Browser template and click Open to add the form to your project.

FIGURE 14.3.

Adding the Browser template to an existing application by using the Add Form dialog box.

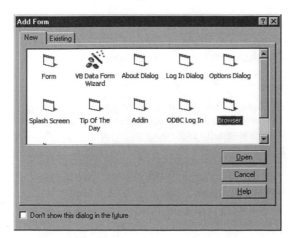

14

By default, the template is added as a child form. Unless you're creating an MDI interface, you need to change the MDIChild property to False before doing anything else.

Open the form in design mode by double-clicking it. You should see the form shown in Figure 14.4.

FIGURE 14.4.

The new browser form added to the application contains many different controls.

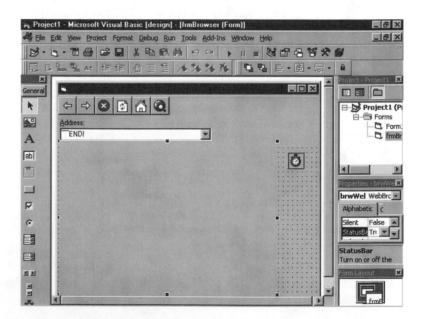

Because the template sets up everything for you, the only other step you need to do is to check the main form's View menu to ensure that a Web browser option is there and has the code to display the correct form. To see how this works, run the application.

Some routines included in the template are no longer defined correctly for the current version of the browser control. For example, the template has a routine defined as follows:

```
Private Sub brwWebBrowser_NavigateComplete(ByVal URL As String)
```

whereas the correct definition would be like so:

```
Private Sub brwWebBrowser_NavigateComplete2(ByVal pDisp As Object, _
URL As Variant)
```

> You must change each incorrect routine before you can execute the application. There will be several of these errors, and the only way to find them all is to have Visual Basic find them as you try to execute the application.

Now, choose View, Web Browser from the menu to display the browser form as shown in Figure 14.5.

FIGURE 14.5.

Browsing the Internet from within your application.

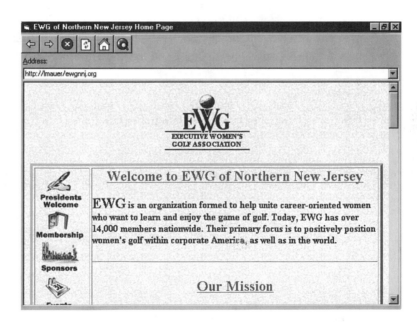

> **Note**
>
> If you aren't already connected to the Internet when you display the browser form, it will use the default connection information on your PC to attempt to connect you.

Compare Figure 14.5 with Figure 14.1 and notice that they look very much alike. At this point, you're connected to the Internet and can browse any Web site that you want.

14

The Web browser that comes with Visual Basic as a template is a simpler version of the full Internet Explorer application (fewer toolbar buttons and no menu). The embedded browser supplies all the common features needed, such as a page previous, next page, and home page. If you click the Search button, Internet Explorer uses Microsoft's search Web site to initiate a search request.

Visual Basic also comes with several other controls you can add to a project that interact with and control the Internet Explorer Web browser. These controls begin with the IE prefix in the Components dialog box and are listed in Table 14.2.

These other IE-related controls do require Internet Explorer in order to be used. They do not work with Netscape.

TABLE 14.2. OTHER INTERNET COMPONENTS.

Name	Description
IE Animated Button	Animated display showing IE's connection
IE Popup Menu	A menu control that appears on the Web page
IE Popup Window	A tabbed window control that opens a new connection window
IE Preloader	Preloads a site before the visible Internet access begins
IE Super Label	A Web page label
IE Timer	Provides timing operations for Internet services

You now have a working Internet browser in your application. If you decide you want to enhance the browser with more features, you can make use of more of the elements supported by the control.

Transferring Files over the Web

You use the File Transfer control to implement two of the most widely used Internet protocols: the Hypertext Transfer Protocol (HTTP) and the File Transfer Protocol (FTP). With the Internet File Transfer control, you can connect to any Web site that uses either protocol and retrieve files by using the control's OpenURL or Execute method. Although you can use this control to retrieve HTML documents, it's more useful in setting up the download/upload of files over the Internet. Some possible uses for this control include the following:

- Add an FTP browser to any application.
- Create an application that automatically downloads files from a public FTP site.
- Parse a Web site for graphics references and download only the graphics.
- Present a custom display of data retrieved from a Web page.

Using this control to download a file is really quite easy. You need to follow these steps to set up an FTP request:

1. Set the AccessType property.
2. Invoke the OpenURL method with a valid URL.
3. Invoke the Execute method with a valid URL and command.
4. Use the GetChunk method to retrieve data from the buffer.

For the purposes of this section, the AccessType property should be set to icDirect. You could use the three access types listed in Table 14.3.

TABLE 14.3. THE AVAILABLE ACCESS TYPES FOR THE FILE TRANSFER CONTROL.

Constant	Value	Description
icUseDefault	0	The control uses the default settings found in the Registry to access the Internet.
icDirect	1	The control has a direct connection to the Internet.
icNamedProxy	2	The control uses the proxy server specified in the Proxy property.

Using the OpenURL Method

Start a new project and place a text box, a command button, and a File Transfer control on the form, as shown in Figure 14.6.

14

FIGURE 14.6.

Creating a new form for the File Transfer example.

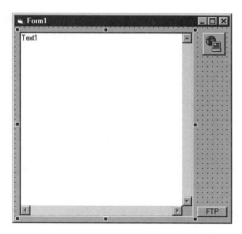

You also need to set the text box properties `Multiline` and `Scrollbar` to `True`, and the File Transfer control property `Protocol` to `icHttp`. When the `AccessType` property is set, you can use the `OpenURL` method to retrieve data from the Internet. When you use the `OpenURL` method, the result will depend on the target URL. For example, add the following code to the command button to see how to return the HTML document found at www.microsoft.com:

```
Text1.Text = Inet1,OpenURL("http://www.microsoft.com")
```

When you run the application and click the command button, the text box will be filled with the HTML source (see Figure 14.7).

FIGURE 14.7.

Retrieving the HTML source of any Web page on the Internet.

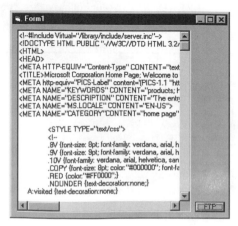

In this case, the action was to return the HTML document located at the URL specified. However, if the URL was pointing to a specific text file, the actual file would be retrieved. For this example, you need to set the Protocol property to icFTP. The following code would retrieve the file and display it in the text box control, as shown in Figure 14.8:

```
Text1.Text = Inet1.OpenURL("ftp://ftp.microsoft.com/disclaimer.txt")
```

FIGURE 14.8.

Retrieving a text file by specifying the URL and filename.

Tip

When you use the OpenURL or Execute method, you don't need to set the Protocol property because the File Transfer control will automatically set itself to the correct protocol.

To save the information returned by the control, you can write the information directly to a file by replacing the code in the command button with the following code:

```
Dim strURL As String
Dim intFileNum As Integer
    IntFileNum = FreeFile()
    StrURL = "http://www.microsoft.com/disclaimer.txt"
    Open "c:\temp\Mssource.txt" for Output As IntFileNum
    Write IntFileNum, Inet1.OpenURL(strURL)
    Close IntFileNum
```

The OpenURL method results in *synchronous* communication, which means that the transfer operation occurs before any other procedures are executed. On the other hand, the Execute method results in *asynchronous* communication, where the transfer operation occurs independently of other procedures, allowing other code to execute while data is being received in the background. This means that you can decide how you want the data transfer to be processed simply by using the appropriate method. For the purposes of an

14

application, coding an FTP function allows users to get updated information for the application directly from the Internet. Another reason for using this function is to provide users with a way of getting upgrades for their application files without waiting for disks to be sent to them.

Using the Execute Method

The Execute method has four arguments: *url*, *operation*, *data*, and *requestHeaders*. FTP operations require only the *operation* and *url* arguments. For example, to get a file from a remote computer, you could use the following code:

```
Inet1.Execute "FTP://ftp.microsoft.com", "GET disclaimer.txt
➥C:\Temp\Disclaimer.txt"
```

If you're used to using FTP to retrieve files from anonymous FTP servers, you'll be familiar with the commands used to navigate through server trees and to retrieve files to a local hard disk. For example, to change directories, you would use the command "CD" with the path of the directory you want to change to. For the most common operations, such as putting a file on a server and retrieving a file from a server, the File Transfer control uses the same or a similar command with the Execute method. For example, the following code uses the "CD" command as an argument of the Execute method to change directories:

```
Inet1.Execute txtURL.Text, "CD " & txtRemotePath.Text
```

Because an asynchronous connection is used when you're downloading data from a remote computer, the StateChanged event is used to determine the status of the operation. For example, using the Execute method with the "GET" operation causes the server to retrieve the requested file. When the process is completed, the State argument returns an icResponseCompleted value. At that point, you can use the GetChunk method to retrieve the data from the buffer, as follows:

```
Private Sub Inet1_StateChanged(ByVal State As Integer)
Dim vtData As Variant
    Select Case State
        Case icResponseCompleted
            Open txtOperation For Binary Access Write As intFileNum
            vtData = Inet1.GetChunk(1024, icString)
            Do While LenB(vtData) > 0
                Put intFileNum, , vtData
                vtData = Inet1.GetChunk(1024, icString)
            Loop
            Put intFileNum, , vtData
            Close intFileNum
    End Select
End Sub
```

Logging On

There are two types of FTP servers: public and private. Public servers are open to any-one; private servers won't let you log on unless you're a verified user of the server. Either way, the FTP protocol requires that you supply a user name and a password, which authenticates users and allows or prevents access.

To log on to public servers, the common practice is to log on as "anonymous" (`UserName` = "anonymous") and send your email name as the password. This process is simplified even further with the Internet Transfer control. By default, if you don't supply `UserName` and `Password` property values, the control sends "anonymous" as your `UserName` and your email name for the `Password`. It gets both pieces of information from your PC's Registry settings. If you're logging on to a private server, simply set the required `UserName`, `Password`, and `URL` properties, and invoke the `Execute` method, as follows:

```
With Inet1
    .URL = "ftp://ftp.someFTPSite.com"
    .UserName = "John Smith"
    .Password = "mAuI&9$6"
    .Execute ,"DIR"
    .Execute ,"CLOSE"
End With
```

After you invoke the `Execute` method, the FTP connection will remain open. You can then continue to use the `Execute` method to perform other FTP operations, such as `CD` and `GET`. After you finish, close the connection by using the `Execute` method with the `CLOSE` operation. You also can close the connection automatically by changing the `URL` property and invoking the `OpenURL` or `Execute` method, which will close the current FTP connection and open a new one.

 Caution | If you set the URL property last, the UserName and Password properties will be set to blanks. Set the URL property before you set any other properties of the File Transfer control.

HTML Coding

Although Visual Basic 5 provides you with everything you need to access the Internet, to fully understand and use the Internet, you should learn two other languages that bring things together: Hypertext Markup Language (HTML) and VBScript. HTML, the for-matting language behind Web pages, is designed to achieve two purposes:

- Format Web pages in columns with graphics and appropriate titles
- Allow the integration of additional Internet service programs, such as VB ActiveX documents and Java (a small programming language that activates Web pages)

14

HTML is known as a *scripting language*, which doesn't get compiled like Visual Basic programs do. Instead, HTML formats Web pages, specifies where graphics and frames go, and allows you to embed activated applications, such as ActiveX documents and Java programs.

VBScript is another scripting language designed by Microsoft to be a subset of the Visual Basic programming language. This means that you'll feel right at home with VBScript. It becomes very useful when you want to add key Visual Basic features to a Web page, such as pop-up messages, input boxes, and loop-through calculations.

HTML Basics

The HTML scripting language isn't complex to learn. Coding in HTML is just as easy as the early word processors that used codes instead of mouse clicks to perform actions. Unfortunately, it's also just as tedious when you forget the closing code of a matched pair. The codes to control the look of a page are always surrounded by a pair of angle brackets (<>). These commands or codes are called *tags*. Some HTML tags are paired, whereas others aren't.

HTML is supported by all browsers and is the reason the Web works the way it does. Even an all-text browser can understand the simplest text tags of HTML; however, when you start using complex tags such as frames, you require a browser that supports these features.

Because every Web page is created by using HTML code, you can view the HTML source code for any Web page that you can see in your Web browser. In Internet Explorer, if you choose View, Source from the menu, you would see the HTML source code for the current Web page, as shown in Figure 14.9.

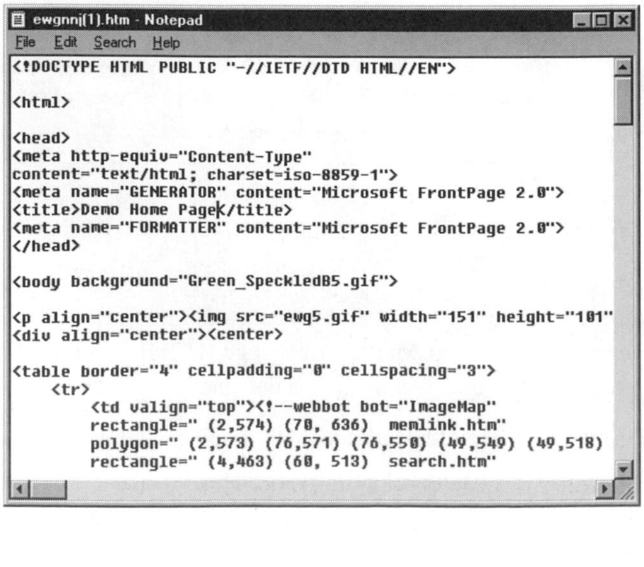

FIGURE 14.9.

Displaying the HTML source of a Web page in Internet Explorer.

```
 ewgnnj(1).htm - Notepad
File  Edit  Search  Help
<!DOCTYPE HTML PUBLIC "-//IETF//DTD HTML//EN">

<html>

<head>
<meta http-equiv="Content-Type"
content="text/html; charset=iso-8859-1">
<meta name="GENERATOR" content="Microsoft FrontPage 2.0">
<title>Demo Home Page</title>
<meta name="FORMATTER" content="Microsoft FrontPage 2.0">
</head>

<body background="Green_Speckled85.gif">

<p align="center"><img src="ewg5.gif" width="151" height="101"
<div align="center"><center>

<table border="4" cellpadding="0" cellspacing="3">
    <tr>
        <td valign="top"><!--webbot bot="ImageMap"
        rectangle=" (2,574) (70, 636)  memlink.htm"
        polygon=" (2,573) (76,571) (76,550) (49,549) (49,518)
        rectangle=" (4,463) (60, 513)  search.htm"
```

If you look at enough Web pages, you'll see that they have several common elements. Every Web page is made of essentially the following lines of HTML code:

```
<html>
<head>
<title>Demo Home Page</title>
</head>
<body>
</body>
</html>
```

This is the basic structure of every HTML file that you'll work with, no matter how complex they get. The tags <head>, <body>, and <html> start sections, and those sections are closed with </head>, </body>, and </html>, respectively. Remember, not all HTML tags have to be closed.

Understanding HTML Tags

HTML pages have their instructions or tags enclosed in brackets, as discussed in the preceding section. These tags aren't displayed in the browser window; they serve to tell the browser how to display the text.

Most tags are closed by duplicating the tag instruction with a slash (/) placed at the beginning of thc tag name. Every HTML page begins with an <HTML> tag and ends with an </HTML> tag. These two tags tell the browser where the Web page begins and ends. Between these HTML tags, every page has two sections—the head and the body. Both sections must be defined for the browser to display the page properly. The head is everything between the <head> and </head>tags, whereas the body is anything between the <body> and </body> tags.

 Tip

It doesn't matter whether the tags are uppercase, but consider capitalizing them to make them easier to find when making changes to the Web page later.

In the head section of Figure 14.9, notice that one line is <title>Demo Home Page</title>. The browser will display the words between those title tags on the title bar of the browser window. Although the average visitor won't pay much attention to the title bar while viewing the Web page, text within the title tag is what browsers usually save with a bookmark or as Favorites in Internet Explorer. Other codes can also appear in the head section of an HTML document. For example, you could use a link tag here to define a relationship between the Web page and yourself as the owner or manager of the Web page. Your link could look like this:

```
<LINK rev=made href="mailto:yourid@youraddress">.
```

14

Another tag you may want to put in the head section is <meta>, a generic tag that you can use to embed information about your document that doesn't fit in the other HTML tags. It's usually used to give the page keywords for indexing in catalogs. An example would be the following:

```
<meta keywords= Ski, Snow, Winter>
```

Everything else in the HTML code is part of the body, which is enclosed in the <body> and </body> tags.

HTML tags allow you to create some very fancy-looking forms. Some must be paired and are listed in Table 14.4; others don't use an ending tag, as shown in Table 14.5.

TABLE 14.4. PAIRED HTML TAGS THAT YOU CAN USE ON A WEB PAGE.

Code Pair	Description
<I>...</I>	Begins and ends italicized text
<B>...</B>	Begins and ends boldfaced text
<BIG>...</BIG>	Displays large type
<A HREF=xxxx>...</A>	Creates a hypertext link to another file or a bookmark within this file
<Address>...</Address>	Begins and ends a formatted section for contact information
<ul>...</ul>	Displays unnumbered lists
<dl>...</dl>	Displays definition lists
<dt>...</dt>	Displays defined terms in a definition list
<dd>...</dd>	Displays definitions in definition list
...	Displays emphasized text
...	Displays boldfaced text
<Hn>...</Hn>	Displays headlines, usually from H1 (the largest) to H6 (the smallest)

TABLE 14.5. NON-PAIRED HTML TAGS THAT YOU CAN USE ON A WEB PAGE.

Tag	Description
<IMG SRC=xxxxx>	Places an image on a Web page
<li>	Displays a list of items
<P>	Creates a paragraph break, a line break, and a blank line
 	Adds a line break, but no blank line
<HR>	Adds a rule between sections

Many more tags are available but aren't covered in today's lesson. If you want a best-selling book on HTML coding, read Laura Lemay's *Teach Yourself Web Publishing with HTML in a Week*, also from Sams Publishing.

Creating an HTML Page

Let's start the process by creating a very simple Web page and then browse it to see how it works. Many HTML editors available, including Microsoft FrontPage97, can help you create the Web pages you need. In this section, you can use Notepad to create your HTML code. Open Notepad and enter the following code to create the simple HTML page:

```
<HTML>
<HEAD>
<TITLE>Demo Page 1</TITLE>
</HEAD>
<BODY>This is a sample web page</BODY>
</HTML>
```

The title element is always inserted in the head of your HTML page, indicated by the <HEAD> and </HEAD> commands. The first few lines of your HTML code won't appear in your actual page—they act as extra information. Any actual page content is inserted in the body section of the file. After you finish, save the file as HTMLDEMO.HTM.

Note

> The .HTM file extension is used to signify a standard HTML file.

To view your first Web page, start your Web browser, choose File, Open, and select the file you just saved. The Web page should look like the one in Figure 14.10.

14

FIGURE 14.10.

The first Web page created by using HTML scripting code.

The first thing that you'll probably put on your Web page is a heading. It's also the first thing that you insert into the body section of the page. After the beginning body tag, add the following line of code to produce the largest sized text heading on the Web page:

```
<H1>My Demo HTML Page</H1>
```

You also can center the text on the page. You must enclose the heading line with this tag pair as follows:

```
<CENTER><H1>My Demo HTML Page</H1></CENTER>
```

Add this line of code to the HTMLDEMO file and save it. Now, in Internet Explorer, refresh the page to see the changes you made (see Figure 14.11).

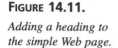

FIGURE 14.11.

*Adding a heading to
the simple Web page.*

Jazzing Up the Page

If you've been browsing the Web for any length of time, you've probably seen nice
background colors used on the Web sites that you've visited. To make your Web page
more pleasant to look at, add some color to the background. Using tags to set the background color requires you to know the hexadecimal RGB values for the color you want
to use. The color value is usually entered by assigning the bgcolor property of the
<body> tag, using the form *#rrggbb* as follows:

```
<body bgcolor="#C0C0C0"> </body>
```

This will change the background color to silver.

Next, you could add an image to the Web page by modifying the <body> tag in the Web
page. The following is an example that adds the background image shown in Figure 14.12
to the page:

```
<body background=file:///C:/temp/CDROM.gif bgcolor="#C0C0C0"> </body>
```

14

FIGURE 14.12.

Displaying images as a background on a Web page.

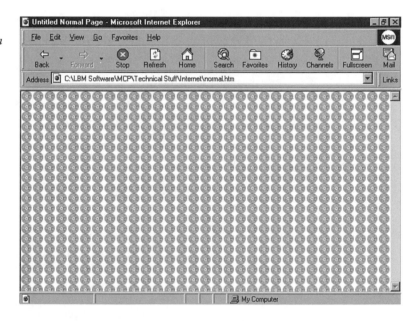

Of course, you have to make sure that the path you specify matches the machine where the Web page will execute from. The background colors and images usually appear as the first item inserted after the <body> tag.

> **Tip**
>
> Internet Explorer users can borrow the background images used in any Web page by right-clicking the background and choosing Save Background Image from the pop-up menu.

Linking to Other Pages

Linking to other pages requires nothing more than coding a hyperlink in your Web page. Hyperlinks are probably the first thing you used when you started browsing the Internet. Used correctly, hyperlinks transport users to interesting and related Web sites.

To create an external link in the HTML code, you would use the <A>. . .</A> tags. The HTML code that links to Microsoft's home page is shown as follows:

```
<A HREF=http://www.microsoft.com>Microsoft HomePage</A>
```

Using VBScript

VBScript, a scaled-down version of Visual Basic, uses fundamental VB syntax but is intended as a scripting language, similar to a DOS batch file. VBScript code is usually found embedded directly in a Web page, as is JavaScript. In the following sections, you'll get a brief overview of VBScript and how to use it, as well as some notes on how it varies from the standard Visual Basic language.

VBScript Overview

VBScript was designed to be a subset of the full Visual Basic language because its code is interpreted as the Web page is displayed. As you already know, the HTML code behind a Web page can also include scripting code to enhance the Web page. Before the introduction of VBScript, JavaScript had established itself as the industry standard for Web page scripting; however, JavaScript is very similar to C++, which made it difficult for VB programmers to use.

The main purpose for Microsoft's developing VBScript was to provide a Web scripting language compatible with Microsoft's industry standard for Windows development, Visual Basic. Because this new language was going to be embedded into Web pages, it needed to be simple enough that it could be interpreted as quickly as JavaScript. To accomplish this, the Visual Basic language needed to be simplified.

VBScript also was scaled down from Visual Basic for security concerns. If VBScript programmers could call the Windows API or perform file I/O, hackers could easily write a virus in VBScript to crash every system that executed their VBScript Web page. To reduce the chances of this happening, all the features of Visual Basic that potentially could be abused were removed.

Perhaps the biggest difference (and source of frustration) between VBScript and standard Visual Basic is that VBScript supports only the `Variant` data type. This means that a statement such as:

```
Dim x As Integer
```

would trigger an error in VBScript because the `Integer` data type isn't supported. Using just the `Variant` data type simplifies the code for the interpreter, thus making execution much faster.

When you start working with VBScript, knowing what commands and features of Visual Basic aren't supported is a good idea. This keeps you from designing a function that can't be coded in VBScript. Table 14.6 lists the features that you can't use in VBScript code.

14

TABLE 14.6. VISUAL BASIC FEATURES NOT SUPPORTED IN VBSCRIPT 2.0.

Category	Feature or Keyword
Array handling	`Option Base`, declaring arrays with lower-bound <> 0
Collection	`Add`, `Count`, `Item`, `Remove`, access to collections by using ! character
Conditional compilation	`#Const`, `#If...Then...#Else`
Control flow	`DoEvents`, `GoSub. . .Return`, `GoTo`, `On Error GoTo`, `On. . .GoSub`, `On. . .GoTo`, line numbers, line labels, `With. . .End With`
Conversion	`CVar`, `CVDate`, `Str`, `Val`
Data types	All intrinsic data types except `Variant`, `Type. . .End Type`
Date/time	`Date` statement, `Time` statement, `Timer`
DDE	`LinkExecute`, `LinkPoke`, `LinkRequest`, `LinkSend`
Debugging	`Debug.Print`, `End`, `Stop`
Declaration	`Declare` (for declaring DLLs), `Property Get`, `Property Let`, `Property Set`, `Public`, `Private`, `Static`, `ParamArray`, `Optional`, `New`
Error handling	`Erl`, `Error`, `On Error. . . Resume`, `Resume`, `Resume Next`
File input/output	All
Financial	All financial functions
Object manipulation	`TypeOf`
Objects	`Clipboard`, `Collection`
Operators	`Like`
Options	`Deftype`, `Option Base`, `Option Compare`, `Option Private Module`
Strings	Fixed-length strings, `LSet`, `Rset`, `Mid` statement, `StrConv`
Using objects	Collection access by using !

Don't worry if the list seems long. The most important features of Visual Basic are included in VBScript, so you still can write powerful scripts. The only difference is that now you have to be more inventive when designing the code. You may find that some tricks you invent to overcome these limitations are so good that you want to use them in your normal Visual Basic applications.

Adding VBScript to an HTML Page

To see how VBScript works, look at what you have to add to a Web page to make it perform some processing. To use VBScript in your Web page, you must add some HTML code that tells the browser that your Web page contains script code. VBScript also doesn't support the forms you're accustomed to using in Visual Basic, meaning that your code must include information about which controls to use and where they should be placed on the page.

To begin using VBScript in an HTML page, you must tell the browser which scripting language you'll be using. This is done by using the `<Script...></Script>` tags, which define the script block in the Web page. For VBScript, the syntax in a Web page would start out as follows:

```
<Script Language="VBScript">
.
.
.
</Script>
```

Immediately after the `<Script>` statement, your VBScript code is added in an HTML comment block (`<!--` and `-->` tags) so that your code isn't displayed by browsers that don't support VBScript. At the end of the comment block, the closing `</Script>` tag tells the browser that there's no more code. Listing 14.1 shows a simple Web page that displays a message box every time the page is accessed.

LISTING 14.1. HTMLDEMO1.HTM—A SIMPLE WEB PAGE THAT DISPLAYS A VISUAL BASIC MESSAGE BOX.

```
<HTML>
<HEAD>
<SCRIPT LANGUAGE="VBScript">
<!--
    MsgBox "Hello World!"
-->
</SCRIPT>
</HEAD>
</HTML>
```

Although you can have code executed when the page is loaded, typically you would want to execute your code in response to an event, the same way as in Visual Basic. To do this, you need a control on the page that users can interact with and an event routine for that control. In Visual Basic, this is done for you when you place a command button on the form, and a `Click` event is created when you double-click the control. In VBScript, you must do everything yourself, but it isn't as difficult as it sounds. Listing 14.2 shows how to create a command button on the Web page and display a message box in response to the `Click` event.

14

LISTING 14.2. CMDBTN.HTM—ADDING AND THEN USING A COMMAND BUTTON ON A WEB PAGE.

```
<HTML>
<HEAD>
<SCRIPT LANGUAGE="VBScript">
<!--
Sub Command1_OnClick()
    MsgBox "Hello World!"
End Sub
-->
</SCRIPT>
<FORM>
    <INPUT NAME="Command1" TYPE="BUTTON" VALUE="Say Hello!">
</FORM>
</HEAD>
</HTML>
```

Now that you've seen how to work with a simple VBScript Web page, you need to modify the HTML page you just created. The code in Listing 14.3 shows how to add a text box and command button to the Web page and then have a subroutine executed whenever users click the command button.

LISTING 14.3. HTMLCODE.HTM—A COMPLETE VBSCRIPT APPLICATION ON A WEB PAGE.

```
<HTML>
<HEAD>
<TITLE>VBScript Demonstration Page</TITLE>
<SCRIPT LANGUAGE="VBScript">
<!--
Option Explicit

Sub SayHello(InputName)
    Dim Reply

    Reply = MsgBox("Hello " & InputName & ", are you ready to compute?", 36)

    If Reply = 6 Then
        MsgBox "Okay, Let's see what we can do!", 64
    Else
        MsgBox "This function has been canceled", 64
    End If

End Sub

Sub Command1_OnClick()
    SayHello Form1.Text1.Value
End Sub
-->
```

```
    </SCRIPT>
    </HEAD>

    <BODY>
    <BR>
    <H3>Enter your name:</H3>
    <P>
    <HR>
    <FORM NAME="Form1">
        <INPUT NAME="Text1" TYPE="TEXT" VALUE="">
        <INPUT NAME="Command1" TYPE="BUTTON" VALUE="Say Hello!">
    </FORM>

    </BODY>
    </HTML>
```

As you can see, VBScript allows you to add complex processing code to your Web-based applications.

Note Don't try to use any of the included Visual Basic constants that you've probably become used to. VBScript doesn't support them, which means that you have to code the numeric values for such constants as vbInformation.

If you start Internet Explorer or Netscape and open this Web page, the resulting display should look like Figure 14.13.

FIGURE 14.13.

Displaying the demo HTML/VBScript Web page in Internet Explorer.

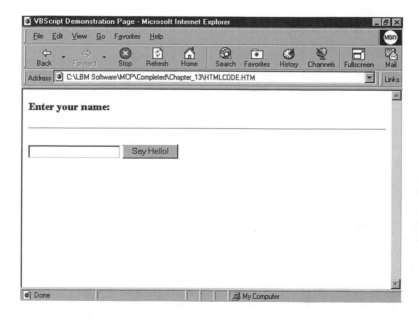

14

Developing a DHTML Application

A DHTML application is really a Visual Basic application that uses both compiled Visual Basic code and Dynamic HTML to produce an interactive, browser-based application. The DHTML application will reside on the browser machine and respond to the actions of the end user. These applications can be as simple as a single HTML page that uses VB code to respond instantly to the actions that occur on the page. This could involve responding to user actions such as mouse movements and clicks, or even actions that the browser performs, such as opening the page. With a more complicated DHTML application, you could

- Retrieve data from the page and use it to access a database
- Update the page's appearance and behavior
- Create HTML elements and insert them onto a page

The Visual Basic code that you add to a DHTML page will replace the processing that was previously performed by VBScript or CGI processing, and much of it can be done without transferring the process to the server.

Creating the DHTML Application

When you begin a DHTML application, you select the DHTML Application project from the New Project tab. This project is really an ActiveX DLL project that will automatically set the correct references you need to access the DHTML designer for your HTML pages. When the project is created, Visual Basic automatically inserts a designer into the project and displays it on the screen (see Figure 14.14). This corresponds to a single HTML page and acts as the base on which you will create the user interface. If you want to add more HTML pages to the application, you would insert additional designers into your project.

FIGURE 14.14.

Starting a DHTML project in Visual Basic will insert an HTML page into the project.

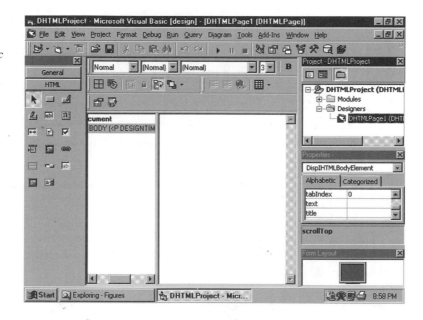

When designing your Web applications, you can choose to create the page layouts by

- Creating the pages from scratch by adding HTML elements from the toolbox and arranging them as desired
- Using an External HTML editor such as FrontPage
- Using a combination of both

If you decide to create the Web pages in Visual Basic, you will add HTML elements to the designer and arrange them on the page. Also, you don't need to know HTML programming to build the page in this way; Visual Basic will create the HTML tags and attributes that you need. Designing pages this way is quick, easy, and allows you to create functional pages without having to learn the details of HTML.

However, Visual Basic is not an advanced HTML editor. If you want to create fancy Web pages, you should use one of the HTML editors that are specifically created to perform this type of process. As an example, you cannot view the source HTML code for your page in the Visual Basic page editor or work with advanced features such as animation.

Adding Visual Basic Code to the Page

Designing and creating an Internet application requires the same amount of time and analysis that a standard Visual Basic application would require. To fully cover the concepts and features of a DHTML application would require a complete discussion of Web

14

programming. In this section, the best that can be hoped for is a brief look at the creation process. When adding code to a DHTML page, you should understand that DHTML coding differs from standard Visual Basic code in certain ways that relate to the HTML process. The starting point for this understanding is in the way events are processed in a DHTML page. Most events in dynamic HTML are similar to the events in Visual Basic, except in the way they are named. All event names in DHTML are preceded by the word *on*. You can locate most common events by looking for them under this prefix. As an example, the Visual Basic `Click` event corresponds to the `onClick` event in a DHTML page.

To see how this actually works, you will create the same HTML page as you did in the previous section; however, this time, you will use the DHTML features. Start a new application, choosing the DHTML application option in the New Project dialog. Once the project is created, you should notice that there is a new toolbox page available (see Figure 14.15) that contains the HTML style controls that you can use in the application.

FIGURE 14.15.

A DHTML project adds a new set of controls to the Visual Basic design interface for use on the HTML page.

To create the same HTML page as before, add Textbox and Command Button controls to the HTML page using the HTML controls as shown in Figure 14.16.

FIGURE 14.16.

Designing an HTML page by adding controls to the HTML work area.

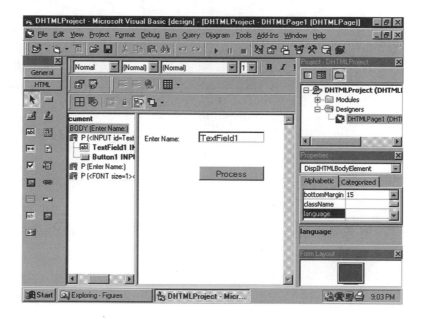

You should notice that as you add these controls to the HTML page, Visual Basic automatically adds the HTML source tags to the page source on the left side of the work area. In addition, you can add labels to the HTML page.

 Note

> You cannot display the code editor for a control by simply double-clicking the control. In the HTML page layout, all the controls are active. To view the code editor, you would right-click the control, and then select the View Source option.

Display the OnClick routine for the command button and place the following code into the routine.

```
BaseWindow.Alert "Hello " & Me.Text1.Value
```

When you run the application, Visual Basic will start the default Web browser on your computer and display the startup page of the application. Then enter your name and click the Command button to execute the code you have added. This will display a message box within the Web browser which contains the message to the user as shown in Figure 14.17.

14

FIGURE 14.17.

Displaying a message box in the Web browser.

As you can see, the code is very similar to the VBScript code that you created in the previous section. At this point, you are probably asking yourself, "Why should I use DHTML"? The answer to this question is the performance that you can provide for a Web-based application by having all of the processing performed on the local computer.

Navigating the Web

In addition to creating a fully functional application, you can also add Hyperlink commands to the HTML pages in the application to give the user the ability to go to other pages in the application, or to other pages on the Internet.

To enable the user to go to another page in the application, you could use the following code example.

```
Private Function Button1_OnClick() As Boolean
    BaseWindow.Navigate "Project1.DHTMLPage2.html"
End Function
```

This example uses the navigate method of the BaseWindow object to move to the specified location. `Project1.DHTMLPage2.html` is the default name that was assigned to the second DHTML page added to the project. By changing the value passed to the navigate method, you can have the user go to any Web site on the Internet.

Distributing the DHTML Application

When you complete the application and compile it, Visual Basic will create a DLL that contains the page designer and any related code that you have added. The HTML pages and their related files are stored separately from the DLL and must be distributed with it. However, to deploy this application properly, you should use the new Package and Deployment Wizard to create the DLL and package it and all other associated files in a cabinet or .cab file. The wizard can then deploy this cabinet and its support files to a location you indicate on the Web server.

In addition to the DLL and cabinet files, the wizard creates the starting HTML page for the application, which, when it is accessed by a user, will start the download process to bring your DHTML application to the user's computer. Once the download is complete, the application will run locally on the user's computer.

Summary

In this lesson, you looked at how to add the hottest thing in computers today. With the Browser control, your users can browse the Internet without having to open any other application. Also, if you have your own Web site, you can point users directly to it and have your application automatically download upgrades for itself. You also saw a little of what it takes to create Web pages and add processing code in the form of VBScript to the HTML page. Unless you're creating a full Internet Web application, these concepts and controls will serve only to add enhancements to any application that you create. Finally, you took a brief look at how to create a Dynamic HTML Visual Basic application, which gives you the ability to design very sophisticated Web-based applications.

Q&A

Q What does the Web-browsing application you generate with Visual Basic's Application Wizard do with the URL you supply?

A The Application Wizard uses the URL to set the starting or default URL page when the browser is opened.

Q What's the difference between an intranet and the Internet?

A An *intranet* is a Web server that's local to the computer you're using (a network or a personal server). The Internet is a worldwide system of linked computer networks that facilitates data communication services such as remote logons, file transfer, electronic mail, and newsgroups. The World Wide Web is a major part of the Internet.

14

Q Which scripting languages work with HTML to enhance the Web page?

A VBScript and JavaScript are used to enhance HTML Web pages.

Q What is the difference between DHTML and other types of server side processing, such as CGI?

A DHTML coding uses standard Visual Basic code that will be executed on the browser's local machine, without requiring any server processing at all.

Workshop

The Workshop provides quiz questions to help solidify your understanding of the material covered, as well as exercises to provide you with experience in using what you've learned. Try to understand the quiz and exercise answers before continuing on to the next day's lesson. Answers are provided in Appendix A, "Answers to Exercises."

Quiz

1. What are the two Internet controls that you can use in your applications?
2. What does the File Transfer control do?
3. What's the difference between Visual Basic and VBScript?

Exercise

Create a Web page that contains three separate headings and asks users to input their first and last names in different text boxes. Then add two command buttons: one to put a message box onscreen saying hello to users, and one to reset the text boxes.

WEEK 2

In Review

The second week took you through the steps to add database access to your application by covering design, creation, SQL programming, and actually building the database. Then, you saw how to use the new ActiveX data control and objects to connect to the database which not only gave you access to your data, it also let you use the latest data reporting and manipulation designers and controls that have been included in Visual Basic.

Database Design and Access

Chapter 8 took you through what you should consider when designing a new database. The different types of databases that can be accessed from within Visual Basic were discussed. This included how to use the functional specifications of your application design to help with the design of the database. At the end of this chapter, you saw how to use the Data Interface wizard to have Visual Basic create the database access forms for your application by using the database table design itself.

Over the next two lessons—Days 9 and 10—you saw how to design a database, and then, using the Visual Data Manager, how to create a Microsoft Access database for use with your Visual Basic application. In addition to the design and creation of the database, you learned about the SQL programming language that is used to access the data in a relational database. Finally, the new ActiveX Data Control and Data Objects were covered, and you saw how to connect to the database using the new OLE DB concepts to build complex entry forms using these controls.

Enhancing the Application

In Days 11 and 12, you saw how to make use of many of the newest controls and features in Visual Basic 6. Using Visual Basic, you can now create data-aware controls that can be used in your application to enhance the user interface. By using these techniques, you can now include a form within an application as a control to fully integrate it into the application. Finally, you worked with the Data Environment designer which allows you to define database connections. The connections give you the ability to create data-bound reports within the application and to design data grid controls that are used to display records in a database in a much more usable manner.

Using Crystal Reports

One of the more important features that is needed to create a professional Windows Application is the ability to create reports from the data entered into the application. Chapter 13 introduced you to Crystal Reports, which is a separate application tool that is included with Visual Basic. Crystal Reports gives you the ability to create any type of report from the very simple to the complex. In addition, you also saw how to incorporate Crystal Reports directly into your application by making use of the Crystal Reports Custom Control that is included with the product.

Accessing the Internet

The last chapter this week (Day 14) introduced you to the Internet controls that are included with Visual Basic. You saw how to add Internet access to your application by using these controls. In addition to these controls, Visual Basic 6 contains the ability to create a Dynamic HTML application. Dynamic HTML, or DHTML, is used to produce Visual Basic applications that are Web-enabled and execute from a Web browser.

WEEK 3

At a Glance

Week 3 covers topics that are normally forgotten about by the average programmer. Error-handling, performance, testing and debugging are all covered during this week. You are also introduced to the concepts and information involved in getting a product to market. In addition, you are instructed on how to create a new ActiveX document application or convert an old Visual Basic application into an ActiveX document application. Finally, you learn how to add a little pizzazz to your application by using some tools that are available from the Microsoft Web site or are included on the Visual Basic CD-ROM.

Day 15 — Adding Advanced Features

Day 15 reintroduces the concept of OLE drag and drop. This feature of Windows has been around for a long time. However, most applications use it to do the simplest of actions. This chapter shows you how to add functionality to your application using the OLE drag-and-drop features. In addition, you will take a look at how to make use of the Systray ActiveX control that is included on the Visual Basic CD-ROM, as well as the new Date controls included with Visual Basic.

Day 16 — Coping with Error Handling

Day 16 covers the forgotten child of programming. The importance of error handling is discussed as well as different

15

16

17

18

19

20

21

issues that may pop-up as you develop an application. In addition, some helpful tips and techniques that you can use in your application will be covered.

Day 17 — Building Online Help

Day 17 introduces you to the Windows Help system. You learn how to design and create a working Help system. This chapter shows you how to incorporate it into your application using the different functions, controls, and features available in Visual Basic. You are also introduced to the latest concept in online help—namely using HTML as a base for the Help system. This means that you can integrate remote help into your local files.

Day 18 — Testing and Debugging the Application

Day 18 covers an area that many programmers do not fully understand. In this chapter, you gain an understanding of what testing really means, why it should be done and how to use the debugging facilities that come with Visual Basic. The concept of regression testing and scripting is also discussed.

Day 19 — Performance and Tuning

Day 19 covers the concepts and techniques that you can use to make your application run faster and use less resources on the computer. You will see different techniques that can be used to enhance the performance of an application.

Day 20 — Finishing the Application

In Day 20, you learn the information you need to package the application you have written. Besides the actual creation of the distribution software, you also learn the other topics and issues that you will have to deal with if you want to sell the application you have created.

Day 21 — Creating an ActiveX Document

Day 21 explains what an ActiveX document is and how it differs from a standard Visual Basic application. In addition, you learn what it takes to create a new ActiveX document; then you see how to convert an existing Visual Basic application into an ActiveX Document using the included wizard.

DAY 15

Adding Advanced Features

In most programming languages, there are always some features that are available, but not usually covered. This chapter is going to cover three very different, yet important features of Visual Basic. The first section will discuss the concepts and features of OLE drag and drop, then you will see how to make use of an unsupported control that comes with Visual Basic to give you the ability to use the System Tray features of Windows 95. Finally, you will see how to use two new controls that add calendar features to your application.

OLE Drag and Drop

Almost every application that you use today has some type of drag-and-drop capability. Even Windows 3.1 had drag and drop in some of the applications. The Windows File Manager enables you to drag files from one directory to another or from disk to disk. OLE drag and drop is the more advanced version of the simple drag-and-drop functionality. Instead of invoking code by dragging one object to another, data is being moved from one control or application to another control or application.

Even the simple Notepad application enables you to drag a text file from the Explorer window into an open Notepad window to display the contents of the file. OLE drag and drop was so useful that when Microsoft developed the initial design for Windows 95, it included OLE drag and drop as one of the main standards that defines a Windows 95–compliant product. These standards are used to determine if a new product meets the requirements to be able to display the Windows 95 Logo on its packaging and documentation.

This chapter includes a review of what drag and drop is, how it works, and how to use it. More importantly, you will learn how to incorporate the concepts of drag and drop into the Address Book application. You will see how to enable the user to drag a name from the TreeView control to an icon on the toolbar that will print the selected entries information or to display it in the data entry control (remember that you have converted the form into an ActiveX custom control).

Defining OLE Drag and Drop

OLE drag and drop is probably the most powerful, if not the most misunderstood, feature available to you when designing your Visual Basic application. By adding the capability to drag object information from one control to another, from a control to another Windows application, or from another application into yours, you are enhancing your application with whatever other applications the user has on his computer.

If you have been coding Visual Basic for any length of time, you should be very familiar with standard drag-and-drop capabilities that are supported by the controls within a Windows application. The concepts you learned to use drag-and-drop functionality are still useful when using the new OLE drag-and-drop features. The difference is that OLE drag and drop opens your Visual Basic application to other applications running on the user's PC.

Most of the controls included with Visual Basic support OLE drag and drop in some manner. Depending on which control you are using, OLE drag and drop can be used without adding any additional code, although you might need to write some code to support the function you require. Three levels of OLE drag and drop support exist; the controls included with Visual Basic all contain support at one of these levels:

- **Level 1**—Supports only manual OLE drag and drop. This requires you to write the code needed to support any drag-and-drop functionality.
- **Level 2**—Supports only automatic drag functions. If you need any drop functionality, you must code for it.
- **Level 3**—Provides full support for the automatic OLE drag-and-drop capabilities.

Even though the drag-and-drop operation is supported by Visual Basic, only Level 3 supported controls can be used without writing any code. To see how the automatic process works, start a new project and place one text box on the form, setting both the OLEDRAGMODE and OLEDROPMODE properties to Automatic. Start the application and then start WordPad.

 Note

> WordPad is being used instead of NotePad because WordPad supports the OLE drag-and-drop methods, whereas NotePad does not.

Select the default text in the text box, drag it to the WordPad work area, and drop it. You will see that the text is moved from your application to WordPad. Table 15.1 lists the controls included with Visual Basic and the level of OLE drag and drop that they support.

TABLE 15.1. VISUAL BASIC CONTROLS AND THEIR OLE DRAG AND DROP SUPPORT LEVELS.

Level	Control
Level 1	Data
	Drive ListBox
	CheckBox
	CommandButton
	Frame
	Label
	OptionButton
Level 2	ComboBox
	Data-bound ComboBox
	Data-bound ListBox
	Directory ListBox
	File ListBox
	ListBox
	ListView
	TreeView
Level 3	Apex data-bound grid
	Image
	MaskedEditBox
	PictureBox
	RichTextBox
	TextBox

Although this list is as current as I can make it, the best way to see if a control supports OLE drag and drop is to place it on a form and then check its property list. If OLEDragMode and OLEDropMode properties are listed, the control supports automatic or manual processing.

Using OLE Drag and Drop

For each drag-and-drop operation, there are events that are triggered on both sides of the operation. Each operation has a source control and a target control. If the control is contained in your application, you can add additional code to enhance the way OLE drag and drop works.

The source control events are generated for both the automatic and manual types of processing. In contrast, the target controls events will only be triggered during a manual drop operation. All of the vents related to OLE drag and drop are listed in Table 15.2.

TABLE 15.2. OLE SOURCE AND TARGET EVENTS DESCRIBED.

Type	Event	Description
Source	OLEStartDrag	Occurs when the OLEDrag method is executed, or when an OLE drag/drop operation is initiated with the OLEDragMode property set to Automatic.
	OLESetData	Occurs for a source control when a target control executes the GetData method, but the data has not yet been loaded.
	OLEGiveFeedback	Occurs after the OLEDragOver event has been executed.
	OLECompleteDrag	Occurs when source data is dropped onto a target control.
Target	OLEDragDrop	Occurs when source data is dropped onto a target control where a drop can occur.
	OLEDragOver	Occurs when one control is dragged over another.

Depending on how you want the OLE drag and drop functionality to perform in your application, you add code only to the events you want the application to respond to. The simplest way to add the functionality is to use both the automatic drag and automatic drop features. In addition to controlling the drag-and-drop process, you can also change the mouse cursor to visually show the user that something is happening.

15

In fact, you can use the different events to have your application respond to the drag-and-drop request based on the mouse button or key (shift, alt, ctrl) that was hit with the mouse button. Also, if you want to analyze or modify the data before it's dropped into the control, or dragged from it, you would need to use the manual OLE drag-and-drop operations. This gives you full control of the drag-and-drop process. If you look back at the simple text box/WordPad example, you will notice that the data is moved from the text box into WordPad. If you want to copy the data, you can use the built-in Windows copy feature by holding the Ctrl key when dragging the data. However, this will only work when both objects involved are supported and using the automatic process.

Because data can be dragged and dropped into many different controls or applications, implementing OLE drag and drop can range in difficulty from straightforward to fairly complex. The easiest method, of course, is dragging and dropping between two automatic objects.

It Starts with a Drag

A manual OLE drag-and-drop operation starts when the user selects and then drags data from an OLE drag source (such as a TextBox control). When this happens, the OLEStartDrag event is triggered, and you can choose to either store the data or simply specify the formats that the source control will support. You also need to specify if copying or moving the data, or both, will be enabled by the source control.

As the data is dragged over a control, the OLEDragOver event is triggered and you would then add code to the event to either refuse the data or accept it while specifying if the drag is a copy or a move. The default is generally set to move; however, you can change the default to copy if you want. When the user drops the data, the OLEGiveFeedback event is triggered to give the user feedback on what action has been taken when the data was dropped (that is, the mouse pointer changes to indicate a copy, move, or "no drop" action). Figure 15.1 shows the three different mouse pointer icons that come with Visual Basic.

FIGURE 15.1.

The default mouse icons used for the OLE drag-and-drop operations.

Finishing the Process

When the user drops the data onto the target, the target's OLEDragDrop event is triggered and the target checks the data from the source object to see whether it is the proper data type. Depending on the outcome, it either retrieves or rejects the data. To see this, add a second text box to the form in the project and set the OLEDROPMODE to Manual. Then place the following code in the form:

```
Private Sub Text2_OLEDragDrop (Data As ComctlLib.DataObject, Effect As Long,_
Button As Integer, Shift As Integer, x As Single, y As Single)
    If Data.GetFormat(vbcfText) then
        MsgBox "This data is text"
    End If
End Sub
```

 Caution Make sure that you use the OLEDragDrop event instead of the DragDrop event, which is used for non-OLE type processing.

Now, run the application and try dragging data from the first text box to the second one. The only thing that should happen is that the message box should be displayed. To have the data in the text box, you would use the GetData method of the Data object that was passed to the control in the Drop event. If the data was stored automatically when the drag was started, the GetData method retrieves the data. If the data wasn't stored when the drag operation started, the source control's OLESetData event is triggered and the SetData method retrieves the data.

When the data is accepted or rejected, the OLECompleteDrag event is triggered and the source can then perform the necessary clean-up. If the data is accepted and a move was requested, the source deletes the data. The most important concept to understand when using OLE drag and drop is knowing when the different events will occur and for which object.

Which One to Use?

Whether you want to use the automatic or manual OLE drag-and-drop process really depends on the type of functionality you want the user to be able to perform when using your application. With automatic drag and drop, all operations are controlled by Windows and the internal Visual Basic process. You can drag text from one TextBox control to another by simply setting the OLEDragMode and OLEDropMode properties of these controls to Automatic. No code is required to respond to any of the OLE drag-and-

15

drop events. Depending on how a given control or application supports it and the type of data being dragged, automatically dragging and dropping data may be the best and simplest method.

When using manual drag and drop, you must code for one or more of the OLE drag-and-drop events. Manual implementation of OLE drag and drop may be the better method when you need greater control over each step in the process or you need to provide the user with customized visual feedback or as you will see, dragging a record key into a complex control to display a row of data from a database. Manual implementation is the only option when a control doesn't support the automatic drag-and-drop features.

The Automatic Process

If the controls you want to use support automatic drag and drop, you can activate the features by setting the control's OLEDragMode or OLEDropMode properties to Automatic. However, automatic support does have its limitations. Some of them are derived from the controls themselves. For example, if you move text from a Word document into a text box, all the rich text formatting in the Word document is stripped out because the standard TextBox control doesn't support this formatting. Similar limitations exist for most controls. The RichTextBox control is the correct control to use for this particular situation.

If you change the text box/WordPad example to a RichTextbox control and Microsoft Word, you would then be able to move formatted text between the two applications.

Understanding the Manual Process

The manual process is more involved, but it gives you complete control over the entire OLE drag-and-drop process. To understand how the manual process works, review the available events, methods and objects and see how they work together.

Starting a manual drag-and-drop operation is as simple as calling the OLEDrag method. You then set the drop effects that you want to support, the supported data formats, and if necessary, you can place data into the DataObject. When the OLEDrag method is executed to start the drag operation, the OLEStartDrag event is triggered to enable you to set the effects and formats.

The DataObject

Because OLE drag and drop is implemented across applications, you would not always know where the data being processed is coming from. The event code must work whether the data is within the same application or from another application such as Word or Excel. Visual Basic provides an object that contains the data being moved, no matter where it comes from. The DataObject object contains the data as it moves from the source to the target. It does this by providing the methods needed to store, retrieve, and analyze the data. Table 15.3 lists the property and methods used by the DataObject object.

TABLE 15.3. THE METHODS AND PROPERTIES OF THE DataObject.

Category	Item	Description
Property	Files	Holds the names of files dragged to or from the Windows Explorer.
Methods	Clear	Clears the content of the DataObject object.
	GetData	Retrieves data from the DataObject object.
	GetFormat	Determines if a specified data format is available in the DataObject object.
	SetData	Places data into the DataObject or sets a specified format.

These methods enable you to manage the data in the DataObject only for the controls in your application. The three important methods are the GetData, SetData, and GetFormat. The first two give you the ability to put data into the DataObject or to retrieve the data it contains. The last one enables you to check the format of the data before you process it, in case the data isn't valid for the target control (such as text being dropped on a picture box). All three methods use the same constants that are listed in Table 15.4 to test or set the format of the data.

TABLE 15.4. OLE DRAG AND DROP VISUAL BASIC–SUPPLIED CONSTANTS.

Constant	Value	Meaning
vbCFText	1	Text
vbCFBitmap	2	Bitmap (.BMP)
vbCFMetafile	3	Metafile (.WMF)
vbCFEMetafile	14	Enhanced metafile (.EMF)
vbCFDIB	8	Device-independent bitmap (.DIB or .BMP)
vbCFPalette	9	Color palette
vbCFFiles	15	List of files
vbCFRTF	16639	Rich text format (.RTF)

15

The syntax is basically the same for all three methods:

```
object.GetData (format)
object.SetData [data], [format]
object.GetFormat (format)
```

The SetData, GetData, and GetFormat methods use the data and format arguments either to return the type of data in the DataObject object or to retrieve the data itself if the format is compatible with the target. In the following example, data in a text box was selected and the format was specified as text (vbCFText). This text is stored in the DataObject so the target control (wherever it is) can retrieve it:

```
Private Sub txtLastName_OLEStartDrag(Data As VB.DataObject,_
AllowedEffects As Long)
    Data.SetData txtLastName.SelText, vbCFText
End Sub
```

The OLEDrag Method

The OLEDrag method is usually executed from an object's Mousemove event. Its primary purpose is to initiate the start of a manual drag operation, which triggers the OLEStartDrag event. The OLEDrag method will only work if the object's OLEDragMode property has been set to Manual.

Note

> If the control supports manual but not automatic OLE drag, it will not have the OLEDragMode property; however, it will still support the OLEDrag method and the OLE drag-and-drop events.

The OLEStartDrag Event

When the OLEStartDrag event has been triggered, you will be able to specify which drop effects and data formats the source requires the target to support. The OLEStartDrag event has two arguments that indicate the supported data formats and whether the data can be copied or moved when data is dropped.

Caution

> If you don't specify any drop effects or data formats in the OLEStartDrag event, the manual drag operation will not start.

The allowed effects argument sets which drop effects the drag source control will support. This argument can be checked in the target control's OLEDragDrop event, and the program can respond based on the current settings. In addition, you can also specify which data formats the source control supports by setting the format argument in the OLEStartDrag event. The SetData method is used to set the format of the data. The code in Listing 15.1 sets the drag effects allowed to Copy and Move, and also assigns the data format of the DataObject to both text and richtext.

LISTING 15.1. STARTDRAG.TXT—CUSTOMIZING THE START DRAG PROCESSING.

```
1: Private Sub tvwBook_OLEStartDrag(Data As VB.DataObject, AllowedEffects _
   As Long)
2:      AllowedEffects = vbDropEffectMove Or vbDropEffectCopy
3:      Data.SetData , vbCFText
4:      Data.SetData , vbCFRTF
5: End Sub
```

Putting Data in Its Place

The DataObject usually has data placed in it at the beginning of a drag operation by executing the SetData method in the OLEStartDrag event as shown in Listing 15.2. This clears the default data formats from the DataObject, sets the current data format of the selected data, and then puts that data into the DataObject.

LISTING 15.2. SETDATA.TXT—SETTING THE DATA FORMAT AND ASSIGNING THE DATA IN THE StartDrag EVENT.

```
1: Private Sub tvwBook_OLEStartDrag(Data As VB.DataObject, AllowedEffects _
   As Long)
2:      Data.Clear
3:      Data.SetData tvwBook.SelText, vbCFText
4: End Sub
```

The OLEDragOver Event

The OLEDragOver event is triggered whenever you drag data over a control. The effect and state arguments of the OLEDragOver event are used to inform the program of the exact properties and status of the data being dragged. The effect argument is used to specify that action should be taken if the data is dropped. Whenever the value of the argument is changed, the source control's OLEGiveFeedback event will be triggered, which can then be used to provide the user with some type of visual feedback. The constants listed in Table 15.5 are used in conjunction with the effect argument to retrieve or set the effects allowed.

15

TABLE 15.5. CONSTANTS FOR THE Effects ARGUMENT.

Constant	Value	Description
vbDropEffectNone	0	Drop target cannot accept the data.
vbDropEffectCopy	1	Drop results in a copy. The original data is untouched by the drag source.
VbDropEffectMove	2	Drag source removes the data.
VbDropEffectScroll	&H80000000&	Scrolling is about to start or is currently occurring in the target.

The state argument enables you to respond to the source data entering, passing over, and leaving the target control. As an example, when the source data is dragged onto the target control, the state argument is set to vbEnter. The constants listed in Table 15.6 are used to check the value of the state argument.

TABLE 15.6. CONSTANTS USED TO CHECK THE STATE ARGUMENT.

Constant	Value	Description
vbEnter	0	Data was dragged within the range of a target.
vbLeave	1	Data was dragged out of the range of a target.
vbOver	2	Data is still within the range of a target, and either the mouse has moved, a mouse or keyboard button has changed, or a certain system-determined amount of time has elapsed.

The code in Listing 15.3 checks the format of the data being dragged over a control and if it is compatible and the data is dropped, a move operation is requested. However, if the data isn't compatible, the effect argument is set to None and a No Drop mouse pointer is displayed.

LISTING 15.3. DRAGOVER.TXT—CHECKING THE DATA FORMAT AND SETTING THE OPERATIONS ALLOWED.

```
1: Private Sub txtTarget_OLEDragOver(Data As VB.DataObject, Effect As Long,_
2: Button As _
3:     Integer, Shift As Integer, X As Single, Y As Single, State As Integer)
4:     If Data.GetFormat(vbCFText) Then
5:         Effect = vbDropEffectMove And Effect
6:     Else
7:         Effect = vbDropEffectNone
8:     End If
9: End Sub
```

Customizing the Feedback

Customized feedback is provided by inserting code into the OLEDragOver event of the target control or the OLEGiveFeedback event of the source control. The OLEGiveFeedback event is triggered automatically whenever the effect argument of the OLEDragOver event is changed. In this event, you can change the default behavior of the mouse pointer based on the effect argument. The OLEGiveFeedback event's two arguments enable you to check the effects allowed and then modify the mouse pointer as needed.

The effect argument, like the other OLE drag-and-drop events, specifies whether data is to be copied, moved, or rejected. The purpose of this argument is to enable you to provide customized feedback to the user by changing the mouse pointer indicating the current action.

The defaultcursors argument specifies whether the default OLE mouse pointers will be used. Setting this argument to False enables you to specify your own cursors using the Screen.MousePointer property of the Screen object.

Tip

Unless you really want unique mousepointers in your application, it is unnecessary to change the default pointers, because the default behavior of the mouse is handled by OLE.

An example of how to specify custom mousepointers for the copy, move, and scroll effects is shown in Listing 15.4.

LISTING 15.4. CUSTOMMOUSE.TXT—CUSTOMIZING THE MOUSE POINTERS IN THE APPLICATION CODE.

```
 1: Private Sub TxtSource_OLEGiveFeedback(Effect As Long, DefaultCursors As _
    Boolean)
 2:     DefaultCursors = False
 3:     If Effect = vbDropEffectNone Then
 4:         Screen.MousePointer = vbNoDrop
 5:     ElseIf Effect = vbDropEffectCopy Then
 6:             Screen.MousePointer = vbCustom
 7:             Screen.MouseIcon = LoadPicture("c:\Program Files\devstudio\_
 8: vb\icons\copy.ico")
 9:     ElseIf Effect = (vbDropEffectCopy Or vbDropEffectScroll) Then
10:             Screen.MousePointer = vbCustom
11:             Screen.MouseIcon = LoadPicture("c:\Program Files\devstudio\_
12: vb\icons\copyscrl.ico")
13:     ElseIf Effect = vbDropEffectMove Then
14:             Screen.MousePointer = vbCustom
```

```
15:            Screen.MouseIcon = LoadPicture("c:\Program Files\devstudio\_
16: vb\icons\move.ico")
17:    ElseIf Effect = (vbDropEffectMove Or vbDropEffectScroll) Then
18:            Screen.MousePointer = vbCustom
19:            Screen.MouseIcon = LoadPicture("c:\Program Files\devstudio\_
20: vb\icons\movescrl.ico")
21:    Else
22:            DefaultCursors = True
23:    End If
24: End Sub
```

Note
The paths used in the preceding code depend on how you installed Visual Basic on your computer.

Caution
You should reset the mousepointers back to the default values in the OLECompleteDrag event, when the operation is finished.

The OLEDragDrop Event

The OLEDragDrop event is triggered when data is dropped onto the target. If data was placed into the DataObject, it can be retrieved by using the GetData method. The following example retrieves data using the DataObject's GetData method and places it into the target control:

```
Private Sub picDisplay_OLEDragDrop(Data As VB.DataObject, Effect As Long,_
Button As _
    Integer, Shift As Integer, X As Single, Y As Single)
      txtLastName.Text = Data.GetData(vbCFText)
End Sub
```

Before accepting the data that is being dropped, you should query the DataObject to check the data type. The GetFormat method is used to check whether the data being dropped is compatible with the target control. If it is, the drop action is completed, as shown in the following code:

```
Private Sub picDisplay_OLEDragDrop(Data As VB.DataObject, Effect As Long,_
Button As _
  Integer, Shift As Integer, X As Single, Y As Single)
    If Data.GetFormat(vbCFText) Then
       picDisplay.Text = Data.GetData(vbCFText)
    End If
End Sub
```

If the data was not placed into the DataObject object when the OLEStartDrag event occurred, the source control's OLESetData event is triggered by the GetData method to retrieve the source control's data. The OLESetData event enables the source control to respond to only one request for a given format of data, as shown in the following code:

```
Private Sub picDisplay_OLESetData(Data As VB.DataObject, DataFormat As _
Integer)
   If DataFormat = vbCFText Then
      Data.SetData txtLastName.SelText, vbCfText
   End If
End Sub
```

Whenever the effect argument is changed in the OLEDragDrop event, the source control's OLECompleteDrag event is triggered. This enables the source control to finish the drag-and-drop process. This event is the last one to be triggered in any drag-and-drop operation.

The OLECompleteDrag Event

The OLECompleteDrag event has only the effect argument, which is used to inform the source control of the action that was taken when the data is dropped. If a move was specified and the data is dropped into the target, the following code deletes the data from the source control:

```
Private Sub txtLastName_OLECompleteDrag(Effect As Long)
   If Effect = vbDropEffectMove Then
      txtLastName.SelText = ""
   End If
End Sub
```

The button and shift arguments in the OLEDragDrop event are used to respond to the state of the mouse buttons and the Shift, Ctrl, and Alt keys. For example, when dragging data into a control, you can enable the user to specify a copy operation by pressing the Ctrl key while dragging the data. In the following code, the shift argument is used to determine if the Ctrl key is pressed when the data is dropped. If it is, a copy is performed, otherwise, a move is performed:

```
Private Sub picDisplay_OLEDragDrop(Data As VB.DataObject, Effect As Long,_
Button As _
        Integer, Shift As Integer, X As Single, Y As Single)
   If Shift And vbCtrlMask Then
       picDisplay.Text = Data.GetData(vbCFText)
       Effect = vbDropEffectCopy
   Else
       picDisplay.Text = Data.GetData(vbCFText)
       Effect = vbDropEffectMove
   End If
End Sub
```

In addition, you can also use the button argument to see which mouse button was clicked, and respond differently for each variation. For instance, you might want to let the user move the data by clicking the right mouse button.

Enhancing the Application with OLE

Now that you have an understanding of what OLE drag and drop can do, how it works, and the events and methods you can use, you are going to add this capability to the address book application that you have been creating. Start by opening the address book project and display the frmMain form. The functions that you are going to add will enable the user to drag a name from the TreeView control to one of three icons on the toolbar to perform the following actions:

- Display the selected entry in the data entry form.
- Delete the selected entry.
- Print the entry using Crystal Reports.

The first step is to add the three PictureBox controls to the toolbar as shown in Figure 15.2 and set the properties that are listed in Table 15.7.

FIGURE 15.2.

Adding the icons to the toolbar for the OLE drag-and-drop functionality.

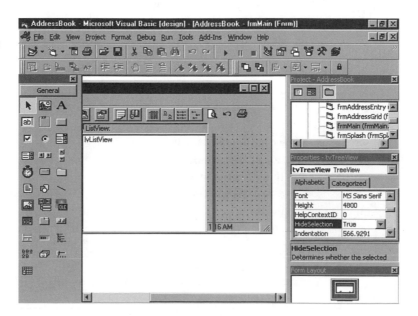

TABLE **15.7.** THE PICTUREBOX CONTROLS AND PROPERTY SETTINGS.

Control	Property	Value
PictureBox	Name	picDisplay
	OLEDropMode	Manual
	Borderstyle	0-None
	Height	330
	Width	360
	Top	60
PictureBox	Name	picDelete
	OLEDropMode	Manual
	Borderstyle	0-None
	Height	330
	Width	360
	Top	60
PictureBox	Name	picPrint
	OLEDropMode	Manual
	Borderstyle	0-None
	Height	330
	Width	360
	Top	60

Choose the pictures you want to represent the three functions. In addition, you need to
set the TreeView control's OLEDRAGMODE property to Automatic to enable the addition of
code to start the drag process. After you have done this, the only step remaining is to add
the code that will place the selected names record key into the DataObject when the drag
process is started, and then when the data is dropped, the PictureBox that it was dropped
on will retrieve the record key and perform the operation specified for that PictureBox
(such as display, delete, or print). The code in Listing 15.5 performs the action for the
display event.

LISTING **15.5.** ADDRESSDRAG.TXT—SETTING THE DRAG OPERATION FOR THE ADDRESS BOOK
APPLICATION.

```
1: Private Sub tvTreeView_OLEStartDrag(Data As ComctlLib.DataObject,_
2: AllowedEffects As Long)
3:     Data.SetData tvTreeView.SelectedItem.Key
4: End Sub
```

15

```
 5:
 6: Private Sub picDisplay_OLEDragDrop(Data As DataObject, Effect As Long,_
 7: Button As Integer, Shift As _
 8:          Integer, X As Single, Y As Single)
 9:     frmAddressEntry.sqlEntry = "select * from [Address Entry] Where_
10: [AddressID] = " & _
11:          Mid(tvTreeView.SelectedItem.Key, 1, 3)
12:     frmAddressEntry.Show
13: End Sub
```

Place this code into your address book main form and try the new functions that you
have just added.

Note

The preceding code assumes that you have modified the data entry form
and converted it into a custom control as discussed on Day 11. If not, you
need to modify the code to call the data entry form instead of displaying
the control.

Using the System Tray control

These days, you want to have many applications running for easy access yet don't want
them displayed all the time. Many of these applications do this by using the Windows
system tray functionality. The *system tray* is the frame on the far right of the Windows
taskbar (see Figure 15.3). The icons displayed in the tray are used to interact with their
associated applications.

FIGURE 15.3.

*The system tray has
many application icons
displayed for easy
access.*

Microsoft provides the system tray control so you can provide this same functionality to
users of your application. To see how to use this control in an application, add it to your
Address Book project. A project such as the Address Book is a good example to use
because many users need quick access to the names and phone numbers in the book but
don't need it to be displayed all the time.

The SysTray control contains only three properties and four events that you'll use to perform any action required (see Table 15.8).

TABLE 15.8. THE SYSTRAY CONTROL'S PROPERTIES AND EVENTS.

Name	Description
	Properties
InTray	Specifies whether the icon will appear in the system tray
TrayTip	Contains the text that's displayed when the mouse pointer is positioned on the icon
TrayIcon	Sets the bitmap used as the system tray icon
	Events
MouseDblClick	Occurs when either mouse button is used to double-click the icon
MouseMove	Occurs when the mouse is moved over the icon
MouseUp	Occurs when either mouse button is released when positioned on the icon
MouseDown	Occurs when either mouse button is pressed when positioned on the icon

Adding the Control

To add the control, first open the Address Book project in Visual Basic. Then, to add the control project, choose File, Add Project and select SYSTRAY.VBP in the Visual Basic /SAMPLES directory. This adds a new project with several objects to the Project Explorer window (see Figure 15.4). When the control is included in the project, its icon appears in the Visual Basic toolbox (see Figure 15.5).

FIGURE 15.4.

Adding the new control to the Address Book application project.

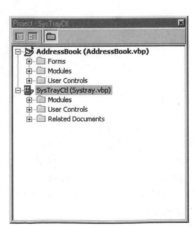

FIGURE 15.5.

The new control is displayed as an icon in the Toolbox window.

As you can see, the custom control that you created and added to the project in an earlier lesson and the SysTray control both have the same icon. This is because neither you nor the person who created the SysTray control set the ToolBoxBitmap property for the control. If you want, you can change this property yourself to make it easier for you to identify which control is which. Close any open form or code window, and then open the frmMain form. Place the SysTray control on the form and set the properties listed in Table 15.9.

TABLE 15.9. THE PROPERTY SETTINGS FOR THE SYSTRAY CONTROL.

Property	Value
Name	sysAdTray
InTray	True
ToolTip	'Address Book Application'
TrayIcon	Set to any valid bitmap that you want to use

For this to work with the address book, you need to add a new item to the main menu to allow users to hide the application when it's not being used. You also will need to add the code to redisplay the application when users double-click the associated tray icon. You can use the following code line in both places because it toggles the form's Visible property from True to False:

```
Me.Visible = Not Me.Visible
```

The one problem when using the system tray control is that if you use an Unload or End statement to end the application, the application terminates abnormally. For the system tray control to work properly, you need to add two Windows API definitions to the application's common code module (see Listing 15.6). Then, in the application's exit routine, you need to add the following code line in place of the Unload statement:

```
PostMessage Me.hwnd, WM_CLOSE, 0&, 0&
```

LISTING 15.6. SYSAPI.TXT—USING WINDOWS API CALLS SO THE SYSTEM TRAY CONTROL CAN WORK.

```
1: Public Declare Function SetForegroundWindow Lib "user32" (ByVal hwnd As _
2: Long) As Long
3: Public Declare Function PostMessage Lib "user32" Alias "PostMessageA" _
4:    (ByVal hwnd As Long, ByVal wMsg As Long, ByVal wParam As Long, ByVal
5:    lParam As Long) As Long
6: Public Const WM_USER = &H400&
7: Public Const WM_CLOSE = &H10&
```

Now, run the application to see how the control works by hiding the application and then double-clicking the tray icon to redisplay it.

Using Menus

If the only function that you can perform with the SysTray control was the one described in the preceding section, it would be a pretty good control. In addition to the basic capability that you've added, you can also add support to display application menu items as pop-ups for the tray icon without displaying the entire application. By using the menus, you can display any non-child form in the application for users to access.

To add pop-up menu capability, you would add the code in Listing 15.7 to the sysAdTray_MouseUp event routine.

LISTING 15.7. SYSMENU.TXT—ADDING POP-UP MENU PROCESSING TO THE SYSTRAY CONTROL.

```
1: Private Sub sysAdTray_MouseUp(Button As Integer, Id As Long)
2:     ' SetForegroundWindow and PostMessage (WM_USER) must wrap all
       ' popup menu's
3:     ' in order to work correctly with the Notification Icons
4:     SetForegroundWindow Me.hwnd
5:
6:     Select Case Button
7:     Case vbRightButton
8:         Me.PopupMenu mnuHelp, vbPopupMenuRightButton
9:     Case vbLeftButton
10:        Me.PopupMenu mnuFile, vbPopupMenuRightButton
11:    End Select
```

```
12:
13:       PostMessage Me.hwnd, WM_USER, 0&, 0&
14: '- - - - - - - - - - - - - - - - - - - - - - - - - - - - - - - - - - - - - - - - - - - - - - - - - - - - - - - - - - - - - - - - - -
15: End Sub
```

15

In this routine, you can see that you can test to see which button was clicked, allowing you to perform different actions based on the mouse button clicked. Also, because of the quirks with using the SysTray control, you need to use the two API calls as shown to set the correct Windows handles.

Add the code in Listing 15.7 to the Address Book application. Now, start the application and use each mouse button to click the tray icon to see the different menus that pop up (see Figure 15.6).

FIGURE 15.6.

Displaying menus by clicking the system tray icon.

Introducing the New Date Controls

Almost every windows application requires the user to enter dates in one format or another. Originally, most programmers used text boxes and then coded all of the edit and input routines required to enable the user to enter dates properly. Then, the Masked Edit control was introduced allowing the programmer to specify an input length and format for the data. Along the way, many Calendar custom controls were created to display a visual calendar to the user, as shown in Figure 15.7.

FIGURE 15.7.

Displaying a calendar in Microsoft Access for the user to select a date.

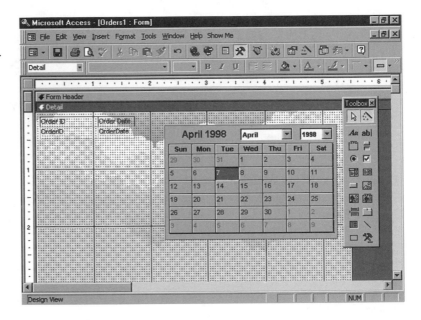

In fact, Visual Basic 5 had an unsupported Calendar control included on the CD-ROM. Now, with Visual Basic 6, there are two new controls that give the programmer the most robust date interaction yet possible. The following are the two new controls:

- **MonthView**—This control makes it easy for users to view and set date information using a calendar interface.
- **DateTimePicker**—This control displays date and/or time information and allows the user to modify this information.

Each of these controls address a particular date display function as discussed in the following sections.

The MonthView Control

The MonthView control should be used whenever you want to display date information to the user in an easy-to-follow calendar-style format. Allowing the user to choose a date using the mouse, instead of typing a date value, makes it easier to work with dates within an application. In addition to the standard one month view, this control has the ability to display up to 12 months at one time on a form. This feature can be used when you want to give the users the ability to view date information around a specified date. Figure 15.8 shows the MonthView control's display.

FIGURE 15.8.

The MonthView control displayed at runtime can be accessed with the mouse or the keyboard.

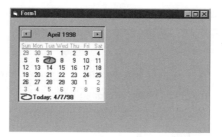

15

Buttons at the top of the control are used to scroll the months in and out of view. The user can navigate using either the keyboard or the mouse. You can also see that the specified date is highlighted while the current date is circled. To see how this control works, start a new project in Visual Basic and add the MonthView control to the Toolbox. Now, add the MonthView control and two command buttons to the form as shown in Figure 15.9.

FIGURE 15.9.

Adding the MonthView control to a form.

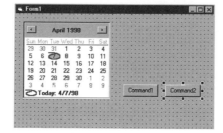

Set the Name properties for the controls as shown in Table 15.10.

TABLE 15.10. SETTING THE PROPERTIES FOR THE MONTHVIEW DEMO.

Control	Property	Value
MonthView	Name	mvDate
Command1	Name	cmdShowDate
	Caption	Show Date
Command2	Name	cmdQuit
	Caption	Quit

In the mvDate_DateClick routine, add the following line of code:

```
MsgBox "You have selected the date: " & DateClicked, vbInformation
```

When you run this application, the above code will display a message dialog telling you the date that you clicked the MonthView control. The controls Value property will be set after the `DateClicked` event is finished processing. Besides the `Value` property that you can use anywhere in the application, the control has several other properties that return specific date information:

- `Month`—Returns a value (1–12) of the month containing the currently selected date.
- `Day`—Returns the day number (1–31) currently selected.
- `DayOfWeek`—Indicates the day of the week the selected date falls on.
- `Year`—Returns the year of the selected date.
- `Week`—Returns the week number the selected date falls in.

Selecting a Date Range

If your application requires the user to enter a date range, you can use the MonthView control to display or select a date range. In order to allow the selection of more than one date, the `MultiSelect` property must be set to `True`. In addition, you can control the maximum number of days that can be selected using the `MaxSelCount` property (the default being seven days). The `SelStart` and `SelEnd` properties will contain the starting and ending dates in a range. However, if only one date is selected, both properties will contain the same date. When a range of dates is selected, they will all be highlighted (see Figure 15.10).

FIGURE 15.10.

Selecting a date range will highlight all of the selected dates on the control.

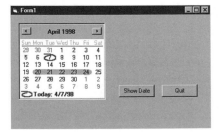

Displaying Multiple Months

To display more than one month on the control, you would use the `MonthRows` and `MonthColumns` properties. These are used to specify how many months will be displayed. To display six months, set the `MonthRows` property to 2 and the `MonthColumns` property to 3. The resulting display would resemble the one in Figure 15.11.

FIGURE 15.11.

Certain types of applications require multiple months displayed at the same time.

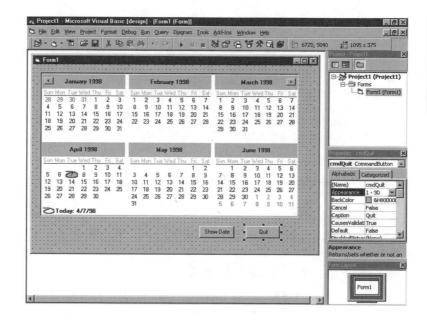

Clicking the arrow buttons at the top of the control would scroll the next six months or the previous six months into view. However, you can see that this takes up large amounts of space on the form.

Formatting the Calendar

Besides the standard type of formatting properties to modify the background and foreground colors of the control, you can also specify which day of the week will appear as the first day by changing the value of the StartOfWeek property. In addition, the ShowWeekNumbers property specifies if week numbers will be displayed in a separate column on the control. Finally, the current date can be displayed at the bottom of the control by setting the ShowToday property to True. Any day's number on the control can have its font set to bold by using the GetDayBold event. This allows you to draw the user's attention to specific dates (such as holidays, vacations, etc.). To bold all of the Sundays on a control—even when new months are scrolled into view—add the following code to the mvDate_GetDayBold event routine in the demo form:

```
Dim I As Integer
I = vbSunday
While I < Count
    State(I — mvDate.StartOfWeek) = True
    I = I + 7
Wend
```

When you run the application, you should see every Sunday bolded as shown in Figure 15.12.

FIGURE 15.12.

Changing the font properties to highlight important dates.

Although this control is very useful, it does take up a lot of space on a form. When you have space requirements or do not need to display a calendar all the time, you should consider using the other new date control—the DateTimePicker control.

The DateTimePicker Control

If you are short of space on a form, but need a date control on the form, you should use the DateTimePicker control. This control presents itself as a drop-down box (see Figure 15.13).

FIGURE 15.13.

Adding a DateTimePicker control takes up as much space as a DropDown control.

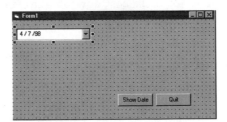

When the DateTimePicker is dropped down, a MonthView calendar is displayed. Depending on whether you are working with dates or times, the control has the following two different modes:

- Drop-down calendar—Enables the user to display a drop-down calendar that can be used to select a date.
- Time format—Allows the user to select a field in the date display, and then press the up/down arrow to set its value.

The control can be used to display the date in several preset formats, and you can also specify custom formats using the standard format strings.

Because the DateTimePicker acts like a MaskedEdit control, each part of the date or time is treated as a separate field within the edit portion of the control.

Try using this control by adding it to the demo form and then executing the application. Then, when you click the arrow button of the control, the MonthView calendar will be displayed as shown in Figure 15.14.

FIGURE 15.14.

Selecting a date from the MonthView calendar that is displayed.

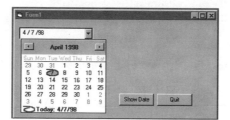

The best feature of these controls is that you can bind them to a date field in the database recordset. This provides a codeless method of inputting and displaying date information from a database.

Summary

In this chapter, you learned what OLE drag and drop is really about and how to add this functionality to your application to give the user another way of accessing the information in the database. By enabling the user to drag an entry item to an icon to request some type of action, you are adding an easier way to work with the application.

Q&A

Q **What is the difference between the standard drag and drop and the OLE drag and drop?**

A OLE drag and drop is used to move information between any two ActiveX controls or between two OLE-enabled applications.

Q **What are the two ways of using OLE drag and drop?**

A OLE drag and drop can be an automatic process where it is supported or a manual process when you need complete control over the drag process.

Q **How do I know if a control supports OLE drag and drop?**

A The best way to see if a control supports OLE drag and drop is by looking at its property list for the OLEDragMode and OLEDropMode properties. If they are present, the control supports OLE drag and drop.

Q Can I make changes to the SysTray custom control code?

A Yes. Because you have the source code, you can make any changes that you think might be beneficial for your application.

Q What does the SysTray control really let me do?

A The SysTray control allows you to give users access to the functions of your application directly from the system tray icon.

Q What is the difference between the MonthView and DateTimePicker controls?

A The biggest difference between these two controls, is that the MonthView control displays a calendar style display at all times, while the DateTimePicker will only display the calendar when the dropdown button is clicked.

Workshop

The Workshop provides quiz questions to help solidify your understanding of the material covered, as well as exercises to provide you with experience in using what you've learned. Try to understand the quiz and exercise answers before continuing on to the next day's lesson. Answers are provided in Appendix A, "Answers to Exercises."

Quiz

1. What is the method used to place data into the `DataObject` during an OLE drag operation?

2. How would you tell the user that something has been processed?

Exercise

Add the code to process the Delete operation when an entry is dragged onto the Delete picture box.

DAY **16**

Coping with Error Handling

In a perfect world, the applications you design would work all the time without errors ever occurring. However, we live in an imperfect world where mistakes are made, disk drives stop working, and files are erased. These types of problems and more cause runtime errors. Runtime errors can be separated into two types: those that are found and corrected before the application is released to the users, and those that must be handled while the application is being used. The second group of runtime errors are spotlighted in this chapter.

To deal with these errors, you need to design error-handling routines in your application code. Through the years, the process of dealing with errors has become a complex issue. Now, with the capability of creating your own ActiveX components, another layer of error handling has been added to the equation. In this chapter, you will learn what the types of errors are that can occur in your application and how you handle them. You will also see how to make use of the Visual Basic Error objects that assist you in catching any errors that might occur in the application. Anther technique that you can use is to create a log file that will provide a way for you to see exactly what happened when the error occurred. In addition, you will learn how a Visual Basic application processes an error.

Types of Errors

Before we start discussing error handling, I would like to make a blanket statement:

Errors will occur, no matter how good you are! So get over it.

This might sound a bit pretentious, but many programmers think that they cannot make a mistake. And as always, that is their first mistake. You can only create good error-handling routines if you accept the fact that you can make a mistake when designing an application.

Unfortunately, no matter how good your testing is, there will always be errors that you did not think of or expect in your application. Because the coding of an error routine isn't easy, fun, or exciting, many programmers fall a little short in the anticipation and prevention of any application errors. When this happens, Visual Basic often takes control and abnormally exits your application. This can result in lost data if the error is severe enough.

Once Visual Basic is involved in handling the error, your application has already been stopped. There is no way at that point for you to undo the damage and allow the application to continue processing. Even more dangerously, if the error doesn't stop your application, it might continue executing with unpredictable results. Like everything else in programming, error handling requires good design skills to create good error-handling routines. In a well-designed application, errors are handled by the application and trapped before Visual Basic ever sees it.

Errors in General

Before handling any errors, you should understand the types of errors that can occur. The term error actually covers a multitude of programming problems that pop up during the design, creation, and testing phases of application development. There are four distinct types of errors:

- Syntax
- Compile
- Logic
- Runtime

In previous releases of Visual Basic, the issue of Syntax errors were dealt with in the code editor. If you entered a line of code incorrectly, the code editor would alert you to the problem before you could continue. With Visual Basic 5, the code editor has been enhanced to display the syntax of the commands you can use and the valid properties, methods, or events that you could use on a given line of code. This enables you to concentrate more on the logic of your application than on your typing. However, after you fix a syntax error it will not occur again.

The next type of error that can occur is a Compile error. These occur when your code doesn't adhere to the Visual Basic command structure standards. Again, these errors are displayed to you when you compile the application, enabling you to fix and then forget them.

Logic errors are the hardest to find in an application because the application will execute without any errors occurring. However, the application will probably not process as you expected.

The final error type, runtime, occurs while the application is executing and causes it to end abnormally. This chapter shows you how to detect and repair runtime errors. Finding and fixing logic errors will be discussed on Day 18, "Testing and Debugging the Application."

Error Types

Runtime errors usually occur in one of four similar groups of problems. The four types of Visual Basic errors are as follows:

- General File errors
- Physical errors
- Code errors
- Database errors

Each different type of error must be handled differently in your application. And, for each group of error, you will see what you can and cannot do to resolve them.

General File Errors

Most general file errors occur because invalid file information is processed by the application. A bad filename or invalid directory path will prevent most applications from continuing to process any information. Usually the user can fix these errors, and the application will continues from where the error occurred. The basic error handler for this type of error is to report the problem to the user and prompt him for the additional information to complete or retry the operation.

File errors are one of the oldest types of errors that can occur in your application and are listed in Table 16.1. These types of errors usually enable you to give the user a chance to correct the problem.

TABLE 16.1. GENERAL VISUAL BASIC FILE ERRORS.

Error Code	Error Message
52	Bad filename or number
53	File not found
54	Bad file mode
55	File already open
58	File already exists
59	Bad record length
61	Disk full
62	Input past end of file
63	Bad record number
64	Bad filename
67	Too many files
74	Can't rename with different drive
75	Path/File access error
76	Path not found

Its important to know that these errors will not occur when you are accessing data within a database. Most of the time, you can create an error routine that anticipates these errors, prompts the user, and then returns the operation that caused the error. In some cases, you will not be able to prompt the user and retry the operation; you would then display a message giving the user the information or at least an error number that will help her identify and, hopefully, fix the problem.

Physical Errors

Another group of older common error is caused by problems that occur with the physical media or hardware on the user's computer. Printers that don't print, disk drives without disks, and disconnected communication ports are the most common examples of physical errors. These errors might or might not be fixed quickly by the user. Usually, you can report the error to the user, wait for them to fix the problem, and then either continue with the process or exit the application. As an example, if the application is trying to copy a file to a disk and there is no disk in the drive, all you need to do is tell the user that they need to insert a disk and then wait for the user to correct the problem and click OK to continue the process.

Code Errors

A program code error cannot be resolved by the user. These are generally programming problems caused by unexpected conditions that have occurred in the application code. The best way to deal with these errors is to tell the user to report the message to you and exit the program. After you have this information, you would need to find the problem in the application code, fix it, recompile the application, and then send the new executable file to the user.

Database Errors

When you start designing and working with database applications, another type of error that occurs is the data-related error. These usually include those errors that deal with data type or field size problems, table access restrictions, duplicate or incorrect data added to the database, any SQL-related errors, or an empty recordset that shouldn't be empty. Database access falls into two categories that you have already worked with earlier in this book, Data Controls and Data Access Objects. The way you handle these access errors is unique to the access type. For most errors, all you need to do is trap the error, report it to the user, and enable the user to return to the data entry or display form to fix the problem.

If you use the Data Control on your data forms, you can take advantage of the automatic database error reporting that is built into the Data Control. When you try to perform an action that is inherently incorrect for the database that the Data Control is connected to, the Data Control will trap the error and display a message to the user. The Data Control provides a complete database error reporting even if you have no error-handling routines in your Visual Basic application. Along with the automatic error handling provided, the Data Control also has an Error event that is triggered each time a data-related error occurs. You can add custom code to this event to fix some of the database errors for the user, or display a better, more understandable error message.

Note

It is usually not a good idea to override the default error routines of the Data Control with your own database error code. Al long as you use the Data Control, you don't need to add database error-handling routines to your application. However, if you need to perform special actions when a database error occurs, you would need to add code to the Data Control's Event routine.

On the other hand, if you are using the Data Access objects instead of the Data Control, you will need to add the error-handling routine to your project. As an example, if you are adding a new record to the database, you will need to trap for any error that might occur during the add process.

> It is a good idea to open database tables in the Form_Load event. That way, if any errors occur, you can catch and fix them before any data access really occurs.

The Error-Handling Process

When you first start to think about creating an error-handling routine for your application, you should realize that error handlers in Visual Basic aren't as straightforward as they might have been in older, more procedure -driven languages such as COBOL or BASIC. There are several reasons why this is true. First, Visual Basic is event-driven, meaning that every event that occurs will trigger some operation or action. Second, Visual Basic uses a call stack to keep track of the routines being processed and to isolate local variables within a routine. When your application exits from a routine, it can lose track of the values of any internal variables it might have been using. This makes resuming execution after the error has been resolved very difficult. Finally, all errors are local. If an error occurs, it should be handled in the routine where it occurred, which means you must write an error handler for each routine that you have included in the application.

Because of the way Visual Basic handles errors, you need to understand how Visual Basic searches application code for an active error routine. In addition, you need to know how to enable an error routine or, as Visual Basic calls it, an error trap. Before looking at the hierarchy of the error processing flow, lets take a look at the commands and methods that are available in Visual Basic to help you handle any errors that occur. There are two main Visual Basic commands that help you control the error process. These are the On Error and Resume statements.

The On Error Statement

The On Error statement gives you the capability of enabling and disabling error traps within the application as well as specifying the location of the error-handling routine to execute for a given routine or form. The On Error statement comes in three different flavors:

- On Error GoTo [*Line* ¦ *Label*]
- On Error Resume Next
- On Error GoTo 0

The first version of this statement will enable the error-handling routine that begins at the line or label specified in the statement. If an error occurs while this error routine is enabled, control will jump to the first line of the code in the error routine. This is the most common way of using the On Error statement.

Before going on to the next version of the statement, investigate the use of line numbers or labels for the error routine. Before Windows programming was done in Visual Basic, most basic programs written for DOS computers were created with line numbers assigned by the basic editor to each line in the program code. This was both good and bad. First, the line numbers had to be set so that the programmer could add new lines in between those that were already there. The good part of line numbers was that when an error occurred, you could have the line number printed where the error occurred, enabling you to find the problem and fix it quicker. This was done using some properties of the Err object that existed even back in the DOS days.

These days, using line numbers in Visual Basic has fallen into a programming black hole. Although they are still supported, most programmers don't use them. The Err object in Visual Basic that is discussed in the next section still supports the line number property.

Getting back to the On Error statement, if the second version of the statement is used, control will jump to the statement immediately following the one where the error occurred. This enables you to trap an error and have the application simply ignore it. Of course, this only works if the line of code that has the error will not effect any of the following code due because of the error.

The third and final version of the On Error statement will disable the error-handling routine in the current procedure. This version can be used to temporarily disable an error routine in a procedure. You would then need to execute the first or second version of the statement to re-enable the error routine. When you add an error routine to an event procedure or to a subroutine or function that you create, it should be placed at the bottom of the routine. In addition, you need to place an Exit Sub statement immediately preceding the error routine label. This will enable the routine to exit normally if execution flows to the bottom of the routine.

16

The Resume Statement

If an error is trapped by an error-handling routine, and control is passed to the error routine, the only way to deactivate and return from the routine is to execute one of the three forms of the Resume statement:

- Resume [*Line* ¦ *Label*]
- Resume Next
- Resume [0]

The first type specifies the line number or the label where you want control of the application execution to be returned. The second type causes execution to continue from the statement immediately following the one that caused the error. Finally, the third version will re-execute the statement that had the error. If the error routine has resolved the reason the error occurred, you can use the third version to retry the operation. The best example of this would be when the user tries to save a file to a disk and there is no disk in the drive. An error will occur and the error routine will be executed. In the error routine, the user is told to insert a disk and click the OK button of the MessageBox. When this is done, the application will retry the save operation. Of course, you should give the user the capability to cancel the operation altogether.

The Built-in Error Objects

Among the many objects that are included in Visual Basic, there are two that you can use to track and report errors that occur during the execution of your application. The Err and Error objects provide useful information about the error that has just occurred.

The Err object exists and can be accessed anywhere in a Visual Basic application. Each time an error occurs in the application the Err object's properties will be populated with the information about the current error. The object contains several properties and two methods, listed in Table 16.2, that you can use in the process.

TABLE 16.2. THE METHODS AND PROPERTIES OF THE ERR OBJECT.

Type	Description
Properties	
Number	The Visual Basic error number
Source	Name of the current Visual Basic file here the error occurred
Description	The description of the error number found in the Number property
HelpFile	The full path and filename of the Help file that supports the reported error
HelpContext	The Help topic ID in the help file indicated in the preceding property

Type	Description
Properties	
LastDLLError	The error code of the last call to a DLL
Methods	
Clear	Clears all of the property settings of the Err object
Raise	Used to generate an error in the application

16

In addition to these properties and methods, there is one other Visual Basic variable that you can use when processing errors. ERL is a global Visual Basic variable that is undocumented, but enables you to access the line number of the code that caused the error. By using both the archaic line numbers in your application code and the ERL variable, you can pinpoint the offending line of code.

Note You don't need to use line numbers in the On Error and Resume statements even if you use them as a numbering scheme for your code. In addition, each module that you use line numbers in should have its own unique numbering scheme to enable you to find the offending line.

The Error object and its related Errors collection are available only when the application is using one of the data access object libraries. The Error object is a child of the DBEngine and is used to obtain additional information about any database error that might occur in your application. The advantage that the Error object has over the Err object is that it contains many more properties that are directly related to the database server that it is connected to. Because many database servers can have several errors occur related to one problem, the Error object can return each of the error numbers in the order they were raised. The Err object only returns the last error that occurred.

When an Error Occurs

When an error occurs in your application, the first question you want to be answered is "What process should be performed?" However, the second question is more important: "Which error routine will be handling the error?" Every time an On Error statement is executed, another error-handling routine is enabled. The only way an On Error statement is disabled is by executing the On Error GoTo 0 statement or by exiting the procedure where the routine was enabled. The active error handler is the one in which code execution is currently taking place. Now the fun begins! When an error occurs within a procedure without an enabled error-handling routine, or an error occurs within the error-handling routine itself, Visual Basic will search the calls list for another enabled error-handling routine. The calls list is the sequence of calls that leads to the currently executing procedure. To display the calls list yourself (see Figure 16.1), choose View, Call Stack from the menu.

FIGURE 16.1.

Viewing the list of procedures in the calls stack when an error occurs.

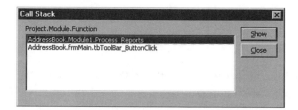

Note

The calls stack is only available when the program is halted because of an error, or because a breakpoint has been set.

To understand how this all works, suppose the following sequence of calls has been made in your application as shown in Figure 16.2. The order of execution is listed here:

1. A command button click event calls subroutine A.

2. Subroutine A then makes a call to Function B.

3. Function B calls subroutine C.

FIGURE 16.2.

A visual diagram of a calls stack list.

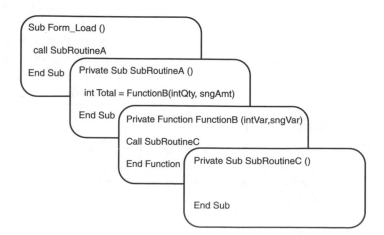

Whichever routine is currently processing, the routines that proceed it are pending, waiting for control to be returned to them. Now, if an error occurs in subroutine C and an error handler isn't enabled or there is none coded for the routine, Visual Basic will search backward through the pending procedures in the calls list. First it will look at Function B, then Subroutine A, then the initial Click event looking for an enabled error-handling routine. The search will go no further back than the top of the current calls list. If it doesn't find any enabled error handler, Visual Basic will present the default error message and halt execution of the application. If an enabled error-handling routine is found, execution will continue in that routine as if the error occurred in the same procedure that contains the error handler itself.

If you haven't caught up to the error yet, here's the problem with all of this. If a Resume or Resume Next statement is executed in the error-handling routine, control will be returned as described in the following list:

- **Resume**—The call to the procedure that was just searched is re-executed.
- **Resume Next**—Execution will return to the statement following the last statement that was executed in the current routine (the one that contains the error-handling routine).

The common thread here is that the statement that will be executed is in the routine where the error-handling routine was found, not necessarily in the routine where the error occurred. If you don't remember this, and don't code an error handler in every routine that you create, your code may perform in ways that you did not intend it to. Also, if the error routine cannot handle the error that occurred, you should use the Raise method to generate an error that will be handled by the error-handling routine in the calling procedure.

Handling Errors

When you have decided how you want to handle the errors that you are anticipating in the routines of your application, you can start writing the actual error-handling code. The first step in any error routine is to add a line label to mark the beginning of the error-handling routine. You should use a descriptive name for the label and it should be followed by a colon (:). The next step is to code the body of the error-handling routine. This is the code that actually handles the error, usually by using a Select statement to check for the error codes that are likely to occur in this procedure, and specifying the action to be taken for each of them. In addition, you should add the else statement to the Select, just in case an error has occurred that you did not anticipate.

Abort, Retry, or Cancel

The hardest part of the error handling process is deciding what you want the application to do when the error occurs. Some errors can be fixed and the application can continue, whereas others require the application to close in order to fix them. Other errors might be ignored if they aren't detrimental to the application process. Before getting into the process of creating an error handler, lets take a look at a standard error handler in Visual Basic. Error handlers have three main parts to them:

- The `On Error GoTo` statement
- The error-handling code
- The exit statement

The `On Error GoTo` statement usually appears at the beginning of a routine and is used to enable the error-handling routine as shown.

```
On Error GoTo CalcTotalError
```

Every time an error occurs in the routine, the program will immediately pass control to the label `CalcTotalError` and begin executing the code that follows the label. Depending on the error and what process you want to perform, the error-handling code can be as simple or as complex as you need it to be. The simplest form of an error handler would just display the error number and description as shown in the following:

```
MsgBox CStr(Err.Number) & " - " & Err.Description
```

The third and final piece to this puzzle is the exit statement. This is the line of code that specifies where to go after the error handler has completed its work. Depending on how you want to exit the routine, you would use one of the three `Resume` statements or the `Exit Sub` or `Exit Function` to immediately exit the routine where the error occurred. The completed error-handling routine would look like the one in the following routine:

```
Private Function CalcTotal(intQty as Integer, sngAmt as Single) as Single
On Error GoTo CalcTotal Error
CalcTotal = intQty * sngAmt
Exit Function
CalcTotalError:
MsgBox CStr(Err.Number) & " - " & Err.Description
End Function
```

To see how to use the basic structure of an error-handling routine, start a new project in Visual Basic and add two text box and label controls and one command button to the default form, as shown in Figure 16.3.

FIGURE 16.3.

Creating a demo application to test the error-handling concepts.

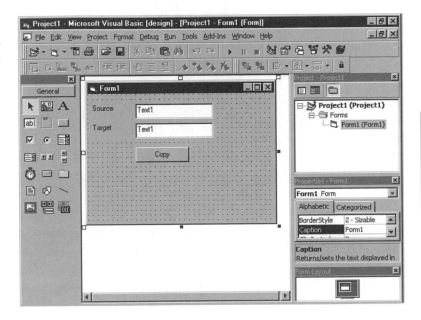

For this example, we will be using the code in Listing 16.1 that you created in the FileCopy project earlier in this book. You may notice that the code has been simplified to enable us to concentrate on the error handler.

LISTING 16.1. FILECOPY.TXT—A SUBSET OF THE FILE COPY CODE FROM CHAPTER 1.

```
1: Private Sub cmdCopy_Click()
2: Dim lngFileSize As Long
3: Dim intLoopCtr As Integer
4: Dim intBufferCount As Integer
5: Dim strInByte As String * 256
6:
7: ' If the destination file exists, ask the user if they
8: ' want to continue
9:     If Dir(txtTargetFile.Text) <> "" Then
10:         If MsgBox(txtTargetFile.Text & vbCrLf & _
11:             " already exists. Copy over old file?", vbOKCancel) =
vbCancel Then
12:             Exit Sub
13:         End If
14:     End If
15:
16: ' Get the size of the file to copy
17: ' and calculate the number of times to loop
```

continues

16

LISTING 16.1. CONTINUED

```
18: ' the copy routine based on moving 256 bytes at a time
19:     lngFileSize = FileLen(txtSourceFile.Text)
20:     intBufferCount = lngFileSize / 256
21:
22: ' Open the source and destination files
23:     Open txtSourceFile.Text For Binary As #1
24:     Open txtTargetFile.Text For Binary As #2
25:
26: ' This routine loops until the entire file is copied
27:     For intLoopCtr = 1 To intBufferCount + 1
28:         Get #1, , strInByte
29:         Put #2, , strInByte
30:     Next intLoopCtr
31:
32: ' After the copy is complete close both files
33:     Close #1     ' Close file.
34:     Close #2     ' Close file.
35: ' Inform the user that the function is complete
36:     MsgBox "Copy function complete", vbInformation
37: End Sub.
```

For a file copy process, the errors that might occur are as follows

- File not found
- File already open
- Device I/O error
- Disk full
- Device unavailable
- Permission denied
- Disk not ready
- Path/File access error
- Path not found

To handle these errors, you would create a routine that resembles the one in Listing 16.2.

LISTING 16.2. ERROREX1.TXT—A SAMPLE ERROR ROUTINE FOR A FILE COPY PROCESS.

```
1: FileCopyError:
2: On Error GoTo 0
3: Select Case Err.Number
4:     Case 53 'File not found
```

```
 5:          MsgBox CStr(Err.Number) & " - " & _
 6:          Err.Description, vbOKOnly, App.Title
 7:      Case 55 'File already open
 8:          MsgBox CStr(Err.Number) & " - " & _
 9:          Err.Description, vbOKOnly, App.Title
10:      Case 57 'Device I/O error
11:          MsgBox CStr(Err.Number) & " - " & _
12:          Err.Description, vbOKOnly, App.Title
13:      Case 61 'Disk full
14:          MsgBox CStr(Err.Number) & " - " & _
15:          Err.Description, vbOKOnly, App.Title
16:      Case 68 'Device unavailable
17:          MsgBox CStr(Err.Number) & " - " & _
18:          Err.Description, vbOKOnly, App.Title
19:      Case 70 'Permission denied
20:          MsgBox CStr(Err.Number) & " - " & _
21:          Err.Description, vbOKOnly, App.Title
22:      Case 71 'Disk Not ready
23:          MsgBox CStr(Err.Number) & " - " & _
24:          Err.Description, vbOKOnly, App.Title
25:      Case 75 'Path/File access error
26:          MsgBox CStr(Err.Number) & " - " & _
27:          Err.Description, vbOKOnly, App.Title
28:      Case 76 'Path Not found
29:          MsgBox CStr(Err.Number) & " - " & _
30:          Err.Description, vbOKOnly, App.Title
31:      Case Else
32:          MsgBox CStr(Err.Number) & " - " & _
33:          Err.Description, vbOKOnly, App.Title
34: End Select
```

16

Note

This error routine will only report what the error was, not correct it. If you want to add code to correct one or more of these errors, you would simply include that code in the case statement for that error. You can then decide if the solution enables you to continue the operation; if it does, you would need to add a Resume statement as well.

This routine would be added to the cmdCopy_Click event routine along with the On Error statement at the beginning of the routine, as shown in the following code:

```
Private Sub cmdCopy_Click()
Dim lngFileSize As Long
Dim intLoopCtr As Integer
Dim intBufferCount As Integer
Dim strInByte As String * 256

On Error GoTo FileCopyError
```

```
'
'BODY OF ROUTINE GOES HERE
'
Exit Sub
'
FileCopyError:
'
'ERROR HANDLING ROUTINE GOES HERE (use code from Listing 15.2)
'
End Sub
```

In addition to handling the anticipated errors, you should also add code that will handle
any unexpected errors. This is usually done by adding the `Case Else` statement to the
`Select...End Select` statement group:

```
Case Else 'Unexpected
    MsgBox(CStr(Err.Number) & " - " & _
        Err.Description, vbOKCancel, App.Title)
```

Add the error-handling routine to the file copy code and enter an incorrect filename. This
will generate an error message telling you that the filename isn't found. You can then re-
enter the name and try again. You should also notice that this error routine doesn't use
the `Resume` statement to exit the error handler. The reason for this is that any of the errors
that have occurred are all related to the copy operation, and after the error has happened,
there is no easy way to continue the copy. It is better to just start over.

Whenever you start adding the error-handling routines to your application, you will
quickly see that some code is being repeated over and over again. This will cause problems when you have to change the way a particular error is being handled. In addition,
the more code you add to the application, the more complex it will become. With some
careful planning, you can reduce the amount of code that you add for error handling by
writing a few procedures that the error routines will call to handle the more common
error situations.

Moving the error-checking code into a function enables you to reduce the amount of
code the program has and simplifies the code that determines if the program can continue. Using the previous code examples, you can see that the `filecopy` routine calls the
error checking routine and uses the return value of the function to determine if it should
continue or not:

```
Private Sub cmdCopy_Click()

On Error GoTo FileCopyError
'
'BODY OF ROUTINE GOES HERE
'
Exit Sub
```

```
'
FileCopyError:
'
If ErrorCheck then
    Resume
Else
    Exit Sub
End If
'
End Sub

Private Function ErrorCheck() as Boolean
    On Error GoTo 0
    Select Case Err.Number
        Case 53 'File not found
            If MsgBox(CStr(Err.Number) & " - " & _
            Err.Description, vbRetryCancel, App.Title) = VbRetry then
                ErrorCheck = True
            Else
                ErrorCheck = False
            End If
        Case Else
            MsgBox CStr(Err.Number) & " - " & _
            Err.Description, vbOKOnly, App.Title
            ErrorCheck = False
    End Select
End Function
```

As you can see, the error-routine is called and returns a value of True or False to signal if the error has been fixed. If the error was fixed, the program can continue.

Testing the Error Routine

When you are creating and testing your application, it is very important to test every error routine that you add to the application. One way to do this is to change the code to produce each error that might happen. An easier way is to use the Raise method of the Err object. This gives you the ability to generate any error that you want from within your code. The syntax of the Raise method is:

```
Err.Raise number, source, description, helpfile, helpcontext
```

Or, you can call the method by passing the name of each argument and its value:

```
Err.Raise Number:=71 ' Test the Disk not Ready error
```

To see how this statement works, add another command button to the form and insert the previous line of code. Now, run the application and click the new command button to see what happens. You should get the message box that you coded in the error-handling routine.

In addition, the `Raise` method of the `Err` object can be used to create custom errors for your application. There may be conditions that can occur in your application that you consider errors, that Visual Basic considers "legal" code processing. For these types of problems, you can create your own error numbers and when they occur, you can `Raise` them and deal with them as you see fit. You can also use the other properties of the `Raise` method to set a topic in a help file that the user can view.

Handling Data Access Errors

Data access errors are more sensitive to the way they can be resolved. There are many more things to worry about when working with a database. As discussed earlier today, with Data Controls, you don't need to code any error routines in the data control's `DataErr` event. However, for Data Access Objects, you do need to trap any data access errors that might occur. Because any errors that occur during database access have the capability to damage or destroy data, the way you handle a particular error is based on what the error is. One of the best ways of coping with data access errors is by using the built-in transaction processing statements. The transaction processing commands enable you to control the final outcome of the data access process:

- `BeginTrans`
- `CommitTrans`
- `RollBack`

These commands enable you to reverse a database function to the original data if an error occurs. After a `BeginTrans` statement is executed, every action that is done to a database can be reversed or rolled back until a `CommitTrans` statement is executed. Using this concept, you can create code that backs out of an error or even enables the user to cancel changes that she already made. The following code is an example of enabling the user to cancel her actions:

```
Private Sub cmdClose_Click()
    If MsgBox("Do you want to save your changes?", vbYesNo) = vbYes Then
        MyWorkspace.CommitTrans
    Else
        MyWorkspace.Rollback
    End If
End Sub
```

Note

You should be aware that the Transaction processing that you get using `CommitTrans` and `Rollback` are not error-handling methods; they are instead a way to inform the database that any changes should either be saved or thrown away.

Summary

In this chapter, you saw what goes into making your application "error free." But, as you well know, there is no such thing as an error-free application. The errors that can occur in the application, and how you handle them, is one of the last major design issues that you must deal with for your application. When designing the error-handling routines, the more time you spend anticipating errors that might occur, the better your application will be. It all depends on how good you want the application to appear to the user. If an error occurs, do you want the user to possibly lose hours of work, or maybe lose important data? Hopefully the answer to both is no.

By coding routines that handle any error that might happen, you are making the application easier to use. You have seen how to use the statements and objects provided by Visual Basic to process the errors and maintain the error-handling routines. In addition, you have learned how to force an error to occur in order to test the error routines that you have created. Finally, using the same Visual Basic methods, you can create your own errors in the application to process any logic errors that you want to handle as an error.

Q&A

Q What types of errors can be fixed in order for the program to continue?

A The errors that can be fixed during execution of the application are usually ones that are non-destructive. This means that the error has not caused any data problems. An example of a fixable error is `Disk Not Ready`.

Q What does an `On Error` command do?

A The `On Error` statement gives you the ability to control the error-handling process.

Q What is an `Err` object?

A The `Err` object contains information about an error that has just occurred.

Workshop

The Workshop provides quiz questions to help solidify your understanding of the material covered, as well as exercises to provide you with experience in using what you've learned. Try to understand the quiz and exercise answers before continuing on to the next day's lesson. Answers are provided in Appendix A, "Answers to Exercises."

Quiz

1. What is an error trap?

2. What are the two types of runtime errors?

3. What are some of the ways to continue after an error has occurred?

Exercise

Open the Address Book application that you have been creating and determine where you might want to add some error handling. Then design and create the error routines and include them in the application. Finally, using the Raise method, test each of the errors that you chose to trap.

DAY 17

Building Online Help

Every Windows application that you've ever used has included some type of help system. Help systems can be as simple or as complex as the application can support. If you've assumed that creating a help system to your application is an impossible task, you're wrong. However, it's a task that requires design-time to decide what should be included in the help system and which available features you should use.

Thankfully, Windows has a built-in help engine that almost every application uses. This allows you to concentrate on the content of the help system, not on how to display it. Today's lesson shows how to design, build, and test the help files you'll need to add to your Visual Basic application. Also, several different techniques that you can use to give your application's users help will be discussed.

Note

With the release of Visual Basic 6 and Visual Studio 6, it appears that Microsoft is changing the look and feel of the Help system by making use of the new Web page technology. Visual Basic will now include both the current standard Help workshop and the New HTML Help workshop, allowing you to choose which one you want to use. Both workshops will be discussed in this chapter.

What today's lesson won't teach you is what you should put into the help system. The content of your application's help system depends entirely on the application and the level of help you want to provide.

Designing a Help System

A help system used to be a help file that could be displayed by itself or from within a computer program. These help files were text files displayed as a scrolling page, with very little in the way of advanced options. These days, a help system is much more complex, including video, pictures, sound, and links to Web sites on the Internet. Thanks to these additions, it takes a great deal of thought and effort to create a help system.

A help system is made up of several different help files that in turn are made up of many different text or topic files. Some of these files will contain the text, graphics, or both that appear in the finished help system, whereas other files will contain the information that specifies how your help system will be displayed and how it will perform. In the compile process, you'll take all these files and turn them into one or more finished help files. The best part of this process is that if you don't like any part of the finished system, you can quickly modify the text and recompile it.

To design and create a help system, you need to know what features are available for you to use in the process. If you've used help at all, you already know some capabilities that you can include in your own help system. WinHelp 4.0, the version of the help engine now included with Windows 95 and Windows NT 4.0, has several changes and enhancements that make using and—more importantly—creating a help system fairly straightforward.

If you've used help before Windows 95 or are using a help system created before WinHelp 4.0 was available, the contents box that you would see when you open the help system would resemble the one shown in Figure 17.1. With WinHelp 4.0, the help system can now show a more sophisticated Contents display known as the Help Topics dialog box (see Figure 17.2).

FIGURE 17.1.

The standard Contents display as used by the original Windows help system.

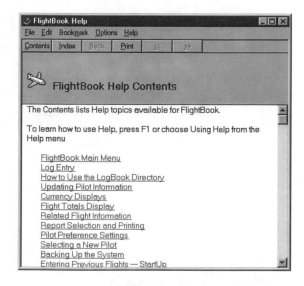

FIGURE 17.2.

The WinHelp 4.0 engine displays the Help Topics dialog box.

Now you have the option of using the New HTML Help design as shown in Figure 17.3.

FIGURE 17.3.

The new HTML format makes it easier to use Help in Windows.

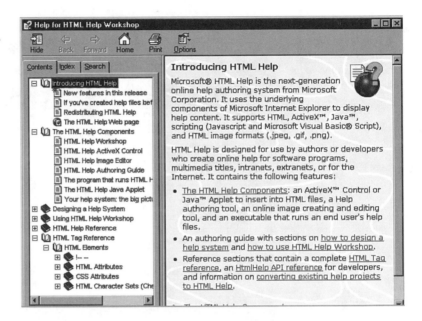

To make full use of these new features and to make maintenance of a help system easier, Visual Basic comes with both the standard and HTML Microsoft Help Workshops. These workshops have the tools and information that you need to create professional-looking help files for Windows.

Note

> Both workshops are included on the Visual Basic product CD-ROM and must be installed manually.

Both Workshop's have easy-to-use interfaces that assist in the help project creation process.

To create your own custom help system, you will need to follow the following general steps:

1. Create the help topic files in an RTF or HTML format by using Microsoft Word or WordPerfect.

2. Create the project file for this help system.

3. Create the contents file to display the table of contents.

4. Use the appropriate Help Workshop to compile and test the help file.

5. Attach your finished help system to your Visual Basic application, where needed.

Help files can be as simple or as complex as you want them to be. To create a topic file, you'll need to perform the following actions:

- Save files in Rich Text Format (RTF) or HTML format
- Insert and display footnotes
- Change line spacing
- Insert graphics into a text document

Note

For the purposes of today's lesson, Microsoft Word is used for all examples. If you use WordPerfect, refer to its help documentation on how to perform the required tasks.

17

The help text or topic files contain topics linked together via hypertext links or special hypergraphics. If the topics weren't linked, they would be isolated sections of information, and your users couldn't move from one topic to another. The way to link topics together is to create hypertext fields that can jump between topics or display a pop-up window. These jumps consist of coded text or graphics that tell the WinHelp engine when to display a different topic in the main help window.

Note

The remainder of this section discusses how to create the topic files for a standard Help system. To see how to create an HTML Help system, see the section "Moving to HTML," later in this chapter.

Building the Topic File

A *topic file* is nothing more than a word processing file saved in Rich Text Format (RTF). A completed help file is a combination of topics that provide users with information. When designing and creating topic files, you want to decide what the flow will be from one topic to another. Each topic is directly related to a single page in the document file. Also, because there are no size restrictions, each topic can be as long as you need it to be.

To create a help text file, you'll work with underlined, double-underlined, and hidden text.

Tip

It's a good idea to reveal all non-printing characters in the Word document while you're creating the RTF file.

A topic file contains the words and graphics that make up your help file. To create most topic files, all you need to do is the following:

- Type text for the topics
- Separate topics with page breaks
- Add footnotes
- Add graphics
- Format characters

When entering text for a topic file, hypertext links are created by double-underlining the link phrases, whereas any pop-up phrases are formatted with single-underlining. Link phrases and pop-up phrases have the format for the context string set as hidden text.

When you're formatting the text to create the links and pop-up phrases, you can't have any spaces between the double-underlined text and the hidden text.

Starting the Topic File

Open hypertext your word processor to start a new topic file. To understand how the process works, see how small text files are used to create a help system that will contain hyperlinks, pop-ups, and other help features. (Actually, sections of previous lessons will be used as the sample text for the help topics.) Figure 17.4 shows the Contents topic page for a completed help file.

FIGURE 17.4.

The Contents page that includes some hypertext formatting.

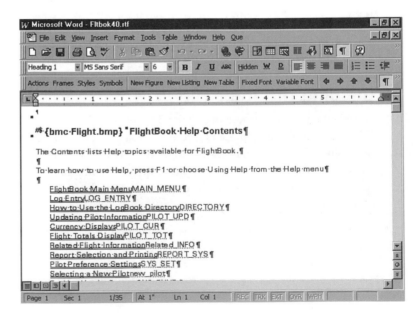

Notice the use of double-underlining in Figure 17.4. Double-underlined words and phrases appear as green, single-underlined hypertext in your help system. When users click the hypertext, WinHelp automatically jumps to the page referenced by hypertext the *jump tag*, the hidden text immediately following the jump phrase. Your help system will actually contain three topic pages, one pop-up page, and one secondary topic; it will also have two separate topic files. The second file will be used to show how you can add multiple files to the help system by using two different techniques.

As the first page of your topic file, enter the following lines of text to list the three topics to be covered in this hypertext example:

```
The Windows Common Dialog In Use

What the Common Dialog is All About

The Many Faces of the Common Dialog
```

Next, insert a page break and then add the text in Listing 17.1 to the second page of your topic hypertext file.

LISTING 17.1. TOPIC1.TXT—TOPIC ONE OF THE EXAMPLE HELP TOPIC FILE.

```
The Windows dialog box allows the application to interact with user with
the same forms that Windows 95 uses. This chapter will review the
different options available in the Common Dialog control and how to use
it. Now, you may be asking yourself, 'Why do I need to review this again'?
Well, if you want to create an application that closely resembles the
Windows 95 standard, you want to understand and use as many of the common
features that are available in Visual Basic as possible. In addition to
the review, you will also get an understanding of why to use the Common
Dialog control and more importantly, when to use it. Finally, you will be
shown another way of accessing the Common Dialog through the use of the
Dialog Automation object which comes with the Visual Basic product CD.
This object can be included in your application instead of the Common
Dialog control.
```

Now, after you add this text, insert another page break to separate this text for the first topic page with the next topic. You must insert a page break between each unique topic page in the file.

Listings 17.2, 17.3, and 17.4 show the text for each of the next three topics. Add the first three text files to the open topic file. Then start a new topic file and add the remaining text files to this second topic document, as described earlier.

LISTING 17.2. TOPIC2.TXT—THIS IS THE NEXT TEXT FILE.

```
When you old DOS based computers underwent the change from black & white
to color displays, many new commands had to be created for the user to
change these new properties. Then, when Windows was introduced, the
developer knew that there would be many activities that would be performed
over and over by the user. The outcome of this knowledge led to the
creation of a 'set' of Windows dialogs that interfaced with the user. As
more and more programs were written for Windows, the dialogs in this set
were copied by many programmers. It was around this time that developers
started calling them the Common Dialogs.
```

LISTING 17.3. TOPIC3.TXT—THIS IS THE NEXT TOPIC.

```
One of the most commonly used functions of the Common Dialog control is
the ability to select a file to open or specify a file name to save. Both
the Open and Save As dialog boxes allows the user to specify a drive,
directory, filename extension, and a filename. If you have been using
older versions of Visual Basic, then you probably think that the code to
display the Open dialog is the following:

DlgGetFile.Action =1
```

LISTING 17.4. TOPIC4.TXT—THIS IS THE NEXT TOPIC.

```
The actual Common Dialog routines are distributed in a dynamic-link
library file call Commdlg.dll. The way in which you as the developer
interact with this library is by using the Common Dialog control. Even
though this control is used in almost every application that you may
create, it is not one of the default controls that is displayed in the
Visual Basic toolbox.
```

After you finish adding these text files, your document should look like the one shown in Figure 17.5. Each page of text will eventually become a topic in your final help system.

FIGURE 17.5.

The final RTF document in your word processor.

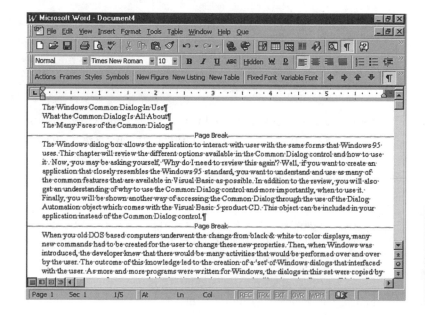

Putting Titles on the Topic

Now that you have five topics, you need to identify each one by assigning a topic ID, which makes it possible for WinHelp to find them. To assign topic IDs and other options to a topic, you create footnotes that are used to define these features. To set up these features of the help system, you use four symbols in the footnote area, as described in Table 17.1.

TABLE 17.1. FOOTNOTE SYMBOLS USED TO DEFINE HELP FEATURES.

Symbol	Description
#	Creates a tag that's used by WinHelp to link from a jump phrase to its associated topic
$	Defines the jump page title, which will appear in the help system's Search list box
+	Defines a browse code to specify the topic's position in a browse sequence
K	Defines a keyword that can be used to search in the Index page

In the footnote section, the # symbol is used to connect a topic page with its jump tag, which identifies each topic in the help system. Each tag must be unique within the help system. Although the compiler can successfully compile topics that don't have jump tags, help system users can't view these topics unless they contain keywords that can be found with the Index page.

The $ symbol defines the title for each help topic in the file. Titles appear at the beginning of the topic, on the Bookmark menu, and in the Search list box, if the topic contains keywords.

Another feature that you can add to the help system is the capability for users to "browse" the topics in a preset order. You must perform two actions to enable this feature. The first is to define the browse sequence in the topics file by using the + symbol in the footnote section of the page, as follows:

```
+ PILOT_TOT:2200
```

A *browse code* is a name common to every topic in a browse sequence, followed by a colon (:) and a number that specifies the position in the browse sequence in which you want a topic to be included.

The final symbol, K, specifies the topic keywords that may be used to search for related topics. The WinHelp system lists matching topics by their titles in the Search dialog box. This symbol is the only one of the four that allows listing of multiple words or phrases. The following footnote example shows a keyword list for the topic titled Pilot, which can be found in a Windows application help system:

```
K Pilot;Information;Medical;IFR;Address;Restrictions;Review;Update;Delete;
AFR;BFR;Add;ICC
```

The custom footnote symbol(s) must be the first items that appear on the jump page, followed by the help topic title (if any) and any text that you want in the topic. To insert a footnote in Word, position the cursor at the beginning of the page and choose Insert, Footnote from the menu. The Footnote and Endnote dialog box appears (see Figure 17.6).

FIGURE 17.6.

Using the Footnote and Endnote dialog box to insert new footnote symbols into the topic.

Click the Custom Mark option button and then enter one of the symbols described in Table 17.1. When you click OK, the screen will split into two separate windows—one showing the topic page and one showing the associated footnote(s) (see Figure 17.7).

FIGURE 17.7.

Displaying the footnotes in the Word document.

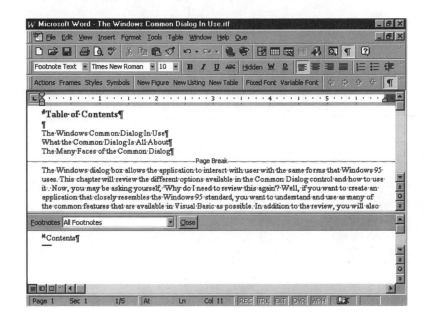

Set the footnotes for the topics file as shown in Table 17.2 by using the link custom footnote symbol of #.

TABLE 17.2. THE FOOTNOTE SETTINGS FOR THE FIRST EXAMPLE HELP FILE.

Page	Footnote Text
1	Contents
2	InUse
3	CDAbout
4	ManyFaces
5	interface

With these footnotes, you can now set the hyperlinks in one topic to allow users to jump from that topic to another topic. To set a link in a topic, you need to format the word or phrases that you want as the links. Follow these steps:

1. On the first page of the help topic file, place the cursor at the end of the word Use and enter the topic ID phrase InUse.

2. Single-underline the entire phrase The Windows Common Dialog In Use.

3. Format the word InUse as hidden text. This instructs the WinHelp system to display a pop-up window showing the text on the Preamble topic page. The hidden text should match the topic ID for the page you want to jump to.

4. Perform the same tasks for Common Dialog on page two, having it jump to the topic ID of CDAbout by using a double-underline to create a jump instead of a pop-up.

5. Set the three topics on the first page to their corresponding topic pages. This will create a contents topic page that will be used if the Help Topics dialog box can't be displayed.

The topics file should now look like the one in Figure 17.8.

FIGURE 17.8.

The topics file containing all the hyperlinks and footnotes needed for the help system.

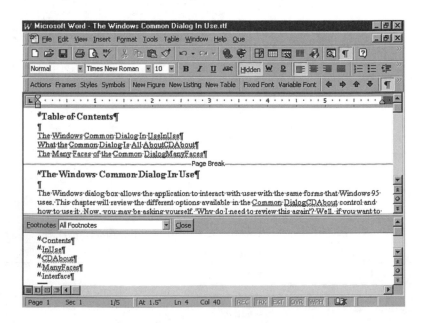

Using the Standard Help Workshop

As you've just seen, the project file contains all the instructions needed to compile your help topic files into a working help file that will be displayed by the WinHelp engine. When you use the Help Workshop to create the project file, the minimum settings you need are specified when you choose File, New from its menu. The remaining settings that you might have to specify depend on the size and complexity of the help file that you've created. To begin the process, start the Help Workshop.

Starting a New Project

After you start the Help Workshop, choose File, New, select Help Project from the New dialog box, and click OK. The Project File Name selection dialog box appears. Enter the name VBHelp as the project name and click Save. Don't worry about the Save as Type box; you can leave it blank at the moment. The default options for your project should appear in the workshop screen, as shown in Figure 17.9.

FIGURE 17.9.

Starting a new project with default option settings specified.

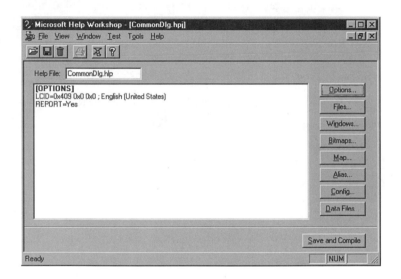

For the help compiler to work properly, you must specify the location and name of each topic file to be included in each .HLP file you create. To specify the files, click the Files button on the right side of the workshop window. In the Topic Files dialog box, you can add or remove the file references to the project (see Figure 17.10).

FIGURE 17.10.

Using the Topic Files dialog box to add the file references to the help project.

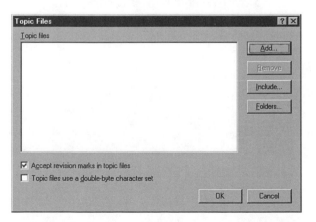

Now, click the Add button to display the Open dialog box, locate each RTF topic file you created previously, and select them. Click the Open button and then OK to add this file to the project. The project file now has the information it needs to compile your topic files into a working help system.

The workshop's toolbar contains two buttons that you'll use to compile and test the help file you create. To compile your help project, click the Compile button. In the Compile a Help File dialog box (see Figure 17.11), set the help project filename to compile. You also can choose to minimize the workshop windows while the project is compiling and then have the help file displayed when the compile is complete.

FIGURE 17.11.

Using the Compile a Help File dialog box to compile your help project.

You can view the progress of the compile or minimize the window. If you're creating the help file for the first time, however, you should watch the process to get an idea of what actually happens. If you didn't choose to have the finished help file displayed when the compile was completed, you need to click the Run WinHelp button, which displays the View Help File dialog box (see Figure 17.12).

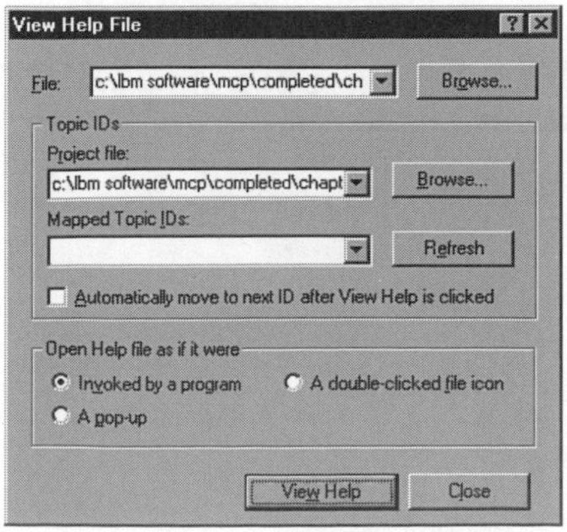

FIGURE 17.12.

Displaying the completed help file by using the View Help File dialog box.

Through this dialog box, you can open the new help file as follows:

- As a program would open it
- As a user by double-clicking its file icon
- As a pop-up help topic by using a mapped topic ID

Select A Double-Clicked File Icon, and then click View Help to display the Table of Contents topic from the new help file (see Figure 17.13).

FIGURE 17.13.

The completed help file's Table of Contents as a user would see it.

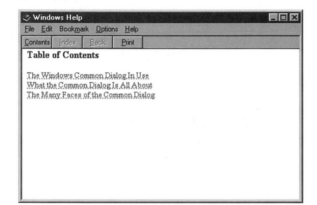

17

Mapping the Topic IDs

If the help system will be displayed only as a standalone system, there would be no reason to assign numeric values to each topic in the help system. These unique numbers reference each help topic directly when the help system is being accessed from within an application. To assign or map a value to a topic ID, click the Map button on the workshop window to open the Map dialog box, which lists the topic IDs that have already been mapped with their related values. To add a new topic ID to this list, click Add to display the Add Map Entry dialog box (see Figure 17.14).

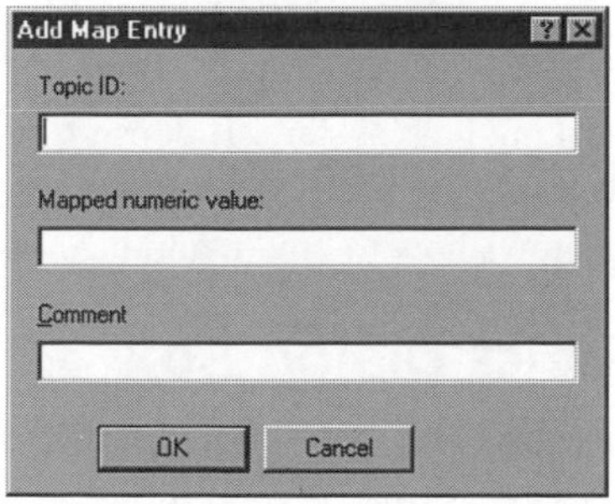

FIGURE 17.14.

Adding new mapped topic IDs to the help project.

In the Add Map Entry dialog box, you can enter only three values:

- The topic ID that defines a topic in the .RTF file
- A unique numeric value
- An optional comment

To see how this works, enter the topic ID as XXXX, and the numeric value of 6. Then, if you want, enter a comment describing this topic. After you're finished, click OK to add this topic to the mapped list. Then click OK again to return to the main workshop window. Your project file will now have a map section included in the list. Recompile the help file and click the Run WinHelp button to display the View Help File dialog box. You should now see the mapped topic that you just added listed in the Mapped Topic IDs drop-down box. Select the mapped value and click OK to display the selected topic (see Figure 17.15).

FIGURE 17.15.

Displaying a specific topic by using the mapped value.

At this point you've created a working help system. It doesn't look any different from the old non-Windows 95 help systems, however, because the new Help Topics dialog box is missing. The next section shows how to create and use this feature.

Creating the Help Topics Dialog Box

A complete help system increases each user's ability to get help when using the application. The help system is usually accessed from several different areas in an application and can be displayed by double-clicking the icon for the help file. In the help file that you've created, notice that the Index button at the top of the help window is grayed out. This is because no keywords are defined in the topic files. Adding keywords to the topics is discussed later in today's lesson.

You can control which tabs appear on the Help Topics dialog box. If you want the Contents tab to appear, you must create a contents file for the help system you created. If you want the Index tab to appear, you need to define keywords for your topics. The Find tab always appears unless you specify otherwise.

The items listed on the Contents page are defined in the contents file that's created by using the Help Workshop. You can dynamically modify the Contents page by adding or removing items from the list independently of the help file. This means that as you enhance the application, you don't have to change the original help files; you just add additional help file(s) to the help system.

As you create the contents file, the Help Workshop displays each item with a book or page icon, depending on the position of the item. This allows you to see the finished Contents list as you create it.

Defining the Contents File

In the Help Workshop, choose File, New, select Help Contents, and then click OK. A window used to create the contents file appears in the Help Workshop (see Figure 17.16).

FIGURE 17.16.

Creating the contents file through the Help Workshop.

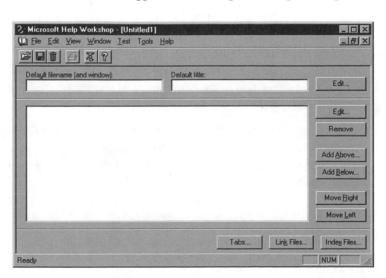

When the contents file is first created, you need to specify default information that's used to locate the entries in the contents file, display the correct title at the top of the Help Topics dialog box, and display the help information in the correct window type. To set this default information, click the Edit button to display the Default Help Information dialog box. Enter the name of your help file in the Default Help Filename text box. Then, in the Default Window text box, enter the window type that you want to use to display the topics in. Finally, you can optionally enter the title that you want to display in the Help Topics dialog box (see Figure 17.17).

Note The window type that you specify must be defined in your help project.

FIGURE 17.17.

WinHelp uses the settings in the Default Help Information dialog box to display your help system topics correctly.

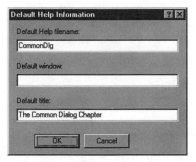

You can modify any of these default settings for individual items in the contents list. You should save the contents file with a name related to the help system. The name you choose will need to be specified in the help project so that the help engine can locate the contents file when needed.

When adding items, remember that headings are identified by book icons that can be double-clicked to display the subheadings or topics that they contain. To add the first entry to the list, click the Add Above or Add Below button (it doesn't matter); the Edit Contents Tab Entry dialog box appears (see Figure 17.18).

FIGURE 17.18.

Adding items to the Contents page of the Help Topics dialog box.

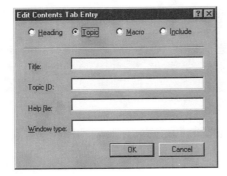

For every item that you enter in the Contents page, you can specify the following:

- Title
- Topic ID
- Help file to look in for the topic ID
- Window type to use when displaying the topic

This is also where you can modify the default settings for the contents file. For the first item, select the Heading option button at the top of the dialog box. Then enter Visual Basic as the Title and click OK. You should see a book icon appear with the title you entered next to it. Next, add the remaining topics and headings as listed in Table 17.3.

TABLE 17.3. THE CONTENTS FILE TOPIC ITEMS TO BE ADDED.

Entry Type	Title	Topic ID
Topic	Windows Common Dialog	InUse
Topic	What is the Common Dialog All About	CDAbout
Heading	New Features	
Topic	The Many Faces of the Common Dialog	ManyFaces

After these items are added, the Contents dialog box should look like the one in Figure 17.19.

17

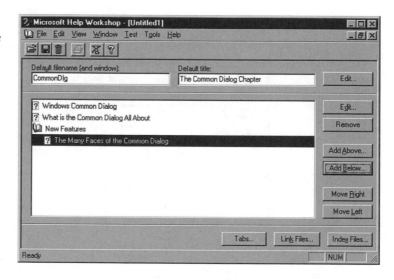

After saving the changes to the contents file, you can test it. Specify the contents filename for your help project on the File page in the Help Workshop's Options dialog box. Click the Run WinHelp button, select Invoked by a Program, and click View Help. This will display the Help Topics dialog box (see Figure 17.20).

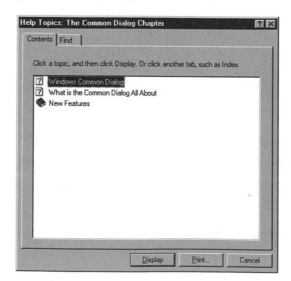

Adding Keywords to the Help Topics

The Index tab appears only if you have K footnotes defined in your topic files. Then, by double-clicking a keyword on the Index tab, users can display the related topic. In the topic files, you add a K footnote to the topics that you want keywords for. Each K footnote can define as many keywords as you need for the topic page. If you assign the same keyword to more than one topic, the keyword appears only once in the index. However, when users double-click that keyword, the Topics Found dialog box appears (see Figure 17.21).

FIGURE 17.21.

Keywords are displayed on the Index page. The Topics Found dialog box displays all topics for a selected keyword.

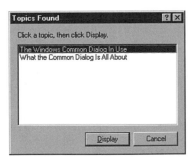

17

Add a few keywords to the help topics by using the techniques and syntax described earlier today. Remember that the K footnote must be an uppercase K and each keyword is separated by a semicolon (;). Unlike the Contents page, you must recompile the help file for the keywords to be included on the Help Topics dialog box. After recompiling, you can display the Help Topics dialog box to see how the Index page works.

Indexes can sometimes contain several levels, just like the Contents page. Second-level entries indented under first-level entries list specific information within that first-level category. You can create the same effect in your help index by defining first- and second-level keywords. The Windows 95 help index shown in Figure 17.22 is a good example of this technique.

FIGURE 17.22.

Second-level indexes are used to display group related keywords.

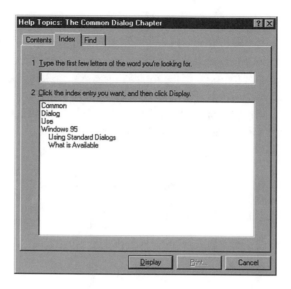

Creating first- and second-level keywords requires only a slight change in how you define the keywords in the footnote. To add a first-level keyword to your help file, add a K footnote and then type the first-level keyword, followed by a comma (,) and a semi-colon (;), as follows:

```
K Constitution,;
```

The comma and the semicolon won't appear in the Index text.

Next, immediately following the semicolon, type the first-level keyword again, followed by a comma, a space, the second-level keyword, and another semicolon:

```
K Constitution,;Constitution, The Constitution of the United States;
```

Enabling the Find Page

The Find page allows users to perform a full-text search through every word in a help file. For example, if users enter the word Print in the Find page in the Windows 95 Help Topics dialog box, every topic that contains that word will be listed. When users click the Find tab for the first time, the Find Setup Wizard will help them set up the full-text search index. Users will have to do this only once, unless they deleted the index file (.FTS) that contains this information.

Note

The only topics included in the Find page search are the ones that have titles defined as $ footnotes.

Adding to Help

Although you can add many additional features to the help file, this section focuses on only a few common ones to give you an idea on how you can enhance your help system. The following list includes features that you can add to your help file:

- Video and sound files
- WinHelp macros
- Context-sensitive help
- Training card help
- Customizing the help display
- Secondary help windows
- Complex graphics with hotspots

17

Adding Secondary Windows

Your help topics can be displayed in one of two types of windows: main and secondary. The main window has a menu bar and a button bar, and can't be sized automatically. There can be only one main window in a help file. The menu bar in the main window contains the Display History option, which allows users to display a list of topics that have been viewed during their session. The Bookmark menu is the other option that allows users to mark a topic to return to later.

A secondary window doesn't have a menu bar, so these features aren't available. However, the secondary window can include a button bar and can be sized automatically. There can be up to 255 different style secondary windows in a help system, with up to a maximum of nine displayed at any one time. To see how this works, you need to define the main window and at least one secondary window in your help project. Click the Windows button to display the Window Properties dialog box (see Figure 17.23), which allows you to define new windows to your project, as well as customize the position, color, buttons, and macros that will appear in the window.

FIGURE 17.23.

*Adding window defini-
tions in the Help
Workshop.*

To create a secondary window, you simply name it. You can then use this name in your project, contents, and topic files to specify which window you want the topic displayed in. In the Help Properties dialog box, click the Add button to display the Add a New Window Type dialog box. The main window is created by using Main as the new window name. Otherwise, enter the name that you want to use, which can include up to eight characters. Then, as a starting point, select one of the three standard window types listed in the drop-down box, as shown in Table 17.4, and then click OK. Think of these window types as templates that you can modify to fit your needs for each window you define.

TABLE 17.4. THE STANDARD WINDOW TYPES USED IN WINDOWS 95 HELP.

Type	Description
Procedure	Normally used to display procedures. It has auto-sizing, contains three buttons on the button bar, and is positioned in the upper-right corner of the screen.
Reference	Normally used to display reference material. It has auto-sizing, contains three buttons on the button bar, and is positioned on the left side of the screen, taking up approximately two-thirds of the screen's width.
Error message	Normally used to display error messages. It has auto-sizing, contains no buttons, and lets WinHelp determine the position (the upper-right corner of the screen is the default, unless users change the position).

To use this new window, you have to change the reference in a topic. In the topic with the ID of InUse, change the hyperlink jump tag to the following:

```
Common DialogMain>window2
```

where *window2* is the name of the secondary window that you just defined. Recompile the help project and open the help file. Navigate to The Windows Common Dialog in Use topic and then click the Common Dialog link. You'll see that rather than change the content of the main window, a secondary window appears (see Figure 17.24).

FIGURE 17.24.

Using secondary windows to highlight certain topics in the help system.

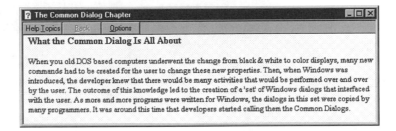

Moving to HTML

HTML Help is the next generation of online help authoring systems that have been created by Microsoft. It uses the underlying components of Microsoft's Internet Explorer to display the Help information, supporting HTML, ActiveX, Java, scripting (both JavaScript and VBScript), and HTML image formats such as .JPEG and .GIF. If you've ever used WinHelp or the standard Help Workshop before, you will be very familiar with many of the features of HTML Help and its associated workshop.

Like WinHelp, HTML Help uses a project file to combine help topic, contents, index, image, and other source files into one compressed help file. HTML Help also provides you with a workshop that helps you create the help file. Unlike WinHelp, HTML Help has no limits to the size of the help file you can create or to the size of any of the other features in the help file. The only limitations that you have are those of the computer and of the Hypertext Markup Language (HTML) might have.

As you have seen, navigation within a standard help system is done by using embedded commands that define which topic should be displayed next. When using the new HTML Help system, these commands have been replaced with HTML tags that instruct the Help browser to locate and display another help topic file. The new interface provides greater ease of movement and a "cleaner" interface to the user, as shown in Figure 17.25.

FIGURE 17.25.

The new HTML Help system interface makes it easier for the user to find the information she needs.

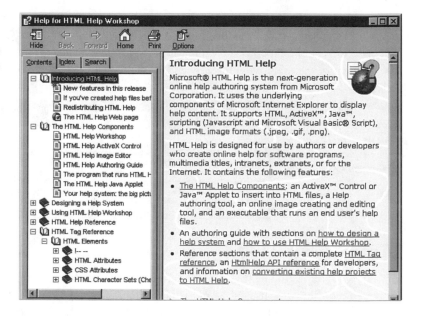

When using the new HTML Help system, the documents you design are created using Hypertext Markup Language or HTML. Each topic you create has a corresponding HTML file. Although each help topic you create appears to be a document with text, graphics, or images on it, the HTML files are actually text documents that contain the HTML formatting codes. The codes, or *tags*, tell the Help browser how to display each page and the locations of any files that are referenced on that page.

Your first task when creating an HTML Help system is to design the overall look of your topic pages. Only then can you continue on and actually create the topic files. By using the Table of Contents tab, users can select an item to view and then navigate from one topic to another, based on what they need to find out. The steps to create an HTML Help system are basically the same as a standard help system, except that you are now creating HTML pages instead of RTF documents.

When you have finished creating the HTML Help system, you only need to distribute the actual help file (.CHM) with your application. Because HTML Help is a relatively new technology, you cannot assume that every user will have the files needed to view the HTML Help. The Package and Deployment Wizard will add a dependency to your application installation for the HTML Help files referenced in your application. To create the topics files, you either need to have a working knowledge of HTML programming to design fancy Help topics or you can use any of the word processors that can save a document in HTML format.

The help text or topics files are linked together by adding HTML <A> tags that include the reference to the next topic file, or you can use a special ActiveX control that comes with the HTML Help workshop to enable the user to click a button and jump to another topic. The process of building topic files has not changed except for one very important item—that is, each topic should now be a separate document that is then converted into HTML format. To create most topics files, all you need to do is the following:

- Enter the text for each topic.
- Add the HTML tags to support the included features (links, images, and so on).

Because you have already seen how to build topic files, take the existing document from the standard help system you created earlier and break it into four separate documents. Then, if your word processor supports it, convert the documents into HTML format. If your word processor does not support this function, you will need to create each HTML file manually and add the text to it.

17

> **Note**
>
> When saving these files as HTML, you should use the listing names as they will be referenced later in this chapter when adding HTML tag codes.

Unlike the old Windows help system, to set a link for a topic, you need to know the name of the HTML file that you want to jump to. This requires you to create most of the topic files before you start adding links and pop-ups to the topic files themselves. This changes the process into a two-step process, one to create the topic files, and the second one to add any required links. To see how to add a link to a topic, open the table of contents file (TOC.HTM) in Notepad, and replace the first item link with the following statement.

```
<A HREF="TOPIC1.HTM">The Windows Common Dialog in Use</A>
```

As you can see, the file that you want to jump to is inserted into the <A> tag. Now, perform the same process for the remaining topic links listed on the table of contents, as shown in Figure 17.26. All three links should use the <A> tag.

FIGURE 17.26.

The Table of Contents topic page showing the links inserted for each main topic listed.

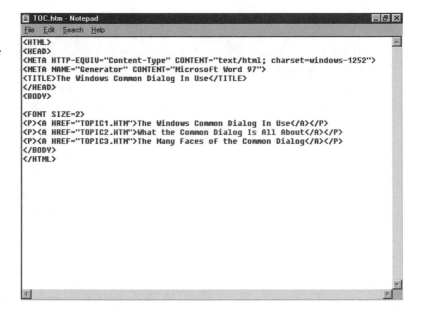

At this point, you have created several HTML files for your help system, but there is nothing that actually makes it into a help system yet. The best you can do with it is display the files in a Web browser. In the next section, you will see how to use the new HTML Help workshop to take these files and create the actual help file for you to use.

Using the HTML Help Workshop

The HTML Help workshop gives you the tools to create an easy-to-use help system that performs much like an Internet Web site. As with the Standard Help system, you need to build a project file that is used by the compiler to create the final HTML Help file. The best way of producing the project file is by using the new HTML Help workshop:

1. Start the HTML Help Workshop from the Start menu.
2. Choose File, New from the Workshop's menu.
3. In the New dialog box, select Project and click OK.

A New Project Wizard is displayed that asks if you want to convert an older WinHelp project. Leave the option unchecked and click Next. Enter VBDemoHTML as the project name and click Next to continue. The next dialog box (see Figure 17.27) lets you specify any files you have already created and want to add to the project.

FIGURE 17.27.

Adding existing files to the new HTML Help project.

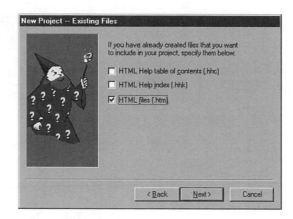

If you check any of these, you are asked to enter the location and name of the file(s). Because you have already created the HTML topic files, click the third selection and click Next. On this dialog box (see Figure 17.28), add the topic files you previously created by clicking Add to select them.

FIGURE 17.28.

Adding the Topic files you have already created.

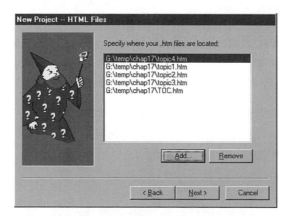

Select all your HTML topic files and click Next, Finish to complete the project's creation. The last step is to set the default topic for the help file. The easiest way to change a project setting is by double-clicking the setting you want to change in the Options list.

Then set the default topic file to TOC.HTM. The project file now has enough information to compile your topic files into a working help file (see Figure 17.29).

17

FIGURE 17.29.

The finished project file contains several parameter sections that were added.

Compile HTML File

View Compiled File

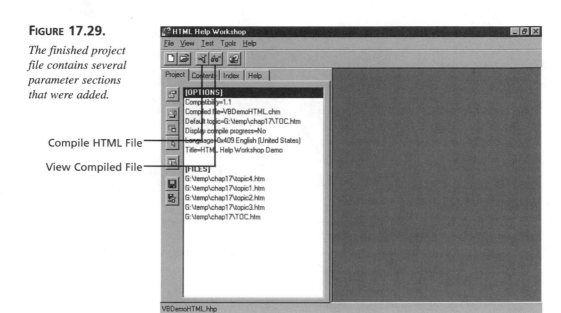

The workshop toolbar in Figure 17.29 contains two buttons that you'll be using to compile and test your Help file. To compile your Help project, click the Compile HTML File button; the Create a Compiled File dialog box appears (see Figure 17.30). This dialog box lets you set the help project filename to compile.

FIGURE 17.30.

Compiling the Help project with the Create a Completed File dialog box.

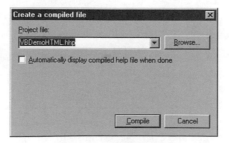

Click the Compile button in the Compile a Help File dialog box to complete the process of compiling the topics files into a help file. When the compile is completed, click the View Compiled File button to display the Table of Contents topic from the new help file (see Figure 17.31).

FIGURE 17.31.

The compiled Table of Contents as the users will see it.

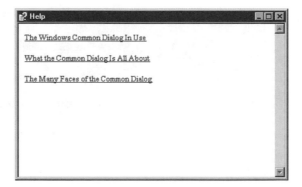

You now have a completed help system; however, you can see that there is no Tab frame to the left of the help information window. This is because you have not created the Contents or Index files. If you want a Contents tab to appear, you must define a contents file within the help project. If you want the Index tab to appear, you must define an Index file that contains keywords for your topics. Finally, the Search tab will appear only if you specify that you want it.

Building the Contents Tab

In the HTML Help Workshop, click the Contents tab to display the Contents window. When you do this for the first time, a dialog box will appear asking if you are creating a new Contents file or using an existing one. Leave the default to create a new one and click OK. The Windows Save As dialog box is displayed for you to enter the new filename. Once again, leave the default name and click Save. An empty Contents window appears in the Help Workshop (see Figure 17.32). This is where you'll create the contents file.

17

FIGURE 17.32.

The Contents tab displays the Contents list as you work.

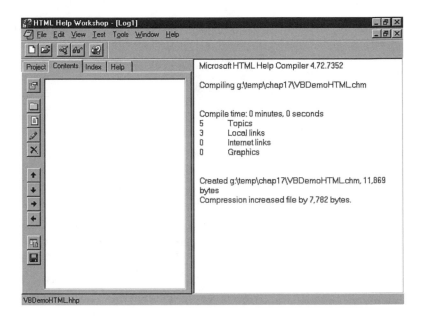

You can add two types of entries to the contents file, each entry giving users the capability of performing a particular function (see Table 17.5).

TABLE 17.5. CONTENTS FILE ENTRY OPTIONS.

Option	Description
Heading	Used to define a category level shown as a Book or Folder icon
Topic	Defines each main page of the Help system

When adding items, remember that headings are identified by book or folder icons that can be double-clicked to display the topics that they contain. To add the first entry to the list, you can click the Insert a Heading or Insert a Page button—it doesn't matter. The Contents Entry dialog box appears (see Figure 17.33).

FIGURE **17.33.**

*Adding entries to the
Contents tab is done
with the Contents
Entry dialog box.*

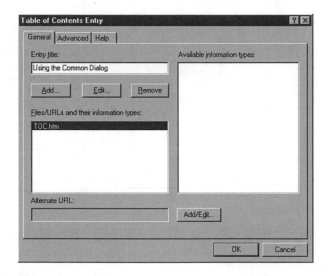

17

The Contents Entry dialog box is where you specify the title of the entry and the associated page or Web link for that item. In fact, headings can now have a topic page associated with them. When you click the Add button, the Path or URL dialog box appears (see Figure 17.34) listing the available HTML file titles (not the filenames) to select from.

FIGURE **17.34.**

*Selecting the HTML
topic files for the
Contents file.*

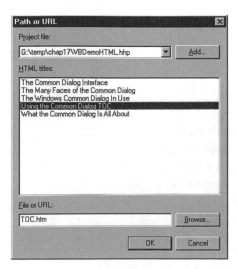

Add the items listed in Table 17.6 to the contents file.

TABLE 17.6. TOPIC ITEMS ADDED TO THE CONTENT FILE.

Entry Type	Title	Topic File
Heading	Using the Common Dialog	TOC
Page	The Common Dialog in Use	TOPIC1
Page	What it is all About	TOPIC2
Heading	The Many Faces of the Common Dialog	
Page	The Common Dialog Interface	TOPIC3

After you add these entries, the Contents tab should look like the one shown in Figure 17.35.

FIGURE 17.35.

The finished Contents tab displayed in the Help Workshop.

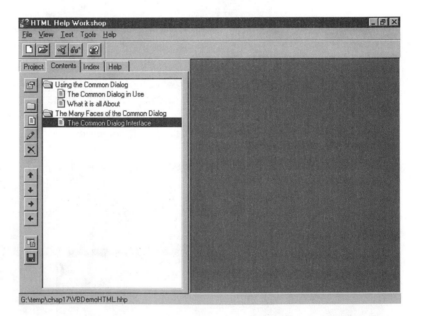

After saving the changes to the contents file, test it by compiling the help file and viewing it. To test the Contents file, click the View Compiled File button to see the new help system, shown in Figure 17.36. Try clicking the book icons and then the item icons to see what happens.

FIGURE 17.36.

The finished help file including a Contents tab.

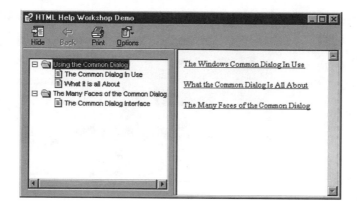

Adding Keywords to the Index Tab

If you recall, the Index tab appears only if you have keywords defined for your topic pages. Then, by double-clicking a keyword displayed on the Index tab, users can display the related topic. You would add keywords to the Index the same way as you added items to the Contents tab. By clicking the Index tab in the HTML Help workshop, you are prompted for the name of the new Index file to create. Also you can add multiple topic pages to a keyword definition, as shown in Figure 17.37.

17

FIGURE 17.37.

Adding multiple topic pages to an Index keyword.

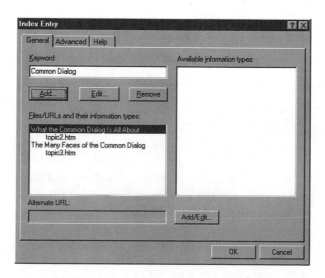

Then, when you are in the help system and click that topic, a selection dialog box is displayed as shown in Figure 17.38.

FIGURE 17.38.

Getting a Related Topics Selection dialog box from the Index tab.

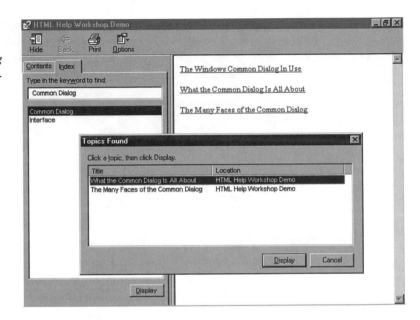

Setting Up the Search Tab

The Search tab enables users to perform a full text search for every word in a help file. For example, if users enter OPEN on the Search tab in the Windows Help browser, every topic that contains the word OPEN is listed. If you choose to have the project compile in a full-text search file (.CHG), you must distribute it with the Help file.

Converting from Older Help Projects

If you are a Visual Basic developer who has already created help systems for your applications, don't panic; The HTML Help workshop has a conversion feature that enables you to easily create an HTML Help project from an existing WinHelp project. The New Project Wizard will convert the WinHelp project file (.HPJ) to an HTML Help project file (.HHP), the topic files (.RTF) to HTML topic files (.HTM), the contents file (.CNT) to the HTML Help contents file (.HHC), and any index files to the new format (.HHK). Any bitmap images you may have in the files will be converted to either .GIF, .JPEG, or .PNG depending on your target browser. If you want, see how this works by converting the Standard Help project that you created at the beginning of this chapter.

Using Advanced HTML Help Features

There are many different components that you can add to your help system by making use of the different HTML code tags. HTML tags support everything from adding images to an HTML page to having animations or movie clips displayed on the HTML page. In addition, by using the HTML Help workshop, you can define different window formats so that you can have certain topics displayed differently than others. The types of windows that you can create or customize are:

- **Default window**—This is the window where topics will automatically appear. You never have to create the default help window, but you can customize them.

- **Secondary window**—This is a custom window in which you can assign topics to display.

- **Embedded window**—This is also a secondary window, but rather than staying on top of the help display, embedded windows are nested into the software program.

To define a new window, go to the Project tab and click the Add/Modify Windows Definition button. Now enter the name for the new window and click OK to go to the Windows Type dialog box shown in Figure 17.39.

17

FIGURE 17.39.

Defining a new window to be used by the help system.

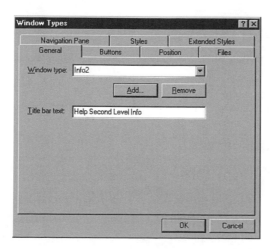

This dialog box enables you to customize almost every aspect of a window frame. Then to use a custom window, you would change the Window property for a given Contents item, as shown in Figure 17.40.

FIGURE 17.40.

*Setting the Window
property of a Content
item to display the
information in a
custom window.*

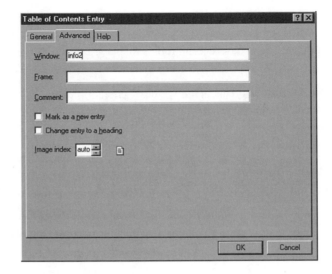

Linking to the Internet

Many newer applications, such as Microsoft Office 97, use jumps in their help systems
to take users to specific pages on the World Wide Web. When creating your help system,
you can also provide users with a way to locate your Web site or any other Internet Web
site. This is done by setting an URL Web address instead of a local help filename.

Adding Multimedia

Another way to enhance your help system is by adding video and sound clips to it. Video
can be useful and fun to include in your help system. Windows uses it in its *Online
User's Guide*. Several topics include animation to explain how to perform a particular
function. Adding any video or audio features to your help system is done by using standard HTML tag commands. The following line of code will add a video to a topic page:

```
<A href="../Images/File.avi"> Click here to see a movie.</A>
```

This will be played using the registered media player on the users computer.

Connecting Help to the Visual Basic Application

After you design and create the help system, which probably includes many of the features discussed, you're ready to add it to your application. You can access help from within your Visual Basic application in three ways:

- The Windows Common Dialog control
- Built-in Visual Basic help context features
- API calls to the WinHelp program

Of these three methods, this lesson covers only the first two, which are more directly connected to the Visual Basic commands that you know. You no longer need to use the third, more advanced method of accessing help in a Visual Basic application. To see how to use the first two methods, you'll create a new project that you'll add the different functions and features available to access the help system.

Using the Common Dialog Control Again

The same Common Dialog control that you used for other Windows functions also can display help by running the WinHelp engine. To see how the Common Dialog control accesses help, create a new Visual Basic project and add the controls in Table 17.7 to the default form, using the property settings listed.

TABLE 17.7. ADDING HELP ACCESS TO THE FORM.

Control	Property	Value
Command Button	Name	cmdClose
	Caption	Close
Command Button	Name	cmdHelp
	Caption	Help
Common Dialog	Name	dlgHelp
	HelpFile	*<path/filename>* of your compiled help system

You can change any other properties for the Common Dialog by using its associated Properties Pages dialog box (see Figure 17.41).

Figure 17.41.

Using the Common Dialog's Property Pages to modify the help action properties.

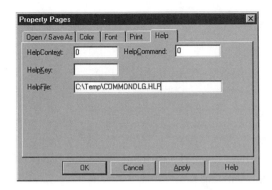

After you add these controls, you next add the code needed to access the help system when a command button is clicked. The code in Listing 17.5 is all that's needed to access the help system. The code to close the application is also included.

Listing 17.5. HELPEX1.TXT—ALL THE CODE REQUIRED TO ACCESS YOUR HELP SYSTEM.

```
1: Const HelpFinder = &h00B
2: Private Sub cmdClose_Click()
3:      End
4: End Sub
5:
6: Private Sub cmdHelp_Click()
7:      dlgHelp.HelpCommand = HelpFinder
8:      dlgHelp.ShowHelp
9: End Sub
```

Note

The `HelpFinder` command has replaced the `HelpContents` and `HelpIndex` commands to display the help file's contents topic and keyword index.

Also, for some reason known only to Microsoft, VB6 doesn't provide a Common Dialog control constant for the `HelpFinder` command. To access the contents topic in a help file, you must explicitly define the constant in your application's general area as follows:

```
Const HelpFinder = &h00B
```

Run the application and click the Help command button to display the Help Topic dialog box.

Adding to the Help Menu

Every Windows application should have a well-defined Help menu, as you can see in Figure 17.42.

FIGURE 17.42.

A standard Windows Help menu.

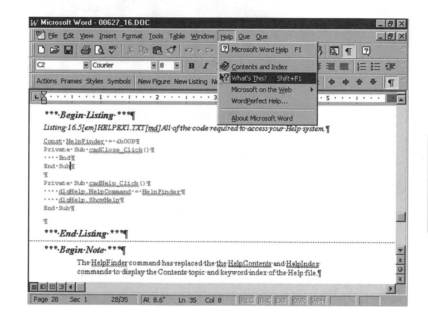

Accessing help from the menu is exactly the same as shown in the previous section. You use the Common Dialog control to perform many actions of the help engine by specifying the action with the supplied Visual Basic constants that can be found in the Visual Basic Object Browser.

To include a Help menu, you need to add the Help menu items by using the VB's Menu Editor (see Figure 17.43).

FIGURE 17.43.

Using the Menu Editor to define Help menu items.

If you used the Application Wizard, it has set up the two main Help items. The wizard, however, uses the API call to the help engine rather than the Common Dialog control. When you've defined the menu items, add the code in Listing 17.6 to the application.

LISTING 17.6. HELPEX2.TXT—ADDING CODE TO THE HELP MENU ITEM ROUTINES.

```
1: Private Sub mnuHelpContents_Click()
2:     dlgHelp.HelpCommand = HelpFinder
3:     dlgHelp.ShowHelp
4: End Sub
5:
6: Private Sub mnuHelpSearchForHelpOn_Click()
7:     dlgHelp.HelpCommand = cdlHelpIndex
8:     dlgHelp.ShowHelp
9: End Sub
```

You'll see that the code calls the different functions of the help system simply by using the different commands available. Try running the application again to see how these functions work.

Summary

You've seen several different concepts today. First, you've seen that the creation process for a professional Windows help system is really quite easy if you use the Help Workshop. Designing and selecting what you want in the help system is the hard part of the job, however. You may have figured out that the design of the help system should be done in parallel with the design and creation of the actual application. This way, you can list what topics you'll need mapped in the help system and how topics there should be. In addition, you have taken the first look at the new HTML Help systems that will become the standard type of help display with the release of Windows 98. Finally, you saw how you can add the help system access directly into the application by using the Common Dialog control and other features of the included Visual Basic objects.

Q&A

Q What does it take to create a help system?

A Creating a help system requires an RTF-capable word processor and the help compiler or workshop supplied with the Visual Basic product. You also need an understanding of what you want to put into the help topics and how to access them from an application.

Q How can hypertext links improve a help system?

A Hypertext links allows users to move from one topic to related topics based on highlighted text defined in the text of the topic they're viewing.

Workshop

The Workshop provides quiz questions to help solidify your understanding of the material covered, as well as exercises to provide you with experience in using what you've learned. Try to understand the quiz and exercise answers before continuing on to the next day's lesson. Answers are provided in Appendix A, "Answers to Exercises."

Quiz

1. How do you connect context-sensitive help to the help topics?
2. How do you add the What's This button to a form?
3. What are some features of the help project file?

Exercise

Create a small help system that you can add to the Address Book application. Try making use of as many of the help functions and features as you can. This will enhance the overall usability of the application.

17

Testing and Debugging the Application

Designing and creating your application is only part of the total process that you have to perform to fully complete the application. When you have finished writing the application, you must test it to make sure it works correctly and then, if there are any problems, debug it and fix those problems. The problem with testing and debugging is that it takes lots of time and effort to do it properly. Unfortunately, most programmers don't want to take the time needed to do it properly. This will cause problems for the users when bugs make themselves known.

Today's lesson will attempt to provide you with some ideas and tips on testing and debugging your application. At the same time, you will review the tools that Visual Basic has included to assist you in the process. Finally, you will see how to use some of the newer Visual Basic commands to help identify where a problem exists, even after the application is in use.

Overview

Before jumping into the tools and techniques of debugging your application, it is a good idea to understand what bugs are and how a user would see a bug. In addition, the differences between testing and debugging and how they are tightly related will be explained.

Someone once said that testing is a never-ending process, or to put it another way, there will always be one more bug. But, what are bugs? How do we find them and then fix them? Back when computers took up whole rooms and used hot vacuum tubes, finding bugs was really quite simple. All you had to do was walk into the computer and remove the dead bugs that were preventing the computer's physical switches from closing. Thus, the term "debugging" was born. Unfortunately, it isn't that simple anymore.

The process is much more complicated, both in terms of what is considered a bug and how bugs are found. A programmer must now test and then debug his application code using time, logic, and the tools that are available from the development system. But, what is testing and what is debugging? Testing is the process by which applications are put through every possible keystroke, mouse click, and input; these test cases hopefully exercise every line of code in the application. It is during this process that any indication of an application error should be located. After a problem is found, the debugging process starts. Debugging is a multi-part process that determines the problem and its location in the code, and then fixes it. When the problem has been fixed, you must go back and rerun the test that caused the error to see if you really fixed it. If the problem has been resolved, you can move on to the next test.

Bugs can mean different things to different people. They range from the annoying (misspellings) to the serious (Windows terminates) to the deadly (load data). To the user of your application, a bug is anything that doesn't conform to her expected results. But, to a programmer, a bug is something that produces unexpected results or prevents the application from executing. Now these two definitions might sound similar, but if you take a closer look, you would find that they are very different. If an application is executing properly but doesn't perform the tasks or actions that were initially required of it, the user could consider it a bug. However, the programmer would say that it is performing as designed. So, to a user, a bug is anything unexpected (even bad answers, as opposed to incorrect answers), whereas the programmer would define a bug as a mistake in the technical design and execution of the application.

When testing and debugging your application, you will face many problems that relate to finding and fixing the bugs. Although this will sound a little trite, the best way to debug the application is to take the time to carefully plan and design the application before you begin coding. Beyond that, you should create a physical list of the tests you want to perform on the application during the testing and debugging process. This will prevent you from 'bouncing' from one test to another without any plan. You should test the application in a logical sequence so that after you have tested a portion of the code, you can be confident that it will work.

Finding the Problems

Finding where a problem happened in a computer program isn't as easy as it sounds. The fact that you are trying to accomplish it in a Windows environment makes it that much more difficult. Because Visual Basic stops the execution of the application when a problem occurs, this enables you to at least identify the section of code to look at. Many times, Visual Basic displays an error message like the one shown in Figure 18.1 that tells you the error. However, it does not tell you where it happened or how to fix it.

FIGURE 18.1.

A typical error message from Visual Basic during the testing process.

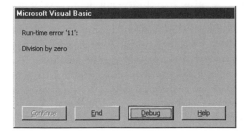

Even more confusing is that the actual problem or error might have occurred earlier, in an entirely different area of the program, but, has manifested at this time. What this means in English, is that you will have to work backwards from the point of the problem to find the real culprit, almost like solving a crime. You have clues, but you have to look carefully for the guilty line of code.

Luckily for you, Visual Basic provides some very good tools to assist you when testing and debugging your application. These tools enable you to look at how the application logic flows from one routine to another. In addition, it enables you to observe how variables and property settings change during the execution of the application. What you're really doing is lifting the hood of your application and looking at the engine.

The testing and debugging process can be made much simpler by simply adhering to the following concepts and techniques:

- Use the Option Explicit statement to prevent misspelled variable and object names.

- Include well-designed error-handling routines to trap many of the problems that can occur.

18

- Keep your routines fairly short and easy to follow.
- Indent all `Loops` and `If` statement code for easier reading.
- If it is possible, use line numbers so that they can be displayed in the error-handling routines.
- Name your forms, objects, and variables logically so that you can instantly know what they are or what they do.

The preceding suggestions will help you resolve many of the problems that can pop up. These are the syntax, compile, or runtime errors. However, the problems that you are really checking for when you test and debug the application are the logic errors in your code.

Logic errors are the toughest type of problem to find and fix because the error usually occurs further down the execution path in the application. For example, an incorrect result may be produced at the conclusion of a long series of calculation. In debugging, the task is to determine what and where something went wrong. It could be that you forgot to initialize a variable, chose the wrong operator or function, or used an incorrect formula. Making matters worse, logic problems are can be caused by bad data input, which means that a particular problem might not always happen.

Sometimes, these problems generate a runtime error that prevents the application from continuing. These bugs are usually found only by checking the results that the application returns against what the results should have been. This means that we have to perform the same functions and operations by hand that the application would do on the computer, enabling us to check the answers. This is known as *desk-checking* the application. This method got its name because programmers sat at their desks reading the application code and performing the actions of the application on paper. These days, supplied debugging tools have taken the place of the pencil and paper in the desk-checking process, although it should really still be done.

Unfortunately, there are no magic tricks in the debugging process, and there is no specific sequence of steps that will work every time you try them. Basically, debugging helps you to understand what is going on during the execution of the application. The Visual Basic–supplied debugging tools give you a snapshot of your application at any given moment in the process. The better you understand how your application works, the faster you can find the bugs.

The Debugging Environment

Visual Basic provides you with several very good tools for testing and debugging your application. These tools include breakpoint processing, Break expressions, Watch expressions, single-step processing, and the capability to display the contents of variables and properties. In addition, you can also modify code and change variable or property values during the execution of the application as well as being able to specify the next statement to be executed. To test and debug an application, you need to understand the three unique modes that you will be working in. Two of these modes you should already be somewhat familiar with.

When you are in the process of creating or coding your application, your are in Visual Basic's Design mode. When you are running the application, you are in Run mode. During the debugging process, you will be working in the third mode, called Break mode, which suspends the execution of the application so you can examine and alter any data or code. To know which mode you are in requires you to look only as far as the Visual Basic title bar. The title bar will always display the current mode as shown in Figure 18.2.

FIGURE 18.2.

The Visual Basic title bar will always display the current mode enclosed in square brackets.

Current Mode Displayed

18

Table 18.1 describes each of these three modes and the actions you can take.

TABLE 18.1. THE ACTIONS OF THE THREE VISUAL BASIC OPERATING MODES.

Mode	Description
Design	Most of the work of creating an application is done at designtime. You can design forms, draw controls, write code, and use the Properties window to set or view any of the property settings. However, you cannot execute any code or use the available debugging tools, except for setting the breakpoints and creating watch expressions.
Run	When you execute the application, you interact with the application the same as a user. You can view code, but you cannot change it.
Break	Execution of the application is suspended. You can view and edit code, examine or modify data, restart the application, stop execution, or continue execution from the same point.

The Debugging Toolbars

On the standard toolbar, Visual Basic provides three buttons that enable you to quickly change from one mode to another (see Figure 18.3).

FIGURE 18.3.

The three mode buttons—Start, Break, and End—on the standard toolbar gives you quick access to control the testing process of the application.

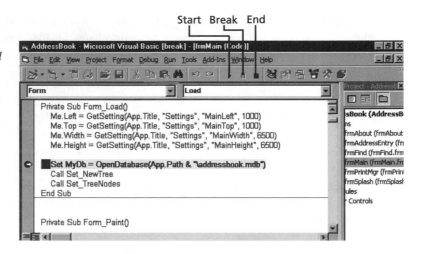

One or more of these buttons will be available depending on whether Visual Basic is in Run, Design, or Break modes. Table 18.2 lists the different modes each button is available in.

TABLE 18.2. THE THREE MODES AND THE AVAILABLE BUTTONS.

Mode	Buttons available
Designtime	Start
Runtime	Break, End
Break	Continue (when in Break mode, the Start button becomes the Continue button), End

In addition to the mode buttons, Visual Basic provides a Debug toolbar (see Figure 18.4) that you can optionally display or you can use the Debug menu instead.

Each of these functions are briefly described in Table 18.3.

TABLE 18.3. THE AVAILABLE DEBUGGING FUNCTIONS AND THEIR PURPOSES.

Debugging Function	Purpose
Breakpoint	Sets a line in the code where Visual Basic suspends execution of the application
Step Into	Executes the next executable line of code in the application and steps into any procedure
Step Over	Executes the next executable line of code in the application without stepping into any procedure

Debugging Function	Purpose
Step Out	Executes the remainder of the current procedure and breaks at the next line in the calling procedure
Locals Window	Displays the current value of any local variables
Immediate Window	Enables you to execute code or display any values while the application is in Break mode
Watch Window	Displays the values of selected expressions
Quick Watch	Lists the current value of an expression while the application is in Break mode
Call Stack	While in Break mode, presents a dialog box that displays all the procedures that have been called but not yet run to completion, as discussed on Day 15

FIGURE 18.4.

The optional Debug toolbar provides many of the debugging functions that Visual Basic has.

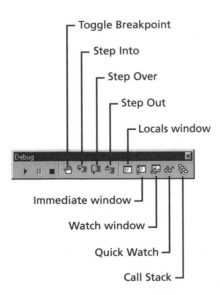

18

As mentioned previously, all these toolbar functions are also available on the Debug menu (see Figure 18.5). Besides the functions from the toolbar, there are also the options to add and remove Watch expressions and show the next executable statement. Also, after you place the cursor at a given line of code, you can have the application execute until it hits the line with the cursor on it.

FIGURE 18.5.

Use the Debug menu to access the debugging tools in Visual Basic.

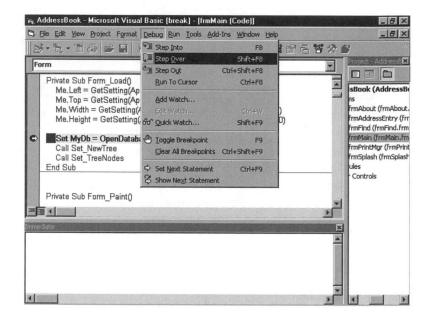

The Debug Windows

There are times when you will need to execute portions of your application code in order to find the cause of a problem. In most cases, you will also have to analyze what is happening to the data as well. You might find that the problem is in a variable or a property with an invalid value in it. What you must do is find out how and why the value was incorrect. With the different debugging windows, you can monitor the values of expressions and variables while stepping through the statements in your application. There are three different debugging windows that you will use during this process:

- Immediate window
- Watch window
- Locals window

Working in conjunction with the code window, you will use these three windows to fully test and debug your application. The Immediate window displays information from one of two possible areas. By using the Debug object (discussed later in this chapter), you can have any value or expression printed in this window during the execution of the application, or when in Break mode, you can use the Print command to display the contents of any variable, property, or calculation as shown in Figure 18.6.

FIGURE 18.6.

Using the Immediate window to visually check the contents of any variable or property value in the application.

The Watches window, on the other hand, will display the values of any Watch expressions that you have chosen to track. There are two types of Watch expressions, those that only display the values of the expressions, and those that stop the execution of the application when the condition you specified becomes True. In the Watches window (see Figure 18.7), the Context column indicates the procedure, module, or modules in which each Watch expression is checked.

FIGURE 18.7.

Using the Watches window to track expressions in the application.

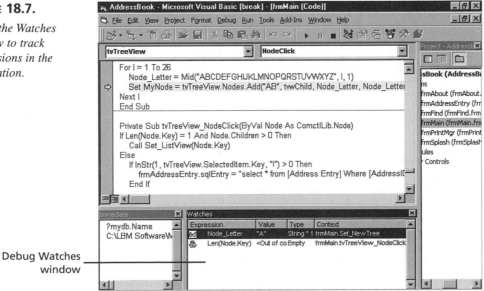

Debug Watches window

If the statement that the application is currently stopped at is within the specified context of the Watch expression, then the value for that expression is displayed. Otherwise, the value column will display a message that the statement isn't in context. Finally, the Locals window displays the value of any variables that are within the scope of the current procedure. As the execution of the application flows from one procedure to another, the Locals window (see Figure 18.8) changes to reflect only those variables applicable to the current procedure.

FIGURE 18.8.

The Locals window displays all local variables and all properties associated with the current form.

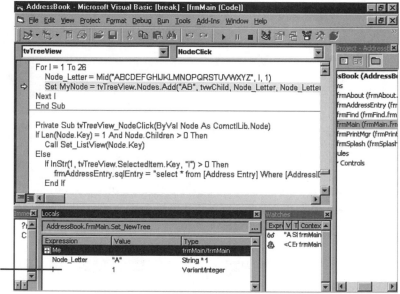

Debug Locals window ——————

Breakpoints in Code

At designtime, you can modify the design or code of the application, but you cannot see how the changes will affect the way the application will execute. At runtime, you can watch how the application will execute, but you cannot change the code or any of the values being processed. By using the Break mode, you can halt the execution of the application and look at a snapshot of its condition at that moment. Variable and property values are retained, so that you can analyze the current state of the application and enter changes that affect how the application executes. The various actions that you can take while the application is in Break mode are:

- Modify application code
- View any changes to the user interface (form changes)
- Determine the procedures that have been called
- Track and display the values of any variables, properties, and statements
- Modify any values necessary
- Specify the next statement you want to be executed
- Execute Visual Basic statements in the Immediate window

When testing and debugging the application, you might want to halt the application at certain places in the code where you think the problem might have started. This is one of the main reasons that Visual Basic provides the capability to set breakpoints. A breakpoint defines a statement or set of conditions (if set in a Watch/Break expression) at which Visual Basic will automatically stop the execution of the application and put it into Break mode without running the statement containing the breakpoint. You can enter Break mode by doing any of the following operations while the application is executing:

- Press the Ctrl+Break keys
- Choose Run, Break
- Click Break on the toolbar

It's possible to suspend execution when the application is between processing of events. When this happens, execution does not stop at a specific line, but Visual Basic switches to Break mode anyway. You can also enter Break mode automatically whenever one of the following conditions occurs:

- A statement generates a runtime error that was not handled by an error handler
- A runtime error was generated and the Break on All Errors option was selected
- A Break expression defined in the Add Watch dialog box changes or becomes True, depending on how you defined it
- Exccution encounters a line that contains a breakpoint
- Execution reaches a Stop statement

Setting a breakpoint in your application code can be done one of three ways, as shown in the following list:

- Select the statement and choose Debug, Toggle Breakpoint from the menu, or hit the F9 shortcut key.
- Select the statement and then right-click it. From the pop-up menu, choose Toggle, Breakpoint.
- Click the mouse in the border to the left of the statement.

When a breakpoint is set, Visual Basis will highlight the selected line in bold, using the colors specified in the Editor Format tab on the Options dialog box from the Tools menu. Additionally, Visual Basic will also highlight the current statement in the code window. Both of these highlights are shown in Figure 18.9 with the associated margin indicators as well.

After you reach a breakpoint and the application has stopped, you can examine the application's current condition by moving the focus among the forms and modules of your application, the Code window, and the debugging windows. A breakpoint stops the application just before executing the line that contains the breakpoint. If you want to observe

18

what happens when that line is executed, you need to use Step Into or Step Over commands to execute that statement.

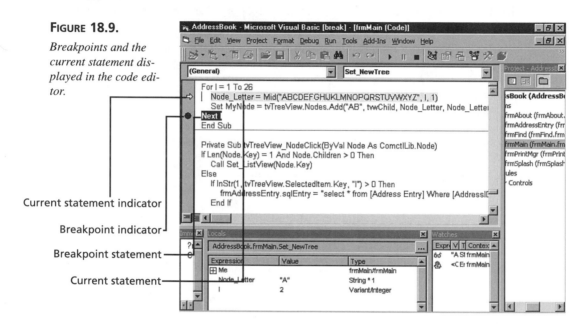

Current statement indicator

Breakpoint indicator

Breakpoint statement

Current statement

To see how this works, open the Address Book project and set a breakpoint on the statement that displays the Address Entry form in the Toolbar click event. Now, run the application and display a book entry. Visual Basic will stop the application at the selected statement, as shown in Figure 18.10.

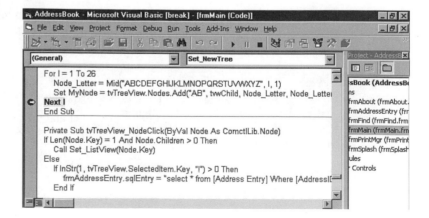

At this point, you can display the variables or set any of the other debugging options. If you can identify the statement that caused the error, a single breakpoint might help you in locating the problem. More often than not, you only know the general section of code that caused the error. A breakpoint will help you isolate the problem area. By using breakpoints, you can step through the logic of your application to see which line or section of code is executed depending on the data being processed.

The Step Into and Step Over commands are used to observe the effect each statement has on the overall process. You can also skip over statements or back up by specifying the line of code to execute. The three step commands that you can use are listed in Table 18.4.

TABLE 18.4. THE AVAILABLE STEP COMMANDS IN VISUAL BASIC.

Command	Description
Step Into	Executes the current statement and then stops at the next line, even if it's in another procedure
Step Over	Executes the entire procedure called by the current statement and then stops at the statement following the current statement
Step Out	Executes the remainder of the current procedure and stops at the statement following the one that called the procedure

Note

These commands are only available when the application is in Break mode.

18

The Step Into command executes the application code one statement at a time. This process, also known as single-stepping through the code, enables you to view the effects each statement has on the overall application. When you click the Step Into button or press the F8 key, Visual Basic temporarily switches to runtime, executes the current statement, moves to the next statement, and then switches back to Break mode. Try this in the Address Book project. You should still be at a breakpoint; press the F8 key and the application will execute the statement you are stopped at and then stop at the next executable statement.

The Step Over command is identical to the Step Into command, except when the current statement contains a call to a procedure. Unlike the Step Into command, which will follow the execution into the called procedure, Step Over will execute the procedure as a unit and then stop at the next statement in the current procedure. Suppose, for example, the current statement calls the procedure SizeControls as shown

```
SizeControls picSplitter.Left
```

If you use Step Into, the Code window jumps to the SizeControls procedure and sets the first executable statement in that procedure to the current statement. This enables you to analyze the code with the SizeControls procedure. However, when using the Step Over command, the Code window continues to display the current procedure. Execution then moves to the statement immediately after the call to SizeControls, unless the procedure contained a breakpoint or Stop statement. Step Over is used if you don't need to analyze the SizeControls procedure, but want to continue single-stepping though the code.

By using the Step Into and Step Over commands together, you can single-step through the application. Then, when you arrive at a procedure call you can choose to either follow the execution into the call or step over it and stop at the statement after the procedure was processed. To see the difference between the commands, stop the Address Book application and set a breakpoint at the beginning of the frmMain's Form_Load routine. Now, execute the application and when you are stopped at the breakpoint, single-step the code by pressing F8 until you get to the call to the Set_NewTree procedure. First, try stepping into the procedure. Then, quit the application and restart it. This time when you get to the breakpoint, single-step to the procedure call and then try the Step Over command by pressing Shift+F8 to see how Visual Basic processes these commands.

The third step command is the Step Out command. This command is similar to the Step Into and Step Over commands, except that it will execute the remainder of the code in the current procedure. If the procedure was called from another procedure, it will continue execution until it gets to the statement immediately following the one that called the procedure. Once again, restart the Address Book application and this time Step Into the Set_NewTree procedure being called. Now press Ctrl+Shift+F8 to perform a Step Out command. You should now be stopped at the statement immediately after the procedure call.

While you are stepping through the application code, you will undoubtedly encounter process loops or long sections of plain, boring code that you don't want to step through. To dynamically "step over" this code, you can use the Run To Cursor command to select a statement further down in your code where you want to stop the execution of the code. In the Address Book application, place the cursor on a statement a few lines further down from where you are stopped. By pressing the Ctrl+F8 keys, you will bypass the code between the cursor and the statement where the code was stopped.

Last but not least is the capability to change the pointer to the next executable statement. Visual Basic enables you to set a different line of code to execute, provided it falls within the current procedure. The effect is similar to using Step Into, except Step Into executes only the next line of code in the procedure. By setting the next statement to execute, you choose which line executes next. To set the next statement to be executed, move the insertion point (cursor) to the line of code you want to execute as shown in Figure 18.11, and then choose Run, Continue from the menu.

FIGURE 18.11.

Moving the current statement pointer to set the next executable statement in the code.

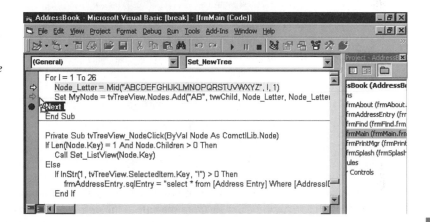

Also, if you have lost track of which statement will be executed next, you can use the Show Next Statement command from the Debug menu to place the cursor on the line that will execute next.

Watching Your Variables

During the debugging process, you may find that a calculation is not producing the results that you want, or problems might be occurring when a certain variable or property contains a particular value. As you have seen, many of the debugging problems are not immediately traceable to a single statement; this requires you to observe the behavior of the variable or expression throughout a procedure or the entire application. The Watch expression tools give you the capability to automatically monitor these variables and expressions in your application. When the application enters the Break mode, the Watch expressions that you specified will appear in the Watches window, where you can observe their values.

In addition, you can use a special version of a Watch expression to halt the execution of the application when a value or expression changes or equals a specified value. For example, if you want to see what a variable contains at a certain point in a loop, you could single-step through the loop until you reach the appropriate counter value, or you could put a Break expression on the loop counter for the value you want to stop at, and then run the application.

18

You can add Watch expressions either at designtime or while the application is in Break mode. The Add Watch dialog box prompts you for the information needed to set the Watch expression (see Figure 18.12).

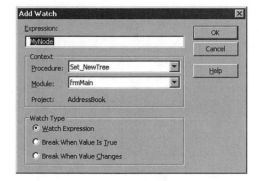

Besides entering the expression, you must set the context for the watch item using the drop-down lists in the Context Option group. This defines in which procedures Visual Basic should monitor the expression. It can watch the expression in a single procedure, a form, a module, or the entire application. Besides the context of the expression, you can also specify the type of watch you are setting. The watch type can just display the contents of the expression as its value changes, break when its value is True or break every time its value changes. If you want to modify the Watch expression, you would select Debug | Edit Watch from the menu. If you want to delete an expression, select the one you want to delete in the Watches window, and then press Delete.

In addition, when you are in Break mode, you can check the value of a property, variable, or expression quickly using the Quick Watch dialog box shown in Figure 18.13.

If you need to continue watching this expression, you can add it to the watch window by clicking Add. This expression would then appear in the Watches window. The fastest way of accessing the Quick Watch function is by selecting the variable or expression and pressing the Shift+F9.

When using the Watches window, you can identify which type of Watch expressions are being displayed by the icon on the left edge of each expression, as shown in Figure 18.14.

FIGURE 18.14.

Identifying the Watch expression types using the displayed icons.

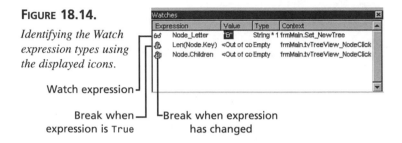

Watch expression

Break when expression is `True`

Break when expression has changed

Using the Immediate Window

When you are debugging your application, you may sometimes have a need to execute individual procedures, evaluate expressions, or assign a new value to a variable or property. The Immediate window is the location where you can accomplish any of these tasks. One of the oldest methods of debugging is to print the contents of variables after each calculation. You can:

- Use `MsgBox` statements to display these values
- Use the Debug object to print the values directly to the Immediate window
- When the application is in Break mode, you can enter `Print` methods directly in the Immediate window

When you are in Break mode, the Immediate window can be used to execute almost any Visual Basic command that you might need. You can print any variable or expression. In addition, if the execution of the application halts within the code that is attached to a form or class, you can also refer to the properties of that form. When doing this, the List Properties/Methods quick list is displayed the same way as when you are entering code during designtime. Besides printing values in the Immediate window, you can also assign values to a variable or property to help isolate the possible cause of an error in the application.

Any of these commands are entered as standard Visual Basic code, as shown in Figure 18.15.

After you set the values of one or more properties and variables, you can continue the execution of the application to see the results, or you can even execute any procedure that is accessible in your application. After entering a statement as shown in the following code, you would press Enter:

```
SaveSetting App.Title, "Settings", "MainHeight", Me.Height
```

FIGURE 18.15.

Entering standard Visual Basic code in the Immediate window.

When you press Enter, Visual Basic actually switches to Run mode to execute the statement, and then returns to Break mode. At that point, you can see the results of the procedure call and test any possible effects it might have had on the variables or properties.

 Caution

If you have Option Explicit specified, any variable that you enter in the Immediate window must have been previously defined in the application.

You can also use the Immediate window to display any error message using its related error number. Put the Address Book application in Break mode and then enter the following line of code in the Immediate window:

```
error 76
```

When you press Enter, this statement will produce a standard MsgBox with the related error message, as shown in Figure 18.16.

FIGURE 18.16.

Displaying error messages directly from the Immediate window.

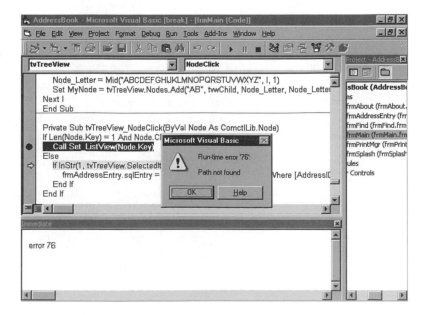

> **Note**
>
> Although most statements are supported in the Immediate window, you can only execute a single line of basic code. To execute multiple statements, you must use colons to separate the statements as shown in the following code:
>
> ```
> For J = 1 to 5 : txtColor(J).Text = VbRed : Next J
> ```

Other Debugging Tools to Use

Besides all of the tools that you have available to use when debugging your application, there are several other features that you can use that are not so much tools as methods and statements in the Visual Basic language. These enable you to build debugging code into the application and then control these statements by using the command line arguments.

Conditional Compiling and Code

Command line arguments can be used to have the application execute certain sections of code only when a particular argument is passed to the application at startup. The user can enter them by choosing Run from the Start menu and then entering the application name, followed by one or more arguments, as shown in Figure 18.17.

18

FIGURE 18.17.

Running the application from the Windows 95 Start, Run menu option, passing debugging arguments on the command line.

This enables you to have debugging code imbedded in your application that will not be executed until you give the user the correct argument to enter on the command line. This is one way of obtaining information from your application when a bug occurs after the application is in use. In addition, this helps you get the information as the user works with the application.

> **Note**
>
> The hardest thing to do is reproduce an error that a user has reported. Without reproducing the error, it is almost impossible to fix the problem.

Command line arguments can also be passed to the application using the Make tab on the Projects Properties dialog box, as shown in Figure 18.18.

FIGURE 18.18.

*Passing command line
arguments in the
Project Properties
Make tab.*

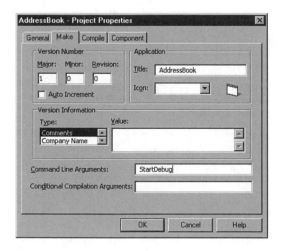

In addition to command line arguments, you can also pass conditional compilation arguments to the application. By using the conditional compilation arguments, you can have whole sections of code included in the application only when you specify certain arguments when you compile the application. This gives you the capability of removing any debugging statements from your application when you distribute the application. An example of conditional code is shown in the following code:

```
#If conFrenchVersion Then
    ' <code specific to the French language version>.
#ElseIf conGermanVersion then
    ' <code specific to the German language version>.
#Else
    ' <code specific to other versions>.
#End If
```

This enables you to add code to your application that can be used in different versions of the application, such as different languages.

Debug Object

The Debug object is used during the testing and debugging of an application to send output directly to the Immediate window or to force an assertion in the code when a specified condition is either True or False.

An assertion is a convenient way to test for conditions that should exist at a given point in your application. In Visual Basic, assertions are created using the Debug object and the

Assert method using the syntax shown in the following code:

Debug.Assert (boolean expression)

When you are testing your application, this statement will cause the application to enter Break mode with the line containing the statement highlighted (that assumes that the expression evaluates to False). The Debug.Assert statement is very similar to setting a Watch expression with the Break When Value Is True option selected, with the exception that it will break when the expression is False.

The other method of the Debug object is also very useful. The Print method is used to print information directly into the Immediate window using the following syntax:

Debug.Print [output list]

By using the Spc and Tab functions, you can even format the information that is printed in the window. The same functionality and syntax for the Basic Print statement is used for the output list of the Debug Print method.

When debugging your application, you can have as much information as you need printed to the Immediate window to help you track down the problem you are trying to fix.

Note

Don't worry about having the Debug methods in your application; when you compile your application, all of the references to the Debug object are ignored by the compiler.

18

Special Debugging Considerations

In any Visual Basic application, certain events can pose some unique problems when debugging your application. It is very important that you are aware of these problems so that you can work around them and not have them confuse you. When using the debugging tools, you are also using some very basic features of your computer—the keyboard and the mouse. But, what happens when the routines that you need to test are the mouse event or keyboard routine?

Breaking During a MouseDown Event

If the execution of the application is halted during a MouseDown event, you may release the mouse button or use the mouse to do any number of other tasks. However, when the application continues, it assumes that the mouse button is still pressed down. You will not get a MouseUp event until you click the mouse button down and then release it. The problem with this scenario is if you have a breakpoint in the MouseDown event. When you click the mouse button down in Run mode, you will press the breakpoint in the

MouseDown event, then when you continue and click the mouse button down again to get to the MouseUp routine, the breakpoint in the MouseDown event will be hit again. Thus, you would never get to the MouseUp event. The only way around this is to remove the breakpoint in the MouseDown event.

Breaking During a KeyDown Event

If you are testing a KeyDown event, the same considerations discussed previously hold true for the KeyDown and KeyUp events.

Summary

On this day, you have seen all of the tools, tips, techniques, and Visual Basic statements that you have available to you when debugging your application. By using all of these together, you will be able to test your application and fix almost every problem that there might be. Of course, I said almost every problem; you will never get your application to a point where problems will never happen again. Debugging can be a very daunting task after you have finally completed your application. However, there are several ways to simplify this task. The following list are just some of the tips that I use when debugging applications that I have created:

- When the application doesn't produce correct results, browse through your code looking for statements that night have caused the problem. Then set breakpoints at one or more of these statements and restart the application.

- When the program breaks, display the values of any important variables and properties by using the Immediate window.

- Use the Break on All Errors option to determine where an error occurred. Then, step through your code, using Watch expressions and the Locals window to monitor how values change during the process.

- If an error occurs in a loop, define a Break expression to determine where the problem occurs.

- If you determine that a variable or property is causing problems in your application, use a Debug.Assert statement to halt execution when the wrong value is assigned to the variable or property.

As you have seen, debugging is something that is learned but not necessarily taught. There is an art to the debugging process, and just because you know how to use the tools, doesn't imply that you will be doing a good job when debugging the application. You should strive to understand the process and think of the application code as whole units instead of statements. This will help you understand and discover where things may be going wrong.

Q&A

Q **What is a breakpoint?**

A A breakpoint is a method of setting automatic stops within the application code to halt the execution of the application at a particular statement in order to debug a problem.

Q **What are the different ways of setting a breakpoint?**

A There are many different ways to set a breakpoint when in a Visual Basic application. You can either set the breakpoints yourself or have Visual Basic do it when you set Break expressions. The most common ways of setting a breakpoint on a particular line of code are:

- Select the statement and choose Debug, Toggle Breakpoint from the menu.
- Select the statement and press F9.
- Select the statement and right-click it to display the pop-up menu. Then choose Toggle, Breakpoint.
- Click the mouse in the border to the left of the statement you want the breakpoint on.

Q **What is a Watch expression?**

A A Watch expression enables you to define a particular condition either for a variable or an expression that Visual Basic will "watch." In this case, watch means displaying any changes to the value of the variable or expression in the Watches window when in Break mode, or a Break expression that will halt application execution of the value of the variable or expression changes.

Q **What is the Immediate window used for?**

A The Immediate window is used to execute any Visual Basic statement or procedure while testing the application. You can also display the value of any variable, property, or expression by using the Print command.

Q **What information does the Calls Stack dialog box give you?**

A The Calls Stack dialog box displays all the procedures that are active and not yet completed at that moment. It can be used to trace the history of calls that got you to the current statement in the application.

Workshop

The Workshop provides quiz questions to help solidify your understanding of the material covered, as well as exercises to provide you with experience in using what you've learned. Try to understand the quiz and exercise answers before continuing on to the next day's lesson. Answers are provided in Appendix A, "Answers to Exercises."

Quiz

1. What is the difference between a Watch expression and a Break expression?

2. How can you set a Watch expression?

3. What information does the Locals window provide you with?

Exercise

In the Address Book application, place several breakpoints to follow the flow of execution when you select a book entry to display. Then choose a variable or expression and set a Watch expression for it. Finally, while at a breakpoint change the value of the AddressID variable to see how it affects the execution of the application.

DAY 19

Performance and Tuning

Making an application run better and faster is every programmer's goal. Performance is the second most important aspect of any application, right behind the application's usability and features. When anyone talks about performance in an application, however, the answer these days is usually, "Get a faster computer." If things were perfect, your application's users would have a computer with the fastest possible processor, plenty of memory, and unlimited disk space.

Unfortunately, reality dictates that for most users, the actual performance of an application is affected by one or more of the preceding factors. In today's world of Pentium Pro processors and MMX technology, however, computer processing speed is quickly passing the 400Mhz range, meaning that users have come to expect better performance out of every application they install on their computer.

As your applications become larger and more complex, the amount of memory it uses and the speed in which is executes becomes very important. To get your application performing the best it can, you need to understand the different code and techniques that affect performance. This is known as *optimizing and tuning* an application.

When you're optimizing the application code, you can use several techniques to increase performance. Some techniques will help make your application faster, whereas others will help make it smaller. One problem that you face when tuning your application is that the changes you make to the code may not always benefit you in the long run. Changes made to the application to improve its performance can cause the code to become more difficult to maintain or change in the future. Sometimes a change can actually decrease an application's performance.

What you have to do is weigh and decide what the final performance of the application will be against the changes you make to affect it. Today's lesson focuses the different tips and techniques that you can use to enhance the performance of an application.

Creating the Right Impression

You know how first impressions are important. If your application takes a long time to load, it can annoy users and appear as though it's not working correctly. The larger and more complex the first form in the application is, the slower it will load. Any custom controls in the form also must be loaded at startup. And if the first form calls procedures in other modules, these modules must be loaded at startup time as well.

As you can see, performance can very quickly become a domino effect. Adding all this up causes the application to slow down. You can resolve the perceived problem by changing how the application is started. Rather than have the application's main form be the first one displayed, use a splash screen instead (see Figure 19.1).

FIGURE 19.1.

*Present users with
a splash screen to
enhance startup
performance.*

This splash screen should have the minimum amount of processing code in it. While the screen is displayed, the main form is loaded. Finally, when the main form is ready to appear, the splash screen is unloaded. The Application Wizard helps you set up the code for this to work, as follows:

```
Sub Main()
    frmSplash.Show
    frmSplash.Refresh
    Set fMainForm = New frmMain
    Load fMainForm
    Unload frmSplash

    fMainForm.Show

End Sub
```

Giving Windows a Chance

Another reason an application appears to slow down occurs when code routines that are processing large amounts of data don't have any commands that require calls to the Windows engine. This will cause users to think that the computer has frozen or locked up. Windows can't process any user input, such as mouse clicks, unless a Visual Basic control command or Windows call is executed. To prevent this from becoming obvious, you should execute a DoEvents statement within the intensive processing code. This statement passes control to the operating system. After the operating system finishes processing the events in its queue and all keys in the SendKeys queue are sent, control is returned to your application.

> **Caution**
>
> Even though the DoEvents statement is an essential and useful tool to allow Windows to do some processing, it has been known to cause some unexpected problems to appear. You should use this statement carefully.

19

Distracting the User

Another way to prevent the perceived impression of a slow application is to display the status of a process (see Figure 19.2). As you saw on Day 1, however, by using a combination of progress bar, text box, and the new animation controls (see Figure 19.3), you can create a professional-looking status display that will do several things: tell users that something is definitely being processed and, in most cases, show users that the computer hasn't locked up.

FIGURE **19.2.**

*Progress bars were
the first attempt to
display the status of an
application process.*

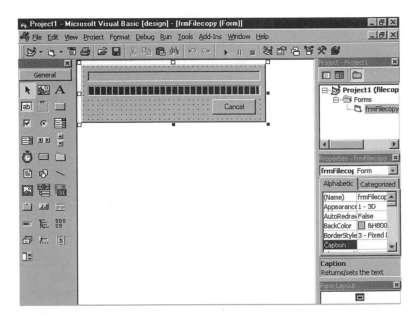

FIGURE **19.3.**

*Adding the Animation
control to the progress
bar adds a little spice
to the status display.*

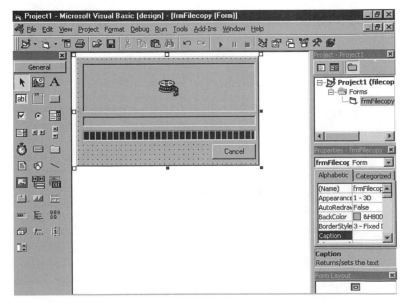

Using Other Tricks to Increase Perceived Speed

In addition to the tips already discussed, you can use other tricks to provide a snappier
look and feel to your application. Each tip helps your application perform better, faster,

and with more efficiency. For example, don't load modules that you don't need. Visual Basic loads code modules on demand, rather than all at once when the application starts. This means that if you never call a procedure in a module, that module will never be loaded. If your startup form or main form calls procedures in several modules, however, all those modules will be loaded as your application starts and before it's displayed.

The following sections discuss other tips and tricks.

Run a Small Visual Basic Application First

Visual Basic spends a large amount of time during the application startup process simply loading the various runtime DLLs used by Visual Basic, ActiveX, and ActiveX controls. If these are already loaded, however, none of that time would be spent by your application. This means that your application would start up faster if another Visual Basic application was already executing on the computer.

Keep Forms Hidden but Loaded

If you intend to use a form again later in the application process, you might consider hiding the form instead of unloading it. This will keep all the controls and variables in memory so that they don't have to be loaded again when the form is needed. The obvious downside to this technique is the amount of memory used by these forms. If you think that users of your application can afford the memory usage, however, this is an excellent way of having forms appear quickly.

Preload Data

Another way to improve the perceived speed of the application is by preloading any data that it might need. For example, if you need to read several files from disk, it's more efficient to read all the files at once rather than read one, read another, then another, and so on. No matter how fast the computer gets, starting disk access always slows down the process. The time spent loading the additional files will probably go unnoticed by users, and you'll have loaded all the required data.

19

Getting the Application to Perform Better

Tuning or optimizing an application is a combination of some programming techniques and some common sense. When you get past the obvious things that you can change in the way the application is process (as discussed in the preceding sections), any other changes will take some thought and possibly designtime before you can implement them. An important part of the process is understanding what you can and can't optimize. You can optimize Visual Basic code, processing algorithms, and data access. But you can do nothing about any operation that occurs outside your control, such as network file access.

A common misconception is that the optimization process takes place at the end of the application development. To create a truly optimized application, you must be optimizing it at the same time that you're developing it. By choosing your algorithms carefully—weighing speed against size and other constraints—you should be able to tell which parts of the application will be fast or slow, large or compact.

If you don't start with a clear goal in mind, you could waste time optimizing the wrong areas of your application. Everything you do should be based on user needs and expectations. The key to the optimization process is to understand the real problem that optimization will address. If you're like most programmers, you don't want to take the time to optimize everything in your application. Because of time, it's obvious that you should focus on the areas that seem to be the slowest or fattest. But to make the results of your efforts count, you should concentrate on the code where a little work will make a lot of difference.

Using the LightWeight Controls

Another way to get the application to perform better is by making use of a new set of controls that come with Visual Basic 6. These controls are called LightWeight controls because they take up less system resources then do the standard versions of the same controls. The set of LightWeight controls consist of the following:

- CheckBox
- ComboBox
- Command button
- Frame
- Horizontal and Vertical Scrollbars
- ListBox
- Option button
- TextBox

These LightWeight controls, sometimes called *windowless controls*, differ from the regular controls in one very significant way, they do not have a Windows Handle property (hWnd). Because of this, they will use fewer resources, making them the controls of choice wherever system resources may be a limiting factor. These controls are contained in the MSWLESS.OCX file; however, they are not automatically installed on your computer.

Note To install these controls, you must copy them from the COMMON\TOOLS\ WINLESS directory on the Visual Basic 6 Product CD-ROM to the WINDOWS\ SYSTEM directory on your computer. Then, you need to register them by double-clicking the MSWINLESS.REG file that is also in the above-mentioned directory.

Directly on a Form

When using these windowless controls, there is no difference between them and the standard controls in how you would use them. Again, because of the lack of an hWnd property, if your application does not need to use APIs that require this property, the windowless versions will interact with the user the same way, but will take up less resources. In addition, your application will load faster increasing the performance ,of the application.

Creating Lightweight Custom User Controls

Another way to make use of the enhanced performance supplied by windowless controls is to create your own custom windowless controls. When designing a custom user control, you should consider creating a windowless control unless the controls design matches one of the following:

- The control contains controls that do not have windowless versions available.
- If the control acts as a designtime container for other controls, it can't be a windowless control.
- The control makes calls to the Windows API that require a window handle as an argument.

Windowless user controls are created by setting the Windowless property to True at designtime. If you attempt to place a standard control on a windowless user control, you will get a designtime error.

Note Not all container programs (such as Visual Basic, Internet Explorer, etc.) support LightWeight controls. If your user control runs in a host that doesn't support it, it will automatically be treated as a standard control. A window handle will be assigned to it by the system.

Optimizing the Code

You can modify your code to enhance performance in many different ways. But unless your application is performing tasks like generating fractals, they're unlikely to be limited

19

by the actual speed of your code. Other factors, such as video speed, network delays, or disk activities, are usually the limiting factor for your application. However, you may find areas in your application where the speed of your code is the limiting factor, especially for frequently called routines. When that's the case, you can use the following techniques to increase your application's speed:

- Avoid using Variant variables
- Use Long integer variables and integer math
- Cache frequently used properties in variables
- Replace procedure calls with inline procedures
- Use constants whenever possible
- Pass arguments ByVal instead of ByRef

Even if you're not optimizing your code for speed, it helps to be aware of these issues and their underlying concepts. As you get into the habit of choosing more efficient methods while you create your code, the gains can add up to a noticeable improvement of your application speed.

Replacing Code with New Functions

Visual Basic 6 includes several new language functions that can be used to replace older less efficient ways of data processing. By replacing these older multiple function statements with the newer functions, the application will perform better. The following section of code was used to search each element of an array for a specific string value and place those elements into a second array:

```
J = 0
For I = 0 To 99
    If Instr(arrInput(I),"Demo") > 0 then
        J = J + 1
        ReDim arrFound(J)
        arrFound(I) = arrInput(I)
    End If
Next I
```

As you can see, while this code works, it does require some processing time from the computer to perform the loop and the If statement test. Using the new Filter function, this process would be reduced to the following one statement:

```
arrFound = Filter(arrInput,"Demo",True,vbTextCompare)
```

By using this statement, you are making use of an internal function to perform the task instead of standard basic code. Table 19.1 lists the new functions and a description. You should take a few minutes to investigate these new commands to see when you can, or should, use them.

TABLE 19.1. NEW BASIC LANGUAGE FUNCTIONS INCLUDED WITH VISUAL BASIC 6.

Name	Description
Filter	Returns a zero-based array containing a subset of the original array based on a specified value
Replace	Returns a string where a specified substring has been replaced with a new substring wherever it was found
Round	Returns a number rounded to a specified number of decimal places
Split	Returns an array containing a specified number of substrings from a single string expression
StrReverse	Reverses the character order of a specified string
Join	Returns a string created by joining all the elements in a string array
WeekdayName	Returns the name of the specified day of the week
MonthName	Returns the name of the specified month

In addition to these new functions, there are several new formatting functions that you can use. The name of these functions basically explain their function and are as follows:

- FormatCurrency
- FormatDateTime
- FormatNumber
- FormatPercent

Avoid Using Variant Variables

You should know that the default data type in Visual Basic is Variant. But because Visual Basic converts all Variant types to the appropriate data type at runtime, any operations involving other simple data types will eliminate this extra step and are faster than their Variant equivalents.

To avoid Variant data types from being defined for you, you should use the Option Explicit statement in the application, which forces you to declare all your variables.

Use Long Integer Variables and Integer Math

If your application performs complex arithmetic operations, you should avoid using Currency, Single, and Double variables. Use Long integer variables whenever you can, particularly in loops; because the Long integer is the 32-bit CPU's native data type, operations that use such integers are very fast. If you can't use Long variables, the Integer or Byte data types are the next best choice.

19

Cache Frequently Used Properties in Variables

You can get and set values of variables faster than those of properties. If you're getting the value of a property frequently (such as in a loop), your code runs faster if you assign the property to a variable outside the loop and then use the variable instead of the property. Variables are generally 10 to 20 times faster than properties of the same type. The following code is very slow:

```
Do Until EOF(F)
    Line Input #F, nextLine
    Text1.Text = Text1.Text + nextLine
Loop
```

This version of the code runs much more quickly:

```
Do Until EOF(F)
    Line Input #F, nextLine
    bufferVar = bufferVar + nextLine
Loop
Text1.Text = bufferVar
```

Replace Procedure Calls with Inline Procedures

Although procedures help make your code more modular, every procedure call involves some additional work and time for your application. If you have a loop that calls a procedure several times, you can eliminate this overhead by placing the body of the procedure directly in the loop.

Use Constants Whenever Possible

Using constants makes your application run faster. Constants also make your code more readable and easier to maintain. If some strings or numbers in your code don't change, declare them as constants. Constants are resolved once at compile time. Because variables must be resolved each time the application runs and finds a variable, the application has to access the variable in memory to get the current value.

Pass Arguments ByVal Instead of ByRef

When writing procedures that include arguments, it's faster to pass the arguments by value (ByVal) than to pass them by reference (ByRef). If you don't need to modify the arguments within the procedure, you should define them as ByVal.

Compiling Versus Using P-Code

When you compile your Visual Basic application, you're actually creating a file that will be interpreted during execution by the Visual Basic dynamic link library (DLL). This type of compilation is called a *P-code executable*. The Professional and Enterprise Editions of Visual Basic include an option to compile your application to a native code .EXE.

In many cases, compiling to native code can provide substantial gains in speed over the interpreted versions of the same application; however, this isn't always the case. You can follow some general guidelines to determine whether native code compilation is the correct method is use:

- Any code that does a lot of primitive operations, such as complex financial calculations or fractal generation, benefits from native code.

- Local process-intensive applications that shuffle a lot of data around within local data structures gain by using native code.

- Applications doing a lot of Windows API calls, COM method calls, and string manipulations don't benefit from using native code.

- Applications that consist mostly of functions from the Visual Basic for Applications runtime library don't see much, if any, advantage from using native code

- If your code involves a lot of subroutine calls, it also will unlikely appear to be much faster using native code.

What native code does is allow programmers to write code procedures never possible before because of performance issues. Enabling these procedures to run much faster can also improve the responsiveness of certain portions of an application, which improves the perceived performance of the overall application.

Finally, if you choose to compile your application to native code, you can use the available compiler options to optimize that type of executable file that will be created. Figures 19.4 and 19.5 show the compiler options that appear on the Compile page of the Project Properties dialog box and the advanced properties available when you click the Advanced Optimizations button.

19

FIGURE 19.4.

Setting the compiler options for a native-code-compiled application.

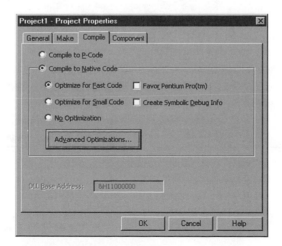

FIGURE 19.5.

*Advanced optimization
options for a native-
code compile.*

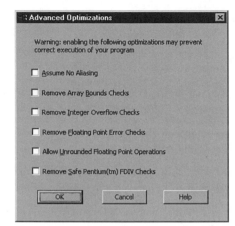

Table 19.2 describes some of the more common compiler options shown in Figures 19.4
and 19.5. If you're unsure of which options to change, the safest thing to do is to use the
default settings.

TABLE 19.2. NATIVE CODE COMPILER OPTIONS.

Option	Description
Optimize for Fast Code	Maximizes the speed of compiled executable files by telling the compiler to favor speed over size.
Optimize for Small Code	Minimizes the size of compiled executable files by telling the compiler to favor size over speed.
No Optimization	Turns off all optimizations so that the compiler generates code that's significantly slower and larger than if optimization for fast or small code is selected.
Favor Pentium Pro	Optimizes code to favor the Pentium Pro (P6) processor. Code generated with this option still runs on earlier processors, but less efficiently. Use this option only if all or most of the machines your program will run on are Pentium Pros.
Remove Array Bounds Checks	Turns off error checking for valid array indexes and the correct number of dimensions of the array.
Remove Integer Overflow Checks	Turns off error checking to ensure that numeric values assigned to integer variables are within the correct range for the data types.

Using Resource Files

One of the easiest things to change in an application that would affect size and speed are the static resources the application uses. Every time you use a string constant for messages or labels, it increases the size of the application, as do picture resources used by the application. If the picture resources are loaded rather than included in the application, the load process also affects the application's speed. All these items are collectively called *application resources* and can be defined in a resource definition file.

Resources are the presentation data that your application uses—that is, no matter what your application does, it uses resources to interact with users. You can divide resources into two main groups: string and binary. String resources contain text string data, such as Hello World or (more realistically) Cannot find Name in Address Book!. Binary resources can contain icons, bitmaps, cursors, sounds, videos, or any other data that's usually stored as binary information.

Using a resource file allows you to collect into one file all the version-specific text, bitmaps, and sounds for an application. This information is kept separate from the code, allowing better control over them. In addition to the obvious optimization effects, resource files are also used to give the application the capability to change its strings, pictures, fonts, sounds, and so on, depending on user input.

A good example for using resource files is when an application is sold in other countries. When an application is distributed in another country, it should display words and images in that country's language. Rather than rewrite the application for each country, you can have a resource file that contains the different country-specific information and then, depending on an installation prompt, uses the correct file.

A resource file is nothing more than a plain text file that consists of the following:

- Preprocessing directives
- Single-line statements
- Multiline statements

By using these commands, you can take most of your memory-intensive resources and define them into a single resource definition file (.RC) and compile them with the actual resource files into a single binary (.RES) file by using the Resource compiler.

Note
The Resource compiler is included on VB's product CD-ROM in the COM-MON/TOOLS/VB/RESOURCE directory. You only need to copy the contents to your hard drive to use it.

19

Creating a Resource File

One way to create a resource file is by using the Application Wizard. Of course, this works only when you're creating a new application. When you use the Application Wizard to create a new application, you're asked whether you want to create a resource file for the application (see Figure 19.6). Then, if you choose to use the resource file, you can edit it later to include more resources as the application grows.

FIGURE **19.6.**

Defining a new Resource file with the Application Wizard.

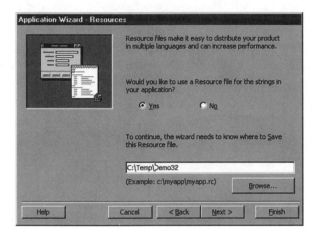

Because a resource file is nothing more than a simple text file, you can use NotePad or Wordpad to create it. Before you start the text editor, however, you should do some design work to decide what you want to include in the file. The resources that you can include in a resource file are divided into two types: *simple resources* are strings and message tables, whereas *complex resources* are binary resources such as bitmaps, sounds, and videos.

To understand how to use a resource file, you must first understand its building blocks. A resource file is created by using one or more of the following commands or statements.

Preprocessing Directives

Preprocessing directives are used to control what the resource compiler will do with the statements included in the definition file. The first directive listed allows you to define variable names and their values to be used later in the file. The remaining directives control which sections of the file will be compiled:

- #define defines a specified name by assigning it a given value.
- #elif marks an optional clause of a conditional-compilation block.
- #else marks the last optional clause of a conditional-compilation block.

- #endif marks the end of a conditional-compilation block.
- #if conditionally compiles the script if a specified expression is true.
- #ifdef conditionally compiles the script if a specified name is defined.
- #ifndef conditionally compiles the script if a specified name isn't defined.
- #include copies the contents of a file into the resource definition file.
- #undef removes the definition of the specified name.

Single-Line Statements

Single-line statements define the resources that require only one line of information for the compiler to understand how to create the resource:

- BITMAP defines a bitmap by naming it and specifying the name of the file that contains it. To use a particular bitmap, the application requests it by name.
- CURSOR defines a cursor by naming it and specifying the name of the file that contains it. To use a particular cursor, the application requests it by name.
- FONT specifies the name of a file that contains a font.
- ICON defines an icon by naming it and specifying the name of the file that contains it. To use a particular icon, the application requests it by name.
- LANGUAGE sets the language for all resources up to the next LANGUAGE statement or to the end of the file. When the LANGUAGE statement appears before BEGIN in an ACCELERATORS, DIALOG, MENU, RCDATA, or STRINGTABLE resource definition, the specified language applies only to that resource.
- MESSAGETABLE defines a message table by naming it and specifying the name of the file that contains it. The file is a binary resource file generated by the Message Compiler.

Multiline Statements

Multiline statements are definitions that require more than one line to fully define the resource:

- ACCELERATORS defines menu accelerator keys.
- DIALOG defines a template that an application can use to create dialog boxes.
- MENU defines the appearance and function of a menu.
- RCDATA defines data resources, which let you include binary data in the executable file.
- STRINGTABLE defines string resources, which are Unicode strings that can be loaded from the executable file.

19

Putting the Resources into the File

The most common resources used in an application are stringtable, bitmap, and icon. Creating a file with these resources should be enough to show you how to create a good resource definition file. To create the file, you can use whichever text editor you are most comfortable with; for this section, however, the NotePad editor will be used.

The first set of statements in the file will define values that will be used later in the file. Enter the following code into the text editor:

```
#define Str_GetName 1
#define Str_GetBirthdate 2
#define Str_DateError 3
#define Str_ExitMessage 4
#define NewIcon 5
#define Open 6
```

This code defines several variables to be used with the following command statements, allowing you to change the ID references without having to search the entire file for each occurrence.

The next step is to add the stringtable, which contains the string statements your application will use. In this example, four strings will be created in this file. The first two will be used as labels in the application; the second two will be used as messages for the `MessageBox` statement. Add this code next in the editor to set these strings:

```
STRINGTABLE DISCARDABLE
BEGIN
        Str_GetName,       "Please Enter Your Name:"
        Str_GetBirthdate,  "Enter Your Birthdate (mm/dd/yy)"
        Str_DateError,     "The date you entered is invalid."
        Str_ExitMessage,   "Okay to Quit?"
END
```

The `DISCARDABLE` option specifies that the resource can be removed from memory if it's no longer being used.

Adding an icon and bitmap resource requires that the following statements be added to the resource definition file:

```
NewIcon    ICON C:\Temp\Point04.ico
Open    BITMAP C:\Temp\Calendar.bmp
```

Include this code in the definition file, using whatever icon and bitmap that you want and have available on your computer.

Caution Because of a problem in the resource compiler that limits the path size that the compiler will accept, keep the files path as short as possible.

After you define all the resources you want in the file, save the file as RESDEMO.RC and then close the text editor. You're now ready to compile this definition file into the finished resource file.

Using the Resource Compiler

The resource compiler is a DOS-based program that allows you to compile the resource definition file into a .RES file, allowing these resources to be used in your application. The Resource Compiler is executed on the command line as follows:

```
rc /r [options] definition-file
```

Table 19.3 shows the parameters used to control the Resource Compiler.

TABLE 19.3. RESOURCE COMPILER PARAMETERS.

Parameter	Description
/r	Specifies that the .RC file only be compiled, not linked to any executable
/?	Displays a list of rc command-line options
/fo filename	Uses filename as the name of the .RES file
/v	Prints progress messages
/d	Defines a symbol
/l	Sets the default language ID in hex
/i	Adds a path for INCLUDE searches
/x	Ignores INCLUDE environment variable
/c	Defines a code page used by NLS conversion
RC file	Specifies the name of the resource definition file (.RC) that contains the names, types, filenames, and descriptions of the resources to be compiled

To compile the completed definition file and name the compiled version DEMO32.RES, you would enter the following command at the DOS prompt:

```
RC /r /fo DEMO32.RES XXXX.RC
```

where *XXXX* is the name of the .RC file that you've just finished creating.

19

Including the Resource File

Now that you have a finished resource file, include it in an application and see how to access the resources defined in it.

You first need to create a new project with command buttons that will display each string defined in the resource file either in a label control or in a message box. There will also be a picture control on the form to display the bitmap. Finally, the icon will be loaded so that it's displayed as part of the command button that loaded it.

Add the six command buttons, PictureBox, and Label controls to the form as shown in Figure 19.7. Then change the properties of these controls as shown in Table 19.4.

FIGURE 19.7.

Creating the Resource demo form in Visual Basic.

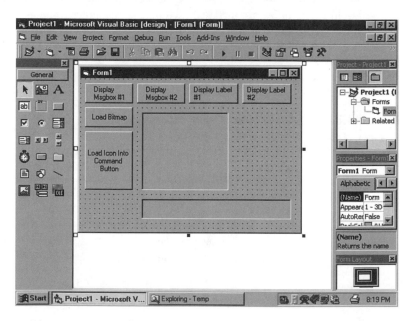

TABLE 19.4. SETTING THE DEMO FORM'S PROPERTIES.

Control	Name	Caption	Style
Command1	cmdMsgbox1	Display Msgbox #1	N/A
Command2	cmdMsgbox2	Display Msgbox #2	N/A
Command3	cmdLabel1	Display Label #1	N/A
Command4	cmdLabel2	Display Label #2	N/A
Command5	cmdBitmap	Load Bitmap	N/A

Control	Name	Caption	Style
Command6	cmdIcon	Load Icon into Command button	Graphical
Picture1	picBitmap	N/A	N/A
Label1	lblString	(blank)	N/A

Now add the resource file to the project. Right-click in the Project window, select the Add option, and then select Add Resource File to display the Open a Resource File dialog box. Locate the resource file that you just created and select it. It's now displayed in the project window in the group Related Documents (see Figure 19.8).

FIGURE 19.8.

Confirming that the resource file has been added correctly to the project.

You can use three commands to retrieve specific resources from the file. The syntax of each command is discussed in the following sections.

LoadResString

```
Lblprompt.caption = LoadResString(index)
```

The required *index* parameter can be an integer value or a string that specifies the identifier (ID) of the data in the resource file.

LoadResPicture

```
PicFrame.Picture = LoadResPicture(index, format)
```

The required *index* parameter can be an integer value or a string that specifies the identifier (ID) of the data in the resource file.

The *format* parameter is also required. The value or constant specifies the format of the data being returned, as follows:

vbResBitmap	0	Bitmap resource
vbResIcon	1	Icon resource
vbResCursor	2	Cursor resource

19

LoadResData

```
StrHolder = LoadResData(index, format)
```

The required *index* parameter can be an integer value or a string that specifies the identifier (ID) of the data in the resource file.

The *format* parameter is also required. The value or constant specifies the original format of the data being returned, as follows:

1	Cursor resource
2	Bitmap resource
3	Icon resource
4	Menu resource
5	Dialog box
6	String resource
7	Font directory resource
8	Font resource
9	Accelerator table
10	User-defined resource
12	Group cursor
14	Group icon

The value can also be the string name of a user-defined resource.

Inserting the Code

When you understand the commands that you can use, the code to use the resources in the resource file is quite easy. Listing 19.1 shows each control event routine needed to perform the necessary actions in the program.

LISTING 19.1. RESOURCE.TXT—COMMAND BUTTON CLICK EVENT ROUTINES TO ACCESS THE RESOURCE FILE.

```
1: Private Sub cmdBitmap_Click()
2: picBitmap.Picture = LoadResPicture(6, vbResBitmap)
   ' Display the Calendar Bitmap
3: End Sub
4:
```

```
 5: Private Sub cmdIcon_Click()
 6: cmdIcon.Picture = LoadResPicture(5, vbResIcon) ' Display the Point04 Icon
 7:
 8: End Sub
 9:
10: Private Sub cmdlabel1_Click()
11: lblString.Caption = LoadResString(1) ' Display the Str_GetName String
12: End Sub
13:
14: Private Sub cmdlabel2_Click()
15: lblString.Caption = LoadResString(2) ' Display the Str_GetBirthDate String
16:
17: End Sub
18:
19: Private Sub cmdMsgbox1_Click()
20: MsgBox (LoadResString(3)) ' Display the Str_DateError String
21: End Sub
22:
23: Private Sub cmdMsgbox2_Click()
24: MsgBox (LoadResString(4)) ' Display the Str_ExitMessage String
25:
26: End Sub.
```

The first and second command buttons will take the first or second strings respectively and use them as the text of a message box. The third and fourth command buttons will display one of two strings in the label on the form. The fifth command button will load the bitmap into the picture box; the sixth button will add an icon to its own picture property.

Executing the Project

Now that the program is coded, the only thing left to do is test it. When you run the program, it should like similar to the Figure 19.9 before you click any command buttons.

FIGURE 19.9.

The demo application before any commands are executed.

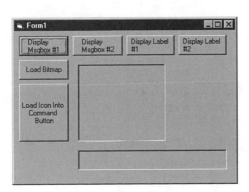

19

Now, see what happens when you click each command button. Your application should now look like the one in Figure 19.10 after you click all the buttons.

FIGURE 19.10.

After executing each command button click routine, the control displays reflect the resources that you've loaded.

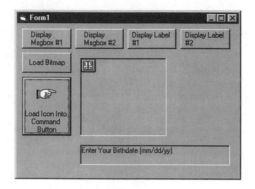

Using the Resource Editor

Now that you've seen how to manually create a resource definition file and have compiled it, you can see how to use a tool to simplify the entire process. Again, Microsoft has a tool installed into the Visual Basic environment that's used to maintain the entire resource file. This tool which was available without charge from the Visual Basic owner's Web site (/www.microsoft.com/vbasic/) is now included with Visual Basic 6. When the editor is installed on your computer, a new reference is added to the Visual Basic Tools menu, as shown in Figure 19.11.

FIGURE **19.11.**

*Accessing the
Resource Editor from
the Tools menu.*

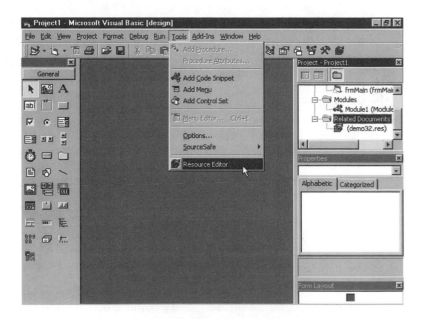

To see how the editor works, choose Tools, Resource Editor. If you already have a
resource file included in the project, the editor will automatically open this file. Otherwise,
you can click the Open button on the toolbar. Figure 19.12 shows the main Resource
Editor dialog box.

 Note

The Resource Editor doesn't contain a menu, only a toolbar.

19

FIGURE **19.12.**

*Working with the
Resource Editor.*

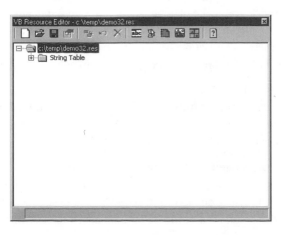

This interface is used to maintain any of the different resources that you can add to the file. As an example of how the editor works, open the String Table folder (if it isn't already open), and then double-click the String Table reference to display the Edit String Tables dialog box (see Figure 19.13).

FIGURE 19.13.

Editing the string resources by using an unbound data grid.

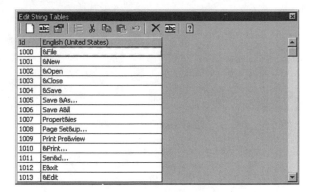

As you can see, the maintenance of the resource definition file has become a simple process with this editor. Now, here's the best part of the Resource Editor: When you finish working with the resource definition file and save the changes, the editor automatically recompiles the information into the .RES file for you.

Summary

In today's lesson, you've seen how the performance of the application can be affected by many different changes, Visual Basic commands, and techniques that you've used in the application. However, performance by itself is a very subjective concept. Making very minor changes in the way the application executes can create the impression of a faster application. Anytime you make changes to increase an application's speed, you should always retest the application to ensure that the changes haven't hurt performance rather than help it. You must also test for reliability after such changes. It's not uncommon for the changes you make to "break" working code somewhere else in the application.

Also, putting many of the more size-intensive resources into its own resource file that your application can access reduces the application's size and increases performance. Finally, VB5's new compile features allow you to create executable files that are optimized for the type of computer the application will probably run on.

The suggestions and techniques that you've seen today are by no means the only ones that you can use to enhance your application. You may think that some suggestions appear too simple to really do anything; however, the best changes you can make to an application are those that require more common sense than complex coding changes.

Q&A

Q Why is using an `Integer` data type more efficient?

A An `Integer` data type is processed more efficiently by the computer than a `Variant` type, which is translated into the appropriate data type for the calculation.

Q What can make an application appear slow?

A An application can appear slow for many different reasons, including very complex forms and large sections of code without any Windows function calls in them.

Q How can you display the first form faster?

A If you display a splash screen while the initial form is being loaded, the application will appear to load faster. Also, remove any unnecessary procedure calls in the first form to reduce the amount of procedure calls the application must do before displaying the first form.

Workshop

The Workshop provides quiz questions to help solidify your understanding of the material covered, as well as exercises to provide you with experience in using what you've learned. Try to understand the quiz and exercise answers before continuing on to the next day's lesson. Answers are provided in Appendix A, "Answers to Exercises."

Quiz

1. What's a resource file?
2. Name three ways to increase application performance.

Exercise

Open the Address Book application and identify any resources or variables that you can change to optimize the process. Also, locate any sections of code that you can modify to tune the process even more.

19

DAY **20**

Finishing the Application

If you're like most new Windows developers, you've spent a lot of time on
what type of application to create, and even more time actually creating it. You
also must have spent time learning the Visual Basic programming language.
Well, you've done it—your application is written, tested, and ready to go. But
go where? Today's lesson covers several topics dealing with the packaging and
deployment of your application.

Unless you work for a company that sells or uses the software you work on,
you'll probably want to sell your application. If this is what you want to do,
you need to worry about many more issues in addition to creating a working
application, such as advertising, customer support, protecting you creation,
and—of course—the actual distribution of the software.

Understanding What Makes Up
a Windows Application

Finishing a Windows application is a lot more than just putting your application
on disks and selling it. The whole process of what the final application package

should be starts right at the beginning. If you're like most programmers, you probably think you have the best application in the world. But if your packaging doesn't look good or the advertising isn't effective, you won't sell many copies. You should start a list of the things you like and don't like about the companies, products, and support that you've dealt with through the years. You also should write down how you think you can improve on these things. The different areas that you must consider when striving for a Windows application package fall into product-related or support-related issues.

Product-Related Issues

When you've decided to create an application, you should realize that you have to consider many topics. Dealing properly with these topics or issues is what eventually will help you create a great application product. Most product-related issues you'll deal with will fall into one of the following categories:

- Program design
- Reporting
- Online help
- Performance
- Error handling
- Printed documentation

Although some of these issues have been discussed to some degree earlier in this book, don't stop here. Make sure that you continue to address each issue as you continue your application's design and development process.

Program Design

Deciding what your application will do and how it should look is the most demanding task in the creation process. Time spent in designing the application will provide you with an easier task when coding the application. Because your application will run in the Windows environment, the overall look of the forms that you design should reflect the type of person who will use it.

Reports

When adding the reporting capability to your application, you have to decide on the type of reporting to give your application's users. Unfortunately, the various reports that might be needed tend to evolve during the creation process. You generally don't know exactly what reports are really needed until the application is completed. However, reports—like weeds—will keep popping up, even when you thought you had covered them all.

Online Help

The Online Help system included with the final application wasn't a walk in the park to create. As you've already seen, designing and creating the Help system is as difficult to do as the application design and creation was. Designing the Help system after the application is done only delays the final application, as you go back and add the Help topic references to the application code and retest the application. What you should really do is design the Help system as you design the application, working with both of them at the same time.

Performance

Performance is a very difficult topic to cover because the idea of performance is as fleeting as the most current PC on the market today. No matter how well you design your application, it will run differently on each and every computer that it's installed on. Because each computer is unique and there are many types and speeds of computer, the best you can hope for is to get your application to run as fast and efficiently as possible.

Error Handling

If everything worked the way it should, there would be no need for error handling in your application. However, we all live in an imperfect world where mistakes happen, files are deleted, and hard disks still run out of space. If you have no error handling in your application, Visual Basic must handle any problems that happen. Unfortunately, Visual Basic isn't as forgiving as you might be when it comes to error handling. If an error occurs, Visual Basic will display a simple default error message and then stop the application's execution. It's your job to code enough error-handling routines to deal with any problems that you think might happen.

Printed Documentation

A good manual for your application is a very difficult thing to produce. Deciding what to put into it and how detailed to get is a complicated procedure. You not only decide what topics are in the manual, but you also have to decide which forms and examples from the application should be placed in the manual. The starting point of any design is to assume that users won't be at the computer when reading the manual. You need to balance the manual's content between text and figures as users read about what the application will do. A good manual usually contains the following sections:

- Table of contents
- Product introduction
- Getting started
- Using the product

20

- Troubleshooting
- Getting technical support
- Index

Each section of the manual should give users enough information to get started, to figure out some of the simpler questions, and to know where to find technical support.

Again, you should look at other product manuals to see which features you like and which features you don't like. If your manual is well laid out and well written, with the online help file, the amount of support calls you receive from users should be fairly low.

Another way of producing a manual, without incurring the cost of printing, is by using a product such as Acrobat. Acrobat and products like it let you create an electronic format of your manual that you would include on your distribution disks. This way, users can view the manual on their computer or, if they want to, print it out themselves.

 Note An online manual isn't an online help file. The manual can be read and searched, but there are no dynamic hyperlinks to other areas in the manual.

Support-Related Issues

Depending on who you talk to, support is different things to different people. This all depends on what the problem, question, or concern might be. When customers call the software company that created an application they use, they want their answers fast, and they want the answers to be correct. What happens when you call a company for support? Do you like the response that you get, or can they do better? Providing customers with a way of getting good application support is part of the overall application package that you must create.

No matter how hard you try, you'll never be able to satisfy everyone who buys your software. Don't be upset if someone returns the software because it doesn't do what they need it to do. (You've returned software for this reason yourself, right?) Most of the time, users call support only when they run out of all the other options they can think of. By the time they call you for support, they're annoyed with the product, and you have to work harder just to calm them down.

When considering the whole concept of support, there's more to this process then just having someone answer a phone when it rings. You must consider the following issues when developing a plan for supporting your application:

- Easy access

- Questions and problems
- Application upgrades and fixes

You need to plan for each of these issue when deciding how to give your users support. If you do this all correctly, your product will be well received by the people who use it.

Easy Access

The entire idea of easy access to technical support has changed over the last year or two. In the past, technical support was usually provided by telephone, fax, or mail. Now, with the increasing use of the Internet, most software providers (a category that you now belong to) provide access to technical support by through a page on their Web site. Depending on the time and money that you want to spend in this area, you can give your users one or all of the following options:

- Direct technical support phone number
- Toll-free technical support
- 24-hour technical support by fax
- Technical support e-mail address
- Interactive Internet support Web page

Every option that you give users comes with its own unique set of problems and—more importantly to you—cost. The best, most used method of offering support to your users is over the phone. However, unless you plan on sitting by the phone 24 hours a day, five to seven days a week, you need some type of answering machine or service to take phone messages. Of course, allowing users to fax in any questions can be useful, but what if you have questions to ask them? The resolution process will tend to get very drawn out and frustrating for users. In my opinion, if you set a standard of getting back to your users within a range of six hours, users will get the impression that you care about the application and their use of it.

The hottest way to offer support these days is by making use of the World Wide Web. If you decide to use this method, you need to obtain space on a Web server, design and build the Web site itself, and then set up a method for checking messages that come into the site, in addition to updating the information on the site. Also, you can have any fixes or upgrades to your application available to your users on the Web for them to download when needed.

Deciding on the type of support that you want to supply to the users of your application really depends on your budget. However, you must pick one or more of these options and then implement them before you start distributing the application.

20

Questions and Problems

Now that you've given users a way of calling, faxing, or emailing their questions and problems to you, how will you handle them? You have to develop a way of tracking the user who sent the question or problem. This way, you can keep track of who your users are. It also allows you to know which questions are being repeated, so you can determine what needs to be changed in your application and whether it's part of the interface or the documentation.

Problems and questions should be dealt with a little differently. With questions that deal with how your application works, you can usually answer them quickly, with a simple answer or instructions on how to do something. With problems, however, you need to obtain enough information to allow you to resolve a problem. When taking a problem report, ask the user for every bit of information that you can think of to figure out the problem. You should request some of the following information when users report a problem:

- The version of the application they're using
- The type and speed of their computer
- The amount of memory the computer has on it
- The exact error message that appeared
- Precisely what users were doing when the error occurred
- Any recent changes made to the PC (hardware, software, or both)

The last item listed is by far the most difficult to get from users. You often hear that a user started the application and then it "blew up." This isn't very specific indication of what happened. You need to know what the user typed, which function keys were pressed, or which command buttons were clicked. These bits of information are very important when you're trying to narrow down the possible problem(s).

Sometimes, when a problem is very hard to resolve, you may come up with a way around it. Called a *workaround*, this stop-gap solution doesn't fix a user's problem, but it allows that user to continue working with the application while you're revising it. Workarounds are important because sometimes a problem takes a long time to fix or can't be fixed without major changes to the application.

Application Upgrades and Fixes

When you decide that it's time to create the next version of your application, you have to figure out what the new features are to be added. Also, you need to think about how your current users will upgrade to this new version. You must give your users the ability to use the new release without having to input their data all over again. Think of how you would feel if you had spent months learning and entering information into an application, only to receive the next release with no way of moving your preexisting data over to it. Keep this in the back of your mind; otherwise, you'll start losing customers soon.

When designing an upgrade to your application, consider how you want to distribute them. If a large number of things have changed in the application, you might consider creating a new set of distribution disks. If only a small amount has changed, you would want to distribute only the changes. Also, you'll want to have two separate sets of distribution disks: one for new users and one for current users upgrading to the new release. Generally, upgrades should contain fixes to problems that have popped up, as well as any new features and functions. This gives current users a good reason to buy the upgrade and new users a reason to try the application.

Distributing the Application

After you complete the development of your application and decide that you've tested it enough, you're ready to make copies of it. Before Windows was around, many applications fit on one disk and were very easy to distribute to users. You would copy the files onto the disk, and then when users purchase the software, they copy it onto their computer.

Well, it's not that easy anymore. These days, Windows 95 and Visual Basic make it a little more than just copying files onto disks. More support files need to be installed with your application than you might realize. Even a small Visual Basic application will require many of the Visual Basic files that provide the access to the controls and database commands that your application uses. In addition, there are many more ways of distributing the application than just using disks. The distribution methods include the following:

- Disk
- CD-ROM
- Network Access
- Internet or intranet access

Each of these methods require a slightly different installation process. The two main steps that you need to perform for your application are:

- **Packaging**—Your application must be packaged into one or more cabinet (.CAB) files that can be deployed to the location you choose.
- **Deployment**—The packaged application needs to be moved to a location from which users can install it. This may mean copying the package to disks or to a local or network drive, or deploying the package to a Web site.

20

> **Note**   A .*CAB* file is a compressed file that is well suited to distribution on both disks or the Internet.

To allow you to more efficiently perform these steps, Visual Basic 6 has included with it the Packaging and Deployment Wizard. This wizard replaces the older Application Setup Wizard that has been included with Visual Basic since version 1. The Package and Deployment Wizard automates much of the work involved in creating and deploying these files. The wizard offers the following three options or functions for you to use:

- **Package option**—Helps you package a project's files into .CAB file(s) that can then be deployed, and in some cases the setup program that installs the .CAB files.
- **Deploy option**—Delivers your packaged applications to the appropriate distribution media, such as disks, a network drive, or to a Web site.
- **Manage Scripts option**—Lets you view and manipulate the scripts you have saved from the previous packaging and deployment sessions.

Packaging the Application

The Packaging and Deployment Wizard helps you to create professional-looking installation packages for your application. In addition to creating a standard installation process, it will also include the files and programs to allow users to uninstall your application if they want to. An application package consists of the .CAB file or files that contain your compressed project files and any other files the user will need to install and use your application. There are two kinds of packages that you can create — standard or Internet packages. If you plan to distribute the application on disk, network drive, or CD-ROM, you should create a *standard package* for the application. However, if you plan on distributing the application through an intranet or Internet site, you should create an Internet package.

No matter which type of package you choose, there are certain steps you need to perform to create the package. These steps are as follows:

1. Select the package type you want to create
2. Specify all the files you need to distribute
3. Set the location to install the files on the user's computer
4. Create the package
5. Deploy the package

When you start the Packaging and Deployment Wizard, you'll be taken through several steps that prompt you for the information needed to build the final installation package. You must do the following:

- Specify your application's project and select whether you are packaging or deploying the application
- Decide how you want to package your application
- Set the destination for the completed package
- Add any files that your application needs, such as the database file
- Save the setup template and actually build the install program

When you finish the process, the Packaging and Deployment Wizard will compress all the selected files included with the application. It will then copy these .CAB files as well as any required install program files to the specified destination. If you had chosen to create a disk installation, you would be asked for disks. You can start the Packaging and Deployment Wizard from the Windows Start menu, as shown in Figure 20.1.

FIGURE 20.1.

Starting the Packaging and Deployment Wizard from the Start menu.

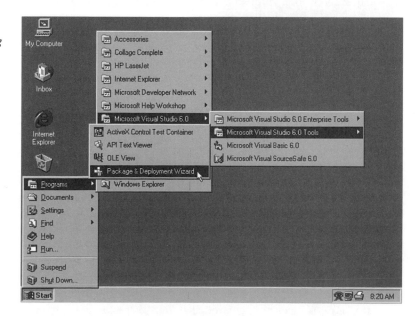

20

The first dialog in the creation process asks you to specify which Visual Basic project you want to work with and presents the three options for you to choose from (see Figure 20.2).

FIGURE 20.2.

Selecting the application project and choosing the processing option.

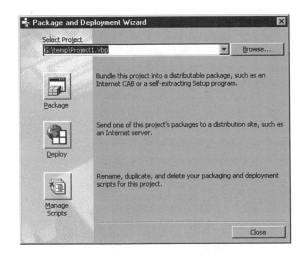

Use the Browse button to locate your application project on your computer. Select the `dlgFileOpenCopy` project that you created during the course of this book. Once you have chosen the project, click the Package button to continue the process. The next dialog (see Figure 20.3) asks you to choose the type of package you are creating.

FIGURE 20.3.

Choosing the packaging type for the application.

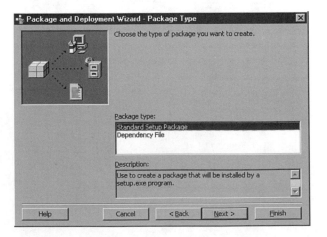

If you're using custom controls that you've created yourself, you should run the Wizard's package option, selecting the Dependency option for each control before you run the wizard for the actual application, to create the dependency file for each the control.

Note   The Packaging and Deployment Wizard uses a dependency file to determine which files are required by an .OCX, .DLL, or ActiveX component.

Select the Standard Setup package and click the Next button to continue. You are now prompted for the directory path that you want to save the package files to, as shown in Figure 20.4.

FIGURE 20.4.

Specifying the build path for the application package files.

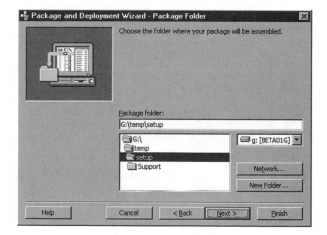

After specifying the directory path, click Next. If the wizard cannot find any of the required files, you will be shown a list of these files and asked to either locate them or ignore them as shown in Figure 20.5.

FIGURE 20.5.

Any missing files are listed, allowing you to locate them on your computer.

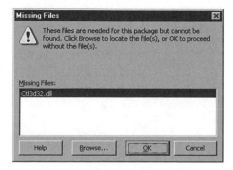

20

If a file that cannot be found is not essential to the package creation, you can choose to proceed without it by clicking the OK button. If your application uses any components that either don't have a dependency file or the file is out of date, they will be displayed and you're asked if you want to proceed. Click the OK button to continue the process. You'll now see all the components that your application requires to execute properly (see Figure 20.6).

FIGURE 20.6.

All of the files for your application are listed on this dialog.

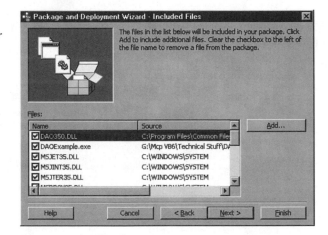

If your application needs any other files, you should add them now. Some of the files that you might have to add are as follows:

- Online help files
- Database-related files
- ReadMe text files
- Any electronic documentation files

When you're finished checking the list of files to include, click the Next button to continue. You now must decide the way you'll be distributing your application. You can choose from the two distribution types, as shown in Figure 20.7.

FIGURE 20.7.

The distribution type you want for your application is selected in this dialog box.

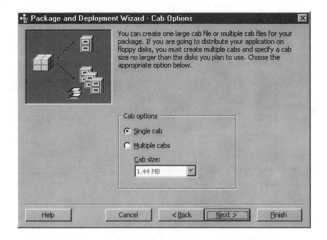

The first type will create a single cabinet file that can be copied to CD-ROM or a network drive for deployment. The second type will create cabinet files that will fit on disks. After selecting the distribution type, click Next to specify the title that will be seen on the installation screen. After entering the title for your application, click Next to continue. The next dialog (see Figure 20.8) allows you to define the start menu group name and items in the group as well as the icons to be used.

FIGURE 20.8.

The Packaging and Deployment Wizard allows you to define exactly what the Start menu group will contain and what icons will be used.

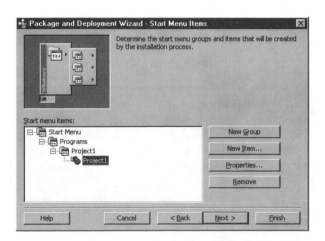

20

Some of the items you might want to put in your application start group are as follows:

- Help menu
- ReadMe text file
- Utility programs

Once you have setup the Startup group, click Next to continue. The next dialog allows you to specify where each of the files in your application will be installed to, as shown in Figure 20.9.

FIGURE 20.9.

Verifying the location that each file will be installed to on the user's computer.

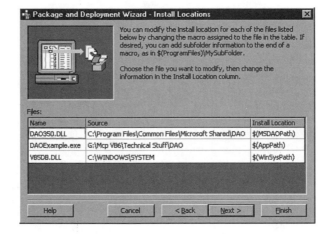

For most of the files, the default locations should be used. However, for any file(s) that are specific to the application (such as database files, help or report files), you should verify the install locations. After you have done this, click Next to specify which files you are deploying can be shared or used by more than one program (see Figure 20.10). Specifying a file as shared will prevent it from being removed during an uninstall until every program which uses them are removed.

FIGURE 20.10.

Marking a file to be shared will prevent it from being removed by another application.

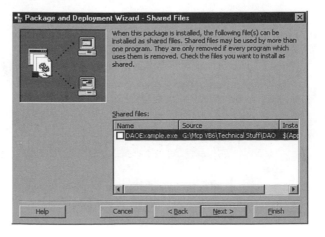

After selecting the shared files, click Next to continue. The final dialog prompts you to name and save the packaging script for you to use at a later time when updating the installation package. Click the Finish button to create the installation package. At this point, you are returned to the main wizard dialog.

Deploying the Package

Now that you have created an installation package for your application, you need to specify the deployment strategy for the application. You can use the deployment option of the wizard to deploy your application to floppy disks, a local or network drive, or to a Web site. Deploying your application requires you to take the following steps:

- Create a package for deployment
- Select the package to deploy
- Choose the deployment method
- Select the files to deploy
- Specify the deployment destination

Starting from the main wizard dialog, select the project you just created the package for and click the Deploy button. This will display a dialog box (scc Figure 20.11) that asks you which package for this project you want to deploy.

FIGURE 20.11.

Choosing the package for deployment.

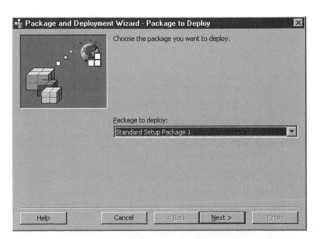

This allows you to support different types of deployment by creating a package for each deployment type. Choose the package you created and click Next. You are now asked which type of deployment you want to perform. The following are the three available deployment types:

- Floppy Disks
- Folders
- WebPost

Each of these requires certain information to process the package.

Floppy Disks

By selecting floppy disks and clicking Next, you will be asked which disk drive to use. Then, click the Next button to save the information as a script and click the Finish button to actually start copying the files to the disks.

Folders

By selecting Folder, you can distribute the package to a folder on either a local or network drive. Clicking Next will display a dialog that asks you to specify the Folder name and location as shown in Figure 20.12.

FIGURE 20.12.

Deploying the package to a specific location on a hard drive.

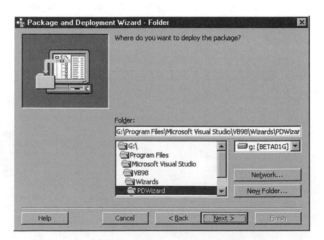

After setting the folder, click Next to save the deployment script, and then click Finish to complete the process.

WebPost

By selecting this option, you can deploy the package across the Internet by posting the package to a Web server. Clicking Next will display the files that are included in the package (see Figure 20.13).

FIGURE 20.13.

Selecting the files you want to post to the Web site.

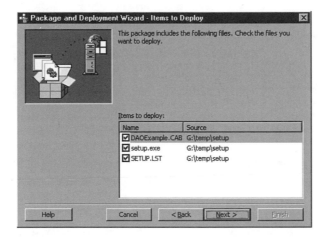

This allows you to select the files you want to deploy. After choosing the files, click Next to continue. The next dialog lets you add other files or folders that you want to deploy along with the package. Once you have added any other files or folders, click Next to continue. At this point you are asked for the WebPost site to display the package to. Only sites registered on your computer PC will appear in the drop-down list. To add a new site, click the New Site button. In the next series of dialog forms, you will be asked for the following:

- A name for the new site
- The type of Web providers to use (for example, FTP, HTTP)
- The posting URL
- The base folder to set on the posting URL

After specifying this information, clicking the Finish button will post (copy) all of the information to the posting URL.

Managing Scripts

The third function the Packaging and Deployment Wizard provides is the ability to manage the scripts that you have saved for a project. By selecting a project on the main wizard dialog and clicking Manage Scripts, a dialog (see Figure 20.14) will be displayed listing both the package and deployment scripts you have previously saved.

20

FIGURE 20.14.

*Manage deploymennt
scripts using the
Package and
Deployment Wizard.*

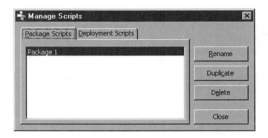

If you need to make modifications to any of the scripts, you can use this feature to either rename or duplicate a script before making changes to it.

Caution

If you remove a packaging script, the deployment function will not recognize the package created from that script as one that it can deploy.

Now that you've finished the packaging and deployment process for your application, you should take the time to test the installation process by installing your application on a different PC. The PC that you use to test the install program shouldn't have Visual Basic installed on it; this would invalidate the test by already having the Visual Basic files on the PC. The purpose of the test is to ensure that all the required files for your application were included in the installation file set.

Ensuring Ownership of Your Code

After working for many weeks, months, or years on designing, creating, and distributing your application, you want to make sure that you own everything about the application. This means dealing with several different legal issues that related to the ownership of the application and the source code that you've written. This all might sound a bit daunting if you work at home. However, with the right amount of information, this issues aren't all that mysterious. You must consider the following issues:

- User registration of the application
- Software theft
- Trademark
- Application copyright

Having users register the purchase of the application and worrying about software theft are really two sides to the same coin. There's really no foolproof way of preventing someone from copying your application disks and giving them to someone else. However, if you require that users register the application with you to obtain technical support, you'll reduce the possibility of this theft from happening. Another way to help in the prevention of product theft is to have a serial number associated with each copy of the application that you produce. Although the serial number can be given with the disks, it makes it a little easier for you to keep track of who really owns a particular copy of the software.

The incentive for users to register the application with you is the availability of support and the notification of any upgrades, fixes, or new versions of the application. When you receive a call from users for support, you should first see if they're already registered; if not, you should ask them for the serial number. If they can't tell you what the serial number is, you must decide whether to refuse to answer their question or to continue with the phone call. At the end of the day, if you do catch someone who doesn't own your software but has a copy of it, you must decide what course of action—legal or otherwise—you want to take.

Protecting Your Application Name

Protecting the name of your application requires you to trademark the name. The decision to trademark the name is the first step in a long legal process, however. Having a trademark for your application prevents someone else from legally using the name. For example, if someone designed a new operating system and wanted to call it Windows, Microsoft would have the legal right to prevent them from doing it. But before you jump into the trademark process, you should know that it takes time and money to get it done. Some developers decide to take a chance and not trademark their application. Unfortunately, if someone decided to trademark the name, the developer would have to change the name of the application wherever it might appear in the application, documentation, and marketing.

As you can probably guess, this decision could be expensive. When applying for a trademark, you need to be aware of many rules. If you can afford it, you should really use a trademark lawyer because this type of lawyer does this type of work daily and knows what to watch for that might cause problems. If you decide to do it yourself, you should know that if the trademark is denied, you don't get your processing fee refunded. To get the information about the trademark process, call or write to the trademark office in Washington, D.C., as soon as you can:

20

U.S. Department of Commerce
Patent and Trademark Office
Washington D.C. 20231
(703) 308-4357

The process can take from three to six months if there are no delays or problems with the trademark submission.

Copyrighting Your Work

Another area that you need to protect yourself is the possible theft of your idea, design, or implementation of your application. If you decide to copyright your application, you're protecting it from any unauthorized copying. Although you can copyright your source code, help files, and documentation, you can't copyright the actual idea or the forms' design that your application uses. If you decide to copyright your application, however, you should apply for the copyright protection before you start selling your application. The actual protection afforded you by obtaining a copyright is directly proportional to your desire to take legal action against the person who has violated the copyright. For more information about obtaining a copyright, call or write the following:

> Publications Section
> LM-455
> Copyright Office
> Library of Congress
> Washington D.C. 20559
> (202) 707-3000

A copyright is considered effective on the date the copyright office receives all the required elements. A return receipt should be used when sending the application to the copyright office so that you know when it gets there.

The Final Decision

When choosing the way you want to sell your product, you have only three real choices: sell your product yourself, sell with the help of another company, or place your application into the wonderful world of shareware. Shareware is a very different way to "sell" your product. Shareware products aren't sold through the use of advertising, direct mail, or catalogs; in fact, they aren't actually sold. They're instead placed in an area on the Internet or on a accessible download area of a service such as America Online (AOL). Anyone who wants to try your application can just copy it from one of these locations. If they like the application, they're supposed to send you the price of a copy of the software. Unfortunately, there's no real way to actually force anyone to pay for the product.

To encourage people to pay for the shareware product if they decide to keep it, most shareware products use one of the following three methods:

- **Use a "Nag" dialog box.** Every time the shareware product is started, users are presented with a dialog box reminding them that the product isn't free and that they should pay the specified amount to get a registered copy and upgrades from the company.
- **Build in a kill switch.** After a shareware product has been used for a preset number of days or occasions, a *kill switch* causes the product to stop working.
- **Disable several of the application's more interesting features.** The only way users can use these features is to purchase the application, at which time you would send them an update of the executable file that would unlock the features.

One of the most successful products on the market today started as a shareware program. PKZIP was originally developed to address the issue of space on a computer disk. It allowed users to compress their files when they weren't needed and to decompress them when they were needed. Because of the way it worked, anyone who used it told everyone they knew about it, until the product became a requirement on a computer.

Many online services today, such as AOL, have areas for posting of shareware products. And catalogs of shareware products have popped up over the years. Of course, the best part of selling your product as shareware is the small amount of money required to do so.

By comparison, the retail world is more costly and much more confusing. Retailing your application often consists of everything but programming. You can advertise your product through the following mediums:

- Magazines
- Newspapers
- Trade journals
- Direct mail
- Television

Each option has its own associated costs and concerns. You should also investigate paying a catalog service to advertise your product for you. If you have a small budget, this is probably one of the best methods of selling a product. The catalog company does all the advertising and order processing for you, at a price (generally, the company takes a percentage of the sale price for its services).

20

Summary

In today's lesson, you've seen the issues that you must resolve before actually distributing your application. There are many different things to worry about when creating an application you want to sell. Technical support is an area that you want to really think about before you actually have to deliver any. Also, you've seen how to use the Packaging and Deployment Wizard to create a professional looking installation program that your users will need to install your application on their computer. Finally, the topics of product security and obtaining trademarks and copyrights were discussed in today's lesson.

Q&A

Q When you develop an application, what are some of the things you must consider?

A Besides worrying about the standard programming issues such as error handling and documentation, you must also consider what you need to do to support users after they purchase the application.

Q What function does the Packaging and Deployment Wizard perform?

A The Packaging and Deployment Wizard helps you build a professional-looking installation program that your users will execute to install your application.

Q Why should you protect your software from theft or copying?

A If you don't protect your software by getting a trademark or copyright, someone could steal your application name or your code and create their own version of the software.

Workshop

The Workshop provides quiz questions to help solidify your understanding of the material covered, as well as exercises to provide you with experience in using what you've learned. Try to understand the quiz and exercise answers before continuing on to the next day's lesson. Answers are provided in Appendix A, "Answers to Exercises."

Quiz

1. Why is customer support so important?
2. What's the difference between selling your application or releasing it as shareware?
3. What's the difference between a trademark and a copyright?

Exercise

Take one of the applications you created earlier in this book and create a set of installation disks for it by using the Packaging and Deployment Wizard.

20

DAY 21

Creating an ActiveX Document

The latest addition to the computer world and business is the Internet and the World Wide Web. It seems that every company and many individuals have Web sites. Creating and maintaining these Web sites involves different levels of support and skill depending on the type of site you are creating. The simplest type of Web site used to contain static Web pages that you could browse, much like a standard Help file. However, as the Internet's popularity has grown, it has become apparent to many that static pages are no longer enough. These days the Internet is used to do the following:

- Obtain software updates from companies
- Find information or reference material, such as phone numbers, addresses, and so on
- Report problems with an owned product
- Send and receive e-mail
- Purchase anything from airline tickets to automobiles

It is now commonplace to see Web sites that act more like standard applications than static images. Creating this interactive "application" environment for a Web site can appear very difficult and confusing. Web programming is still a fairly new area and many people are not yet sure what can and cannot be done in a Web application.

The answer to this is really contained in the development tool you are using. When the topic of Web programming comes up, many different terms come to mind, such as HTML, Perl, CGI, Java, VBScript, and ActiveX Server Pages to name just a few. These are the backbone components of any Web application and are supported by just as many Web development tools, such as Microsoft Visual InterDev and Microsoft FrontPage. Each of these languages and tools has its own strengths and weaknesses.

Today's lesson covers ActiveX documents, which are only one possible option that you have as a Visual Basic programmer creating an Internet application. As you will see, ActiveX documents may not be the best choice for all of your Web needs, but they do make it easy for you to start programming for the Internet.

ActiveX Documents Defined

During this book, you looked at adding a Web browser to your Visual Basic application and reviewed the concepts of HTML and VBScript. However, to understand what an ActiveX document does and how to create it, you need to understand the three levels of HTML/Web processing that exist. The three levels of processing listed in Table 21.1 define when and if any scripting code is executed by a Web page.

TABLE 21.1. THE THREE LEVELS OF WEB PROCESSING.

Level	Description
Simple	Standard HTML pages without any scripting code
Client Side	HTML that contains scripting code that will be executed by the browser
Server Side	HTML that contains scripting code that is processed by the server before being sent to the browser

The capability of embedding code in a Web page allows you to create very robust Web-based applications. These applications can be created to run either on the server to retrieve or process information to be displayed, or on the client or browser PC for locally processed information.

So, what does this all mean in relation to an ActiveX document? To keep it simple, an ActiveX document is a Visual Basic application that is designed to run inside a browser like Internet Explorer instead of running as a stand-alone application, as shown in Figure 21.1.

FIGURE 21.1.

Using a simple ActiveX document application from within Internet Explorer.

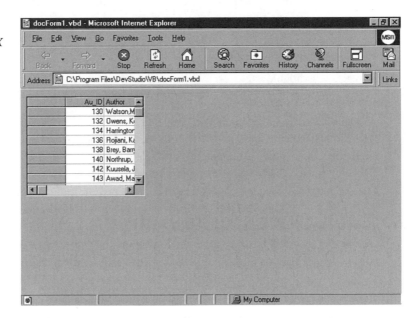

Calling this application a "document" comes from the way word-processing or spreadsheet files have historically been handled. All of these files contain data, but must be accessed by an application in order to be viewed or edited. For example, you can create a document in Excel and store it in a file, but if you send the file to another user, he can't do anything with it without having a copy of Excel on his PC. An ActiveX document works the same way; you can create and store an ActiveX document in a file, but if you send it to someone, she must have an application capable of supporting ActiveX documents before she can work with it.

These days, there are several container applications that support the ActiveX document format, including Internet Explorer, Microsoft Office 97 binders, and the Visual Basic IDE. Using one of these applications, your user would be able to run your ActiveX document.

Because there are many different ways to create an Internet application, you should know the advantages and disadvantages of using ActiveX documents. The primary reason to use ActiveX documents in Visual Basic is to create Internet-enabled applications.

21

Because they are created using the Visual Basic IDE, you immediately have several advantages, including the following:

- All of your Visual Basic expertise can be applied to creating ActiveX documents.
- You can design your Internet application using the Visual Basic design environment.
- You also have access to Visual Basic's debugging environment for testing the code and fixing any problems.
- The available Hyperlink object makes it easy to navigate to other pages from the browser.

So, Visual Basic makes it easy to create an ActiveX document, but why create one instead of just creating a standard application? The answer, if you don't already know it, is the Internet. ActiveX documents take you away from the standard distribution methods that you have already learned how to use. If you stay with a standard application design, you need to use disks or CD-ROMs to distribute your application. However, with ActiveX documents, you can set up your application to be downloaded from a Web browser when the user opens a specific Web page. Using HTML codes embedded in the Web page instructs Internet Explorer to download a cabinet (.CAB) file to the user's PC. This file will contain all of the necessary files and components that your application needs to execute properly. This approach makes it very easy for you to maintain the application code and keep everyone running the same version.

Note

When creating any type of application for the Internet that will give browsers access to data, you need to consider what security options you might have available to you for the Internet.

Creating a New ActiveX Document

Creating an ActiveX document is much the same as creating a standard Visual Basic application. However, there are a few things that make it different. To better understand how to work with an ActiveX document project, you will create a small, fairly simple ActiveX document application and then execute it on your Web browser. You will see from the exercise that everything you learned so far about using Visual Basic is still applicable.

Starting an ActiveX Document Project

The first step in creating any ActiveX document is to start a new project in Visual Basic. Then from the New Project dialog box, select the ActiveX Document .EXE by double-clicking the icon. This opens the new project and displays a blank UserDocument form on the screen, as shown in Figure 21.2.

FIGURE 21.2.

A new project showing a UserDocument *object for the ActiveX Document application.*

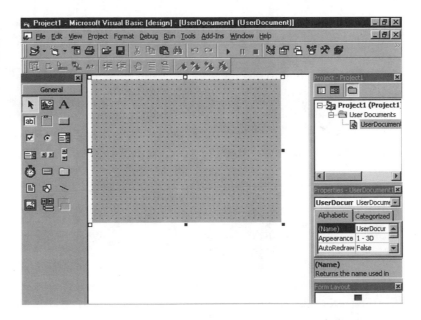

Notice that the UserDocument looks a lot like a form without any border. In fact, the UserDocument looks exactly like the UserControl object that you used to create the ActiveX custom control earlier in this book. This UserDocument is where you will create the user interface for the application. After you have created the project, change the default value of the Name property for the project and the UserDocument to something a little more descriptive.

When you save this project, you will notice that the naming of the files is slightly different than for a standard project. The source code for ActiveX documents is saved much the same way a form is saved. The description of the UserDocument object and any included controls are stored along with the code of the document in a file with the extension .DOB. This is similar to the forms .FRM file. If there are any graphical components of the interface, these are stored in a .DOX file, instead of an .FRX file. When you compile your ActiveX document, you will be creating either an .EXE or .DLL file along with a .VBD file. The .VBD file is the one that is accessed by the Internet Explorer and is considered the "document" part of the file.

Creating the Document Interface

The ActiveX document interface is created by drawing the required controls on the UserDocument object the same way you would for a standard form. Almost any Visual Basic control can be used in the creation of the document. The only exception is that you

21

cannot use the OLE container control as part of an ActiveX document. Add the controls listed in Table 21.2 to the UserDocument as shown in Figure 21.3.

FIGURE 21.3.

Creating a Database Viewer as an ActiveX document.

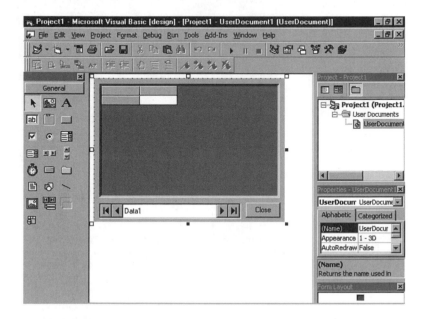

As you can see, you are creating a simple database viewer display using the supplied Biblio database. When you have completed adding the controls to the document, set the following properties for each control as shown in Table 21.2.

TABLE 21.2. ADDING THE CONTROLS TO THE ACTIVEX DOCUMENT.

Control	Property	Value
Data Control	Name	docDataCtl
	DatabaseName	C:\program files\devstudio\vb\biblio.mdb
	Recordsource	Authors
Command Button	Name	cmdClose
	Caption	Close
MSFlexGrid	Name	docFlexGrid
	DataSource	docDataCtl

For this example, the only code you need to add is the End statement in the cmdClose click event.

Testing the ActiveX Document

After adding the code and saving your document, you are ready to test the code. Testing an ActiveX document is a little different than testing a standard program because the document must run inside another application. To test your code, follow these steps:

1. Run your document by clicking the Start button on the toolbar. Visual Basic will not display the user interface of the application, so don't worry.

2. Start Internet Explorer and choose File, Open from Internet Explorer's menu. This will display an Open dialog box where you can enter the name of the ActiveX document to open.

3. Specify the path of your ActiveX document and the name. The name will be the value of the Name property of the UserDocument object, followed by a .VBD extension.

> When running your document within Visual Basic, the file is located in the same folder as Visual Basic (that is, C:\PROGRAM FILES\).

4. Click OK in the Open dialog box to load your document. The new database viewer document will be executed in Internet Explorer, as shown in Figure 21.4.

FIGURE 21.4.

Executing the Database Viewer ActiveX document.

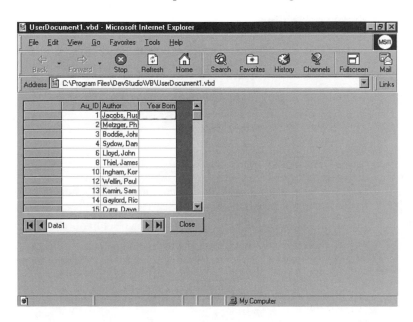

21

If you happen to receive an error message, you can use all of Visual Basic's debugging tools to track down and eliminate the errors. Using the Visual Basic debug environment, you can set breakpoints in your code, set Watches to observe the values of variables, and step through the code line by line to locate an error.

.Terminating your application without closing Internet Explorer may cause errors in Internet Explorer. Therefore, you should close and restart Internet Explorer each time you run your document.

Compiling the Document

After you are satisfied that the ActiveX document works properly, you are ready to compile the document. Choosing File, Make from the Visual Basic menu will open the Make Project dialog box shown in Figure 21.5 to enable you to specify the name and location of the completed .EXE or .DLL file.

FIGURE 21.5.

Using the Make Project dialog box to compile the ActiveX document.

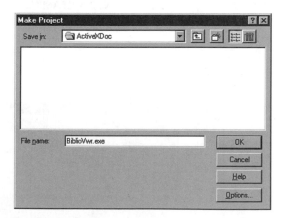

The name of the .VBD file is based on the Name property of the UserDocument object. This file is placed in the same folder that you specified for the .EXE file. After compilation, your document can be used in any of the applications that support ActiveX documents. If you want to put your ActiveX Document on the Internet, you need to first run the Setup Wizard with the Internet Download Setup option. The wizard will create a .CAB file containing required components, as well as sample HTML shown in Listing 21.1 that shows you how to include your document on a Web page. It also creates a SUPPORT directory with the components in the .CAB file, should you need to modify anything.

LISTING 21.1. CABHTML.HTM—THE HTML FILE THAT IS GENERATED DURING THE SETUP WIZARD PROCESS.

```
 1: <HTML>
 2: <HEAD>
 3: <TITLE>Project1.CAB</TITLE>
 4: </HEAD>
 5: <BODY>
 6: <OBJECT ID="Form1"
 7: CLASSID="CLSID:920C5568-8EBD-11D1-ABBA-40C109C10000"
 8: CODEBASE="Project1.CAB#version=1,0,0,0">
 9: </OBJECT>
10:
11: <SCRIPT LANGUAGE="VBScript">
12: Sub Window_OnLoad
13:     Document.Open
14:     Document.Write "<FRAMESET>"
15:     Document.Write "<FRAME SRC=""Form1.VBD"">"
16:     Document.Write "</FRAMESET>"
17:     Document.Close
18: End Sub
19: </SCRIPT>
20: </BODY>
21: </HTML>
```

Note   The Clsid value in the preceding example will be different because it is generated by the Setup Wizard on your computer.

Exploring the UserDocument Object

The UserDocument object is the key part of any ActiveX document. It provides the container for all the controls that you need to create the user interface of the document. You can place any controls on the UserDocument or use graphics methods and the Print method to display other information directly on the document.

Although the UserDocument is similar in many respects to a form, there are also some key differences. Understanding what those differences are enables you to better control the ActiveX document. The events of a form that are not supported by the UserDocument object as follows:

- Activate
- Deactivate
- Load
- Unload

21

On the other hand, the UserDocument supports the following events that the form doesn't support:

- AsycReadComplete—Occurs when the container holding the document has finished an asynchronous read request.
- EnterFocus—Occurs when the ActiveX document receives focus.
- ExitFocus—Occurs when the ActiveX document loses focus.
- Hide—Occurs when the user navigates from the current ActiveX document to another document.
- InitProperties—Occurs when the document is first loaded. However, if any properties have been saved using the PropertyBag, the ReadProperties event will occur instead.
- ReadProperties—Occurs in place of the InitProperties event if items are stored in a PropertyBag. This event also occurs as the document is first loaded.
- Scroll—Occurs when the user uses the scrollbar of the container in which the ActiveX document is running.
- Show—Occurs when the user navigates from another document to the ActiveX document.
- WriteProperties—Occurs as the program is about to be terminated. This event happens right before the Terminate event, but only occurs if the PropertyChanged statement has been used to indicate that a change in a property's value has occurred.

Using Properties for a UserDocument

Because a UserDocument is a stand-alone object, if you are creating an application that uses more than one form, you need to use properties the way a user control does. All three objects—form, UserControl, and UserDocument—enable you to create properties and methods to extend their capabilities. However, only the UserControl and the UserDocument have the capability to use the PropertyBag object, which along with some special events, is used to store values of public properties so that settings are remembered between sessions, and enable you to pass parameters between ActiveX documents.

To see how this works, add a text box and a command button to the UserDocument as shown in Figure 21.6.

FIGURE 21.6.

Adding the controls to call another ActiveX document passing it an argument.

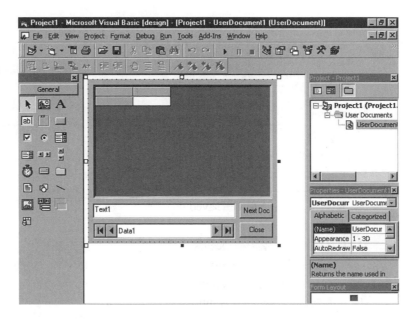

Now add the code in Listing 21.2 to the first document's code.

LISTING 21.2. PROPCODE.TXT—THE CALLING DOCUMENT WILL SET ITS PROPERTIES.

```
 1: Public docBag As docMainFrm
 2:
 3: Private Sub cmdCallNext_Click ()
 4:     Set docBag = Me 'add the reference to this document
 5:     Hyperlink.NavigateTo "C:\Temp\docSecondFrm"
 6: End Sub
 7: Public Property Get strProp() As String
 8:     strProp = Text1.Text
 9: End Property
10:
11: Public Property Let strProp(ByVal _
12: NewStrProp As String)
13:     Text1.Text = NewStrDocProp
14: End Property
```

Then add another `UserDocument` to the project using the normal Visual Basic procedures and put one text box on the form. Then add the code in Listing 21.3.

21

LISTING 21.3. PASSARG.TXT—USING PROPERTIES TO PASS ARGUMENTS BETWEEN DOCUMENTS.

```
1: Private Sub docSecondFrm_Show()
2:     If Not docBag Is Nothing Then
3:         Text1.Text = docBag.strProp
4:         Set docBag = Nothing
5:     End If
6: End Sub
```

Now, rerun the application and test it from your Web browser. Enter some text in the text box and then click the command button to display the next document. The second document should be displayed with the text that you have just entered in the first documents text box.

Using the `Hyperlink` Object

One object of extreme importance in ActiveX documents is the `Hyperlink` object. This object has no properties and only three methods. However, the `Hyperlink` object is what enables an ActiveX document to call other ActiveX documents or to navigate to a Web site. The following are the three methods of the `Hyperlink` object:

- `NavigateTo`—This method causes the container holding the ActiveX document to jump to a file or URL specified in the method. This is the method to use to move from one ActiveX document to another.

- `GoBack`—This method performs a hyperlink jump to the previous document in the history list of a container.

- `GoForward`—This method causes the container to move to the next document in the history list.

Adding Menus to the ActiveX Document

Using the Menu Editor, you can add a menu to your ActiveX document. However, because an ActiveX document cannot have a menu, the menu you create will be merged with the application you used to view the ActiveX document. Thus, you must consider menu negotiation when adding a menu to an ActiveX document. When users navigate to your ActiveX document, they may not know its origin. To fix this, you should always include an About form with your ActiveX document.

Instead of displaying an About box as an ActiveX document, you should display as a standard form using the `Show` command, as shown in the following code:

```
frmAbout.Show VbModal
```

Try this by adding a single menu item that will execute the preceding line of code. Of course, you need to add a standard form to your project. After you have done this, re-test the application in the Web browser and select the menu option.

Converting an Existing Visual Basic Application

So far, you have seen how to create an ActiveX document from scratch. But, if you have a lot of time and effort invested in creating standard Visual Basic applications, you really want some way to capitalize on the work you have already done. Fortunately, Visual Basic provides a tool called the ActiveX Document Migration Wizard, which helps you convert forms from an existing application into UserDocument objects for an ActiveX document.

However, because an ActiveX document doesn't support all of the properties, methods, and events that a standard form does, the Migration Wizard will not create a complete ActiveX document directly from your standard application. The following lists what the wizard does do:

- Copies the properties of the form to a new user document.

- Copies menu items from the source form to the new user document.

- Copies all controls from the source form and retains their relative positions on the form. All control properties are retained except for any OLE container controls and embedded OLE objects, which are not copied.

- Copies the code from the form event procedures to the corresponding procedures in the user document. This includes all event procedures associated with the component controls.

- Comments out code statements that are not supported by ActiveX documents, such as Load, Unload, and End.

Although the Migrate Wizard can do a lot of the work of converting a document for you, there are some things that it cannot handle. You will have to do some coding work before you can compile and distribute your document.

First, you need to remove unsupported events such as Load and Unload. Although the wizard will comment out the Load and Unload statements, it will not remove the event procedures code. If you use these events to initialize the properties of a form or its controls; you may want to move some of the code from the Load event to the Initialize event of the UserDocument. Also, you may want to move some of the code from the Unload event to the Terminate event of the UserDocument.

21

In addition, any statements that Load or Show a form must be changed to a NavigateTo statement, so that you are now calling the other ActiveX documents. Also, if different forms are passing parameters, you must use properties as discussed earlier.

Using the ActiveX Document Migration Wizard

To run the ActiveX Document Migration Wizard, it must be available in the Visual Basic Add-Ins menu. After you have access to the Wizard, you can run it by choosing the ActiveX Document Migration Wizard item from the Add-Ins menu.

To begin converting the forms of a project into ActiveX documents, you must first open the project whose forms you want to convert. The wizard will only work correctly from within the project. To see how this works, open the Address Book project and then start the ActiveX Document Migration Wizard, which displays the introductory dialog box telling you a little of what the wizard can and cannot do for you. Click Next to continue.

The second dialog box, shown in Figure 21.7, enables you to select the forms from the current project that you want to convert to ActiveX documents. All the forms of the current project are shown in the Forms list. You can select any form by clicking the check box next to its name. Because this is a going to be a Web application, there is no compelling reason to have a Splash dialog box, so select all of the forms except for the Splash form and click Next to continue the process.

FIGURE 21.7.

Selecting your forms from the project list.

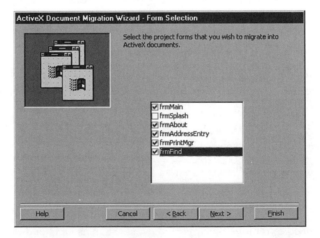

The next dialog box is the Options page shown in Figure 21.8, which enables you to control how the wizard will process the forms you have selected. The three options are:

- Choose to comment out invalid code. This option will comment out statements such as Load, Unload, or End that are not supported by ActiveX documents.

- Remove original forms after conversion. This option will remove the forms from the current project after the conversion is made. Typically, you will *not* want to check this option, because you will want your original project intact.

- Choose whether to convert your project to an ActiveX EXE or ActiveX DLL project. The option defaults to ActiveX EXE.

FIGURE 21.8.

Choosing the Migration options.

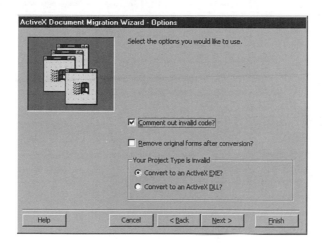

If you choose to have the invalid code commented out, the Form_Load event would be modified as shown in the following code:

```
'[AXDW] The following line was commented out by the ActiveX
' Document Migration Wizard.
'     Me.Left = GetSetting(App.Title, "Settings", "MainLeft", 1000)
```

After selecting the option you want, click Next to continue. The final page of the wizard asks if you would like to see a summary report after the conversion has been completed. Choose Yes and then click Finish to begin the actual conversion. The summary report, shown in Figure 21.9, describes what additional activities you need to perform in order to complete the conversion process.

21

FIGURE 21.9.

Using the Summary report to know what steps you need to complete.

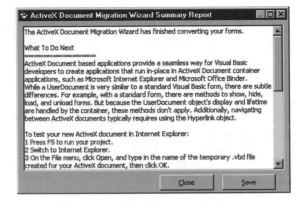

When the Wizard has completed its process, the newly created `UserDocument` objects are placed in the same project as the original forms, as shown in Figure 21.10.

FIGURE 21.10.

The Projects Explorer window showing the new Documents that have been added.

The document source files are stored in the same folder as the original form files and given similar names, with the appropriate extension. For example, a form stored in the file frmdemo.frm would create a `UserDocument` stored in the file docDemo.dob.

Of course, before you can actually run your new ActiveX document, you will need to modify any of the code that uses methods that are not supported in the document object. There are two things you must do before being able to start the testing process. First, search for any wizard comments such as the following line:

```
'[AXDW] The following statement may be invalid in a User Document:':Width'
```

If you compare this comment with the one shown earlier, you notice that this one states that the related *may* be invalid and it is up to you to determine if it is and what to do about. In addition, because you did not choose the Splash form to include in the Web application, you must change the StartUp Object reference in the Projects Properties dialog box from Sub Main to None. When you have completed this code change, the final result would have the main address book form displayed as a Web page, as shown in Figure 21.11.

FIGURE 12.1.

The final Address Book application as an ActiveX document application.

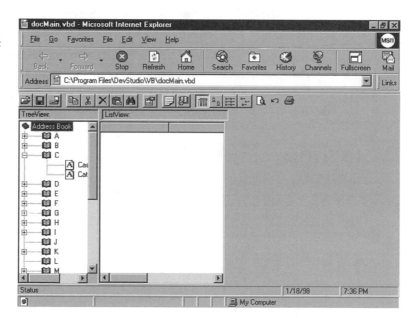

Summary

Today you learned how to use your Visual Basic knowledge to create one type of Web application using ActiveX documents. Even though ActiveX documents are not for every Web application that you might create, they do enable you to create full function applications that run from a Web browser. However, the limitation is that they have no server side scripting in it. This means that any database access is performed locally and requires the database to reside on the user's PC.

Besides learning how to create an ActiveX document from scratch, you also saw how to use the Migration Wizard that is included with Visual Basic to enable you to convert an existing application into ActiveX documents. However, you also saw that there is still plenty of work for you do perform on the converted documents before you can deploy the new application to the Web.

21

In either case, you have seen that creating a Web application using ActiveX documents enables you to have complex applications, but there are still several design issues that you need to deal with that are different from a standard Visual Basic application.

Q&A

Q What are some of the languages that can be used to create Web applications?

A The languages you can use include Java, HTML, VBScript, and Visual Basic.

Q Why is ActiveX a good method of creating Web applications?

A Because you can make use of the Visual Basic IDE and use all of your Visual Basic programming knowledge when creating an ActiveX document Web application, it makes the development process fairly easy because you already know the language and the environment.

Workshop

The Workshop provides quiz questions to help solidify your understanding of the material covered, as well as exercises to provide you with experience in using what you've learned. Try to understand the quiz and exercise answers before continuing on to the next day's lesson. Answers are provided in Appendix A, "Answers to Exercises."

Quiz

1. What are some of the properties and events that are not supported by an ActiveX document?

2. Can an ActiveX document display a standard Visual Basic form?

Exercise

Because of the nature of today's lesson, there are no exercises.

WEEK 3

In Review

Week 3 covered many of the topics that are normally forgotten by the average programmer. These include error handling with an application, performance and tuning of the application, and the concepts of testing and debugging the application to fix any problems. In addition, the Help system and workshops were covered to allow you to add Help to your application. Finally, you saw what it takes to get a Windows application to market and how to add some fancy pizzazz to your application.

Additional Features and Help

There are many features that you can add to your application that help the user make use of the application. In Day 15, you saw one of these features which gives you the ability to move data from one area of the application to another or from/to another application. OLE drag and drop gives you the ability to perform this functionality in the application. You also saw how to use the new date controls to display calendar type controls to the user for data selection and display. Finally, the unsupported System Tray control was covered, which allows you to add your application's functionality to the Windows system tray in the Task bar. Then, in Day 17, you learned how to design an application Help system and then create it using both the standard and new HTML Help workshops that are included with Visual Basic.

15

16

17

18

19

20

21

Tuning the Application

Days 16 and 18 covered all of the issues that help you to create an application that handles any errors that might occur when the application is being used. In addition, you saw how to use the debugging tools that are included with Visual Basic to test and fix any errors that might be found. Then in Day 19, you were introduced to the concepts, tips, and techniques that you can use to enhance the performance of your application. This includes using the Resource Editor to compile strings and pictures externally to the application, which reduces the size of the actual application.

Finishing the Application

In Days 20 and 21, the information that you need to know in order to package and sell your application was presented to you along with the different issues that you should think about when finishing your application. Finally, you learned how to convert your application into an ActiveX document that can then be executed from the Internet. Overall, this book covered the different tips, techniques, and skills that you need in order to design, build, and distribute your application in a professional manner.

Appendix A

Answers to Exercises

Day 1, "Writing Professional Visual Basic Applications"

Quiz

1. An application consists of many unique programs combined into one larger related package. This package can usually perform several different functions that all relate to each other.

2. The major steps in a standard life cycle are design, coding, testing and debugging, and documentation.

3. With the Animation control, you can display small .AVI files to users while your application performs some other task.

4. Testing is the process of detecting errors in your application as they occur, whereas debugging is the process of identifying the cause of an error and correcting it.

Exercise

To change the file-copy function to a move-file function, you need to add only one Visual Basic statement to the routine. After you successfully copy the file to the destination, you have to delete it from the source directory. To do so, insert the following line of code immediately after the two `Close` statements:

```
Kill strFrom_Filename
```

This statement deletes the file referenced by the variable.

Day 2, "The Windows Common Dialog in Use"

Quiz

1. The Dialog Automation Object doesn't access the Windows help engine.

2. The help function doesn't have its own dialog box to display; instead, it accesses the Windows help engine to display the referenced help file.

3. To use the Common Dialog's Open dialog box, you need to set these properties:

Filter	DefaultExt
FilterIndex	InitDir
Flags	MaxFileSize
Filename	

Exercise

Any answers or example code that I could put here would match what's already in the chapter. So for this exercise, you can decide for yourself what the answer is, and it's not even cheating.

Day 3, "Changing the Face of the Application"

Quiz

1. You can create an MDI application by adding an MDI parent form to your project and then setting other forms' `MDIChild` property to `True`.

A

2. The Explorer interface uses the ListView, TreeView, PictureBox, and Label controls to create the two-pane work area.

3. The Application Wizard that comes with Visual Basic that helps you to create a functioning application skeleton in one of the three interface styles.

Exercise

Because you can enhance an application in many different ways, I'll leave it up to you to decide how the changes should be done and how they should look.

Day 4, "Creating Form Templates"

Quiz

1. A toolbar requires an ImageList and Toolbar control to be on the form.

2. Yes, a toolbar can display text, pictures, or both.

3. The Toolbar Builder allows you to select the different buttons that you want on the toolbar, and then adds those images to an ImageList control it places on the form and then creates the toolbar with the buttons on it and the generic code to work with.

4. You can have as many top-level menu items as you want; however, too many will make your application very hard to use.

5. No. At any given level of a menu item, only one hotkey can use a particular letter.

6. There can be at most 79 shortcut keys in any application.

Exercise

To give users a selection list of color names to choose from on the toolbar, add a combo box control to the toolbar by using the placeholder style of button and changing its width to match that of the combo box control plus 150 twips. The toolbar would look like the one shown in Figure A.1.

FIGURE A.1.

Using drop-down combo box controls on the toolbar.

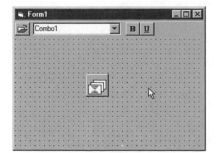

Day 5, "Objects, Collections, and Array Processing"

Quiz

1. There are two functions available in Visual Basic to determine the class of an object: the `TypeOf` and `TypeName` functions.

2. The `With...End With` statements are efficient only when you are working with many properties of a control. When assigning only one or two properties it is better to just code the full statements.

3. All collections share four objects:

    *   `Add` method
    *   `Remove` method
    *   `Item` method
    *   `Count` property

4. You can create a new instance of a class or an object by declaring it in the Declarations section as follows:

    ```
    Private myObj as New [object]
    ```

    The object is created on the first reference in the code.

Exercise

To create an application that places new controls on the form when a command button is clicked, you must place one copy of the control on the form and set its visible property to `False` and its `Index` property to `0`. This will properly create the control array. Then, every time you must add another copy of the control to the form, load the next element in the array and make it visible. The code for this exercise is shown in Listing A.1.

LISTING A.1. CHAP5EXE.TXT—THE FINISHED CODE FOR THE EXERCISE.

```
Dim txtTop As Integer
Dim txtLeft As Integer
Dim txtCount As Integer
Dim txtHeight As Integer
Dim txtWidth As Integer

Private Sub Command1_Click()
txtCount = txtCount + 1
Load Text1(txtCount)
Text1(txtCount).Top = txtTop
Text1(txtCount).Left = txtLeft
txtTop = Text1(txtCount).Top + txtHeight + 120
```

```
Text1(txtCount).Visible = True
End Sub

Private Sub Form_Load()
txtTop = 120
txtLeft = 120
txtHeight = 495
txtWidth = 1215
txtCount = 0
End Sub
```

However, this code will keep adding controls on this form even if there is no longer any room for them to be displayed.

Day 6, "Procedures, Functions, and Logic"

Quiz

1. A function can return only a single value; however, by using the `byRef` keyword, the function can modify any of the variables that were passed to it.

2. The only difference between a subroutine and a function is that a function returns a value, while a subroutine does not.

3. Using public variables is not recommended because they can be accessed anywhere in the application code, and you could wind up accidentally modifying a value. This would result in unexpected errors in the application.

4. You can leave any subroutine or object's event routine by using the `Exit Sub` statement.

Exercise

The first part of this exercise will print all the variables because the procedure-level variables are in the routine that will be printing them. However, the second part of the exercise will result in a runtime error because the procedure-level variables are not accessible. Listing A.2 shows the code to perform the tasks for this exercise. You will also need to add a module to the application as shown in Listing A.3.

LISTING A.2. CHAP6EX1.TXT—FORM MODULE CODE FOR THE EXERCISE.

```
Option Explicit

Private mVar1 As Integer
Private mVar2 As String
```

continues

LISTING A.2. CONTINUED

```
Private Sub myPrint()
Dim pVar1 As Integer
    pVar1 = 5
    Print "Var1=", Var1
    Print "Var2=", Var2
    Print "mVar1=", mVar1
    Print "mVar2=", mVar2
    Print "Constant txtInput=", txtInput
    Print "pVar1=", pVar1
End Sub

Private Sub Command1_Click()
    Call myPrint
End Sub

Private Sub Command2_Click()
    Print "Var1=", Var1
    Print "Var2=", Var2
    Print "mVar1=", mVar1
    Print "mVar2=", mVar2
    Print "Constant txtInput=", txtInput
    Print "pVar1=", pVar1
End Sub

Private Sub Form_Load()
    Var1 = 1
    Var2 = 2
    mVar1 = 3
    mVar2 = "this is a string variable"
End Sub
```

LISTING A.3. CHAP6EX2.TXT—MODULE-LEVEL CODE FOR THE EXERCISE.

```
Public Var1 As Integer
Public Var2 As Integer
Public Const txtInput = "Please enter your name"
```

Day 7, "Building Complex Forms"

Quiz

1. The following six design concepts result in well-designed forms:

   • Make the forms as consistent as possible within an application.

   • Apply the same standards throughout the application.

- Place the command buttons on all forms in the same position and order whenever possible.
- Use color to highlight important information.
- Don't clutter the forms with too much information.
- Keep the data entry forms simple.

2. No, the only objects that can be placed directly on the MDI parent form are the picture box, menus, and any custom control that supports the `Align` property, such as the Statusbar control.

3. Although both interface styles use a single form as the main application form, the Explorer interface uses many different controls to create the unique display.

Exercise

To create this application, you need two forms in the new project, the MDI parent and one child form with its visible property set to `False`. The child form should contain only the following code:

```
Private Sub Form_Resize()
    txtInput.Height = ScaleHeight
    txtInput.Width = ScaleWidth
End Sub
```

The MDI parent form will contain a menu, toolbar, and a status bar and should have the code from Listing A.4 included.

LISTING A.4. CHAP7EXE.TXT—THE MDI PARENT CODE FOR THE FINAL EXERCISE.

```
Dim intFormCtr As Integer
Private Sub Toolbar1_ButtonClick(ByVal Button As ComctlLib.Button)
    On Error Resume Next
    Select Case Button.Key
        Case "New"
            Call mnuFileNew_Click
    End Select
End Sub

Private Sub MDIForm_Load()
    intFormCtr = 1
    frmNote.Caption = "NotePad Version " & intFormCtr
End Sub

Private Sub mnuFileNew_Click()
    Dim NewNote As New frmNote
    intFormCtr = intFormCtr + 1
    NewNote.Show
    NewNote.Caption = "NotePad Version " & intFormCtr
End Sub
```

Day 9, "Database Processing"

Quiz

1. When you design a database, you want to meet as many of the following objectives as possible:

   - Remove repetitive data

   - Have the ability to find unique records quickly

   - Keep the database easy to maintain

   - Allow changes to the database structure easy to perform

2. You can use five main SQL commands to access the data contained within a database: SELECT, INSERT INTO, UPDATE, DELETE FROM, and TRANSFORM.

3. Although Microsoft Access is the better tool for creating a Jet database, the Visual Data Manager is integrated with the Visual Basic development environment, which makes it easier to make changes to the database during the design process.

Exercise

When creating a database design, the first step is to list the tables and columns that will be created. Table A.1 lists the suggested tables and columns for an address book application.

TABLE A.1. SUGGESTED TABLES AND COLUMNS FOR THE EXAMPLE APPLICATION.

Table	Columns
Address Entry	Entry Key
	Date Updated
	First Name
	Middle Initial
	Last Name
	Address
	City
	State
	Zip Code
	Home Phone
Phones	Phone Key
	Entry Fkey
	Phone Type
	Phone Number

Day 10, "Accessing the Database"

Quiz

1. A Data control provides automatic access to many of the standard data-access features and functions. This way, you can create a data-access application without creating any code.

2. The `MoveComplete` event is called whenever the database recordset that's attached to a Data control is moved to another row.

3. To delete a record, you can use the `Delete` method of the Data control or the `Delete` method of a recordset.

4. A bound control updates the underlying database attached to a Data control.

Exercise

To add a search form to the application, add a new toolbar button to show the new form, and then create the form as shown in Figure A.2. Then add the code in Listing A.5; change the `Name` properties of the different controls to match the ones in the code.

FIGURE A.2.

Adding a search form to the application.

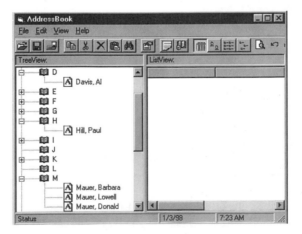

LISTING A.5. CH10EXAMPLE.TXT—THE CODE TO SEARCH THE DATABASE AND DISPLAY A LIST OF FOUND NAMES.

```
Private Sub cmdNew_Click()
lstNames.Visible = False
txtSearch.Text = ""
End Sub

Private Sub cmdQuit_Click()
```

continues

LISTING A.5. CONTINUED

```
Unload Me
End Sub

Private Sub cmdSearch_Click()
If optLastName Then
    ADODC1.RecordSource = "Select addressid, LastName, firstname, _
    firstname & "" _
        "" & Lastname as fullname from [address entry] where lastname _
    like '" _
        & txtSearch.Text & "*'"
ElseIf optFirstname Then
    ADODC1.RecordSource = "Select addressid, LastName, firstname, _
    firstname & "" _
        "" & Lastname as fullname from [address entry] where firstname _
    like '" _
        & txtSearch.Text & "*'"
End If
ADODC1.Requery
lstNames.Refresh
lstNames.Visible = True
End Sub

Private Sub Form_Load()
txtSearch.Text = ""
End Sub

Private Sub lstNames_DblClick()
ADODC1.RecordSet.Find "fullname = '" & lstNames.BoundText & "'", _
    adSearchForward
frmAddressEntry.sqlEntry = "select * from [Address Entry] Where _
[AddressID] = "  & Data1.Recordset.Fields("addressid")
frmAddressEntry.Show

End Sub
```

After adding all the controls, resize the DBListbox to fill the area as shown in Figure A.3. Also, set the DBListbox's Visible property to False.

Day 11, "Enhancing the Application"

Quiz

1. A project group includes several different projects, such as a Standard EXE project and one or more ActiveX control projects.

FIGURE A.3.

The DBListbox fills the entire area of the form.

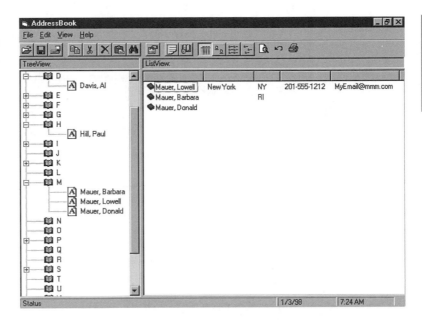

A

2. The SelectionChanged event is triggered whenever the Change property of the Property Page has been set to True, allowing you to update the properties of the custom control when the property page is closed.

3. Property Pages group all the custom controls associated properties that you might want to modify when adding the control to a form.

Exercise

This is an exercise that only you will know if you found the correct answer.

Day 12, "Enhancing Database Access"

Quiz

1. The Data Environment Designer can support as many different commands that you need for your application.

2. The Data Environment Designer allows you to group all of the application's database access commands in one area for easier support and maintenance.

3. While you can add functions directly to a Data Report using supplied controls in the toolbox and add aggregate fields in the Data Environment Designer for a command, calculated fields must be added directly in the SQL statement.

4. Yes, you can use any data-bound control with the Data Repeater control; however, the Data Repeater is most useful when you use a custom data-bound control to display data in a given format.

5. The Data ActiveX Data Control can also be used with the Data Repeater control.

Exercise

The design of the actual report is based on individual preferences. However, to create the report, you need to perform the following tasks:

- Add a Data Environment Designer.
- Define a SQL command with the required fields.
- Add a Data Report Designer.
- Choose the fields for the report and position them on the report.
- Add a button to the toolbar that will show the Data Report form.

Day 13, "Working with Crystal Reports"

Quiz

1. Crystal Reports can access any type of database that you might use. It can access most PC local databases directly, although it needs an ODBC connection for network or remote databases.

2. No, Crystal Reports enables you to build reports without any need to learn SQL.

Exercise

The only code that you must change in the frmMain form is to add a Crystal Reports control to the form and name it rptAddress. Then add a button to the toolbar that will display the frmPrintMgr form. Also, you need to add the frmPrintMgr form to the project and remove the Crystal Reports control from that form. Finally, you need to change the references in the frmPrintMgr form from rptAddress for the Crystal Reports control to frmMain!rptAddress. This will access the Crystal Reports control on the main form.

Day 14, "Internet Programming"

Quiz

1. The Browser and File Transfer controls are the two main objects that you can use to add Internet access to your application.

A

2. The File Transfer control allows you to add the code that would download or upload files from the Internet.

3. Visual Basic is the programming language used to create Windows applications, whereas VBScript is a subset of the Visual Basic language used to enhance HTML Web pages.

Exercise

This Web page is created by using HTML and VBScript, as shown in Listing A.6.

LISTING A.6. EXERCISE.HTM—SAMPLE CODE FOR DAY 14'S EXERCISE.

```
<HTML>
<HEAD>
<TITLE>VBScript/HTML Exercise Page</TITLE>
<SCRIPT LANGUAGE="VBScript">
<!--
Option Explicit

Sub SayHello_OnClick()
    MsgBox "Hello " & Form1.fname.Value & " " & Form1.lname.Value & _
      ", are you ready to compute?", 36
End Sub
Sub Reset_OnClick()
    Form1.fname.Value = ""
    Form1.lname.Value = ""
    msgbox "Text has been Cleared.",36
End Sub
-->
</SCRIPT>
</HEAD>

<BODY>
<BR>
<H1> This is the exercise for Chapter 13</H1>
<H2> Please enter your first and last name</H2>
<H3> A message box will be displayed.</H3>
<P>
<HR>
<FORM NAME="Form1">
    <INPUT NAME="FName" TYPE="TEXT" VALUE="">
    <INPUT NAME="LName" TYPE="TEXT" VALUE="">
    <INPUT NAME="SayHello" TYPE="BUTTON" VALUE="Say Hello!">
    <INPUT NAME="Reset" TYPE="BUTTON" VALUE="Reset">
</FORM>

</BODY>
</HTML>
```

Day 15, "Adding Advanced Features"

Quiz

1. The SetData method is used to place data into the DataObject when the OLEStartDrag event is triggered, or it can be used in the OLESetData event.

2. Feedback is given to the user when the OLE drag-and-drop operation has been completed in the OLECompleteDrag event, which is triggered when the process is finished.

Exercise

The best way to process a delete is to use the delete routine already present in the frmAddressEntry form. The code in Listing A.7 shows how to do this without users seeing the entry form itself.

LISTING A.7. DELETEENTRY.TXT—DELETING AN ENTRY WITH THE cmdDelete CLICK EVENT
ROUTINE IN THE AddressEntry FORM.

```
Private Sub picDelete_OLEDragDrop(Data As DataObject, Effect As Long, _
    Button As Integer, Shift As Integer, X As Single, Y As Single)
    frmAddressEntry.sqlEntry = "select * from [Address Entry] Where _
            [AddressID] = " & Mid(tvTreeView.SelectedItem.Key, 1, 3)
    frmAddressEntry.Load
    frmAddressEntry.Visible = False
    frmAddressEntry.cmdDelete.Value = True
End Sub
```

Day 16, "Coping with Error Handling"

Quiz

1. An *error trap* is a term that describes the detection of an error during the execution of an application.

2. The first type is one that can be found and corrected during the testing process; the other type must be handled during the normal execution of the application.

3. There are three ways to have your application code continue after an error has occurred. You can use any of the Resume statement versions: Resume [Line ¦ Label], Resume Next, or Resume.

Exercise

Because of the nature of error handling, there is no easy way to show an answer to the exercise. It is entirely up to you as to how the error routines will look and work.

Day 17, "Building Online Help"

Quiz

1. You connect context-sensitive help to its related topics by mapping numeric values to the topic IDs defined for the topic pages.

2. The What's This button is added by setting the following properties of a form:

Property	Setting
WhatsThisHelp	True
WhatsThisButton	True
ControlBox	True
MinButton and MaxButton	False
BorderStyle	Fixed Single or Sizable

3. The help project file can contain definitions for secondary windows, mapped topic IDs, toolbar buttons, bitmap references, and topic file references.

Exercise

I can't put any answers here that would match what you would do. The design, creation, and inclusion of a help system into a Visual Basic application is a very unique and personal thing. As long as the help system can be accessed and the information in it makes sense in regards to the application, you did it correctly.

Day 18, "Testing and Debugging the Application"

Quiz

1. A Break expression is a special form of a Watch expression. While a Watch expression will track the values of specified variables, properties or expressions, the Break expression will actually halt the execution of the application when the value of the specified variable, property or expression has changed or become True.

2. A Watch expression is set by using the Tools, Add Watch menu option, pressing Shift+F9, or by right-clicking the variable and choosing Add Watch from the pop-up menu.

3. Whenever you are stopped at a breakpoint or Break expression in a procedure, the Locals window will display the values of all variables and properties that are currently available within that procedure.

Exercise

Because of the way breakpoints work, the only thing I can show you is what it would look like on my computer, not necessarily what you would see on your computer. For that reason, there is no answers for this chapter.

Day 19, "Performance and Tuning"

Quiz

1. A resource file contains all the string constants and picture objects that your application will use. It also allows you to quickly change the language of all messages and labels in the application.

2. You can increase the performance of your application in many different ways, including the following:

   - By keeping forms hidden instead of unloading them
   - By using more efficient Visual Basic variables and processing
   - When appropriate, by compiling the application into a native code executable

Exercise

This is another exercise that only you will know if you found the correct answer.

Day 20, "Finishing the Application"

Quiz

1. If you can't support your application after you sell it, your users won't recommend it to other people they talk to.

2. When selling your application, you need to advertise and set up a process by which customers can purchase your software. By selling as shareware, however, all you need to do is put in on a shareware server and wait for the money to start coming in.

A

3. A copyright protects you from someone stealing your code and idea of the application you've created. A trademark protects only the name or symbol that you've chosen for that application.

Exercise

Because there is no way for me to show you how the finished installation disks that you've created will look, there's no answer here for the exercise.

Day 21, "Creating an ActiveX Document"

Quiz

1. An ActiveX document doesn't support the Load and Unload events for a form, or the Width and Height properties of any controls on the document.

2. An ActiveX document can display a standard Visual Basic form, or it can display another ActiveX document using hyperlink navigation.

APPENDIX B

Adding Some Character to Your Application

Well, you've made it to the end of this book. In the past three weeks, you've looked at many standard Visual Basic controls, tools, and concepts from a slightly different point of view than you might have expected. You've learned how to combine all the things you know about Visual Basic programming to create more professional-looking applications. You've also seen how to convert standard forms into custom controls to enhance the interface for users. When using other applications on your computer, however, you probably noticed other "nice" stuff that you would use in your application if you knew how.

As the need for new, catchy components evolved, Microsoft has managed to add another great component to the collection that you can use when developing standard and Web-style applications. This new component, Microsoft Agent, is a set of programmable software objects that presents animated characters within the Windows application environment. Developers can use these characters as an interactive assistant to introduce, guide, entertain, and enhance the application as well as the standard windows, menus, and controls.

This system doesn't replace the conventional Windows interface; instead, these characters can be easily blended with the rest of the application interface. The Agent's programming interface makes it easy to animate a character to respond to user input. Animated characters appear in their own window, providing maximum flexibility. This is all accomplished with an included ActiveX control that makes its services accessible to Visual Basic.

Getting the Agent

The Microsoft Agent is available from Microsoft's Web site at `http://www.microsoft.com/intdev/agent/agent-f.htm` (see Figure B.1). This Web site contains all the different components you can use to work with the Agent, including all the documentation on how to use the different components.

FIGURE B.1.

The Microsoft Agent Web site home page.

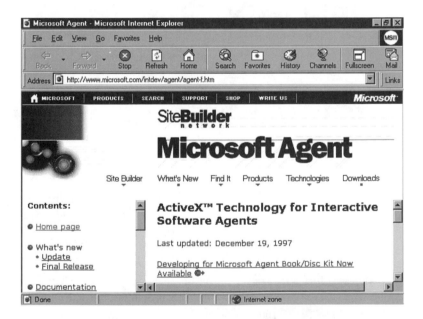

You then have to download the components that you want to use. The minimum number of components are the Agent Server, the ActiveX control, and at least one character file set. Figure B.2 shows the three different characters that you can choose from.

FIGURE B.2.

The three available Agent characters that you can download.

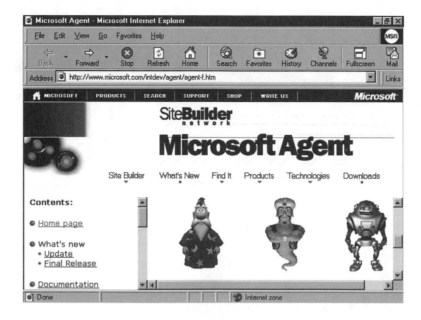

The Microsoft Agent is now royalty-free; before you distribute it with your application, however, you should check the Web site for any changes to this policy.

Accessing the Agent

You can use the Microsoft Agent by writing directly to the Agent's services by using its Automation server interface. An easier method is to use the available ActiveX control.

The Agent consists of many advanced tools that allow you to record your own voice for the characters, create or edit the character animations, and use the characters in an application. To show how to use all these tools would require almost an entire book. To get an idea of what the Agent can do and how to use it, start a new project and place an instance of the control on the form.

 Note

You have to add AGENTCTL.DLL to the Components dialog box to access the control on the toolbox.

B

You now have access to all the Agent's objects, events, and methods. You'll probably never use many events and methods for a standard application, so today's lesson covers only the ones you'll use most often. The two objects that you'll work with are `Characters` and `Request`.

Using the `Characters` Object

The Agent control can support one or more characters using the `Characters` object. To access a character, use the `Load` method to load the character's data (.ACS file) into the `Characters` collection and specify that the item in the collection uses the methods and properties supported for that character. The `Characters` object supports the following methods:

- `Load` loads a character into the `Characters` collection.
- `Unload` unloads the character data for the specified character ID.
- `Character` isn't required for Visual Basic programs because Visual Basic supports collections.

The `Characters` collection also has methods that enable the character to appear, move to a particular location onscreen, gesture at something on the form, talk to users, and disappear:

- `GestureAt` plays the gesturing animation for the character at the specified location.
- `Hide` hides the specified character.
- `MoveTo` moves the specified character to the specified location.
- `Play` plays the specified animation for the specified character.
- `Show` makes the specified character visible and plays its Showing animation.
- `Speak`, by using the character voice, "speaks" the specified text.
- `Stop` stops the animation for the specified character.
- `Wait` has the specified character wait for the specified request to complete before continuing.

When you load a character, you assign it an ID that you'll use to reference the character from within the application. In your new application, place the following code into the `Form_Load` event to load the character data into the application:

```
Agent1.Characters.Load "Genie", _
    "c:\program files\microsoft agent\characters\genie.acs"
```

Note   The examples in today's lesson use the GENIE.ACS character file, but you can use either of the other two characters instead.

To make it easier to access the character in the code, add the following definition to the form:

```
Dim MyAgent As IAgentCtlCharacter
```

This definition allows you to refer to the character by the object name instead of the fully qualified `Agent1.Characters` name. To use this object, add the following line of code immediately after the `Load` statement:

```
Set MyAgent = Agent1.Characters("Genie")
```

With just these three code segments, you now have complete access to the character from within the application. To see how this works, add a command button to the form so that you can display the character. Add the following code line to the command button click event:

```
MyAgent.Show
```

Now, run the application and click the command button to display the character, as shown in Figure B.3.

FIGURE B.3.

Displaying the character from within the application.

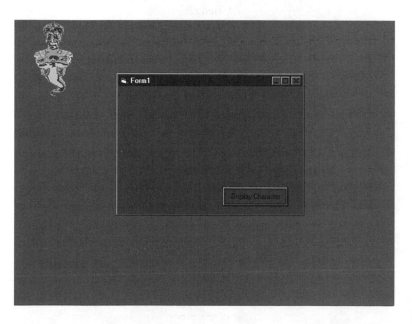

Notice that the character appears at the top, left of the screen. This is the default position. By using the `MoveTo` method, you can position the character anywhere you want, before or after it's displayed. Add the following code immediately before the `Show` statement:

```
MyAgent.MoveTo 320, 240
```

Note

> The x and y coordinates are based on the current screen display size. The values in the preceding statement assume that the screen is set at 640×480.

Now, run the application and click the command button. The character should now appear in the middle of the screen. To have a little fun with this, move the MoveTo command after the Show statement to see the "move" animation for the character.

Using the Request Object

Before looking at other animations you can have the character perform, you need to know how to tell when the character finishes processing a request. Because the server asynchronously processes some methods (such as Load, Play, and Speak), your application code can continue to execute while the method is completing. When an application calls one of these methods, the control creates and returns a Request object for the request. You can use this object to check the status of the method by defining an object and then setting it to the request made. The following code shows how this is done:

```
Dim MyRequest As Object
Set MyRequest = Agent1.Characters.Load("Genie", _
  "c:\program files\microsoft agent\characters\Genie.acs")
```

The Request object has a Status property that can be used to check for the current status of a request. Table B.1 lists the five status codes that can occur for a character.

TABLE B.1. USING THE Request OBJECT'S Status PROPERTY.

Status	Definition
0	Successfully completed
1	Failed
2	Pending
3	Interrupted
4	In progress

This property would be used with some type of loop process to keep the application from continuing until the request was completed.

Animating the Character

In addition to the MoveTo and GestureAt methods, each character has a long list of animations that you can "play" when needed. Each animation interacts with users when something happens in the application, or you can use the Speak method to inform users of something. Table B.2 is a short list of what types of animations you have available to use.

TABLE B.2. AVAILABLE GENIE CHARACTER ANIMATIONS.

Animation Name	Description
Announce	Raises hand
Confused	Scratches head
Congratulate	Thumbs-up gesture
Decline	Raises hands and shakes head
Processing	Spins (looping animation)
Reading	Reads (looping animation)
Suggest	Displays a light bulb
Think	Looks up with hand on chin
Uncertain	Raises eyebrow with hand on chin
Writing	Writes (looping animation)

For each animation is a corresponding animation with the word Return attached to the original name (for example, AnnounceReturn). Remember that with the looping animations, you must use the Stop method before playing any other animation.

Note

Each character has a Word document that lists all the available animations. You can find this document on the Microsoft Agent's Web site.

The animation name is passed to the Play method to tell the character which animation to play. To see how this works, add the following code line to the command button's click event:

```
MyAgent.Play "Congratulate"
```

Caution

If you're playing a looping animation, you must use the Stop method to clear it before other animations can be played.

B

When you run the application and click the command button, you'll see the character perform this request. Finally, you can have the character "speak" to users by passing the required text to the Speak method, as follows:

```
MyAgent.Speak "when in the course of human events"
```

If your computer has sound capabilities, you'll hear as well as see the text as it's spoken (see Figure B.4).

FIGURE B.4.

Displaying the text as it's spoken.

Try putting a Speak statement into the code and running the application again. Then, when the character is displayed, just let the application run for a few minutes; the character will eventually run a built-in animation that shows it waiting for you to do something.

Using the Character in an Application

Wrap this all up by having the character do something useful in the application. To use the character properly, you'll want to position it at the appropriate control. For example, if you want the character to tell users how to display an entry, you would move the character to the TreeView list and have it tell users what to do. While the character is talking, you should have the application wait until it's done before continuing its execution. One way of making it easy to use the character is by creating a routine that actually calls the different methods. You would pass the routine the animation name, any text you want spoken, and the location to move the character to. Listing B.1 shows an example of this routine.

LISTING B.1. AGENTSUB.TXT—USING A ROUTINE TO CENTRALIZE THE AGENT CALLS.

```
 1: Public Sub Call_Character(PlayAni As String, PlayText As String, x As _
 2:Integer,y As Integer)
 3: Dim MyRequest As Object
 4: If x <> 0 And y <> 0 Then
 5:     MyAgent.MoveTo x, y
 6: End If
 7: If PlayAni <> "" Then
 8:     MyAgent.Play PlayAni
 9: End If
10: If PlayText <> "" Then
11:     Set MyRequest = MyAgent.Speak(PlayText)
12: End If
13: Do Until MyRequest.status = 0
14:     DoEvents
15: Loop
16: End Sub
```

You can see in Listing B.1 that it's using the Request object to prevent the application from continuing until the text is completely finished. To move the character to a particular area on the form, use the Left and Top properties to calculate the correct position.

When you're finished with the character, use the Hide method to have the character "vanish" from the screen. In the project, add a text box to the form. When users double-click the text box, the character appears near the text box, points to the text box, describes what users should enter into it, and then disappears. To perform this sequence of events, use the code in Listing B.2. Then for each text box, combo box, or any other control, you can use the same method to give users information.

LISTING B.2. AGTDEMO.TXT—USING THE AGENT CHARACTER TO TELL USERS WHAT TO TYPE INTO THE TEXT BOX.

```
 1: Private Sub Text1_DblClick()
 2:     Dim MyRequest As Object
 3:     MyAgent.MoveTo Text1.Left / 15 + frmAgent.Left / 15 + Text1.Width _
 4:     / 15, frmAgent.Top / 15 + Text1.Top / 15 + Text1.Height / 15
```

continues

B

LISTING B.2. CONTINUED

```
 5:     MyAgent.Show
 6:     MyAgent.GestureAt 20, 20
 7:     Set MyRequest = _
 8:        MyAgent.Speak("Please enter your first and last name in this _
           box.")
 9:     Do Until MyRequest.status = 0
10:        DoEvents
11:     Loop
12:     MyAgent.Hide
13:
14: End Sub
```

Run the application and double-click the text box to see what happens. The end result should resemble Figure B.5.

FIGURE B.5.

When you double-click the text box, the character will appear and talk to users.

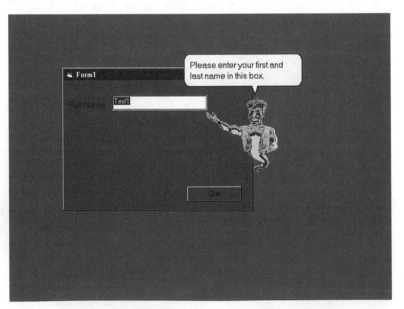

> **Tip**
>
> You can use Agent characters in place of message boxes to inform users of a problem.

Appendix C

Stuff Included with Visual Basic 6

When you purchase the Professional or Enterprise Edition of Visual Basic, you receive several other applications and tools on the Visual Basic CD-ROM. In this appendix, you will learn what a few of these tools are, what they can do for you, and a little on how they work. A new application is included with the Visual Basic product. The Visual Component Manager, included with all releases of Visual Basic 6, gives you more control over the design process of a Visual Basic application.

The Visual SourceSafe application is included only in the Enterprise Edition. You can use the Visual Basic Code Profiler tool to find unused routines in your applications and also see some important statistics about your application. Another tool that comes with Visual Basic is the Image Editor, which gives you a sophisticated way to create and edit icons, bitmaps, and cursors.

Take the time to browse the \TOOLS directory of the Visual Basic CD-ROM. You'll find many helpful tools, applications, and even some neat controls and programs that you can use but aren't supported by Microsoft. A list of what's included in the \TOOLS directory is included at the end of this appendix.

Visual Component Manager

The Visual Component Manager gives you the ability to manage all available components that exist on your computer or network that can be used in a Visual Basic application. To access the Visual Component Manager, you first need to add it to the Visual Basic development environment by using the AddIns manager. After it has been added, a new button is added to the Visual Basic toolbar, as shown in Figure C.1.

FIGURE C.1.

Accessing the Visual Component Manager from within the Visual Basic development environment.

When you start the manager, it displays the available objects and components available in an Explorer-style interface, as shown in Figure C.2.

FIGURE C.2.

The Visual Component Manager displays the available components that you can add to the Visual Basic project.

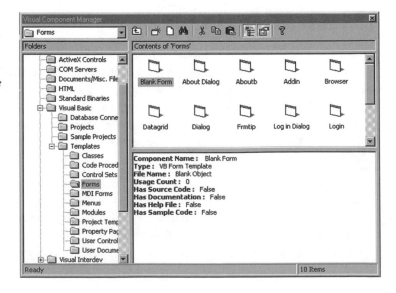

Simply by selecting a component and double-clicking on it, you can add it to the current project. This new application gives you the ability to find any component that you have on your computer without having to search the different directory paths and drives that exist, thus making the development of a Visual Basic application that much easier. Although this addition provides an important function, it is fairly simple to work with.

Visual SourceSafe

When you start developing applications, you soon find out that controlling the changes made to that application over any period of time is one of the hardest things to do. The need to control the source code as it changes has given rise to many different types of methods over the years. Before the advent of personal computers, most of these applications were bulky and hard to use. Now with Windows 95 and Visual Basic comes an easy-to-use product called Visual SourceSafe.

Microsoft Visual SourceSafe can be used by individuals working at home or by large corporate development teams across networks to track the components of an application and what changes are being made to them. This latest version of Visual SourceSafe is included with Visual Basic (Enterprise Edition only), or it can be purchased separately. What you'll see in this brief look at Visual SourceSafe is why source control is important and how SourceSafe addresses these needs.

Why Should You Use It?

The concept of source control is very important if you consider yourself a serious programmer. Every time you modify anything in your application project, you are, in effect, dealing with source control. When you save the changes, are you keeping the previous version intact, just in case the changes don't work? Or are you relying on your memory to remove these changes? How many versions of changes do you keep or remember? Other issues that become important in team projects are who's modifying the code and how many other programmers are modifying the same section of code.

From these few questions, you can get a feeling for the overall scope of the source-control issue. By using a source code control tool such as Visual SourceSafe, the issues about which copy of the code is the current copy and what changes are being made are no longer something you need to worry about. Source control enables you to create components that can be included in as many different applications as you need. This sharing of source code eliminates the worry of which version you're now using for a particular application. If you don't know which version is the most current, it's possible that the application you create might not work correctly. In short, you now have complete control over the project and any related files, text, documents, or binary data that may be included in your application package.

C

The Visual SourceSafe product supports team development by allowing team members to share files, modify then independently, and later merge all the changes back into the current copy of the file. Team members can use the tool to review a file's history to see the changes that have been made and, of course, back up to an earlier version of the file, if needed. Visual SourceSafe is designed to support any size project with any number of programmers. It also can be executed as a standalone product, however; the most common commands that you would use are available from the Visual Basic Add-Ins menu, enabling you to access these functions without leaving your project environment. The remaining functions are always available from the Visual SourceSafe Explorer interface.

Whenever you're working with an existing project, you need to perform a certain set of functions to have your project protected by using source-control concepts:

- Checking files in and out to control the retrieval process
- Logging all file activity
- Merging any changes made back into the master or current copy
- Controlling versions

Rather than have you rely on your memory or disk copies of the project to keep track of your changes, Visual SourceSafe performs these functions.

As its name suggests, the most important feature of Visual SourceSafe is that it keeps your source files safe. Using SourceSafe with your project files is like renting video tapes: You need to give the files back when you're done using them. Some advantages that you gain by using SourceSafe include the following:

- Sharing common code between projects without needing separate copies
- Adding comments to describe the changes made when checking a file back in
- Preventing accidental deletion of files

Also, a history function keeps the "journal" for your project. By knowing the history of any given file, you can determine what changes were made and when. This allows you to choose the correct version to use.

A Quick Look Around

When Visual SourceSafe is installed, you'll actually have two separate applications installed:

- Visual SourceSafe Administrator creates the SourceSafe database, which all users of the tool have access to.

- Visual SourceSafe Explorer gives you access to the Visual SourceSafe functions and registers Visual SourceSafe on your computer so that the Visual Basic environment can find it.

When Visual SourceSafe is installed, it creates an empty database that's used by the Administrator and Explorer to control the SourceSafe environment. This database is used to store all the master copies of the files, the history records, and the project structures. A project is always contained within one database, but the database can contain many projects.

The administration of the SourceSafe environment requires you to define at least one user ID. This user ID is how you access any SourceSafe functions. You use Visual SourceSafe Administrator to set up the user ID and its associated properties (see Figure C.3).

FIGURE C.3.

Maintaining Visual SourceSafe's user list for access to any project files.

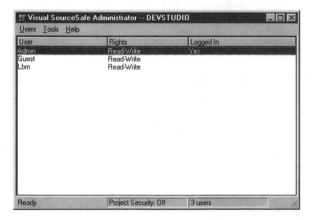

The user list shows every user ID that has access to the Visual SourceSafe environment. By default, two user IDs are already defined to the database:

- **Admin**—There's only one Admin user ID. This user ID can't be deleted or be renamed. Admin has full access rights to any projects controlled by SourceSafe and the capability to undo changes made by other users.

- **Guest**—This user provides access to the Visual SourceSafe database for occasional or first-time users. When you've created other user IDs, you can delete the Guest ID or change its access rights.

If you are the only user of SourceSafe (that is, you work at home), you can use the guest ID if you want or create a new one. The different options available for users can be modified by selecting a user and then choosing Tools, Options from the menu to display the SourceSafe Options dialog box (see Figure C.4).

FIGURE C.4.

Project and security options for a user are maintained on the SourceSafe Options dialog box.

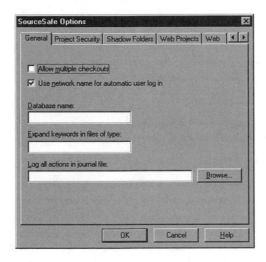

The pages in the SourceSafe Options dialog box cover several different areas of the Visual SourceSafe environment that you can modify to uniquely define the user and its capabilities when accessing Visual SourceSafe:

- General has settings that affect all users defined in the user list.
- Project Security controls whether security is on or off for a project. If security is on, you can set default access rights for users.
- Shadow Folders is used to set the shadow folder for a particular project. A shadow folder is a central folder that contains current versions of all files in a project.
- Web Projects sets the information that's applicable to a single Web project.
- Web sets options for all Web projects at once rather than for an individual Web project.
- File Types sets the types of files that users can store in Visual SourceSafe.

On a regular basis, you should back up the entire Visual SourceSafe database.

Because of the way the database is maintained, never try to perform an incremental backup of it. This will cause problems with the data, and you could possibly lose all your project information.

To cover all the topics involved with using Visual SourceSafe would take more than one lesson, let alone a section of an appendix. The documentation that comes with the product is very detailed and includes many examples to help you get started.

The Visual Basic Interface

When you use Visual Basic with Visual SourceSafe, you get all the product's features, many of which are integrated into the Visual Basic development environment. Whether you're working with an existing Visual Basic project or starting a new one, Visual SourceSafe is around to ensure that your project is protected, if you want it to be.

Let's see how to use the Visual SourceSafe functions when performing the following tasks:

- Creating a new Visual Basic application
- Working with an application that's not already controlled by Visual SourceSafe

When Visual SourceSafe is installed and registered properly, a new selection appears on the Visual Basic Tools menu (see Figure C.5). Then, when you choose SourceSafe, a secondary menu appears (see Figure C.6). The most important of these choices is Options. When you select Options, the Source Code Control Options dialog box appears (see Figure C.7). Through the dialog box, you can customize how Visual Basic automatically interacts with Visual SourceSafe.

FIGURE C.5.

New SourceSafe menu option in Visual Basic.

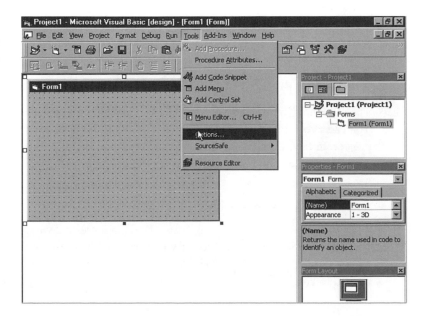

FIGURE C.6.

Visual SourceSafe functionality in Visual Basic.

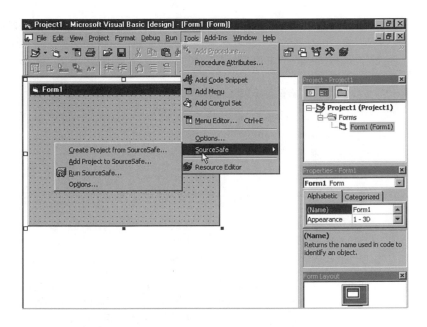

FIGURE C.7.

Setting the options to control how SourceSafe performs.

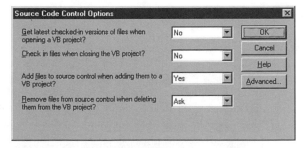

The remaining choices on the SourceSafe submenu are your gateway into SourceSafe. You can check files in and out, display a form's history, and even add new files to the project. In fact, if you right-click a form or module in the Project Explorer, the pop-up menu that appears includes the four main SourceSafe options at the bottom (see Figure C.8).

Creating a New Project

After you create a new project in Visual Basic and are ready to save it for the first time, Visual SourceSafe will ask whether you want to include this project in the SourceSafe database. If you click Yes, Visual SourceSafe prompts you for the required information needed to create the SourceSafe project from your new Visual Basic project.

FIGURE C.8.

SourceSafe options accessible from the pop-up menu.

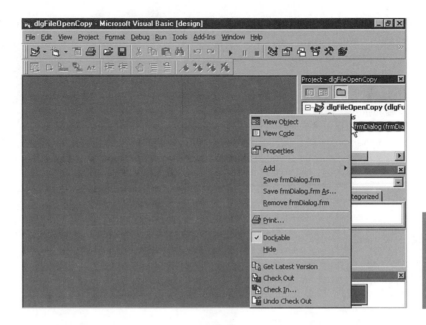

Using an Existing Project

When you open a project that's already on your PC, you'll be asked whether you want to add the project to Visual SourceSafe. If you respond Yes, you must log on to Visual SourceSafe. You're then prompted to select the SourceSafe folder to which to add this project (see Figure C.9). When you select a folder, all the files in your project are displayed (see Figure C.10), allowing you to select the files you want to protect.

FIGURE C.9.

Adding the project folder is the first step in protecting your work.

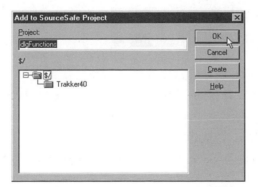

When the include process is finished, you'll see something new in the title bar of any file that you open. The label (Read Only) that now appears next to the name of the file means that you must check out the form or module file before you can make any changes to it. To do so, right-click the file in the Project Explorer and choose Check Out from the menu. After you choose Check Out, the file is ready to use.

FIGURE C.10.

Choosing the files to include in the SourceSafe process.

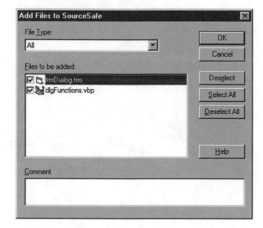

Opening a Protected Project

If you open a project that's protected by Visual SourceSafe, you'll be prompted to log in before you can continue. After the project is open, you need to check out the files to work with, as described in the preceding section. At all times the Project Explorer shows which files (forms, modules, classes, and so on) are checked in or out by the displayed icons, as shown in Figure C.11.

FIGURE C.11.

Visual Basic file icons in the Project Explorer reflect the status of the file within SourceSafe.

Visual Basic Code Profiler

The Code Profiler is a powerful code-analyzing tool that helps you optimize your Visual Basic applications. It identifies which parts of your Visual Basic project are used most often and which ones aren't used at all. It also captures performance information about your application, such as how long it takes to run routines or parts of routines.

The first step in using the Visual Basic Code Profiler is to install it, a process that's quite simple. To install the Code Profiler, you need to copy VBCP.DLL to your Visual Basic directory on your computer and then register it with the REGSVR32.EXE program (which can be found in \TOOLS\REGUTILS on the Visual Basic CD-ROM). To use REGSVR32.EXE, copy it into your Visual Basic directory and then drag and drop the VBCP.DLL file onto the Regsvr32 icon to register the DLL on your computer.

The last step to install this tool is to add the following line to the VBADDIN.INI file, which is found in your Windows directory:

```
[Add-Ins32]
VBCP.VBCPClass=0
```

The next time you start Visual Basic, you need to add the Code Profiler to your Add-Ins menu by using the Add-In Manager. When all this is completed, you can use the Code Profiler with your projects.

What Does It Do for Me?

You can use the Code Profiler to analyze the performance of your application. To get the information about your application, the Code Profiler places extra code into your project. You then run your application, testing as much of it as needed. Then, after you finish running your application, the Code Profiler creates a report on the activity it analyzed. From the analysis report, you can tell which functions are executed most often and where the computer spends most of its time during processing. You can also time your code to see how efficiently it runs. Based on what the report shows you, you can make changes to your code, allowing you to tune your application or remove unused code that takes up space.

You also can take the data and save it as a tab-delimited file that you can then open in a spreadsheet program such as Microsoft Excel. This allows you to graph the data or view in different ways.

Because this all sounds fairly complicated, you may be wondering what exactly happens to the application code and whether you can undo it. When you open a project in Visual Basic, it's automatically opened in the Code Profiler (if the add-in is running). When you

C

select a profile type and click the Add Profiler Code button, the Code Profiler copies the forms and modules in your project. The original files are renamed to the same name, except with a tilde (~) in place of the last character of the filename extension. The copies are then used to create a working copy of your project. Finally, the analysis code is added to the code in your project.

When you finish analyzing your code, you can view the analysis results by choosing File | View Results from the menu. Then when you're ready, you can remove the added code by clicking the Remove Profiler Code button, which deletes the working copies and restores the original files to your project.

Note   Your original code isn't affected by the Code Profiler; only the working copies are affected. However, you should back up your project before running the Code Profiler, just in case.

Using It with Your Application

Using the Code Profiler is really quite simple. To show you what it does, I'll use the VISDATA.VBP project that comes in the Visual Basic \SAMPLES directory. Start Visual Basic and open the VISDATA project. From the Add-Ins menu, choose Code Profiler to display its dialog box (see Figure C.12).

FIGURE C.12.

The Code Profiler dia-log box is where all the action takes place when you're analyzing your project.

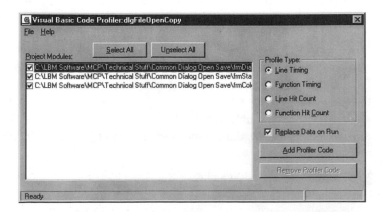

You can see that the modules and forms for your project are listed in the list box. You also start the Code Profiler first and then open your project; the Code Profiler then loads the project's forms and modules automatically.

Next, select the modules and forms you want to analyze. The default is to have all the files selected. You then choose the type of analysis that you want to perform from the Profile Type options:

- Line Timing records how long it takes for single lines of code to execute.
- Function Timing determines how long functions take to execute.
- Line Hit Count counts the number of times each line of code is executed.
- Function Hit Count counts how many times a function was executed.

Finally, click the Add Profiler Code button to add the profiler code to your project. At this point, if you view any of your code, you will see exactly what has been added by the Code Profiler (see Figure C.13). Notice that two lines of code were added for each line of code or function being analyzed.

FIGURE C.13.

The Visual Basic code editor showing the profiler code added to analyze your project's performance.

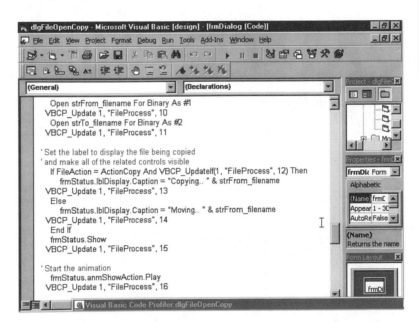

Now, run your application and exercise the functions that you want to test. After you stop your application, you can view the output of the profiler by viewing the results in the analysis grid (see Figure C.14). The columns that appear in the grid depend on which Profile Type you selected. Table C.1 lists all the possible columns the grid can display.

FIGURE C.14.

The Code Profiler uses the analysis grid to display the recorded results of the data.

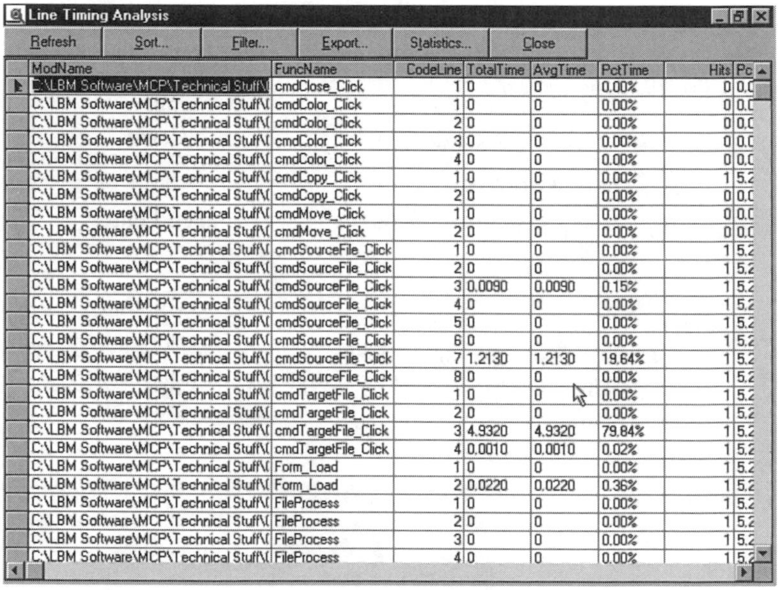

ModName	FuncName	CodeLine	TotalTime	AvgTime	PctTime	Hits	Pc
C:\LBM Software\MCP\Technical Stuff\	cmdClose_Click	1	0	0	0.00%	0	0.0
C:\LBM Software\MCP\Technical Stuff\	cmdColor_Click	1	0	0	0.00%	0	0.0
C:\LBM Software\MCP\Technical Stuff\	cmdColor_Click	2	0	0	0.00%	0	0.0
C:\LBM Software\MCP\Technical Stuff\	cmdColor_Click	3	0	0	0.00%	0	0.0
C:\LBM Software\MCP\Technical Stuff\	cmdColor_Click	4	0	0	0.00%	0	0.0
C:\LBM Software\MCP\Technical Stuff\	cmdCopy_Click	1	0	0	0.00%	1	5.2
C:\LBM Software\MCP\Technical Stuff\	cmdCopy_Click	2	0	0	0.00%	0	0.0
C:\LBM Software\MCP\Technical Stuff\	cmdMove_Click	1	0	0	0.00%	0	0.0
C:\LBM Software\MCP\Technical Stuff\	cmdMove_Click	2	0	0	0.00%	0	0.0
C:\LBM Software\MCP\Technical Stuff\	cmdSourceFile_Click	1	0	0	0.00%	1	5.2
C:\LBM Software\MCP\Technical Stuff\	cmdSourceFile_Click	2	0	0	0.00%	1	5.2
C:\LBM Software\MCP\Technical Stuff\	cmdSourceFile_Click	3	0.0090	0.0090	0.15%	1	5.2
C:\LBM Software\MCP\Technical Stuff\	cmdSourceFile_Click	4	0	0	0.00%	1	5.2
C:\LBM Software\MCP\Technical Stuff\	cmdSourceFile_Click	5	0	0	0.00%	1	5.2
C:\LBM Software\MCP\Technical Stuff\	cmdSourceFile_Click	6	0	0	0.00%	1	5.2
C:\LBM Software\MCP\Technical Stuff\	cmdSourceFile_Click	7	1.2130	1.2130	19.64%	1	5.2
C:\LBM Software\MCP\Technical Stuff\	cmdSourceFile_Click	8	0	0	0.00%	1	5.2
C:\LBM Software\MCP\Technical Stuff\	cmdTargetFile_Click	1	0	0	0.00%	1	5.2
C:\LBM Software\MCP\Technical Stuff\	cmdTargetFile_Click	2	0	0	0.00%	1	5.2
C:\LBM Software\MCP\Technical Stuff\	cmdTargetFile_Click	3	4.9320	4.9320	79.84%	1	5.2
C:\LBM Software\MCP\Technical Stuff\	cmdTargetFile_Click	4	0.0010	0.0010	0.02%	1	5.2
C:\LBM Software\MCP\Technical Stuff\	Form_Load	1	0	0	0.00%	1	5.2
C:\LBM Software\MCP\Technical Stuff\	Form_Load	2	0.0220	0.0220	0.36%	1	5.2
C:\LBM Software\MCP\Technical Stuff\	FileProcess	1	0	0	0.00%	1	5.2
C:\LBM Software\MCP\Technical Stuff\	FileProcess	2	0	0	0.00%	1	5.2
C:\LBM Software\MCP\Technical Stuff\	FileProcess	3	0	0	0.00%	1	5.2
C:\LBM Software\MCP\Technical Stuff\	FileProcess	4	0	0	0.00%	1	5.2

TABLE C.1. THE ANALYSIS GRID COLUMNS.

Column	*Description*	*Related Profile Type*
ModName	The name of the module or form	All
FuncName	The function name	All
CodeLine	The relative number of the analysis code line	Line Timing, Line Hit Count
TotalTime	Total time spent executing a line or function	Line Timing, Function Timing
AvgTime	The average time spent on a line or function	Line Timing, Function Timing
PctTime	The percentage of time spent on a line or function, compared with the entire application	Line Timing, Function Timing
Hits	The number of times a line or function was executed	All
PctHits	The percentage of hits a particular line or function had, compared with	Line Timing, Line Hit Count, Function Hit Count

Column	Description	Related Profile Type
	the entire application	
LineText	The line of executable code from the function	Line Timing, Line Hit Count

The types of analysis you decide to perform depend entirely on your needs. The Code Profiler performs two primary types of testing:

- *Code coverage* is a process of discovering whether a particular function or line of code has run. The two hit count profile types (Line Hit Count and Function Hit Count) are useful in determining whether a particular function or line of code executed. You might find that certain code in your application is never executed.

- *Code optimization* is a process that determines which functions or lines of code are run most often or take the most time to execute. The two timing profile types (Line Timing and Function Timing) are useful in determining how long it takes a particular function or line of code to execute, as well as how often it's run.

Tip

> To have effective testing, I recommend that you create a script to follow when profiling your application, rather than test it at random. Following a script ensures that your application gets a complete and uniform test.

The Hits column contains the total number of times a function or code line was executed. If this number is zero, you should investigate why; if the code is really never used, delete it from your application. When trying to optimize your application, you should find the values in the TotalTime, AvgTime, and PctTime columns very useful. Also, a very high Hits value for a particular function or code line can mean that you have a recursive routine or a possible design problem. The Code Profiler helps you to uncover these issues.

Caution

> If you determine that you need to make changes after profiling your code, be sure to make the changes in your original code files, not in your working copies (the file copies that have profiler code embedded in them). If you change the working copy of a form or module, those changes will be discarded and lost after you click the Remove Profiler Code button.

C

Image Editor

The Image Editor is a simple application that you can use to create or modify custom icons, bitmaps, and cursor to use within your applications. To install the Image Editor on your computer, you only need to copy the files from \TOOLS\IMAGEEDIT on the CD-ROM to a directory on your computer. You also should create a shortcut to the executable file in your Start menu. When you start the Image Editor, the main window is displayed with a color selection dialog box (see Figure C.15).

FIGURE C.15.

The Image Editor interface consists of a dialog box for color selection and a window for designing the images.

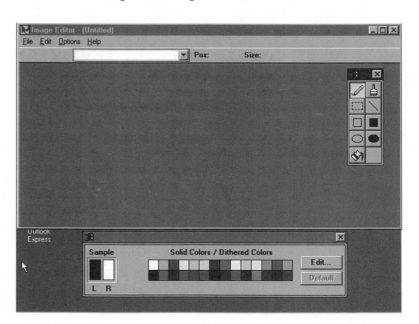

When creating a file, you must choose the type of image you want to create. Each file type serves a different purpose in your application. You can create cursor (.CUR) and icon (.ICO) files that include multiple images. Multiple images are used by Windows to match displays (that is, VGA, EGA, CGA, or black-and-white monitors) with the proper image in the file. When you choose File | New from the menu, the Resource Type dialog box appears, allowing you to choose the image type (see Figure C.16).

After choosing the file type and clicking OK, you're asked for the values for the type of image you're creating. You're now ready to start creating the image. If you follow these general design rules, you'll create more effective images:

- Begin by designing your images in black and white. If the they look good in black and white, they will look even better in color.

- Use 3D effects to emphasize functions, such as when a button is "pressed." Use black, white, light gray, and dark gray to create these shading effects.

- Check out your designs on different backgrounds. They won't always appear on white or gray backgrounds.

- Because black and white are the only opaque colors available for the creation of cursors, it's very important to check cursors on black screens and on white screens. To make sure that the cursor remains visible, outline it in the opposite color.

FIGURE C.16.

Choosing the Image type is the first task when using the Image Editor.

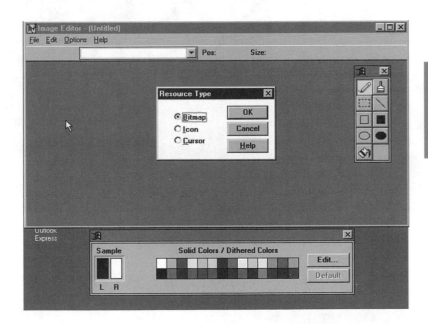

As you can see, the Image Editor is very useful as well as very easy to use.

You can take an existing image and modify it, if you want to. When you're working on an image, you will actually be working on the larger version of the image on the left of the screen, while the actual image is displayed in another window (see Figure C.17).

Included Folders List

The different tools, applications, and controls included with Visual Basic are useful depending on your environment. You've already seen how to use some of these tools from lessons in this book. The more interesting tools will help you determine which tools you can use and which aren't needed:

FIGURE C.17.

The Image Editor displays a working-size version of the image and the actual-sized image.

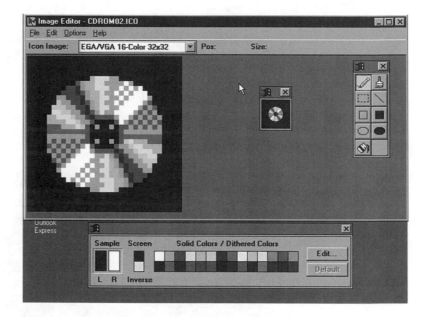

- **Controls**—This directory contains all the ActiveX controls that shipped with Visual Basic 4 and are no longer shipped with Visual Basic 6. If you've removed VB4 from your computer, you might find that some older projects won't load properly because of missing .OCX files.

- **DCOM95**—The Distributed Component Object is an enhancement to the Windows 95 environment. It enables transparent access to objects in remote processes, just as the standard COM object allows clients to access objects in a local process.

- **NTSP3**—This contains the service pack 3 for Windows NT 4.0.

- **Pview**—The PVIEW.EXE process viewer allows you to view or terminate any process on your computer. If you've used Windows NT 4.0, you've already seen this functionality on the task manager.

- **Regutils**—The three tools in this directory are used for registering in-process OLE servers such as .OCX and .DLL files.

- **Unsupprt**—This folder contains several subfolders with completely unsupported tools or projects. You can use these at your own risk; however, I use many of them regularly without any problems.

Checking In at the Web

The Visual Studio Web site www.microsoft.com/vstudio has a section for Visual Basic owners. You should check this Web site periodically to see whether any new controls, tools, or service packs have been made available from Microsoft.

C

INDEX

Symbols

< > (angle brackets), 388
* (asterisk), 246
: (colon), 166
$ (dollar sign), 467
! (exclamation point), 135
| (pipe character), 52
+ (plus sign), 467
# (pound symbol), 467
/? option (rc command), 543
1NF (first normal form), 239-240
2NF (second normal form), 240-241
3NF (third normal form), 242

A

<A> tag (HTML), 390
About dialog box, 191
ACCELERATORS statement, 541
Access, 258-259
access
   data-access forms, 229-233
      columns, 230
      command buttons, 231
      styles, 230
   Data Environments, 324-326
   error handling, 456
   help systems
      common dialog control, 497-498
      Help menu, 499-500
   Microsoft Agent, 617
   multiple tables, 247

   resource files
      control event routines, 546-547
      LoadResData function, 546
      LoadResPicture function, 545
      LoadResString function, 545
   Universal Data Access, 212-213
ActiveControl property (MDI), 81
ActiveForm property (MDI), 81
ActiveX controls
   adding
      to ActiveX documents, 581-582
      to Explorer interface, 313
   Animated Button control, 382

T

Add to Your Sams Library Today with the Best Books for Programming, Operating Systems, and New Technologies

To order, visit our Web site at www.mcp.com or fax us at

1-800-835-3202

ISBN	Quantity	Description of Item	Unit Cost	Total Cost
0-672-31309-X		Visual Basic 6 Unleashed	$49.99	
0-672-31308-1		Sams Teach Yourself Database Programming with Visual Basic 6 in 21 Days	$45.00	
0-672-31251-4		Sams Teach Yourself Visual InterDev 6 in 21 Days	$34.99	
0-672-31299-9		Sams Teach Yourself OOP with Visual Basic in 21 Days	$39.99	
		Shipping and Handling: See information below.		
		TOTAL		

Shipping and Handling

Standard	$5.00
2nd Day	$10.00
Next Day	$17.50
International	$40.00

201 W. 103rd Street, Indianapolis, Indiana 46290   1-800-835-3202 — Fax

Book ISBN 0-672-31307-3

Visual Basic 6 Unleashed

Rob Thayer

Visual Basic 6 Unleashed provides comprehensive coverage of the most sought after topics in Visual Basic programming. *Visual Basic 6 Unleashed* provides the means for a casual level Visual Basic programmer to quickly become productive with the new release of Visual Basic. This book provides the reader with a comprehensive reference to virtually all the topics that are used in today's leading-edge Visual Basic applications. This book looks to take advantage of the past success of the Unleashed series along with the extremely large size of the Visual Basic market. The integration of the text and CD-ROM makes this an invaluable tool for accomplished Visual Basic programmers—everything they need to know as well as the tools and utilities to make it work. Includes topics important to developers such as creating and using ActiveX controls, creating Wizards, adding and controlling RDO, tuning and optimization, and much more. Targeted towards the beginning-to-intermediate level programmer who needs additional step-by-step guidance in learning the more detailed features of Visual Basic. The reader can use this book as a building block to step to the next level from *Sams Teach Yourself Visual Basic 6 in 21 Days.*

Price: $49.99 USA/$71.95 CAN   *SAMS*

ISBN: 0-672-31318-9   *1000 pages*

Sams Teach Yourself Database Programming With Visual Basic 6 in 21 Days

Curtis Smith

Sams Teach Yourself Database Programming with Visual Basic 6 in 21 Days is a tutorial that allows the reader to learn about working with databases in a set amount of time. The book presents the reader with a step-by-step approach to learning what can be a critical topic for developing applications. Each week will focus on a different aspect of database programming with Visual Basic.

Week 1—Data Controls and Microsoft Access Databases. Learn about issues related to building simple database applications using the extensive collection of data controls available with VB. Week 2—Programming with the Microsoft Jet Engine. Concentrate on techniques for creating database applications using Visual Basic code. Week 3—Programming with ODBC Interface and SQL. Study advanced topics such as SQL data definition and manipulation language, and issues for multiuser applications such as locking schemes, database integrity, and application-level security.

Price: $45.00 USA/$64.95 CAN   *SAMS*

ISBN: 0-672-31308-1   *900 pages*

Sams Teach Yourself Visual InterDev 6 in 21 Days

Michael Van Hoozer

This book is organized in the familiar day-by-day format of the *Sams Teach Yourself* series. Each lesson provides an overview of the topic being presented as well as hands-on examples. Each chapter ends with a summary as well as quiz questions and exercises to verify the reader's learning. The book covers a number of key topics related to Visual InterDev, including: designing and developing of dynamic Web sites; editing Web pages; working with images and multimedia; client-side scripting; working with databases; using the visual data tool; understanding database components; and more! In addition to an overall revision of the book for the new version, the following specific changes have been made: exercises added to all the chapters; the weeks in review expanded to include hardcore example applications incorporating the elements of the previous week; coverage of new Visual InterDev features added including Dynamic HTML, scriptlets; and more. After only a year in release, the first version of Microsoft Visual InterDev is used by over 225,000 professional developers worldwide, making it the leading Web application development tool, with nearly twice as many users as its nearest competitor. Visual InterDev is Microsoft's primary development tool for creating dynamic Internet, intranet, and Web-based applications.

Price: $34.99 USA/$50.95 CAN   SAMS

ISBN: 0-672-31251-4   *750 pages*

Sams Teach Yourself Object-Oriented Programming With Visual Basic in 21 Days

John Conley

In just 21 days, you'll have all the skills you need to get up and running efficiently. With this complete tutorial, you'll master the basics and then move on to the more advanced features and concepts. Understand the fundamentals of object-oriented programming with Visual Basic. Master all of the new and advanced features that object-oriented programming with Visual Basic offers. Learn how to effectively use the latest tools and features by following practical, real-world examples. Get expert tips from a leading authority on implementing object-oriented programming with Visual Basic in the corporate environment. This book is designed for the way you learn. Go chapter by chapter through the step-by-step lessons, or just choose those lessons that interest you the most.

Price: $39.99 USA/$57.95 CAN   SAMS

ISBN: 0-672-31299-9   *600 pages*

What's New in This Edition

With every release of Visual Basic, Microsoft has added new functionality to enhance the applications that can be created. Visual Basic 5 took the first real step towards a client/server development tool that was capable of creating a robust Windows application. The previous edition, *Sams Teach Yourself More Visual Basic 5 in 21 Days*, covered many of the more advanced features of Visual Basic 5.

So, you are probably wondering, "Why should I buy this book?" The answer is simple— Microsoft has done it again. Microsoft has dramatically enhanced data access from within Visual Basic 6 using the new ActiveX technology in the form of ActiveX Data Controls and Data Objects, while adding many new designers and controls to display and report the information from the database. The new Dynamic HTML and HTML Help features are also discussed in this book.

In addition, for every topic in this book, there have been additions and enhancements that are discussed. You will see how to incorporate these new features, functions, and controls into your applications. We think you will find this book both informative and useful as a reference once you start coding your applications. Have fun and good luck!